The
Henrik Ibsen
Collection

A Doll's House   3

The Wild Duck   77

Hedda Gabler   180

An Enemy of the People   274

A Doll's House

Henrik Ibsen

Table of Contents

Characters of the Play

Act 1

Act 2

Act 3

Characters of the Play

Torvald Helmer.

Nora, his wife.

Doctor Rank.

Mrs. Linde.

Nils Krogstad.

Helmer's three young children.

Anne, their nurse.

A Housemaid.

A Porter.

(The action takes place in Helmer's house.)

Act 1

(SCENE. — A room furnished comfortably and tastefully, but not extravagantly. At the back, a door to the right leads to the entrance-hall, another to the left leads to Helmer's study. Between the doors stands a piano. In the middle of the left-hand wall is a door, and beyond it a window. Near the window are a round table, armchairs and a small sofa. In the right-hand wall, at the farther end, another door; and on the same side, nearer the footlights, a stove, two easy chairs and a rocking-chair; between the stove and the door, a small table. Engravings on the wall; a cabinet with china and other small objects; a small book-case with well-bound books. The floors are carpeted, and a fire burns in the stove. It is winter.

A bell rings in the hall; shortly afterwards the door is heard to open. Enter NORA, humming a tune and in high spirits. She is in out-door dress and carries a number of parcels; these she lays on the table to the right. She leaves the outer door open after her, and through it is seen a PORTER who is carrying a Christmas Tree and a basket, which he gives to the MAID who has opened the door.)

Nora. Hide the Christmas Tree carefully, Helen. Be sure the children do not see it till this evening, when it is dressed. (To the PORTER, taking out her purse.) How much?

Porter. Sixpence.

Nora. There is a shilling. No, keep the change. (The PORTER thanks her, and goes out. NORA shuts the door. She is laughing to herself, as she takes off her hat and coat. She takes a packet of macaroons from her pocket and eats one or two; then goes cautiously to her husband's door and listens.) Yes, he is in. (Still humming, she goes to the table on the right.)

Helmer (calls out from his room). Is that my little lark twittering out there?

Nora (busy opening some of the parcels). Yes, it is!

Helmer. Is it my little squirrel bustling about?

Nora. Yes!

Helmer. When did my squirrel come home?

Nora. Just now. (Puts the bag of macaroons into her pocket and wipes her mouth.) Come in here, Torvald, and see what I have bought.

Helmer. Don't disturb me. (A little later, he opens the door and looks into the room, pen in hand.) Bought, did you say? All these things? Has my little spendthrift been wasting money again?

Nora. Yes, but, Torvald, this year we really can let ourselves go a little. This is the first Christmas that we have not needed to economize.

Helmer. Still, you know, we can't spend money recklessly.

Nora. Yes, Torvald, we may be a wee bit more reckless now, mayn't we? Just a tiny wee bit! You are going to have a big salary and earn lots and lots of money.

Helmer. Yes, after the New Year; but then it will be a whole quarter before the salary is due.

Nora. Pooh! we can borrow till then.

Helmer. Nora! (Goes up to her and takes her playfully by the ear.) The same little featherhead! Suppose, now, that I borrowed fifty pounds today, and you spent it all in the Christmas week, and then on New Year's Eve a slate fell on my head and killed me, and —

Nora (putting her hands over his mouth). Oh! don't say such horrid things.

Helmer. Still, suppose that happened — what then?

Nora. If that were to happen, I don't suppose I should care whether I owed money or not.

Helmer. Yes, but what about the people who had lent it?

Nora. They? Who would bother about them? I should not know who they were.

Helmer. That is like a woman! But seriously, Nora, you know what I think about that. No debt, no borrowing. There can be no freedom or beauty about a home life that depends on borrowing and debt. We two have kept bravely on the straight road so far, and we will go on the same way for the short time longer that there need be any struggle.

Nora (moving towards the stove). As you please, Torvald.

Helmer (following her). Come, come, my little skylark must not droop her wings. What is this! Is my little squirrel out of temper? (Taking out his purse.) Nora, what do you think I have got here?

Nora (turning round quickly). Money!

Helmer. There you are. (Gives her some money.) Do you think I don't know what a lot is wanted for housekeeping at Christmas-time?

Nora (counting). Ten shillings — a pound — two pounds! Thank you, thank you, Torvald; that will keep me going for a long time.

Helmer. Indeed it must.

Nora. Yes, yes, it will. But come here and let me show you what I have bought. And ah so cheap! Look, here is a new suit for Ivar, and a sword; and a horse and a trumpet for Bob; and a doll and dolly's bedstead for Emmy. — they are very plain, but anyway she will soon break them in pieces. And here are dress-lengths and handkerchiefs for the maids; old Anne ought really to have something better.

Helmer. And what is in this parcel?

Nora (crying out). No, no! you mustn't see that till this evening.

Helmer. Very well. But now tell me, you extravagant little person, what would you like for yourself?

Nora. For myself? Oh, I am sure I don't want anything.

Helmer. Yes, but you must. Tell me something reasonable that you would particularly like to have.

Nora. No, I really can't think of anything — unless, Torvald —

Helmer. Well?

Nora (playing with his coat buttons, and without raising her eyes to his). If you really want to give me something, you might — you might —

Helmer. Well, out with it!

Nora (speaking quickly). You might give me money, Torvald. Only just as much as you can afford; and then one of these days I will buy something with it.

Helmer. But, Nora —

Nora. Oh, do! dear Torvald; please, please do! Then I will wrap it up in beautiful gilt paper and hang it on the Christmas Tree. Wouldn't that be fun?

Helmer. What are little people called that are always wasting money?

Nora. Spendthrifts — I know. Let us do as you suggest, Torvald, and then I shall have time to think what I am most in want of. That is a very sensible plan, isn't it?

Helmer (smiling). Indeed it is — that is to say, if you were really to save out of the money I give you, and then really buy something for yourself. But if you spend it all on the housekeeping and any number of unnecessary things, then I merely have to pay up again.

Nora. Oh but, Torvald —

Helmer. You can't deny it, my dear, little Nora. (Puts his arm round her waist.) It's a sweet little spendthrift, but she uses up a deal of money. One would hardly believe how expensive such little persons are!

Nora. It's a shame to say that. I do really save all I can.

Helmer (laughing). That's very true — all you can. But you can't save anything!

Nora (smiling quietly and happily). You haven't any idea how many expenses we skylarks and squirrels have, Torvald.

Helmer. You are an odd little soul. Very like your father. You always find some new way of wheedling money out of me, and, as soon as you have got it, it seems to melt in your hands. You never know where it has gone. Still, one must take you as you are. It is in the blood; for indeed it is true that you can inherit these things, Nora.

Nora. Ah, I wish I had inherited many of papa's qualities.

Helmer. And I would not wish you to be anything but just what you are, my sweet little skylark. But, do you know, it strikes me that you are looking rather — what shall I say — rather uneasy today?

Nora. Do I?

Helmer. You do, really. Look straight at me.

Nora (looks at him). Well?

Helmer (wagging his finger at her). Hasn't Miss Sweet-Tooth been breaking rules in town today?

Nora. No; what makes you think that?

Helmer. Hasn't she paid a visit to the confectioner's?

Nora. No, I assure you, Torvald —

Helmer. Not been nibbling sweets?

Nora. No, certainly not.

Helmer. Not even taken a bite at a macaroon or two?

Nora. No, Torvald, I assure you really —

Helmer. There, there, of course I was only joking.

Nora (going to the table on the right). I should not think of going against your wishes.

Helmer. No, I am sure of that; besides, you gave me your word —(Going up to her.) Keep your little Christmas secrets to yourself, my darling. They will all be revealed tonight when the Christmas Tree is lit, no doubt.

Nora. Did you remember to invite Doctor Rank?

Helmer. No. But there is no need; as a matter of course he will come to dinner with us. However, I will ask him when he comes in this morning. I have ordered some good wine. Nora, you can't think how I am looking forward to this evening.

Nora. So am I! And how the children will enjoy themselves, Torvald!

Helmer. It is splendid to feel that one has a perfectly safe appointment, and a big enough income. It's delightful to think of, isn't it?

Nora. It's wonderful!

Helmer. Do you remember last Christmas? For a full three weeks beforehand you shut yourself up every evening till long after midnight, making ornaments for the Christmas Tree and all the other fine things that were to be a surprise to us. It was the dullest three weeks I ever spent!

Nora. I didn't find it dull.

Helmer (smiling). But there was precious little result, Nora.

Nora. Oh, you shouldn't tease me about that again. How could I help the cat's going in and tearing everything to pieces?

Helmer. Of course you couldn't, poor little girl. You had the best of intentions to please us all, and that's the main thing. But it is a good thing that our hard times are over.

Nora. Yes, it is really wonderful.

Helmer. This time I needn't sit here and be dull all alone, and you needn't ruin your dear eyes and your pretty little hands —

Nora (clapping her hands). No, Torvald, I needn't any longer, need I! It's wonderfully lovely to hear you say so! (Taking his arm.) Now I will tell you how I have been thinking we ought to arrange things, Torvald. As soon as Christmas is over —(A bell rings in the hall.) There's the bell. (She tidies the room a little.) There's someone at the door. What a nuisance!

Helmer. If it is a caller, remember I am not at home.

Maid (in the doorway). A lady to see you, ma'am — a stranger.

Nora. Ask her to come in.

Maid (to HELMER). The doctor came at the same time, sir.

Helmer. Did he go straight into my room?

Maid. Yes, sir.

(HELMER goes into his room. The MAID ushers in MRS. LINDE, who is in traveling dress, and shuts the door.)

Mrs Linde (in a dejected and timid voice). How do you do, Nora?

Nora (doubtfully). How do you do —

Mrs. Linde. You don't recognize me, I suppose.

Nora No, I don't know — yes, to be sure, I seem to —(Suddenly.) Yes! Christine! Is it really you?

Mrs. Linde. Yes, it is I.

Nora. Christine! To think of my not recognising you! And yet how could I—(In a gentle voice.) How you have altered, Christine!

Mrs. Linde. Yes, I have indeed. In nine, ten long years —

Nora. Is it so long since we met? I suppose it is. The last eight years have been a happy time for me, I can tell you. And so now you have come into the town, and have taken this long journey in winter — that was plucky of you.

Mrs. Linde. I arrived by steamer this morning.

Nora. To have some fun at Christmas-time, of course. How delightful! We will have such fun together! But take off your things. You are not cold, I hope. (Helps her.) Now we will sit down by the stove, and be cosy. No, take this arm-chair; I will sit here in the rocking-chair. (Takes her hands.) Now you look like your old self again; it was only the first moment — You are a little paler, Christine, and perhaps a little thinner.

Mrs. Linde. And much, much older, Nora.

Nora. Perhaps a little older; very, very little; certainly not much. (Stops suddenly and speaks seriously.) What a thoughtless creature I am, chattering away like this. My poor, dear Christine, do forgive me.

Mrs. Linde. What do you mean, Nora?

Nora (gently). Poor Christine, you are a widow.

Mrs. Linde. Yes; it is three years ago now.

Nora. Yes, I knew; I saw it in the papers. I assure you, Christine, I meant ever so often to write to you at the time, but I always put it off and something always prevented me.

Mrs. Linde. I quite understand, dear.

Nora. It was very bad of me, Christine. Poor thing, how you must have suffered. And he left you nothing?

Mrs. Linde. No.

Nora. And no children?

Mrs. Linde. No.

Nora. Nothing at all, then?

Mrs. Linde. Not even any sorrow or grief to live upon.

Nora (looking incredulously at her). But, Christine, is that possible?

Mrs. Linde (smiles sadly and strokes her hair). It sometimes happens, Nora.

Nora. So you are quite alone. How dreadfully sad that must be. I have three lovely children. You can't see them just now, for they are out with their nurse. But now you must tell me all about it.

Mrs. Linde. No, no; I want to hear about you.

Nora. No, you must begin. I mustn't be selfish today; today I must only think of your affairs. But there is one thing I must tell you. Do you know we have just had a great piece of good luck?

Mrs. Linde. No, what is it?

Nora. Just fancy, my husband has been made manager of the Bank!

Mrs. Linde. Your husband? What good luck!

Nora. Yes tremendous! A barrister's profession is such an uncertain thing, especially if he won't undertake unsavoury cases; and naturally Torvald has never been willing to do that, and I quite agree with him. You may imagine how pleased we are! He is to take up his work in the Bank at the New Year, and then he will have a big salary and lots of commissions. For the future we can live quite differently — we can do just as we like. I feel so relieved and so happy, Christine! It will be splendid to have heaps of money and not need to have any anxiety, won't it?

Mrs. Linde. Yes, anyhow I think it would be delightful to have what one needs.

Nora. No, not only what one needs, but heaps and heaps of money.

Mrs. Linde (smiling). Nora, Nora, haven't you learnt sense yet? In our schooldays you were a great spendthrift.

Nora (laughing). Yes, that is what Torvald says now. (Wags her finger at her.) But "Nora, Nora" is not so silly as you think. We have not been in a position for me to waste money. We have both had to work.

Mrs. Linde. You too?

Nora. Yes; odds and ends, needlework, crochet-work, embroidery, and that kind of thing. (Dropping her voice.) And other things as well. You know Torvald left his office when we were married? There was no prospect of promotion there, and he had to try and earn more than before. But during the first year he overworked himself dreadfully. You see, he had to make money every way he could, and he worked early and late; but he couldn't stand it, and fell dreadfully ill, and the doctors said it was necessary for him to go south.

Mrs. Linde. You spent a whole year in Italy, didn't you?

Nora. Yes. It was no easy matter to get away, I can tell you. It was just after Ivar was born; but naturally we had to go. It was a wonderfully beautiful journey, and it saved Torvald's life. But it cost a tremendous lot of money, Christine.

Mrs. Linde. So I should think.

Nora. It cost about two hundred and fifty pounds. That's a lot, isn't it?

Mrs. Linde. Yes, and in emergencies like that it is lucky to have the money.

Nora. I ought to tell you that we had it from papa.

Mrs. Linde. Oh, I see. It was just about that time that he died, wasn't it?

Nora. Yes; and, just think of it, I couldn't go and nurse him. I was expecting little Ivar's birth every day and I had my poor sick Torvald to look after. My dear, kind father — I never saw him again, Christine. That was the saddest time I have known since our marriage.

Mrs. Linde. I know how fond you were of him. And then you went off to Italy?

Nora. Yes; you see we had money then, and the doctors insisted on our going, so we started a month later.

Mrs. Linde. And your husband came back quite well?

Nora. As sound as a bell!

Mrs Linde. But — the doctor?

Nora. What doctor?

Mrs Linde. I thought your maid said the gentleman who arrived here just as I did, was the doctor?

Nora. Yes, that was Doctor Rank, but he doesn't come here professionally. He is our greatest friend, and comes in at least once every day. No, Torvald has not had an hour's illness since then, and our children are strong and healthy and so am I. (Jumps up and claps her hands.) Christine! Christine! it's good to be alive and happy! — But how horrid of me; I am talking of nothing but my own affairs. (Sits on a stool near her, and rests her arms on her knees.) You mustn't be angry with me. Tell me, is it really true that you did not love your husband? Why did you marry him?

Mrs. Linde. My mother was alive then, and was bedridden and helpless, and I had to provide for my two younger brothers; so I did not think I was justified in refusing his offer.

Nora. No, perhaps you were quite right. He was rich at that time, then?

Mrs. Linde. I believe he was quite well off. But his business was a precarious one; and, when he died, it all went to pieces and there was nothing left.

Nora. And then? —

Mrs. Linde. Well, I had to turn my hand to anything I could find — first a small shop, then a small school, and so on. The last three years have seemed like one long working-day, with no rest. Now it is at an end, Nora. My poor mother needs me no more, for she is gone; and the boys do not need me either; they have got situations and can shift for themselves.

Nora. What a relief you must feel it —

Mrs. Linde. No, indeed; I only feel my life unspeakably empty. No one to live for any more. (Gets up restlessly.) That is why I could not stand the life in my little backwater any longer. I hope it may be easier here to find something which will busy me and occupy my thoughts. If only I could have the good luck to get some regular work — office work of some kind —

Nora. But, Christine, that is so frightfully tiring, and you look tired out now. You had far better go away to some watering-place.

Mrs. Linde (walking to the window). I have no father to give me money for a journey, Nora.

Nora (rising). Oh, don't be angry with me.

Mrs. Linde (going up to her). It is you that must not be angry with me, dear. The worst of a position like mine is that it makes one so bitter. No one to work for, and yet obliged to be always on the look-out for chances. One must live, and so one becomes selfish. When you told me of the happy turn your fortunes have taken — you will hardly believe it — I was delighted not so much on your account as on my own.

Nora. How do you mean? — Oh, I understand. You mean that perhaps Torvald could get you something to do.

Mrs. Linde. Yes, that was what I was thinking of.

Nora. He must, Christine. Just leave it to me; I will broach the subject very cleverly — I will think of something that will please him very much. It will make me so happy to be of some use to you.

Mrs. Linde. How kind you are, Nora, to be so anxious to help me! It is doubly kind in you, for you know so little of the burdens and troubles of life.

Nora. I—? I know so little of them?

Mrs Linde (smiling). My dear! Small household cares and that sort of thing! — You are a child, Nora.

Nora (tosses her head and crosses the stage). You ought not to be so superior.

Mrs. Linde. No?

Nora. You are just like all the others. They all think that I am incapable of anything really serious —

Mrs. Linde. Come, come —

Nora. — that I have gone through nothing in this world of cares.

Mrs. Linde. But, my dear Nora, you have just told me all your troubles.

Nora. Pooh! — those were trifles. (Lowering her voice.) I have not told you the important thing.

Mrs. Linde. The important thing? What do you mean?

Nora. You look down upon me altogether, Christine — but you ought not to. You are proud, aren't you, of having-worked so hard and so long for your mother?

Mrs. Linde. Indeed, I don't look down on any one. But it is true that I am both proud and glad to think that I was privileged to make the end of my mother's life almost free from care.

Nora. And you are proud to think of what you have done for your brothers.

Mrs. Linde. I think I have the right to be.

Nora. I think so, too. But now, listen to this; I too have something to be proud and glad of.

Mrs. Linde. I have no doubt you have. But what do you refer to?

Nora. Speak low. Suppose Torvald were to hear! He mustn't on any account — no one in the world must know, Christine, except you.

Mrs. Linde. But what is it?

Nora. Come here. (Pulls her down on the sofa beside her.) Now I will show you that I too have something to be proud and glad of. It was I who saved Torvald's life.

Mrs. Linde. "Saved"? How?

Nora. I told you about our trip to Italy. Torvald would never have recovered if he had not gone there —

Mrs. Linde. Yes, but your father gave you the necessary funds.

Nora (smiling). Yes, that is what Torvald and all the others think, but —

Mrs. Linde. But. —

Nora. Papa didn't give us a shilling. It was I who procured the money.

Mrs. Linde. You? All that large sum?

Nora. Two hundred and fifty pounds. What do you think of that?

Mrs. Linde. But, Nora, how could you possibly do it? Did you win a prize in the Lottery?

Nora (contemptuously). In the Lottery? There would have been no credit in that.

Mrs. Linde. But where did you get it from, then?

Nora (humming and smiling with an air of mystery). Hm, hu! Aha!

Mrs. Linde. Because you couldn't have borrowed it.

Nora. Couldn't I? Why not?

Mrs. Linde. No, a wife cannot borrow without her husband's consent.

Nora (tossing her head). Oh, if it is a wife who has any head for business — a wife who has the wit to be a little bit clever —

Mrs. Linde. I don't understand it at all, Nora.

Nora. There is no need you should. I never said I had borrowed the money. I may have got it some other way. (Lies back on the sofa.) Perhaps I got it from some other admirer. When anyone is as attractive as I am —

Mrs. Linde. You are a mad creature.

Nora. Now, you know you're full of curiosity, Christine.

Mrs. Linde. Listen to me, Nora dear. Haven't you been a little bit imprudent?

Nora (sits up straight). Is it imprudent to save your husband's life?

Mrs. Linde. It seems to me imprudent, without his knowledge, to —

Nora. But it was absolutely necessary that he should not know! My goodness, can't you understand that? It was necessary he should have no idea what a dangerous condition he was in. It was to me that the doctors came and said that his life was in danger, and that the only thing to save him was to live in the south. Do you suppose I didn't try, first of all, to get what I wanted as if it were for myself? I told him how much I should love to travel abroad like other young wives; I tried tears and entreaties with him; I told him that he ought to remember the condition I was in, and that he ought to be kind and indulgent to me; I even hinted that he might raise a loan. That nearly made him angry, Christine. He said I was thoughtless, and that it was his duty as my husband not to indulge me in my whims and caprices — as I believe he called them. Very well, I thought, you must be saved — and that was how I came to devise a way out of the difficulty —

Mrs. Linde. And did your husband never get to know from your father that the money had not come from him?

Nora. No, never. Papa died just at that time. I had meant to let him into the secret and beg him never to reveal it. But he was so ill then — alas, there never was any need to tell him.

Mrs. Linde. And since then have you never told your secret to your husband?

Nora. Good Heavens, no! How could you think so? A man who has such strong opinions about these things! And besides, how painful and humiliating it would be for Torvald, with his manly independence, to know that he owed me anything! It would upset our mutual relations altogether; our beautiful happy home would no longer be what it is now.

Mrs. Linde. Do you mean never to tell him about it?

Nora (meditatively, and with a half smile.) Yes — some day, perhaps, after many years, when I am no longer as nice-looking as I am now. Don't laugh at me! I mean, of course, when Torvald is no longer as devoted to me as he is now; when my dancing and dressing-up and reciting have palled on him; then it may be a good thing to have something in reserve —(Breaking off,) What nonsense! That time will never come. Now, what do you think of my great secret, Christine? Do you still think I am of no use? I can tell you, too, that this affair has caused me a lot of worry. It has been by no means easy for me to meet my engagements punctually. I may tell you that there is something that is called, in business, quarterly interest, and another thing called payment in instalments, and it is always so dreadfully difficult to manage them. I have had to save a little here and there, where I could, you understand. I have not been able to put aside much from my housekeeping money, for Torvald must have a good table. I couldn't let my children be shabbily dressed; I have felt obliged to use up all he gave me for them, the sweet little darlings!

Mrs. Linde. So it has all had to come out of your own necessaries of life, poor Nora?

Nora. Of course. Besides, I was the one responsible for it. Whenever Torvald has given me money for new dresses and such things, I have never spent more than half of it; I have always bought the simplest and cheapest things. Thank Heaven, any clothes look well on me, and so Torvald has never noticed it. But it was often very hard on me, Christine — because it is delightful to be really well dressed, isn't it?

Mrs. Linde. Quite so.

Nora. Well, then I have found other ways of earning money. Last winter I was lucky enough to get a lot of copying to do; so I locked myself up and sat writing every evening until quite late at night. Many a time I was desperately tired; but all the same it was a tremendous pleasure to sit there working and earning money. It was like being a man.

Mrs. Linde. How much have you been able to pay off in that way?

Nora. I can't tell you exactly. You see, it is very difficult to keep an account of a business matter of that kind. I only know that I have paid every penny that I could scrape together. Many a time I was at my wits' end. (Smiles.) Then I used to sit here and imagine that a rich old gentleman had fallen in love with me —

Mrs. Linde. What! Who was it?

Nora. Be quiet! — that he had died; and that when his will was opened it contained, written in big letters, the instruction: "The lovely Mrs. Nora Helmer is to have all I possess paid over to her at once in cash."

Mrs. Linde. But, my dear Nora — who could the man be?

Nora. Good gracious, can't you understand? There was no old gentleman at all; it was only something that I used to sit here and imagine, when I couldn't think of any way of procuring money. But it's all the same now; the tiresome old person can stay where he is, as far as I am concerned; I don't care about him or his will either, for I am free from care now. (Jumps up.) My goodness, it's delightful to think of, Christine! Free from care! To be able to be free from care, quite free from care; to be able to play and romp with the children; to be able to keep the house beautifully and have everything just as Torvald likes it! And, think of it, soon the spring will come and the big blue sky! Perhaps we shall be able to take a little trip — perhaps I shall see the sea again! Oh, it's a wonderful thing to be alive and be happy. (A bell is heard in the hall.)

Mrs. Linde (rising). There is the bell; perhaps I had better go.

Nora. No, don't go; no one will come in here; it is sure to be for Torvald.

Servant (at the hall door). Excuse me, ma'am — there is a gentleman to see the master, and as the doctor is with him —

Nora. Who is it?

Krogstad (at the door). It is I, Mrs. Helmer. (Mrs. LINDE starts, trembles, and turns to the window.)

Nora (takes a step towards him, and speaks in a strained low voice). You? What is it? What do you want to see my husband about?

Krogstad. Bank business — in a way. I have a small post in the Bank, and I hear your husband is to be our chief now —

Nora. Then it is —

Krogstad. Nothing but dry business matters, Mrs. Helmers; absolutely nothing else.

Nora. Be so good as to go into the study then. (She bows indifferently to him and shuts the door into the hall; then comes back and makes up the fire in the stove.)

Mrs. Linde. Nora — who was that man?

Nora. A lawyer, of the name of Krogstad.

Mrs. Linde. Then it really was he.

Nora. Do you know the man?

Mrs. Linde. I used to — many years ago. At one time he was a solicitor's clerk in our town.

Nora. Yes, he was.

Mrs. Linde. He is greatly altered.

Nora. He made a very unhappy marriage.

Mrs. Linde. He is a widower now, isn't he?

Nora. With several children. There now, it is burning up. (Shuts the door of the stove and moves the rocking-chair aside.)

Mrs. Linde. They say he carries on various kinds of business.

Nora. Really! Perhaps he does; I don't know anything about it. But don't let us think of business; it is so tiresome.

Doctor Rank (comes out of HELMER'S study. Before he shuts the door he calls to him). No, my dear fellow, I won't disturb you; I would rather go in to your wife for a little while. (Shuts the door and sees Mrs. LINDE.) I beg your pardon; I am afraid I am disturbing you too.

Nora. No, not at all. (Introducing him.) Doctor Rank, Mrs. Linde.

Rank. I have often heard Mrs. Linde's name mentioned here. I think I passed you on the stairs when I arrived, Mrs. Linde?

Mrs. Linde. Yes, I go up very slowly; I can't manage stairs well.

Rank. Ah! some slight internal weakness?

Mrs. Linde. No, the fact is I have been overworking myself.

Rank. Nothing more than that? Then I suppose you have come to town to amuse yourself with our entertainments?

Mrs. Linde. I have come to look for work.

Rank. Is that a good cure for overwork?

Mrs. Linde. One must live, Doctor Rank.

Rank. Yes, the general opinion seems to be that it is necessary.

Nora. Look here, Doctor Rank — you know you want to live.

Rank. Certainly. However wretched I may feel, I want to prolong the agony as long as possible. All my patients are like that. And so are those who are morally diseased; one of them, and a bad case, too, is at this very moment with Helmer —

Mrs. Linde (sadly). Ah!

Nora. Whom do you mean?

Rank. A lawyer of the name of Krogstad, a fellow you don't know at all. He suffers from a diseased moral character, Mrs. Helmer; but even he began talking of its being highly important that he should live.

Nora. Did he? What did he want to speak to Torvald about?

Rank. I have no idea; I only heard that it was something about the Bank.

Nora. I didn't know this — what's his name — Krogstad had anything to do with the Bank.

Rank. Yes, he has some sort of appointment there. (To Mrs. LINDE.) I don't know whether you find also in your part of the world that there are certain people who go zealously snuffing about to smell out moral corruption, and, as soon as they have found some, put the person concerned into some lucrative position where they can keep their eye on him. Healthy natures are left out in the cold.

Mrs. Linde. Still I think the sick are those who most need taking care of.

Rank (shrugging his shoulders). Yes, there you are. That is the sentiment that is turning Society into a sick-house.

(NORA, who has been absorbed in her thoughts, breaks out into smothered laughter and claps her hands.)

Rank. Why do you laugh at that? Have you any notion what Society really is?

Nora. What do I care about tiresome Society? I am laughing at something quite different, something extremely amusing. Tell me, Doctor Rank, are all the people who are employed in the Bank dependent on Torvald now?

Rank. Is that what you find so extremely amusing?

Nora (smiling and humming). That's my affair! (Walking about the room.) It's perfectly glorious to think that we have — that Torvald has so much power over so many people. (Takes the packet from her pocket.) Doctor Rank, what do you say to a macaroon?

Rank. What, macaroons? I thought they were forbidden here.

Nora. Yes, but these are some Christine gave me.

Mrs. Linde. What! I? —

Nora. Oh, well, don't be alarmed! You couldn't know that Torvald had forbidden them. I must tell you that he is afraid they will spoil my teeth. But, bah! — once in a way — That's so, isn't it, Doctor Rank? By your leave! (Puts a macaroon into his mouth.) You must have one too, Christine. And I shall have one, just a little one — or at most two. (Walking about.) I am tremendously happy. There is just one thing in the world now that I should dearly love to do.

Rank. Well, what is that?

Nora. It's something I should dearly love to say, if Torvald could hear me.

Rank. Well, why can't you say it?

Nora, No, I daren't; it's so shocking.

Mrs. Linde. Shocking?

Rank. Well, I should not advise you to say it. Still, with us you might. What is it you would so much like to say if Torvald could hear you?

Nora. I should just love to say — Well, I'm damned!

Rank. Are you mad?

Mrs. Linde. Nora, dear —!

Rank. Say it, here he is!

Nora (hiding the packet). Hush! Hush! Hush! (HELMER comes out of his room, with his coat over his arm and his hat in his hand.)

Nora. Well, Torvald dear, have you got rid of him?

Helmer. Yes, he has just gone.

Nora. Let me introduce you — this is Christine, who has come to town.

Helmer. Christine —? Excuse me, but I don't know —

Nora. Mrs. Linde, dear; Christine Linde.

Helmer. Of course. A school friend of my wife's, I presume?

Mrs. Linde. Yes, we have known each other since then.

Nora. And just think, she has taken a long journey in order to see you.

Helmer. What do you mean?

Mrs. Linde. No, really, I—

Nora. Christine is tremendously clever at book-keeping, and she is frightfully anxious to work under some clever man, so as to perfect herself —

Helmer. Very sensible, Mrs. Linde.

Nora. And when she heard you had been appointed manager of the Bank — the news was telegraphed, you know — she traveled here as quick as she could, Torvald, I am sure you will be able to do something for Christine, for my sake, won't you?

Helmer. Well, it is not altogether impossible. I presume you are a widow, Mrs. Linde?

Mrs. Linde. Yes.

Helmer. And have had some experience of bookkeeping?

Mrs. Linde. Yes, a fair amount.

Helmer. Ah! well it's very likely I may be able to find something for you —

Nora (clapping her hands). What did I tell you? What did I tell you?

Helmer. You have just come at a fortunate moment, Mrs. Linde.

Mrs. Linde. How am I to thank you?

Helmer. There is no need. (Puts on his coat.) But today you must excuse me —

Rank. Wait a minute; I will come with you. (Brings his fur coat from the hall and warms it at the fire.)

Nora. Don't be long away, Torvald dear.

Helmer. About an hour, not more.

Nora. Are you going too, Christine?

Mrs. Linde (putting on her cloak). Yes, I must go and look for a room.

Helmer. Oh, well then, we can walk down the street together.

Nora (helping her). What a pity it is we are so short of space here; I am afraid it is impossible for us —

Mrs. Linde. Please don't think of it! Good-bye, Nora dear, and many thanks.

Nora. Good-bye for the present. Of course you will come back this evening. And you too, Dr. Rank. What do you say? If you are well enough? Oh, you must be! Wrap yourself up well. (They go to the door all talking together. Children's voices are heard on the staircase.)

Nora. There they are. There they are! (She runs to open the door. The NURSE comes in with the children.) Come in! Come in! (Stoops and kisses them.) Oh, you sweet blessings! Look at them, Christine! Aren't they darlings?

Rank. Don't let us stand here in the draught.

Helmer. Come along, Mrs. Linde; the place will only be bearable for a mother now!

(RANK, HELMER, and MRS. LINDE go downstairs. The NURSE comes forward with the children; NORA shuts the hall door.)

Nora. How fresh and well you look! Such red cheeks! — like apples and roses. (The children all talk at once while she speaks to them.) Have you had great fun? That's splendid! What, you pulled both Emmy and Bob along on the sledge? — both at once? — that was good. You are a clever boy, Ivar. Let me take her for a little, Anne. My sweet little baby doll! (Takes the baby from the MAID and dances it up and down.) Yes, yes, mother will dance with Bob too. What! Have you been snow-balling? I wish I had been there too! No, no, I will take their things off, Anne; please let me do it, it is such fun. Go in now, you look half frozen. There is some hot coffee for you on the stove.

(The NURSE goes into the room on the left. Nora takes off the children's things and throws them about, while they all talk to her at once.)

Nora. Really! Did a big dog run after you? But it didn't bite you? No, dogs don't bite nice little dolly children. You mustn't look at the parcels, Ivar. What are they? Ah, I daresay you would like to know. No, no — it's something nasty! Come, let us have a game. What shall we play at? Hide and Seek? Yes, we'll play Hide and Seek. Bob shall hide first. Must I hide? Very well, I'll hide first. (She and the children laugh and shout, and romp in and out of the room; at last Nora hides under the table the children rush in and look for her, but do not see her; they hear her smothered laughter run to the table, lift up the cloth and find her. Shouts of laughter. She crawls forward and pretends to frighten them. Fresh laughter. Meanwhile there has been a knock at the hall door, but none of them has noticed it. The door is half opened, and KROGSTAD appears. He waits a little; the game goes on.)

Krogstad. Excuse me, Mrs. Helmer.

Nora (with a stifled cry, turns round and gets up on to her knees). Ah! what do you want?

Krogstad. Excuse me, the outer door was ajar; I suppose someone forgot to shut it.

Nora (rising). My husband is out, Mr. Krogstad.

Krogstad. I know that.

Nora. What do you want here, then?

Krogstad. A word with you.

Nora. With me? —(To the children, gently.) Go in to nurse. What? No, the strange man won't do mother any harm. When he has gone we will have another game. (She takes the children into the room on the left, and shuts the door after them.) You want to speak to me?

Krogstad. Yes, I do.

Nora. Today? It is not the first of the month yet.

Krogstad. No, it is Christmas Eve, and it will depend on yourself what sort of a Christmas you will spend.

Nora. What do you want? Today it is absolutely impossible for me —

Krogstad. We won't talk about that till later on. This is something different. I presume you can give me a moment?

Nora. Yes — yes, I can — although —

Krogstad. Good. I was in Olsen's Restaurant and saw your husband going down the street —

Nora. Yes?

Krogstad. With a lady.

Nora. What then?

Krogstad. May I make so bold as to ask if it was a Mrs. Linde?

Nora. It was.

Krogstad. Just arrived in town?

Nora. Yes, today.

Krogstad. She is a great friend of yours, isn't she?

Nora: She is. But I don't see —

Krogstad. I knew her too, once upon a time.

Nora. I am aware of that.

Krogstad. Are you? So you know all about it; I thought as much. Then I can ask you, without beating about the bush — is Mrs. Linde to have an appointment in the Bank?

Nora. What right have you to question me, Mr. Krogstad? — You, one of my husband's subordinates! But since you ask, you shall know. Yes, Mrs. Linde is to have an appointment. And it was I who pleaded her cause, Mr. Krogstad, let me tell you that.

Krogstad. I was right in what I thought, then.

Nora (walking up and down the stage). Sometimes one has a tiny little bit of influence, I should hope. Because one is a woman, it does not necessarily follow that —. When anyone is in a subordinate position, Mr. Krogstad, they should really be careful to avoid offending anyone who — who —

Krogstad. Who has influence?

Nora. Exactly.

Krogstad (changing his tone). Mrs. Helmer, you will be so good as to use your influence on my behalf.

Nora. What? What do you mean?

Krogstad. You will be so kind as to see that I am allowed to keep my subordinate position in the Bank.

Nora. What do you mean by that? Who proposes to take your post away from you?

Krogstad. Oh, there is no necessity to keep up the pretence of ignorance. I can quite understand that your friend is not very anxious to expose herself to the chance of rubbing shoulders with me; and I quite understand, too, whom I have to thank for being turned off.

Nora. But I assure you —

Krogstad. Very likely; but, to come to the point, the time has come when I should advise you to use your influence to prevent that.

Nora. But, Mr. Krogstad, I have no influence.

Krogstad. Haven't you? I thought you said yourself just now —

Nora. Naturally I did not mean you to put that construction on it. I! What should make you think I have any influence of that kind with my husband?

Krogstad. Oh, I have known your husband from our student days. I don't suppose he is any more unassailable than other husbands.

Nora. If you speak slightly of my husband, I shall turn you out of the house.

Krogstad. You are bold, Mrs. Helmer.

Nora. I am not afraid of you any longer, As soon as the New Year comes, I shall in a very short time be free of the whole thing.

Krogstad (controlling himself). Listen to me, Mrs. Helmer. If necessary, I am prepared to fight for my small post in the Bank as if I were fighting for my life.

Nora. So it seems.

Krogstad. It is not only for the sake of the money; indeed, that weighs least with me in the matter. There is another reason — well, I may as well tell you. My position is this. I daresay you know, like everybody else, that once, many years ago, I was guilty of an indiscretion.

Nora. I think I have heard something of the kind.

Krogstad. The matter never came into court; but every way seemed to be closed to me after that. So I took to the business that you know of. I had to do something; and, honestly, don't think I've been one of the worst. But now I must cut myself free from all that. My sons are growing up; for their sake I must try and win back as much respect as I can in the town. This post in the Bank was like the first step up for me — and now your husband is going to kick me downstairs again into the mud.

Nora. But you must believe me, Mr. Krogstad; it is not in my power to help you at all.

Krogstad. Then it is because you haven't the will; but I have means to compel you.

Nora. You don't mean that you will tell my husband that I owe you money?

Krogstad. Hm! — suppose I were to tell him?

Nora. It would be perfectly infamous of you. (Sobbing.) To think of his learning my secret, which has been my joy and pride, in such an ugly, clumsy way — that he should learn it from you! And it would put me in a horribly disagreeable position —

Krogstad. Only disagreeable?

Nora (impetuously). Well, do it, then! — and it will be the worse for you. My husband will see for himself what a blackguard you are, and you certainly won't keep your post then.

Krogstad. I asked you if it was only a disagreeable scene at home that you were afraid of?

Nora. If my husband does get to know of it, of course he will at once pay you what is still owing, and we shall have nothing more to do with you.

Krogstad (coming a step nearer). Listen to me, Mrs. Helmer. Either you have a very bad memory or you know very little of business. I shall be obliged to remind you of a few details.

Nora. What do you mean?

Krogstad. When your husband was ill, you came to me to borrow two hundred and fifty pounds.

Nora. I didn't know any one else to go to.

Krogstad. I promised to get you that amount —

Nora. Yes, and you did so.

Krogstad. I promised to get you that amount, on certain conditions. Your mind was so taken up with your husband's illness, and you were so anxious to get the money for your journey, that you seem to have paid no attention to the conditions of our bargain. Therefore it will not be amiss if I remind you of them. Now, I promised to get the money on the security of a bond which I drew up.

Nora. Yes, and which I signed.

Krogstad. Good. But below your signature there were a few lines constituting your father a surety for the money; those lines your father should have signed.

Nora. Should? He did sign them.

Krogstad. I had left the date blank; that is to say your father should himself have inserted the date on which he signed the paper. Do you remember that?

Nora. Yes, I think I remember —

Krogstad. Then I gave you the bond to send by post to your father. Is that not so?

Nora. Yes.

Krogstad. And you naturally did so at once, because five or six days afterwards you brought me the bond with your father's signature. And then I gave you the money.

Nora. Well, haven't I been paying it off regularly?

Krogstad. Fairly so, yes. But — to come back to the matter in hand — that must have been a very trying time for you, Mrs. Helmer?

Nora. It was, indeed.

Krogstad. Your father was very ill, wasn't he?

Nora. He was very near his end.

Krogstad. And died soon afterwards?

Nora. Yes.

Krogstad. Tell me, Mrs. Helmer, can you by any chance remember what day your father died? — on what day of the month, I mean.

Nora. Papa died on the 29th of September.

Krogstad. That is correct; I have ascertained it for myself. And, as that is so, there is a discrepancy (taking a paper from his pocket) which I cannot account for.

Nora. What discrepancy? I don't know —

Krogstad. The discrepancy consists, Mrs. Helmer, in the fact that your father signed this bond three days after his death.

Nora. What do you mean? I don't understand —

Krogstad. Your father died on the 29th of September. But, look here; your father dated his signature the 2nd of October. It is a discrepancy, isn't it? (NORA is silent.) Can you explain it to me? (NORA is still silent.) It is a remarkable thing, too, that the words "2nd of October," as well as the year, are not written in your father's handwriting but in one that I think I know. Well, of course it can be explained; your father may have forgotten to date his signature, and someone else may have dated it haphazard before they knew of his death. There is no harm in that. It all depends on the signature of the name; and that is genuine, I suppose, Mrs. Helmer? It was your father himself who signed his name here?

Nora (after a short pause, throws her head up and looks defiantly at him). No, it was not. It was I that wrote papa's name.

Krogstad. Are you aware that is a dangerous confession?

Nora. In what way? You shall have your money soon.

Krogstad. Let me ask you a question; why did you not send the paper to your father?

Nora. It was impossible; papa was so ill. If I had asked him for his signature, I should have had to tell him what the money was to be used for; and when he was so ill himself I couldn't tell him that my husband's life was in danger — it was impossible.

Krogstad. It would have been better for you if you had given up your trip abroad.

Nora. No, that was impossible. That trip was to save my husband's life; I couldn't give that up.

Krogstad. But did it never occur to you that you were committing a fraud on me?

Nora. I couldn't take that into account; I didn't trouble myself about you at all. I couldn't bear you, because you put so many heartless difficulties in my way, although you knew what a dangerous condition my husband was in.

Krogstad. Mrs. Helmer, you evidently do not realise clearly what it is that you have been guilty of. But I can assure you that my one false step, which lost me all my reputation, was nothing more or nothing worse than what you have done.

Nora. You? Do you ask me to believe that you were brave enough to run a risk to save your wife's life.

Krogstad. The law cares nothing about motives.

Nora. Then it must be a very foolish law.

Krogstad. Foolish or not, it is the law by which you will be judged, if I produce this paper in court.

Nora. I don't believe it. Is a daughter not to be allowed to spare her dying father anxiety and care? Is a wife not to be allowed to save her husband's life? I don't know much about law; but I am certain that there must be laws permitting such things as that. Have you no knowledge of such laws — you who are a lawyer? You must be a very poor lawyer, Mr. Krogstad.

Krogstad. Maybe. But matters of business — such business as you and I have had together — do you think I don't understand that? Very well. Do as you please. But let me tell you this — if I lose my position a second time, you shall lose yours with me. (He bows, and goes out through the hall.)

Nora (appears buried in thought for a short time, then tosses her head). Nonsense! Trying to frighten me like that! — I am not so silly as he thinks. (Begins to busy herself putting the children's things in order.) And yet —? No, it's impossible! I did it for love's sake.

The Children (in the doorway on the left.) Mother, the stranger man has gone out through the gate.

Nora. Yes, dears, I know. But, don't tell anyone about the stranger man. Do you hear? Not even papa.

Children. No, mother; but will you come and play again?

Nora. No no — not now.

Children. But, mother, you promised us.

Nora. Yes, but I can't now. Run away in; I have such a lot to do. Run away in, sweet little darlings. (She gets them into the room by degrees and shuts the door on them; then sits down on the sofa, takes up a piece of needlework and sews a few stitches, but soon stops.) No! (Throws down the work, gets up, goes to the hall door and calls out.) Helen, bring the Tree in. (Goes to the table on the left, opens a drawer, and stops again.) No, no! it is quite impossible!

Maid (coming in with the Tree). Where shall I put it, ma'am?

Nora. Here, in the middle of the floor.

Maid. Shall I get you anything else?

Nora. No, thank you. I have all I want.

[Exit MAID

Nora (begins dressing the tree). A candle here — and flowers here —. The horrible man! It's all nonsense — there's nothing wrong. The Tree shall be splendid! I will do everything I can think of to please you, Torvald! — I will sing for you, dance for you —(HELMER comes in with some papers under his arm.) Oh! are you back already?

Helmer. Yes. Has anyone been here?

Nora. Here? No.

Helmer. That is strange. I saw Krogstad going out of the gate.

Nora. Did you? Oh yes, I forgot Krogstad was here for a moment.

Helmer. Nora, I can see from your manner that he has been here begging you to say a good word for him.

29

Nora. Yes.

Helmer. And you were to appear to do it of your own accord; you were to conceal from me the fact of his having been here; didn't he beg that of you too?

Nora. Yes, Torvald, but —

Helmer. Nora, Nora, and you would be a party to that sort of thing? To have any talk with a man like that, and give him any sort of promise? And to tell me a lie into the bargain?

Nora. A lie —?

Helmer. Didn't you tell me no one had been here? (Shakes his finger at her.) My little song-bird must never do that again. A song-bird must have a clean beak to chirp with — no false notes! (Puts his arm round her waist.) That is so, isn't it? Yes, I am sure it is. (Lets her go.) We will say no more about it. (Sits down by the stove.) How warm and snug it is here! (Turns over his papers.)

Nora (after a short pause, during which she busies herself with the Christmas Tree). Torvald!

Helmer. Yes.

Nora: I am looking forward tremendously to the fancy dress ball at the Stensborgs' the day after tomorrow.

Helmer. And I am tremendously curious to see what you are going to surprise me with.

Nora. It was very silly of me to want to do that.

Helmer. What do you mean?

Nora. I can't hit upon anything that will do; everything I think of seems so silly and insignificant.

Helmer. Does my little Nora acknowledge that at last?

Nora (standing behind his chair with her arms on the back of it). Are you very busy, Torvald?

Helmer. Well —

Nora. What are all those papers?

Helmer. Bank business.

Nora. Already?

Helmer. I have got authority from the retiring manager to undertake the necessary changes in the staff and in the rearrangement of the work; and I must make use of the Christmas week for that, so as to have everything in order for the new year.

Nora. Then that was why this poor Krogstad —

Helmer. Hm!

Nora (leans against the back of his chair and strokes his hair). If you hadn't been so busy I should have asked you a tremendously big favour, Torvald.

Helmer. What is that? Tell me.

Nora. There is no one has such good taste as you. And I do so want to look nice at the fancy-dress ball. Torvald, couldn't you take me in hand and decide what I shall go as, and what sort of a dress I shall wear?

Helmer. Aha! so my obstinate little woman is obliged to get someone to come to her rescue?

Nora. Yes, Torvald, I can't get along a bit without your help.

Helmer Very well, I will think it over, we shall manage to hit upon something.

Nora. That is nice of you. (Goes to the Christmas Tree. A short pause.) How pretty the red flowers look —. But, tell me, was it really something very bad that this Krogstad was guilty of?

Helmer. He forged someone's name. Have you any idea what that means?

Nora. Isn't it possible that he was driven to do it by necessity?

Helmer. Yes; or, as in so many cases, by imprudence. I am not so heartless as to condemn a man altogether because of a single false step of that kind.

Nora. No you wouldn't, would you, Torvald?

Helmer. Many a man has been able to retrieve his character, if he has openly confessed his fault and taken his punishment.

Nora. Punishment —?

Helmer. But Krogstad did nothing of that sort; he got himself out of it by a cunning trick, and that is why he has gone under altogether.

Nora. But do you think it would —?

Helmer. Just think how a guilty man like that has to lie and play the hypocrite with everyone, how he has to wear a mask in the presence of those near and dear to him, even before his own wife and children. And about the children — that is the most terrible part of it all, Nora.

Nora. How?

Helmer. Because such an atmosphere of lies infects and poisons the whole life of a home. Each breath the children take in such a house is full of the germs of evil.

Nora (coming nearer him). Are you sure of that?

Helmer. My dear, I have often seen it in the course of my life as a lawyer. Almost everyone who has gone to the bad early in life has had a deceitful mother.

Nora. Why do you only say — mother?

Helmer. It seems most commonly to be the mother's influence, though naturally a bad father's would have the same result. Every lawyer is familiar with the fact. This Krogstad, now, has been persistently poisoning his own children with lies and dissimulation; that is why I say he has lost all moral character. (Holds out his hands to her.) That is why my sweet little Nora must promise me not to plead his cause. Give me your hand on it. Come, come, what is this? Give me your hand. There now, that's settled. I assure you it would be quite impossible for me to work with him; I literally feel physically ill when I am in the company of such people.

Nora (takes her hand out of his and goes to the opposite side of the Christmas Tree). How hot it is in here; and I have such a lot to do.

Helmer (getting up and putting his papers in order). Yes, and I must try and read through some of these before dinner; and I must think about your costume, too. And it is just possible I may have something ready in gold paper to hang up on the Tree. (Puts his hand on her head.) My precious little singing-bird! (He goes into his room and shuts the door after him.)

Nora (after a pause, whispers). No, no — it isn't true. It's impossible; it must be impossible.

(The NURSE opens the door on the left.)

Nurse. The little ones are begging so hard to be allowed to come in to mamma.

Nora. No, no, no! Don't let them come in to me! You stay with them, Anne.

Nurse. Very well, ma'am. (Shuts the door.)

Nora (pale with terror). Deprave my little children? Poison my home? (A short pause. Then she tosses her head.) It's not true. It can't possibly be true.

Act 2

(THE SAME SCENE— The Christmas Tree is in the corner by the piano, stripped of its ornaments and with burnt-down candle-ends on its dishevelled branches. NORA'S cloak and hat are lying on the sofa. She is alone in the room, walking about uneasily. She stops by the sofa and takes up her cloak.)

Nora (drops the cloak). Someone is coming now! (Goes to the door and listens.) No — it is no one. Of course, no one will come today, Christmas Day — nor tomorrow either. But, perhaps — (opens the door and looks out.) No, nothing in the letter-box; it is quite empty. (Comes forward.) What rubbish! of course he can't be in earnest about it. Such a thing couldn't happen; it is impossible — I have three little children.

(Enter the NURSE from the room on the left, carrying a big cardboard box.)

Nurse. At last I have found the box with the fancy dress.

Nora. Thanks; put it on the table.

Nurse (doing so). But it is very much in want of mending.

Nora. I should like to tear it into a hundred thousand pieces.

Nurse. What an idea! It can easily be put in order — just a little patience.

Nora. Yes, I will go and get Mrs. Linde to come and help me with it.

Nurse. What, out again? In this horrible weather? You will catch cold, ma'am, and make yourself ill.

Nora. Well, worse than that might happen. How are the children?

Nurse. The poor little souls are playing with their Christmas presents, but —

Nora. Do they ask much for me?

Nurse. You see, they are so accustomed to have their mamma with them.

Nora. Yes, but, nurse, I shall not be able to be so much with them now as I was before.

Nurse. Oh well, young children easily get accustomed to anything.

Nora. Do you think so? Do you think they would forget their mother if she went away altogether?

Nurse. Good heavens! — went away altogether?

Nora. Nurse, I want you to tell me something I have often wondered about — how could you have the heart to put your own child out among strangers?

Nurse. I was obliged to, if I wanted to be little Nora's nurse.

Nora. Yes, but how could you be willing to do it?

Nurse. What, when I was going to get such a good place by it? A poor girl who has got into trouble should be glad to. Besides, that wicked man didn't do a single thing for me.

Nora. But I suppose your daughter has quite forgotten you.

Nurse. No, indeed she hasn't. She wrote to me when she was confirmed, and when she was married.

Nora (putting her arms round her neck). Dear old Anne, you were a good mother to me when I was little.

Nurse. Little Nora, poor dear, had no other mother but me.

Nora. And if my little ones had no other mother, I am sure you would — What nonsense I am talking! (Opens the box.) Go in to them. Now I must —. You will see tomorrow how charming I shall look.

Nurse. I am sure there will be no one at the ball so charming as you, ma'am. (Goes into the room on the left.)

Nora (begins to unpack the box, but soon pushes it away from her). If only I dared go out. If only no one would come. If only I could be sure nothing would happen here in the meantime. Stuff and nonsense! No one will come. Only I mustn't think about it. I will brush my muff. What lovely, lovely gloves! Out of my thoughts, out of my thoughts! One, two, three, four, five, six — (Screams.) Ah! there is someone coming —. (Makes a movement towards the door, but stands irresolute.)

(Enter MRS. LINDE from the hall, where she has taken off her cloak and hat.)

Nora. Oh, it's you, Christine. There is no one else out there, is there? How good of you to come!

Mrs. Linde. I heard you were up asking for me.

Nora. Yes, I was passing by. As a matter of fact, it is something you could help me with. Let us sit down here on the sofa. Look here. Tomorrow evening there is to be a fancy-dress ball at the Stenborgs', who live above us; and Torvald wants me to go as a Neapolitan fisher-girl, and dance the Tarantella that I learnt at Capri.

Mrs. Linde. I see; you are going to keep up the character.

Nora. Yes, Torvald wants me to. Look, here is the dress; Torvald had it made for me there, but now it is all so torn, and I haven't any idea —

Mrs. Linde. We will easily put that right. It is only some of the trimming come unsewn here and there. Needle and thread? Now then, that's all we want.

Nora. It is nice of you.

Mrs. Linde (sewing). So you are going to be dressed up tomorrow, Nora. I will tell you what — I shall come in for a moment and see you in your fine feathers. But I have completely forgotten to thank you for a delightful evening yesterday.

Nora (gets up, and crosses the stage). Well I don't think yesterday was as pleasant as usual. You ought to have come to town a little earlier, Christine. Certainly Torvald does understand how to make a house dainty and attractive.

Mrs. Linde. And so do you, it seems to me; you are not your father's daughter for nothing. But tell me, is Doctor Rank always as depressed as he was yesterday?

Nora. No; yesterday it was very noticeable. I must tell you that he suffers from a very dangerous disease. He has consumption of the spine, poor creature. His father was a horrible man who committed all sorts of excesses; and that is why his son was sickly from childhood, do you understand?

Mrs. Linde (dropping her sewing). But, my dearest Nora, how do you know anything about such things?

Nora (walking about). Pooh! When you have three children, you get visits now and then from — from married women, who know something of medical matters, and they talk about one thing and another.

Mrs. Linde (goes on sewing. A short silence). Does Doctor Rank come here every day?

Nora. Every day regularly. He is Torvald's most intimate friend, and a great friend of mine too. He is just like one of the family.

Mrs. Linde. But tell me this — is he perfectly sincere? I mean, isn't he the kind of a man that is very anxious to make himself agreeable?

Nora. Not in the least. What makes you think that?

Mrs. Linde. When you introduced him to me yesterday, he declared he had often heard my name mentioned in this house; but afterwards I noticed that your husband hadn't the slightest idea who I was. So how could Doctor Rank —?

Nora. That is quite right, Christine. Torvald is so absurdly fond of me that he wants me absolutely to himself, as he says. At first he used to seem almost jealous if I mentioned any of the dear folk at home, so naturally I gave up doing so. But I often talk about such things with Doctor Rank, because he likes hearing about them.

Mrs. Linde. Listen to me, Nora. You are still very like a child in many ways, and I am older than you in many ways and have a little more experience. Let me tell you this — you ought to make an end of it with Doctor Rank.

Nora. What ought I to make an end of?

Mrs. Linde. Of two things, I think. Yesterday you talked some nonsense about a rich admirer who was to leave you money —

Nora. An admirer who doesn't exist, unfortunately! But what then?

Mrs. Linde. Is Doctor Rank a man of means?

Nora. Yes, he is.

Mrs. Linde. And has no one to provide for?

Nora. No, no one; but —

Mrs. Linde. And comes here every day?

Nora. Yes, I told you so.

Mrs. Linde. But how can this well-bred man be so tactless?

Nora. I don't understand you at all.

Mrs. Linde. Don't prevaricate, Nora. Do you suppose I don't guess who lent you the two hundred and fifty pounds.

Nora. Are you out of your senses? How can you think of such a thing! A friend of ours, who comes here every day! Do you realise what a horribly painful position that would be?

Mrs. Linde. Then it really isn't he?

Nora. No, certainly not. It would never have entered into my head for a moment. Besides, he had no money to lend then; he came into his money afterwards.

Mrs. Linde. Well, I think that was lucky for you, my dear Nora.

Nora. No, it would never have come into my head to ask Doctor Rank. Although I am quite sure that if I had asked him —

Mrs. Linde. But of course you won't.

Nora. Of course not. I have no reason to think it could possibly be necessary. But I am quite sure that if I told Doctor Rank —

Mrs. Linde. Behind your husband's back?

Nora. I must make an end of it with the other one, and that will be behind his back too. I must make an end of it with him.

Mrs. Linde. Yes, that is what I told you yesterday, but —

Nora (walking up and down). A man can put a thing like that straight much easier than a woman —

Mrs. Linde. One's husband, yes.

Nora. Nonsense! (Standing still.) When you pay off a debt you get your bond back, don't you?

Mrs. Linde. Yes, as a matter of course.

Nora. And can tear it into a hundred thousand pieces, and burn it up — the nasty, dirty paper!

Mrs. Linde (looks hard at her, lays down her sewing and gets up slowly). Nora, you are concealing something from me.

Nora. Do I look as if I were?

Mrs. Linde. Something has happened to you since yesterday morning. Nora, what is it?

Nora (going nearer to her). Christine! (Listens.) Hush! there's Torvald come home. Do you mind going in to the children for the present? Torvald can't bear to see dressmaking going on. Let Anne help you.

Mrs. Linde (gathering some of the things together). Certainly — but I am not going away from here till we have had it out with one another. (She goes into the room, on the left, as Helmer comes in from, the hall.)

Nora (going up to HELMAR). I have wanted you so much, Torvald dear.

Helmer. Was that the dressmaker?

Nora. No, it was Christine; she is helping me to put my dress in order. You will see I shall look quite smart.

Helmer. Wasn't that a happy thought of mine, now?

Nora. Splendid! But don't you think it is nice of me, too, to do as you wish?

Helmer. Nice? — because you do as your husband wishes? Well, well, you little rogue, I am sure you did not mean it in that way. But I am not going to disturb you; you will want to be trying on your dress, I expect.

Nora. I suppose you are going to work.

Helmer. Yes. (Shows her a bundle of papers.) Look at that. I have just been into the bank. (Turns to go into his room.)

Nora. Torvald.

Helmer. Yes.

Nora. If your little squirrel were to ask you for something very, very prettily —?

Helmer. What then?

Nora. Would you do it?

Helmer. I should like to hear what it is, first.

Nora. Your squirrel would run about and do all her tricks if you would be nice, and do what she wants.

Helmer. Speak plainly.

Nora. Your skylark would chirp about in every room, with her song rising and falling —

Helmer. Well, my skylark does that anyhow.

Nora. I would play the fairy and dance for you in the moonlight, Torvald.

Helmer. Nora — you surely don't mean that request you made of me this morning?

Nora (going near him). Yes, Torvald, I beg you so earnestly —

Helmer. Have you really the courage to open up that question again?

Nora. Yes, dear, you must do as I ask; you must let Krogstad keep his post in the bank.

Helmer. My dear Nora, it is his post that I have arranged Mrs. Linde shall have.

Nora. Yes, you have been awfully kind about that; but you could just as well dismiss some other clerk instead of Krogstad.

Helmer. This is simply incredible obstinacy! Because you chose to give him a thoughtless promise that you would speak for him, I am expected to —

Nora. That isn't the reason, Torvald. It is for your own sake. This fellow writes in the most scurrilous newspapers; you have told me so yourself. He can do you an unspeakable amount of harm. I am frightened to death of him —

Helmer. Ah, I understand; it is recollections of the past that scare you.

Nora. What do you mean?

Helmer. Naturally you are thinking of your father.

Nora. Yes — yes, of course. Just recall to your mind what these malicious creatures wrote in the papers about papa, and how horribly they slandered him. I believe they would have procured his dismissal if the Department had not sent you over to inquire into it, and if you had not been so kindly disposed and helpful to him.

Helmer. My little Nora, there is an important difference between your father and me. Your father's reputation as a public official was not above suspicion. Mine is, and I hope it will continue to be so, as long as I hold my office.

Nora. You never can tell what mischief these men may contrive. We ought to be so well off, so snug and happy here in our peaceful home, and have no cares — you and I and the children, Torvald! That is why I beg you so earnestly —

Helmer. And it is just by interceding for him that you make it impossible for me to keep him. It is already known at the Bank that I mean to dismiss Krogstad. Is it to get about now that the new manager has changed his mind at his wife's bidding —

Nora. And what if it did?

Helmer. Of course! — if only this obstinate little person can get her way! Do you suppose I am going to make myself ridiculous before my whole staff, to let people think that I am a man to be swayed by all sorts of outside influence? I should very soon feel the consequences of it, I can tell you. And besides, there is one thing that makes it quite impossible for me to have Krogstad in the bank as long as I am manager.

Nora. Whatever is that?

Helmer. His moral failings I might perhaps have overlooked, if necessary —

Nora. Yes, you could — couldn't you?

Helmer. And, I hear he is a good worker, too. But I knew him when we were boys. It was one of those rash friendships that so often prove an incubus in after life. I may as well tell you plainly, we were once on very intimate terms with one another. But this tactless fellow lays no restraint upon himself when other people are present. On the contrary, he thinks it gives him the right to adopt a familiar tone with me, and every minute it is "I say, Helmer, old fellow!" and that sort of thing. I assure you it is extremely painful to me. He would make my position in the bank intolerable.

Nora. Torvald, I don't believe you mean that.

Helmer. Don't you? Why not?

Nora. Because it is such a narrow-minded way of looking at things.

Helmer. What are you saying? Narrow-minded? Do you think I am narrow-minded?

Nora. No, just the opposite, dear — and it is exactly for that reason.

Helmer. It's the same thing. You say my point of view is narrow-minded, so I must be so, too. Narrow-minded! Very well — I must put an end to this. (Goes to the hall door and calls.) Helen!

Nora. What are you going to do?

Helmer (looking among his papers). Settle it. (Enter MAID.) Look here; take this letter and go downstairs with it at once. Find a messenger and tell him to deliver it, and be quick. The address is on it, and here is the money.

Maid. Very well, sir. (Exit with the letter.)

Helmer (putting his papers together). Now, then, little Miss Obstinate.

Nora (breathlessly). Torvald — what was that letter?

Helmer. Krogstad's dismissal.

Nora. Call her back, Torvald! There is still time. Oh Torvald, call her back! Do it for my sake — for your own sake, for the children's sake! Do you hear me, Torvald? Call her back! You don't know what that letter can bring upon us.

Helmer. It's too late.

Nora. Yes, it's too late.

Helmer. My dear Nora, I can forgive the anxiety you are in, although really it is an insult to me. It is, indeed. Isn't it an insult to think that I should be afraid of a starving quill-driver's vengeance? But I forgive you, nevertheless, because it is such eloquent witness to your great love for me. (Takes her in his arms.) And that is as it should be, my own darling Nora. Come what will, you may be sure I shall have both courage and strength if they be needed. You will see I am man enough to take everything upon myself.

Nora (in a horror-stricken voice). What do you mean by that?

Helmer. Everything I say —

Nora (recovering herself). You will never have to do that.

Helmer. That's right. Well, we will share it, Nora, as man and wife should. That is how it shall be. (Caressing her.) Are you content now? There! There! — not these frightened dove's eyes! The whole thing is only the wildest fancy! — Now, you must go and play through the Tarantella and practice with your tambourine. I shall go into the inner office and shut the door, and I shall hear nothing; you can make as much noise as you please. (Turns back at the door.) And when Rank comes, tell him where he will find me. (Nods to her, takes his papers and goes into his room, and shuts the door after him.)

Nora (bewildered with anxiety, stands as if rooted to the spot, and whispers). He was capable of doing it. He will do it. He will do it in spite of everything. — No, not that! Never, never! Anything rather than that! Oh, for some help, some way out of it. (The door-bell rings.) Doctor Rank! Anything rather than that — anything, whatever it is! (She puts her hands over her face, pulls herself together, goes to the door and opens it. RANK is standing without, hanging up his coat. During the following dialogue it begins to grow dark.)

Nora. Good-day, Doctor Rank. I knew your ring. But you mustn't go into Torvald now; I think he is busy with something.

Rank. And you?

Nora (brings him in and shuts the door after him). Oh, you know very well I always have time for you.

Rank. Thank you. I shall make use of as much of it as I can.

Nora. What do you mean by that? As much of it as you can.

Rank. Well, does that alarm you?

Nora. It was such a strange way of putting it. Is anything likely to happen?

Rank. Nothing but what I have long been prepared for. But I certainly didn't expect it to happen so soon.

Nora (gripping him by the arm). What have you found out? Doctor Rank, you must tell me.

Rank (sitting down by the stove). It is all up with me. And it can't be helped.

41

Nora (with a sigh of relief). Is it about yourself?

Rank. Who else? It is no use lying to one's self. I am the most wretched of all my patients, Mrs. Helmer. Lately I have been taking stock of my internal economy. Bankrupt! Probably within a month I shall lie rotting in the church-yard.

Nora. What an ugly thing to say!

Rank. The thing itself is cursedly ugly, and the worst of it is that I shall have to face so much more that is ugly before that. I shall only make one more examination of myself; when I have done that, I shall know pretty certainly when it will be that the horrors of dissolution will begin. There is something I want to tell you. Helmer's refined nature gives him an unconquerable disgust of everything that is ugly; I won't have him in my sick-room.

Nora. Oh, but, Doctor Rank —

Rank. I won't have him there. Not on any account. I bar my door to him. As soon as I am quite certain that the worst has come, I shall send you my card with a black cross on it, and then you will know that the loathsome end has begun.

Nora. You are quite absurd to-day. And I wanted you so much to be in a really good humour.

Rank. With death stalking beside me? — To have to pay this penalty for another man's sin! Is there any justice in that? And in every single family, in one way or another, some such inexorable retribution is being exacted —

Nora (putting her hands over her ears). Rubbish! Do talk of something cheerful.

Rank. Oh, it's a mere laughing matter, the whole thing. My poor innocent spine has to suffer for my father's youthful amusements.

Nora (sitting at the table on the left). I suppose you mean that he was too partial to asparagus and pate de foie gras, don't you?

Rank. Yes, and to truffles.

Nora. Truffles, yes. And oysters too, I suppose?

Rank. Oysters, of course, that goes without saying.

Nora. And heaps of port and champagne. It is sad that all these nice things should take their revenge on our bones.

Rank. Especially that they should revenge themselves on the unlucky bones of those who have not had the satisfaction of enjoying them.

Nora. Yes, that's the saddest part of it all.

Rank (with a searching look at her). Hm! —

Nora (after a short pause). Why did you smile?

Rand. No, it was you that laughed.

Nora. No, it was you that smiled, Doctor Rank!

Rank (rising). You are a greater rascal than I thought.

Nora. I am in a silly mood today.

Rank. So it seems.

Nora (putting her hands on his shoulders). Dear, dear Doctor Rank, death mustn't take you away from Torvald and me.

Rank. It is a loss you would easily recover from. Those who are gone are soon forgotten.

Nora (looking at him anxiously). Do you believe that?

Rank. People form new ties, and then —

Nora. Who will form new ties?

Rank. Both you and Helmer, when I am gone. You yourself are already on the high road to it, I think. What did that Mrs. Linde want here last night?

Nora. Oho! — you don't mean to say you are jealous of poor Christine?

Rank. Yes, I am. She will be my successor in this house. When I am done for, this woman will —

Nora. Hush! don't speak so loud. She is in that room.

Rank. To-day again. There, you see.

Nora. She has only come to sew my dress for me. Bless my soul, how unreasonable you are! (Sits down on the sofa.) Be nice now, Doctor Rank, and to-morrow you will see how beautifully I shall dance, and you can imagine I am doing it all for you — and for Torvald too, of course. (Takes various things out of the box.) Doctor Rank, come and sit down here, and I will show you something.

Rank (sitting down). What is it?

Nora. Just look at those.

Rank. Silk stockings.

Nora. Flesh-coloured. Aren't they lovely? It is so dark here now, but to-morrow —. No, no, no! you must only look at the feet. Oh, well, you may have leave to look at the legs too.

Rank. Hm! —

Nora. Why are you looking so critical? Don't you think they will fit me?

Rank. I have no means of forming an opinion about that.

Nora (looks at him for a moment). For shame! (Hits him lightly on the ear with the stockings.) That's to punish you. (Folds them up again.)

Rank. And what other nice things am I to be allowed to see?

Nora. Not a single thing more, for being so naughty. (She looks among the things, humming to herself.)

Rank (after a short silence). When I am sitting here, talking to you as intimately as this, I cannot imagine for a moment what would have become of me if I had never come into this house.

Nora (smiling). I believe you do feel thoroughly at home with us.

Rank (in a lower voice, looking straight in front of him). And to be obliged to leave it all —

Nora. Nonsense, you are not going to leave it.

Rank (as before). And not be able to leave behind one the slightest token of one's gratitude, scarcely even a fleeting regret — nothing but an empty place which the first comer can fill as well as any other.

Nora. And if I asked you now for a —? No!

Rank. For what?

Nora. For a big proof of your friendship —

Rank. Yes, yes.

Nora. I mean a tremendously big favour —

Rank. Would you really make me so happy for once?

Nora. Ah, but you don't know what it is yet.

Rank. No — but tell me.

Nora. I really can't, Doctor Rank. It is something out of all reason; it means advice, and help, and a favour —

Rank. The bigger a thing it is the better. I can't conceive what it is you mean. Do tell me. Haven't I your confidence?

Nora. More than anyone else. I know you are my truest and best friend, and so I will tell you what it is. Well, Doctor Rank, it is something you must help me to prevent. You know how devotedly, how inexpressibly deeply Torvald loves me; he would never for a moment hesitate to give his life for me.

Rank (leaning toward her). Nora — do you think he is the only one —?

Nora (with a slight start). The only one —?

Rank. The only one who would gladly give his life for your sake.

Nora (sadly). Is that it?

Rank. I was determined you should know it before I went away, and there will never be a better opportunity than this. Now you know it, Nora. And now you know, too, that you can trust me as you would trust no one else.

Nora (rises deliberately and quietly). Let me pass.

Rank (makes room for her to pass him, but sits still). Nora!

Nora (at the hall door). Helen, bring in the lamp. (Goes over to the stove.) Dear Doctor Rank, that was really horrid of you.

Rank. To have loved you as much as anyone else does? Was that horrid?

Nora. No, but to go and tell me so. There was really no need —

Rank. What do you mean? Did you know —? (MAID enters with lamp, puts it down on the table, and goes out.) Nora — Mrs. Helmer — tell me, had you any idea of this?

Nora. Oh, how do I know whether I had or whether I hadn't. I really can't tell you — To think you could be so clumsy, Doctor Rank! We were getting on so nicely.

Bank. Well, at all events you know now that you can command me, body and soul. So won't you speak out?

Nora (looking at him). After what happened?

Rank. I beg you to let me know what it is.

Nora. I can't tell you anything now.

Rank. Yes, yes. You mustn't punish me in that way. Let me have permission to do for you whatever a man may do.

Nora. You can do nothing for me now. Besides, I really don't need any help at all. You will find that the whole thing is merely fancy on my part. It really is so — of course it is! (Sits down in the rocking-chair, and looks at him with a smile.) You are a nice sort of man, Doctor Rank! — don't you feel ashamed of yourself, now the lamp has come?

Rank. Not a bit. But perhaps I had better go — forever?

Nora. No, indeed, you shall not. Of course you must come here just as before. You know very well Torvald can't do without you.

Rank. Yes, but you?

Nora. Oh, I am always tremendously pleased when you come.

Rank. It is just that, that put me on the wrong track. You are a riddle to me. I have often thought that you would almost as soon be in my company as in Helmer's .

Nora. Yes — you see there are some people one loves best, and others whom one would almost always rather have as companions.

Rank. Yes, there is something in that.

Nora. When I was at home, of course I loved papa best. But I always thought it tremendous fun if I could steal down into the maids' room, because they never moralized at all, and talked to each other about such entertaining things.

Rank. I see — it is their place I have taken.

Nora (jumping-up and going to him). Oh, dear, nice Doctor Rank, I never meant that at all. But surely you can understand that being with Torvald is a little like being with papa —(Enter MAID from the hall.)

Maid. If you please, ma'am. (Whispers and hands her a card.)

Nora (glancing at the card). Oh! (Puts it in her pocket.)

Rank. Is there anything wrong?

Nora. No, no, not in the least. It is only something — It is my new dress —

Rank. What? Your dress is lying there.

Nora. Oh, yes, that one; but this is another. I ordered it. Torvald mustn't know about it —

Rank. Oho! Then that was the great secret.

Nora. Of course. Just go in to him; he is sitting in the inner room. Keep him as long as —

Rank. Make your mind easy; I won't let him escape. (Goes into HELMER'S room.)

Nora (to the MAID). And he is standing waiting in the kitchen?

Maid. Yes; he came up the back stairs.

Nora. But didn't you tell him no one was in?

Maid. Yes, but it was no good.

Nora. He won't go away?

Maid. No; he says he won't until he has seen you, ma'am.

Nora. Well, let him come in — but quietly. Helen, you mustn't say anything about it to any one. It is a surprise for my husband.

Maid. Yes, ma'am, I quite understand. (Exit.)

Nora. This dreadful thing is going to happen. It will happen in spite of me! No, no, no, it can't happen — it shan't happen! (She bolts the door of HELMER'S room. The MAID opens the hall door for KROGSTAD and shuts it after him. He is wearing a fur coat, high boots and a fur cap.)

Nora (advancing towards him). Speak low — my husband is at home.

Krogstad. No matter about that.

Nora. What do you want of me?

Krogstad. An explanation of something.

Nora. Make haste then. What is it?

Krogstad. You know, I suppose, that I have got my dismissal.

Nora. I couldn't prevent it, Mr. Krogstad. I fought as hard as I could on your side, but it was no good.

Krogstad. Does your husband love you so little, then? He knows what I can expose you to, and yet he ventures —

Nora. How can you suppose that he has any knowledge of the sort?

Krogstad. I didn't suppose so at all. It would not be the least like our dear Torvald Helmer to show so much courage —

Nora. Mr. Krogstad, a little respect for my husband, please.

Krogstad. Certainly — all the respect he deserves. But since you have kept the matter so carefully to yourself, I make bold to suppose that you have a little clearer idea than you had yesterday, of what it actually is that you have done?

Nora. More than you could ever teach me.

Krogstad. Yes, such a bad lawyer as I am.

Nora. What is it you want of me?

Krogstad. Only to see how you were, Mrs. Helmer. I have been thinking about you all day long. A mere cashier — a quill-driver, a — well, a man like me — even he has a little of what is called feeling, you know.

Nora. Show it, then; think of my little children.

Krogstad. Have you and your husband thought of mine? But never mind about that. I only wanted to tell you that you need not take this matter too seriously. In the first place there will be no accusation made on my part.

Nora. No, of course not; I was sure of that.

Krogstad. The whole thing can be arranged amicably; there is no reason why anyone should know anything about it. It will remain a secret between us three.

Nora. My husband must never get to know anything about it.

Krogstad. How will you be able to prevent it? Am I to understand that you can pay the balance that is owing?

Nora. No, not just at present.

Krogstad. Or perhaps that you have some expedient for raising the money soon?

Nora. No expedient that I mean to make use of.

Krogstad. Well, in any case, it would have been of no use to you now. If you stood there with ever so much money in your hand, I would never part with your bond.

Nora. Tell me what purpose you mean to put it to.

Krogstad. I shall only preserve it — keep it in my possession. No one who is not concerned in the matter shall have the slightest hint of it. So that if the thought of it has driven you to any desperate resolution —

Nora. It has.

Krogstad. If you had it in your mind to run away from your home —

Nora. I had.

Krogstad. Or even something worse —

Nora. How could you know that?

Krogstad. Give up the idea.

Nora. How did you know I had thought of that?

Krogstad. Most of us think of that at first. I did, too — but I hadn't the courage.

Nora (faintly). No more had I.

Krogstad (in a tone of relief). No, that's it, isn't it — you hadn't the courage either?

Nora. No, I haven't — I haven't.

Krogstad. Besides, it would have been a great piece of folly. Once the first storm at home is over —. I have a letter for your husband in my pocket.

Nora. Telling him everything?

Krogstad. In as lenient a manner as I possibly could.

Nora (quickly). He mustn't get the letter. Tear it up. I will find some means of getting money.

Krogstad. Excuse me, Mrs. Helmer, but I think I told you just how —

Nora. I am not speaking of what I owe you. Tell me what sum you are asking my husband for, and I will get the money.

Krogstad. I am not asking your husband for a penny.

Nora. What do you want, then?

Krogstad. I will tell you. I want to rehabilitate myself, Mrs. Helmer; I want to get on; and in that your husband must help me. For the last year and a half I have not had a hand in anything dishonourable, and all that time I have been struggling in most restricted circumstances. I was content to work my way up step by step. Now I am turned out, and I am not going to be satisfied with merely being taken into favour again. I want to get on, I tell you. I want to get into the Bank again, in a higher position. Your husband must make a place for me —

Nora. That he will never do!

Krogstad. He will; I know him; he dare not protest. And as soon as I am in there again with him, then you will see! Within a year I shall be the manager's right hand. It will be Nils Krogstad and not Torvald Helmer who manages the Bank.

Nora. That's a thing you will never see!

Krogstad. Do you mean that you will —?

Nora. I have courage enough for it now.

Krogstad. Oh, you can't frighten me. A fine, spoilt lady like you —

Nora. You will see, you will see.

Krogstad. Under the ice, perhaps? Down into the cold, coal-black water? And then, in the spring, to float up to the surface, all horrible and unrecognizable, with your hair fallen out —

Nora. You can't frighten me.

Krogstad. Nor you me. People don't do such things, Mrs. Helmer. Besides, what use would it be? I should have him completely in my power all the same.

Nora. Afterwards? When I am no longer —

Krogstad. Have you forgot that it is I who have the keeping of your reputation? (Nora stands speechlessly looking at him.) Well, now, I have warned you. Do not do anything foolish. When Helmer has had my letter, I shall expect a message from him. And be sure you remember that it is your husband himself who has forced me into such ways as this again. I will never forgive him for that. Good-bye, Mrs. Helmer. (Exit through the hall.)

Nora (goes to the hall door, opens it slightly and listens). He is going. He is not putting the letter in the box. Oh, no, no, that's impossible! (Opens the door by degrees.) What is that? He is standing outside. He is not going downstairs. Is he hesitating? Can he —? (A letter drops into the box; then KROGSTAD'S footsteps are heard, till they die away as he goes downstairs. NORA utters a stifled cry, and runs across the room to the table by the sofa. A short pause.)

Nora. In the letter-box. (Steals across to the hall-door.) There it lies — Torvald, Torvald, there is no hope for us now!

(MRS. LINDE comes in from the room on the left, carrying the dress.)

Mrs. Linde. There, I can't see anything more to mend now. Would you like to try it on —?

Nora (in a hoarse whisper). Christine, come here.

Mrs. Linde (throwing the dress down on the sofa). What is the matter with you? You look so agitated!

Nora. Come here. Do you see that letter? There, look — you can see it through the glass in the letter-box.

Mrs. Linde. Yes, I see it.

Nora. That letter is from Krogstad.

Mrs. Linde. Nora — it was Krogstad who lent you the money!

Nora. Yes, and now Torvald will know all about it.

Mrs. Linde. Believe me, Nora, that's the best thing for both of you.

Nora. You don't know all. I forged a name.

Mrs. Linde. Good heavens —!

Nora. I only want to say this to you, Christine — you must be my witness.

Mrs. Linde. Your witness! What do you mean? What am I to —?

Nora. If I should go out of my mind — and it might easily happen —

Mrs. Linde. Nora!

Nora. Or if anything else should happen to me — anything, for instance, that might prevent my being here —

Mrs. Linde. Nora! Nora! you are quite out of your mind.

Nora. And if it should happen that there were someone who wanted to take all the responsibility, all the blame, you understand —

Mrs. Linde. Yes, yes — but how can you suppose —?

Nora. Then you must be my witness, that it is not true, Christine. I am not out of my mind at all; I am in my right senses now, and I tell you no one else has known anything about it; I and I alone, did the whole thing. Remember that.

Mrs. Linde. I will, indeed. But I don't understand all this.

Nora. How should you understand it? A wonderful thing is going to happen.

Mrs. Linde. A wonderful thing?

Nora. Yes, a wonderful thing! — But it is so terrible, Christine; it mustn't happen, not for all the world.

Mrs. Linde. I will go at once and see Krogstad.

Nora. Don't go to him; he will do you some harm.

Mrs. Linde. There was a time when he would gladly do anything for my sake.

Nora. He?

Mrs. Linde. Where does he live?

Nora. How should I know —? Yes (feeling in her pocket) here is his card. But the letter, the letter —!

Helmer (calls from his room, knocking at the door). Nora.

Nora (cries out anxiously). Oh, what's that? What do you want?

Helmer. Don't be so frightened. We are not coming in; you have locked the door. Are you trying on your dress?

Nora. Yes, that's it. I look so nice, Torvald.

Mrs. Linde (who has read the card) I see he lives at the corner here.

Nora. Yes, but it's no use. It is hopeless. The letter is lying there in the box.

Mrs. Linde. And your husband keeps the key?

Nora. Yes, always.

Mrs. Linde. Krogstad must ask for his letter back unread, he must find some pretence —

Nora. But it is just at this time that Torvald generally —

Mrs. Linde. You must delay him. Go in to him in the meantime. I will come back as soon as I can. (She goes out hurriedly through the hall door.)

Nora (goes to HELMER'S door, opens it and peeps in). Torvald!

Helmer (from the inner room). Well? May I venture at last to come into my own room again? Come along, Rank, now you will see —(Halting in the doorway.) But what is this?

Nora. What is what, dear?

Helmer. Rank led me to expect a splendid transformation.

Rank (in the doorway). I understood so, but evidently I was mistaken.

Nora. Yes, nobody is to have the chance of admiring me in my dress until to-morrow.

Helmer. But, my dear Nora, you look so worn out. Have you been practising too much?

Nora. No, I have not practised at all.

Helmer. But you will need to —

Nora. Yes, indeed I shall, Torvald. But I can't get on a bit without you to help me; I have absolutely forgotten the whole thing.

Helmer. Oh, we will soon work it up again.

Nora. Yes, help me, Torvald. Promise that you will! I am so nervous about it — all the people —. You must give yourself up to me entirely this evening. Not the tiniest bit of business — you mustn't even take a pen in your hand. Will you promise, Torvald dear?

Helmer. I promise. This evening I will be wholly and absolutely at your service, you helpless little mortal. Ah, by the way, first of all I will just —(Goes toward the hall-door.)

Nora. What are you going to do there?

Helmer. Only see if any letters have come.

Nora. No, no! don't do that, Torvald!

Helmer. Why not?

Nora. Torvald, please don't. There is nothing there.

Helmer. Well, let me look. (Turns to go to the letter-box. NORA, at the piano, plays the first bars of the Tarantella. HELMER stops in the doorway.) Aha!

Nora. I can't dance to-morrow if I don't practise with you.

Helmer (going up to her). Are you really so afraid of it, dear?

Nora. Yes, so dreadfully afraid of it. Let me practise at once; there is time now, before we go to dinner. Sit down and play for me, Torvald dear; criticise me, and correct me as you play.

Helmer. With great pleasure, if you wish me to. (Sits down at the piano.)

Nora (takes out of the box a tambourine and a long variegated shawl. She hastily drapes the shawl round her. Then she springs to the front of the stage and calls out). Now play for me! I am going to dance!

(HELMER plays and NORA dances. RANK stands by the piano behind HELMER, and looks on.)

Helmer (as he plays). Slower, slower!

Nora. I can't do it any other way.

Helmer. Not so violently, Nora!

Nora. This is the way.

Helmer (stops playing). No, no — that is not a bit right.

Nora (laughing and swinging the tambourine). Didn't I tell you so?

Rank. Let me play for her.

Helmer (getting up). Yes, do. I can correct her better then.

(RANK sits down at the piano and plays. Nora dances more and more wildly. HELMER has taken up a position beside the stove, and during her dance gives her frequent instructions. She does not seem to hear him; her hair comes down and falls over her shoulders; she pays no attention to it, but goes on dancing. Enter MRS. LINDE.)

Mrs. Linde (standing as if spell-bound in the doorway). Oh! —

Nora (as she dances). Such fun, Christine!

Helmer. My dear darling Nora, you are dancing as if your life depended on it.

Nora. So it does.

Helmer. Stop, Rank; this is sheer madness. Stop, I tell you. (RANK stops playing, and, NORA suddenly stands still. HELMER goes up to her.) I could never have believed it. You have forgotten everything I taught you.

Nora (throwing away the tambourine). There, you see.

Helmer. You will want a lot of coaching.

Nora. Yes, you see how much I need it. You must coach me up to the last minute. Promise me that, Torvald!

Helmer. You can depend on me.

Nora. You must not think of anything but me, either to-day or to-morrow; you mustn't open a single letter — not even open the letter-box —

Helmer. Ah, you are still afraid of that fellow ——

Nora. Yes, indeed I am.

Helmer. Nora, I can tell from your looks that there is a letter from him lying there.

Nora. I don't know; I think there is; but you must not read anything of that kind now. Nothing horrid must come between us till this is all over.

Rank (whispers to HELMER). You mustn't contradict her.

Helmer (taking her in his arms). The child shall have her way. But to-morrow night, after you have danced —

Nora. Then you will be free. (The MAID appears in the doorway to the right.)

Maid. Dinner is served, ma'am.

Nora. We will have champagne, Helen.

Maid. Very good, ma'am.

Helmer. Hullo! — are we going to have a banquet? (Exit.)

Nora. Yes, a champagne banquet till the small hours. (Calls out.) And a few macaroons, Helen — lots, just for once!

Helmer. Come, come, don't be so wild and nervous. Be my own little skylark, as you used.

Nora. Yes, dear, I will. But go in now and you too, Doctor Rank. Christine, you must, help me to do up my hair.

Rank (whispers to HELMER as they go out). I suppose there is nothing — she is not expecting anything?

Helmer. Far from it, my dear fellow; it is simply nothing more than this childish nervousness I was telling you of. (They go into the right-hand room.)

Nora. Well!

Mrs. Linde. Gone out of town.

Nora. I could tell from your face.

Mrs. Linde. He is coming home tomorrow evening. I wrote a note for him.

Nora. You should have let it alone; you must prevent nothing. After all, it is splendid to be waiting for a wonderful thing to happen.

Mrs. Linde. What is it that you are waiting for?

Nora, Oh, you wouldn't understand. Go in to them. I will come in a moment. (MRS. LINDE goes into the dining-room. NORA stands still for a little while, as if to compose herself. Then she looks at her watch.) Five o'clock. Seven hours till midnight; and then four-and-twenty hours till the next midnight. Then the Tarantella will be over. Twenty-four and seven? Thirty-one hours to live.

Helmer (from the doorway on the right). Where's my little skylark?

Nora (going to him with her arms out-stretched). Here she is!

Act 3

(THE SAME SCENE— The table has been placed in the middle of the stage, with chairs around it. A lamp is burning on the table. The door into the hall stands open. Dance music is heard in the room above. MRS. LINDE is sitting at the table idly turning over the leaves of a book; she tries to read, but does not seem able to collect her thoughts. Every now and then she listens intently for a sound at the outer door.)

Mrs. Linde (looking at her watch). Not yet — and the time is nearly up. If only he does not —. (Listens again.) Ah, there he is. (Goes into the hall and opens the outer door carefully. Light footsteps are heard on the stairs. She whispers.) Come in. There is no one here.

Krogstad (in the doorway). I found a note from you at home. What does this mean?

Mrs. Linde. It is absolutely necessary that I should have a talk with you.

Krogstad. Really? And is it absolutely necessary that it should be here?

Mrs. Linde. It is impossible where I live; there is no private entrance to my rooms. Come in; we are quite alone. The maid is asleep, and the Helmers are at the dance upstairs.

Krogstad (coming into the room). Are the Helmers really at a dance tonight?

Mrs. Linde. Yes, why not?

Krogstad. Certainly — why not?

Mrs. Linde. Now, Nils, let us have a talk.

Krogstad. Can we two have anything to talk about?

Mrs. Linde. We have a great deal to talk about.

Krogstad. I shouldn't have thought so.

Mrs. Linde. No, you have never properly understood me.

Krogstad. Was there anything else to understand except what was obvious to all the world — a heartless woman jilts a man when a more lucrative chance turns up.

Mrs. Linde. Do you believe I am as absolutely heartless as all that? And do you believe that I did it with a light heart?

Krogstad. Didn't you?

Mrs. Linde. Nils, did you really think that?

Krogstad. If it were as you say, why did you write to me as you did at the time?

Mrs. Linde. I could do nothing else. As I had to break with you, it was my duty also to put an end to all that you felt for me.

Krogstad (wringing his hands). So that was it. And all this — only for the sake of money.

Mrs. Linde. You must not forget that I had a helpless mother and two little brothers. We couldn't wait for you, Nils; your prospects seemed hopeless then.

Krogstad. That may be so, but you had no right to throw me over for any one else's sake.

Mrs. Linde. Indeed I don't know. Many a time did I ask myself if I had a right to do it.

Krogstad (more gently). When I lost you, it was as if all the solid ground went from under my feet. Look at me now — I am a shipwrecked man clinging to a bit of wreckage.

Mrs. Linde. But help may be near.

Krogstad. It was near; but then you came and stood in my way.

Mrs. Linde. Unintentionally, Nils. It was only today that I learnt it was your place I was going to take in the bank.

Krogstad. I believe you, if you say so. But now that you know it, are you not going to give it up to me?

Mrs. Linde. No, because that would not benefit you in the least.

Krogstad. Oh, benefit, benefit — I would have done it whether or no.

Mrs. Linde. I have learnt to act prudently. Life, and hard, bitter necessity have taught me that.

Krogstad. And life has taught me not to believe in fine speeches.

Mrs. Linde. Then life has taught you something very reasonable. But deeds you must believe in?

Krogstad. What do you mean by that?

Mrs. Linde. You said you were like a shipwrecked man clinging to some wreckage.

Krogstad. I had good reason to say so.

Mrs. Linde. Well, I am like a shipwrecked woman clinging to some wreckage — no one to mourn for, no one to care for.

Krogstad. It was your own choice.

Mrs. Linde. There was no other choice, then.

Krogstad. Well, what now?

Mrs. Linde. Nils, how would it be if we two shipwrecked people could join forces?

Krogstad. What are you saying?

Mrs. Linde. Two on the same piece of wreckage would stand a better chance than each on their own.

Krogstad. Christine!

Mrs. Linde. What do you suppose brought me to town?

Krogstad. Do you mean that you gave me a thought?

Mrs. Linde. I could not endure life without work. All my life, as long as I can remember, I have worked, and it has been my greatest and only pleasure. But now I am quite alone in the world — my life is so dreadfully empty and I feel so forsaken. There is not the least pleasure in working for one's self. Nils, give me someone and something to work for.

Krogstad. I don't trust that. It is nothing but a woman's overstrained sense of generosity that prompts you to make such an offer of your self.

Mrs. Linde. Have you ever noticed anything of the sort in me?

Krogstad. Could you really do it? Tell me — do you know all about my past life?

Mrs. Linde. Yes.

Krogstad. And do you know what they think of me here?

Mrs. Linde. You seemed to me to imply that with me you might have been quite another man.

Krogstad. I am certain of it.

Mrs. Linde. Is it too late now?

Krogstad. Christine, are you saying this deliberately? Yes, I am sure you are. I see it in your face. Have you really the courage, then —?

Mrs. Linde. I want to be a mother to someone, and your children need a mother. We two need each other. Nils, I have faith in your real character — I can dare anything together with you.

Krogstad (grasps her hands). Thanks, thanks, Christine! Now I shall find a way to clear myself in the eyes of the world. Ah, but I forgot —

Mrs. Linde (listening). Hush! The Tarantella! Go, go!

Krogstad. Why? What is it?

Mrs. Linde. Do you hear them up there? When that is over, we may expect them back.

Krogstad. Yes, yes — I will go. But it is all no use. Of course you are not aware what steps I have taken in the matter of the Helmers.

Mrs. Linde. Yes, I know all about that.

Krogstad. And in spite of that have you the courage to —?

Mrs. Linde. I understand very well to what lengths a man like you might be driven by despair.

Krogstad. If I could only undo what I have done!

Mrs. Linde. You cannot. Your letter is lying in the letter-box now.

Krogstad. Are you sure of that?

Mrs. Linde. Quite sure, but —

Krogstad (with a searching look at her). Is that what it all means? — that you want to save your friend at any cost? Tell me frankly. Is that it?

Mrs. Linde. Nils, a woman who has once sold herself for another's sake, doesn't do it a second time.

Krogstad. I will ask for my letter back.

Mrs. Linde. No, no.

Krogstad. Yes, of course I will. I will wait here till Helmer comes; I will tell him he must give me my letter back — that it only concerns my dismissal — that he is not to read it —

Mrs. Linde. No, Nils, you must not recall your letter.

Krogstad. But, tell me, wasn't it for that very purpose that you asked me to meet you here?

Mrs. Linde. In my first moment of fright, it was. But twenty-four hours have elapsed since then, and in that time I have witnessed incredible things in this house. Helmer must know all about it. This unhappy secret must be enclosed; they must have a complete understanding between them, which is impossible with all this concealment and falsehood going on.

Krogstad. Very well, if you will take the responsibility. But there is one thing I can do in any case, and I shall do it at once.

Mrs. Linde (listening). You must be quick and go! The dance is over; we are not safe a moment longer.

Krogstad. I will wait for you below.

Mrs. Linde. Yes, do. You must see me back to my door.

Krogstad. I have never had such an amazing piece of good fortune in my life! (Goes out through the outer door. The door between the room and the hall remains open.)

Mrs. Linde (tidying up the room and laying her hat and cloak ready). What a difference! What a difference! Someone to work for and live for — a home to bring comfort into. That I will do, indeed. I wish they would be quick and come. (Listens.) Ah, there they are now. I must put on my things. (Takes up her hat and cloak. HELMER'S and NORA'S voices are heard outside; a key is turned, and HELMER brings NORA almost by force into the hall. She is in an Italian costume with a large black shawl round her; he is in evening dress, and a black domino which is flying open.)

Nora (hanging back in the doorway, and struggling with him). No, no, no! — don't take me in. I want to go upstairs again; I don't want to leave so early.

Helmer. But, my dearest Nora —

Nora. Please, Torvald dear — please, please — only an hour more.

Helmer. Not a single minute, my sweet Nora. You know that was our agreement. Come along into the room; you are catching cold standing there. (He brings her gently into the room, in spite of her resistance.)

Mrs. Linde. Good evening.

Nora. Christine!

Helmer. You here, so late, Mrs. Linde?

Mrs. Linde. Yes, you must excuse me; I was so anxious to see Nora in her dress.

Nora. Have you been sitting here waiting for me?

Mrs. Linde. Yes, unfortunately I came too late, you had already gone upstairs; and I thought I couldn't go away again without having seen you.

Helmer (taking off NORA'S shawl). Yes, take a good look at her. I think she is worth looking at. Isn't she charming, Mrs. Linde?

Mrs. Linde. Yes, indeed she is.

Helmer. Doesn't she look remarkably pretty? Everyone thought so at the dance. But she is terribly self-willed, this sweet little person. What are we to do with her? You will hardly believe that I had almost to bring her away by force.

Nora. Torvald, you will repent not having let me stay, even if it were only for half an hour.

Helmer. Listen to her, Mrs. Linde! She had danced her Tarantella, and it had been a tremendous success, as it deserved — although possibly the performance was a trifle too realistic — little more so, I mean, than was strictly compatible with the limitations of art. But never mind about that! The chief thing is, she had made a success — she had made a tremendous success. Do you think I was going to let her remain there after that, and spoil the effect? No, indeed! I took my charming little Capri maiden — my capricious little Capri maiden, I should say — on my arm; took one quick turn round the room; a curtsey on either side, and, as they say in novels, the beautiful apparition disappeared. An exit ought always to be effective, Mrs. Linde; but that is what I cannot make Nora understand. Pooh! this room is hot. (Throws his domino on a chair, and opens the door of his room.) Hullo! it's all dark in here. Oh, of course — excuse me —. (He goes in, and lights some candles.)

Nora (in a hurried and breathless whisper). Well?

Mrs. Linde. (in a low voice). I have had a talk with him.

Nora. Yes, and —

Mrs. Linde. Nora, you must tell your husband all about it.

Nora (in an expressionless voice). I knew it.

Mrs. Linde. You have nothing to be afraid of as far as Krogstad is concerned; but you must tell him.

Nora. I won't tell him.

Mrs. Linde. Then the letter will.

Nora. Thank you, Christine. Now I know what I must do. Hush —!

Helmer (coming in again). Well, Mrs. Linde, have you admired her?

Mrs. Linde. Yes, and now I will say good-night.

Helmer. What, already? Is this yours, this knitting?

Mrs. Linde (taking it). Yes, thank you, I had very nearly forgotten it.

Helmer. So you knit?

Mrs. Linde. Of course.

Helmer. Do you know, you ought to embroider?

Mrs. Linde. Really? Why?

Helmer. Yes, it's far more becoming. Let me show you. You hold the embroidery thus in your left hand, and use the needle with the right — like this — with a long, easy sweep. Do you see?

Mrs. Linde. Yes, perhaps —

Helmer. But in the case of knitting — that can never be anything but ungraceful; look here — the arms close together, the knitting-needles going up and down — it has a sort of Chinese effect —. That was really excellent champagne they gave us.

Mrs. Linde. Well — good-night, Nora, and don't be self-willed any more.

Helmer. That's right, Mrs. Linde.

Mrs. Linde. Good-night, Mr. Helmer.

Helmer (accompanying her to the door). Good-night, good-night. I hope you will get home all right. I should be very happy to — but you haven't any great distance to go. Good-night, good-night. (She goes out; he shuts the door after her and comes in again.) Ah! — at last we have got rid of her. She is a frightful bore, that woman.

Nora. Aren't you very tired, Torvald?

Helmer. No, not in the least.

Nora. Nor sleepy?

Helmer. Not a bit. On the contrary, I feel extraordinarily lively. And you? — you really look both tired and sleepy.

Nora. Yes, I am very tired. I want to go to sleep at once.

Helmer. There, you see it was quite right of me not to let you stay there any longer.

Nora. Everything you do is quite right, Torvald.

Helmer (kissing her on the forehead). Now my little skylark is speaking reasonably. Did you notice what good spirits Rank was in this evening?

Nora. Really? Was he? I didn't speak to him at all.

Helmer. And I very little, but I have not for a long time seen him in such good form. (Looks for a while at her and then goes nearer to her.) It is delightful to be at home by ourselves again, to be all alone with you — you fascinating, charming little darling!

Nora. Don't look at me like that, Torvald.

Helmer. Why shouldn't I look at my dearest treasure? — at all the beauty that is mine, all my very own?

Nora (going to the other side of the table). You mustn't say things like that to me tonight.

Helmer (following her). You have still got the Tarantella in your blood, I see. And it makes you more captivating than ever. Listen — the guests are beginning to go now. (In a lower voice.) Nora — soon the whole house will be quiet.

Nora. Yes, I hope so.

Helmer. Yes, my own darling Nora. Do you know, when I am out at a party with you like this, why I speak so little to you, keep away from you, and only send a stolen glance in your direction now and then? — do you know why I do that? It is because I make believe to myself that we are secretly in love, and you are my secretly promised bride, and that no one suspects there is anything between us.

Nora. Yes, yes — I know very well your thoughts are with me all the time.

Helmer. And when we are leaving, and I am putting the shawl over your beautiful young shoulders — on your lovely neck — then I imagine that you are my young bride and that we have just come from the wedding, and I am bringing you for the first time into our home — to be alone with you for the first time — quite alone with my shy little darling! All this evening I have longed for nothing but you. When I watched the seductive figures of the Tarantella, my blood was on fire; I could endure it no longer, and that was why I brought you down so early —

Nora. Go away, Torvald! You must let me go. I won't —

Helmer. What's that? You're joking, my little Nora! You won't — you won't? Am I not your husband —? (A knock is heard at the outer door.)

Nora (starting). Did you hear —?

Helmer (going into the hall). Who is it?

Rank (outside). It is I. May I come in for a moment?

Helmer (in a fretful whisper). Oh, what does he want now? (Aloud.) Wait a minute? (Unlocks the door.) Come, that's kind of you not to pass by our door.

Rank. I thought I heard your voice, and felt as if I should like to look in. (With a swift glance round.) Ah, yes! — these dear familiar rooms. You are very happy and cosy in here, you two.

Helmer. It seems to me that you looked after yourself pretty well upstairs too.

Rank. Excellently. Why shouldn't I? Why shouldn't one enjoy everything in this world? — at any rate as much as one can, and as long as one can. The wine was capital —

Helmer. Especially the champagne.

Rank. So you noticed that too? It is almost incredible how much I managed to put away!

Nora. Torvald drank a great deal of champagne tonight, too.

Rank. Did he?

Nora. Yes, and he is always in such good spirits afterwards.

Rank. Well, why should one not enjoy a merry evening after a well-spent day?

Helmer. Well spent? I am afraid I can't take credit for that.

Rank (clapping him on the back). But I can, you know!

Nora. Doctor Rank, you must have been occupied with some scientific investigation today.

Rank. Exactly.

Helmer. Just listen! — little Nora talking about scientific investigations!

Nora. And may I congratulate you on the result?

Rank. Indeed you may.

Nora. Was it favourable, then.

Rank. The best possible, for both doctor and patient — certainty.

Nora (quickly and searchingly). Certainty?

Rank. Absolute certainty. So wasn't I entitled to make a merry evening of it after that?

Nora. Yes, you certainly were, Doctor Rank.

Helmer. I think so too, so long as you don't have to pay for it in the morning.

Rank. Oh well, one can't have anything in this life without paying for it.

Nora. Doctor Rank — are you fond of fancy-dress balls?

Rank. Yes, if there is a fine lot of pretty costumes.

Nora. Tell me — what shall we two wear at the next?

Helmer. Little featherbrain! — are you thinking of the next already?

Rank. We two? Yes, I can tell you. You shall go as a good fairy —

Helmer. Yes, but what do you suggest as an appropriate costume for that?

Rank. Let your wife go dressed just as she is in every-day life.

Helmer. That was really very prettily turned. But can't you tell us what you will be?

Rank. Yes, my dear friend, I have quite made up my mind about that.

Helmer. Well?

Rank. At the next fancy-dress ball I shall be invisible.

Helmer That's a good joke!

Rank. There is a big black hat — have you never heard of hats that make you invisible? If you put one on, no one can see you.

Helmer (suppressing a smile). Yes, you are quite right.

Rank. But I am clean forgetting what I came for. Helmer, give me a cigar — one of the dark Havanas.

Helmer. With the greatest pleasure. (Offers him his case.)

Rank (takes a cigar and cuts off the end). Thanks.

Nora (striking a match). Let me give you a light.

Rank. Thank you. (She holds the match for him to light his cigar.) And now good-bye!

Helmer. Good-bye, good-bye, dear old man!

Nora. Sleep well, Doctor Rank.

Rank. Thank you for that wish.

Nora. Wish me the same.

Rank. You? Well, if you want me to sleep well! And thanks for the light. (He nods to them both and goes out.)

Helmer (in a subdued voice). He has drunk more than he ought.

Nora (absently). Maybe. (HELMER takes a bunch of keys out of his pocket and goes into the hall.) Torvald! what are you going to do there?

Helmer. Empty the letter-box; it is quite full; there will be no room to put the newspaper in to-morrow morning.

Nora. Are you going to work to-night?

Helmer. You know quite well I'm not. What is this? Some one has been at the lock.

Nora. At the lock?

Helmer. Yes, someone has. What can it mean? I should never have thought the maid —. Here is a broken hairpin. Nora, it is one of yours.

Nora (quickly). Then it must have been the children —

Helmer. Then you must get them out of those ways. There, at last I have got it open. (Takes out the contents of the letter-box, and calls to the kitchen.) Helen! — Helen, put out the light over the front door. (Goes back into the room and shuts the door into the hall. He holds out his hand full of letters.) Look at that — look what a heap of them there are. (Turning them over.) What on earth is that?

Nora (at the window). The letter — No! Torvald, no!

Helmer. Two cards — of Rank's .

Nora. Of Doctor Rank's?

Helmer (looking at them). Doctor Rank. They were on the top. He must have put them in when he went out.

Nora. Is there anything written on them?

Helmer. There is a black cross over the name. Look there — what an uncomfortable idea! It looks as If he were announcing his own death.

Nora. It is just what he is doing.

Helmer. What? Do you know anything about it? Has he said anything to you?

Nora. Yes. He told me that when the cards came it would be his leave-taking from us. He means to shut himself up and die.

Helmer. My poor old friend. Certainly I knew we should not have him very long with us. But so soon! And so he hides himself away like a wounded animal.

Nora. If it has to happen, it is best it should be without a word — don't you think so, Torvald?

Helmer (walking up and down). He has so grown into our lives. I can't think of him as having gone out of them. He, with his sufferings and his loneliness, was like a cloudy background to our sunlit happiness. Well, perhaps it is best so. For him, anyway. (Standing still.) And perhaps for us too, Nora. We two are thrown quite upon each other now. (Puts his arms around her.) My darling wife, I don't feel as if I could hold you tight enough. Do you know, Nora, I have often wished that you might be threatened by some great danger, so that I might risk my life's blood, and everything, for your sake.

Nora (disengages herself, and says firmly and decidedly). Now you must read your letters, Torvald.

Helmer. No, no; not tonight. I want to be with you, my darling wife.

Nora. With the thought of your friend's death —

Helmer. You are right, it has affected us both. Something ugly has come between us — the thought of the horrors of death. We must try and rid our minds of that. Until then — we will each go to our own room.

Nora (hanging on his neck). Good-night, Torvald — Good-night!

Helmer (kissing her on the forehead). Good-night, my little singing-bird. Sleep sound, Nora. Now I will read my letters through. (He takes his letters and goes into his room, shutting the door after him.)

Nora (gropes distractedly about, seizes HELMER'S domino, throws it round her, while she says in quick, hoarse, spasmodic whispers). Never to see him again. Never! Never! (Puts her shawl over her head.) Never to see my children again either — never again. Never! Never! — Ah! the icy, black water — the unfathomable depths — If only it were over! He has got it now — now he is reading it. Good-bye, Torvald and my children! (She is about to rush out through the hall, when HELMER opens his door hurriedly and stands with an open letter in his hand.)

Helmer. Nora!

Nora. Ah! —

Helmer. What is this? Do you know what is in this letter?

Nora. Yes, I know. Let me go! Let me get out!

Helmer (holding her back). Where are you going?

Nora (trying to get free). You shan't save me, Torvald!

Helmer (reeling). True? Is this true, that I read here? Horrible! No, no — it is impossible that it can be true.

Nora. It is true. I have loved you above everything else in the world.

Helmer. Oh, don't let us have any silly excuses.

Nora (taking a step towards him). Torvald —!

Helmer. Miserable creature — what have you done?

Nora. Let me go. You shall not suffer for my sake. You shall not take it upon yourself.

Helmer. No tragedy airs, please. (Locks the hall door.) Here you shall stay and give me an explanation. Do you understand what you have done? Answer me? Do you understand what you have done?

Nora (looks steadily at him and says with a growing look of coldness in her face). Yes, now I am beginning to understand thoroughly.

Helmer (walking about the room). What a horrible awakening! All these eight years — she who was my joy and pride — a hypocrite, a liar — worse, worse — a criminal! The unutterable ugliness of it all! — For shame! For shame! (NORA is silent and looks steadily at him. He stops in front of her.) I ought to have suspected that something of the sort would happen. I ought to have foreseen it. All your father's want of principle — be silent! — all your father's want of principle has come out in you. No religion, no morality, no sense of duty — How I am punished for having winked at what he did! I did it for your sake, and this is how you repay me.

Nora. Yes, that's just it.

Helmer. Now you have destroyed all my happiness. You have ruined all my future. It is horrible to think of! I am in the power of an unscrupulous man; he can do what he likes with me, ask anything he likes of me, give me any orders he pleases — I dare not refuse. And I must sink to such miserable depths because of a thoughtless woman!

Nora. When I am out of the way, you will be free.

Helmer. No fine speeches, please. Your father had always plenty of those ready, too. What good would it be to me if you were out of the way, as you say? Not the slightest. He can make the affair known everywhere; and if he does, I may be falsely suspected of having been a party to your criminal action. Very likely people will think I was behind it all — that it was I who prompted you! And I have to thank you for all this — you whom I have cherished during the whole of our married life. Do you understand now what it is you have done for me?

Nora (coldly and quietly). Yes.

Helmer. It is so incredible that I can't take it in. But we must come to some understanding. Take off that shawl. Take it off, I tell you. I must try and appease him some way or another. The matter must be hushed up at any cost. And as for you and me, it must appear as if everything between us were as before — but naturally only in the eyes of the world. You will still remain in my house, that is a matter of course. But I shall not allow you to bring up the children; I dare not trust them to you. To think that I should be obliged to say so to one whom I have loved so dearly, and whom

I still —. No, that is all over. From this moment happiness is not the question; all that concerns us is to save the remains, the fragments, the appearance —

(A ring is heard at the front-door bell.)

Helmer (with a start). What is that? So late! Can the worst —? Can he —? Hide yourself, Nora. Say you are ill.

(NORA stands motionless. HELMER goes and unlocks the hall door.)

Maid (half-dressed, comes to the door). A letter for the mistress.

Helmer. Give it to me. (Takes the letter, and shuts the door.) Yes, it is from him. You shall not have it; I will read it myself.

Nora. Yes, read it.

Helmer (standing by the lamp). I scarcely have the courage to do it. It may mean ruin for both of us. No, I must know. (Tears open the letter, runs his eye over a few lines, looks at a paper enclosed, and gives a shout of joy.) Nora! (She looks at him, questioningly.) Nora! No, I must read it once again —. Yes, it is true! I am saved! Nora, I am saved!

Nora. And I?

Helmer. You too, of course; we are both saved, both saved, both you and I. Look, he sends you your bond back. He says he regrets and repents — that a happy change in his life — never mind what he says! We are saved, Nora! No one can do anything to you. Oh, Nora, Nora! — no, first I must destroy these hateful things. Let me see —. (Takes a look at the bond.) No, no, I won't look at it. The whole thing shall be nothing but a bad dream to me. (Tears up the bond and both letters, throws them all into the stove, and watches them burn.) There — now it doesn't exist any longer. He says that since Christmas Eve you —. These must have been three dreadful days for you, Nora.

Nora. I have fought a hard fight these three days.

Helmer. And suffered agonies, and seen no way out but —. No, we won't call any of the horrors to mind. We will only shout with joy, and keep saying, "It's all over! It's all over!" Listen to me, Nora. You don't seem to realise that it is all over. What is this? — such a cold, set face! My poor little Nora, I quite understand; you don't feel as if you could believe that I have forgiven you. But it is true, Nora, I swear it; I have forgiven you everything. I know that what you did, you did out of love for me.

Nora. That is true.

Helmer. You have loved me as a wife ought to love her husband. Only you had not sufficient knowledge to judge of the means you used. But do you suppose you are any the less dear to me, because you don't understand how to act on your own responsibility? No, no; only lean on me; I will advise you and direct you. I should not be a man if this womanly helplessness did not just give you a double attractiveness in my eyes. You must not think any more about the hard things I said in my first moment of consternation, when I thought everything was going to overwhelm me. I have forgiven you, Nora; I swear to you I have forgiven you.

Nora. Thank you for your forgiveness. (She goes out through the door to the right.)

Helmer. No, don't go —. (Looks in.) What are you doing in there?

Nora (from within). Taking off my fancy dress.

Helmer (standing at the open door). Yes, do. Try and calm yourself, and make your mind easy again, my frightened little singing-bird. Be at rest, and feel secure; I have broad wings to shelter you under. (Walks up and down by the door.) How warm and cosy our home is, Nora. Here is shelter for you; here I will protect you like a hunted dove that I have saved from a hawk's claws; I will bring peace to your poor beating heart. It will come, little by little, Nora, believe me. To-morrow morning you will look upon it all quite differently; soon everything will be just as it was before. Very soon you won't need me to assure you that I have forgiven you; you will yourself feel the certainty that I have done so. Can you suppose I should ever think of such a thing as repudiating you, or even reproaching you? You have no idea what a true man's heart is like, Nora. There is something so indescribably sweet and satisfying, to a man, in the knowledge that he has forgiven his wife — forgiven her freely, and with all his heart. It seems as if that had made her, as it were, doubly his own; he has given her a new life, so to speak; and she is in a way become both wife and child to him. So you shall be for me after this, my little scared, helpless darling. Have no anxiety about anything, Nora; only be frank and open with me, and I will serve as will and conscience both to you —. What is this? Not gone to bed? Have you changed your things?

Nora (in everyday dress). Yes, Torvald, I have changed my things now.

Helmer. But what for? — so late as this.

Nora. I shall not sleep tonight.

Helmer. But, my dear Nora —

Nora (looking at her watch). It is not so very late. Sit down here, Torvald. You and I have much to say to one another. (She sits down at one side of the table.)

Helmer. Nora — what is this? — this cold, set face?

Nora. Sit down. It will take some time; I have a lot to talk over with you.

Helmer (sits down at the opposite side of the table). You alarm me, Nora! — and I don't understand you.

Nora. No, that is just it. You don't understand me, and I have never understood you either — before tonight. No, you mustn't interrupt me. You must simply listen to what I say. Torvald, this is a settling of accounts.

Helmer. What do you mean by that?

Nora (after a short silence). Isn't there one thing that strikes you as strange in our sitting here like this?

Helmer. What is that?

Nora. We have been married now eight years. Does it not occur to you that this is the first time we two, you and I, husband and wife, have had a serious conversation?

Helmer. What do you mean by serious?

Nora. In all these eight years — longer than that — from the very beginning of our acquaintance, we have never exchanged a word on any serious subject.

Helmer. Was it likely that I would be continually and forever telling you about worries that you could not help me to bear?

Nora. I am not speaking about business matters. I say that we have never sat down in earnest together to try and get at the bottom of anything.

Helmer. But, dearest Nora, would it have been any good to you?

Nora. That is just it; you have never understood me. I have been greatly wronged, Torvald — first by papa and then by you.

Helmer. What! By us two — by us two, who have loved you better than anyone else in in the world?

Nora (shaking her head). You have never loved me. You have only thought it pleasant to be in love with me.

Helmer. Nora, what do I hear you saying?

Nora. It is perfectly true, Torvald. When I was at home with papa, he told me his opinion about everything, and so I had the same opinions; and if I differed from him I concealed the fact, because he would not have liked it. He called me his doll-child, and he played with me just as I used to play with my dolls. And when I came to live with you —

Helmer. What sort of an expression is that to use about our marriage?

Nora (undisturbed). I mean that I was simply transferred from papa's hands into yours. You arranged everything according to your own taste, and so I got the same tastes as you — or else I pretended to, I am really not quite sure which — I think sometimes the one and sometimes the other. When I look back on it, it seems to me as if I had been living here like a poor woman — just from hand to mouth. I have existed merely to perform tricks for you, Torvald. But you would have it so. You and papa have committed a great sin against me. It is your fault that I have made nothing of my life.

Helmer. How unreasonable and how ungrateful you are, Nora! Have you not been happy here?

Nora. No, I have never been happy. I thought I was, but it has never really been so.

Helmer. Not — not happy!

Nora. No, only merry. And you have always been so kind to me. But our home has been nothing but a playroom. I have been your doll-wife, just as at home I was papa's doll-child; and here the children have been my dolls. I thought it great fun when you played with me, just as they thought it great fun when I played with them. That is what our marriage has been, Torvald.

Helmer. There is some truth in what you say — exaggerated and strained as your view of it is. But for the future it shall be different. Playtime shall be over, and lesson-time shall begin.

Nora. Whose lessons? Mine, or the children's?

Helmer. Both yours and the children's, my darling Nora.

Nora. Alas, Torvald, you are not the man to educate me into being a proper wife for you.

Helmer. And you can say that!

Nora. And I— how am I fitted to bring up the children?

Helmer. Nora!

Nora. Didn't you say so yourself a little while ago — that you dare not trust me to bring them up?

Helmer. In a moment of anger! Why do you pay any heed to that?

Nora. Indeed, you were perfectly right. I am not fit for the task. There is another task I must undertake first. I must try and educate myself — you are not the man to help me in that. I must do that for myself. And that is why I am going to leave you now.

Helmer (springing up). What do you say?

Nora. I must stand quite alone, if I am to understand myself and everything about me. It is for that reason that I cannot remain with you any longer.

Helmer. Nora, Nora!

Nora. I am going away from here now, at once. I am sure Christine will take me in for the night —

Helmer. You are out of your mind! I won't allow it! I forbid you!

Nora. It is no use forbidding me anything any longer. I will take with me what belongs to myself. I will take nothing from you, either now or later.

Helmer. What sort of madness is this!

Nora. Tomorrow I shall go home — I mean to my old home. It will be easiest for me to find something to do there.

Helmer. You blind, foolish woman!

Nora. I must try and get some sense, Torvald.

Helmer. To desert your home, your husband and your children! And you don't consider what people will say!

Nora. I cannot consider that at all. I only know that it is necessary for me.

Helmer. It's shocking. This is how you would neglect your most sacred duties.

Nora. What do you consider my most sacred duties?

Helmer. Do I need to tell you that? Are they not your duties to your husband and your children?

Nora. I have other duties just as sacred.

Helmer. That you have not. What duties could those be?

Nora. Duties to myself.

Helmer. Before all else, you are a wife and mother.

Nora. I don't believe that any longer. I believe that before all else I am a reasonable human being, just as you are — or, at all events, that I must try and become one. I know quite well, Torvald, that most people would think you right, and that views of that kind are to be found in books; but I can no longer content myself with what most people say, or with what is found in books. I must think over things for myself and get to understand them.

Helmer. Can you not understand your place in your own home? Have you not a reliable guide in such matters as that? — have you no religion?

Nora. I am afraid, Torvald, I do not exactly know what religion is.

Helmer. What are you saying?

Nora. I know nothing but what the clergyman said, when I went to be confirmed. He told us that religion was this, and that, and the other. When I am away from all this, and am alone, I will look into that matter too. I will see if what the clergyman said is true, or at all events if it is true for me.

Helmer. This is unheard of in a girl of your age! But if religion cannot lead you aright, let me try and awaken your conscience. I suppose you have some moral sense? Or — answer me — am I to think you have none?

Nora. I assure you, Torvald, that is not an easy question to answer. I really don't know. The thing perplexes me altogether. I only know that you and I look at it in quite a different light. I am learning, too, that the law is quite another thing from what I supposed; but I find it impossible to convince myself that the law is right. According to it a woman has no right to spare her old dying father, or to save her husband's life. I can't believe that.

Helmer. You talk like a child. You don't understand the conditions of the world in which you live.

Nora. No, I don't. But now I am going to try. I am going to see if I can make out who is right, the world or I.

Helmer. You are ill, Nora; you are delirious; I almost think you are out of your mind.

Nora. I have never felt my mind so clear and certain as to-night.

Helmer. And is it with a clear and certain mind that you forsake your husband and your children?

Nora. Yes, it is.

Helmer. Then there is only one possible explanation.

Nora. What is that?

Helmer. You do not love me any more.

Nora. No, that is just it.

Helmer. Nora! — and you can say that?

Nora. It gives me great pain, Torvald, for you have always been so kind to me, but I cannot help it. I do not love you any more.

Helmer (regaining his composure). Is that a clear and certain conviction too?

Nora. Yes, absolutely clear and certain. That is the reason why I will not stay here any longer.

Helmer. And can you tell me what I have done to forfeit your love?

Nora. Yes, indeed I can. It was to-night, when the wonderful thing did not happen; then I saw you were not the man I had thought you.

Helmer. Explain yourself better — I don't understand you.

Nora. I have waited so patiently for eight years; for, goodness knows, I knew very well that wonderful things don't happen every day. Then this horrible misfortune came upon me; and then I felt quite certain that the wonderful thing was going to happen at last. When Krogstad's letter was lying out there, never for a moment did I imagine that you would consent to accept this man's conditions. I was so absolutely certain that you would say to him: Publish the thing to the whole world. And when that was done —

Helmer. Yes, what then? — when I had exposed my wife to shame and disgrace?

Nora. When that was done, I was so absolutely certain, you would come forward and take everything upon yourself, and say: I am the guilty one.

Helmer. Nora —!

Nora. You mean that I would never have accepted such a sacrifice on your part? No, of course not. But what would my assurances have been worth against yours? That was the wonderful thing which I hoped for and feared; and it was to prevent that, that I wanted to kill myself.

Helmer. I would gladly work night and day for you, Nora — bear sorrow and want for your sake. But no man would sacrifice his honour for the one he loves.

Nora. It is a thing hundreds of thousands of women have done.

Helmer. Oh, you think and talk like a heedless child.

Nora. Maybe. But you neither think nor talk like the man I could bind myself to. As soon as your fear was over — and it was not fear for what threatened me, but for what might happen to you — when the whole thing was past, as far as you were concerned it was exactly as if nothing at all had happened. Exactly as before, I was your little skylark, your doll, which you would in future treat with doubly gentle care, because it was so brittle and fragile. (Getting up.) Torvald — it was then it dawned upon me that for eight years I had been living here with a strange man, and had borne him three children —. Oh! I can't bear to think of it! I could tear myself into little bits!

Helmer (sadly). I see, I see. An abyss has opened between us — there is no denying it. But, Nora, would it not be possible to fill it up?

Nora. As I am now, I am no wife for you.

Helmer. I have it in me to become a different man.

Nora. Perhaps — if your doll is taken away from you.

Helmer. But to part! — to part from you! No, no, Nora, I can't understand that idea.

Nora (going out to the right). That makes it all the more certain that it must be done. (She comes back with her cloak and hat and a small bag which she puts on a chair by the table.)

Helmer. Nora, Nora, not now! Wait till tomorrow.

Nora (putting on her cloak). I cannot spend the night in a strange man's room.

Helmer. But can't we live here like brother and sister —?

Nora (putting on her hat). You know very well that would not last long. (Puts the shawl round her.) Good-bye, Torvald. I won't see the little ones. I know they are in better hands than mine. As I am now, I can be of no use to them.

Helmer. But some day, Nora — some day?

Nora. How can I tell? I have no idea what is going to become of me.

Helmer. But you are my wife, whatever becomes of you.

Nora. Listen, Torvald. I have heard that when a wife deserts her husband's house, as I am doing now, he is legally freed from all obligations towards her. In any case I set you free from all your obligations. You are not to feel yourself bound in the slightest way, any more than I shall. There must be perfect freedom on both sides. See, here is your ring back. Give me mine.

Helmer. That too?

Nora. That too.

Helmer. Here it is.

Nora. That's right. Now it is all over. I have put the keys here. The maids know all about everything in the house — better than I do. Tomorrow, after I have left her, Christine will come here and pack up my own things that I brought with me from home. I will have them sent after me.

Helmer. All over! All over! — Nora, shall you never think of me again?

Nora. I know I shall often think of you and the children and this house.

Helmer. May I write to you, Nora?

Nora. No — never. You must not do that.

Helmer. But at least let me send you —

Nora. Nothing — nothing —

Helmer. Let me help you if you are in want.

Nora. No. I can receive nothing from a stranger.

Helmer. Nora — can I never be anything more than a stranger to you?

Nora (taking her bag). Ah, Torvald, the most wonderful thing of all would have to happen.

Helmer. Tell me what that would be!

Nora. Both you and I would have to be so changed that —. Oh, Torvald, I don't believe any longer in wonderful things happening.

Helmer. But I will believe in it. Tell me? So changed that —?

Nora. That our life together would be a real wedlock. Good-bye. (She goes out through the hall.)

Helmer (sinks down on a chair at the door and buries his face in his hands). Nora! Nora! (Looks round, and rises.) Empty. She is gone. (A hope flashes across his mind.) The most wonderful thing of all —?

(The sound of a door shutting is heard from below.)

The Wild Duck

Henrik Ibsen

Table of Contents

Characters

Act 1

Act 2

Act 3

Act 4

Act 5

Characters

WERLE, a merchant, manufacturer, etc.

GREGERS WERLE, his son.

OLD EKDAL.

HIALMAR EKDAL, his son, a photographer.

GINA EKDAL, Hjalmar's wife.

HEDVIG, their daughter, a girl of fourteen.

MRS. SORBY, Werle's housekeeper.

RELLING, a doctor.

MOLVIK, student of theology.

GRABERG, Werle's bookkeeper.

PETTERSEN, Werle's servant.

JENSEN, a hired waiter.

A FLABBY GENTLEMAN.

A THIN-HAIRED GENTLEMAN.

A SHORT-SIGHTED GENTLEMAN.

SIX OTHER GENTLEMEN, guests at Werle's dinner-party.

SEVERAL HIRED WAITERS.

The first act passes in WERLE'S house, the remaining acts at HJALMAR EKDAL'S.

Pronunciation of Names:
GREGERS WERLE = Grayghers Verle; HIALMAR EKDAL = Yalmar Aykdal; GINA = Cheena; GRABERG = Groberg; JENSEN = Yensen.

Act 1

[At WERLE'S house. A richly and comfortably furnished study; bookcases and upholstered furniture; a writing-table, with papers and documents, in the centre of the room; lighted lamps with green shades, giving a subdued light. At the back, open folding-doors with curtains drawn back. Within is seen a large and handsome room, brilliantly lighted with lamps and branching candle-sticks. In front, on the right (in the study), a small baize door leads into WERLE'S Office. On the left, in front, a fireplace with a glowing coal fire, and farther back a double door leading into the dining-room.]

[WERLE'S servant, PETTERSEN, in livery, and JENSEN, the hired waiter, in black, are putting the study in order. In the large room, two or three other hired waiters are moving about, arranging things and lighting more candles. From the dining-room, the hum of conversation and laughter of many voices are heard; a glass is tapped with a knife; silence follows, and a toast is proposed; shouts of "Bravo!" and then again a buzz of conversation.]

Pettersen. [lights a lamp on the chimney-place and places a shade over it.] Hark to them, Jensen! now the old man's on his legs holding a long palaver about Mrs. Sorby.

Jensen [pushing forward an arm-chair.] Is it true, what folks say, that they're — very good friends, eh?

Pettersen. Lord knows.

Jensen. I've heard tell as he's been a lively customer in his day.

Pettersen. May be.

Jensen. And he's giving this spread in honour of his son, they say.

Pettersen. Yes. His son came home yesterday.

Jensen. This is the first time I ever heard as Mr. Werle had a son.

Pettersen. Oh yes, he has a son, right enough. But he's a fixture, as you might say, up at the Hoidal works. He's never once come to town all the years I've been in service here.

A Waiter [in the doorway of the other room.] Pettersen, here's an old fellow wanting —

Pettersen [mutters.] The devil — who's this now?

[OLD EKDAL appears from the right, in the inner room. He is dressed in a threadbare overcoat with a high collar; he wears woollen mittens, and carries in his hand a stick and a fur cap. Under his arm, a brown paper parcel. Dirty red-brown wig and small grey moustache.]

Pettersen [goes towards him.] Good Lord — what do you want here?

Ekdal [in the doorway.] Must get into the office, Pettersen.

Pettersen. The office was closed an hour ago, and —

Ekdal. So they told me at the front door. But Graberg's in there still. Let me slip in this way, Pettersen; there's a good fellow. [Points towards the baize door.] It's not the first time I've come this way.

81

Pettersen. Well, you may pass. [Opens the door.] But mind you go out again the proper way, for we've got company.

Ekdal. I know, I know — h'm! Thanks, Pettersen, good old friend! Thanks! [Mutters softly.] Ass!

[He goes into the Office; PETTERSEN shuts the door after him.]

Jensen. Is he one of the office people?

Pettersen. No he's only an outside hand that does odd jobs of copying. But he's been a tip-topper in his day, has old Ekdal.

Jensen. You can see he's been through a lot.

Pettersen. Yes; he was an army officer, you know.

Jensen. You don't say so?

Pettersen. No mistake about it. But then he went into the timber trade or something of the sort. They say he once played Mr. Werle a very nasty trick. They were partners in the Hoidal works at the time. Oh, I know old Ekdal well, I do. Many a nip of bitters and bottle of ale we two have drunk at Madam Eriksen's.

Jensen. He don't look as if held much to stand treat with.

Pettersen. Why, bless you, Jensen, it's me that stands treat. I always think there's no harm in being a bit civil to folks that have seen better days.

Jensen. Did he go bankrupt then?

Pettersen. Worse than that. He went to prison.

Jensen. To prison!

Pettersen. Or perhaps it was the Penitentiary. [Listens.] Sh! They're leaving the table.

[The dining-room door is thrown open from within, by a couple of waiters. MRS. SORBY comes out conversing with two gentlemen. Gradually the whole company follows, amongst them WERLE. Last come HIALMAR EKDAL and GREGERS WERLE.]

Mrs. Sorby [in passing, to the servant.] Tell them to serve the coffee in the music-room, Pettersen.

Pettersen. Very well, Madam.

[She goes with the two Gentlemen into the inner room, and thence out to the right. PETTERSEN and JENSEN go out the same way.]

A Flabby Gentleman [to a THIN-HAIRED GENTLEMAN.] Whew! What a dinner! — It was no joke to do it justice!

The Thin-haired Gentleman. Oh, with a little good-will one can get through a lot in three hours.

The Flabby Gentleman. Yes, but afterwards, afterwards, my dear Chamberlain!

A Third Gentleman. I hear the coffee and maraschino are to be served in the music-room.

The Flabby Gentleman. Bravo! Then perhaps Mrs. Sorby will play us something.

The Thin-haired Gentleman [in a low voice.] I hope Mrs. Sorby mayn't play us a tune we don't like, one of these days!

The Flabby Gentleman. Oh no, not she! Bertha will never turn against her old friends.

[They laugh and pass into the inner room.]

Werle [in a low voice, dejectedly.] I don't think anybody noticed it, Gregers.

Gregers [looks at him.] Noticed what?

Werle. Did you not notice it either?

Gregers. What do you mean?

Werle. We were thirteen at table.

Gregers. Indeed? Were there thirteen of us?

Werle [glances towards HIALMAR EKDAL.] Our usual party is twelve. [To the others.] This way, gentlemen!

[WERLE and the others, all except HIALMAR and GREGERS, go out by the back, to the right.]

Hialmar [who has overheard the conversation.] You ought not to have invited me, Gregers.

Gregers. What! Not ask my best and only friend to a party supposed to be in my honour — ?

Hialmar. But I don't think your father likes it. You see I am quite outside his circle.

Gregers. So I hear. But I wanted to see you and have a talk with you, and I certainly shan't be staying long. — Ah, we two old schoolfellows have drifted far apart from each other. It must be sixteen or seventeen years since we met.

Hialmar. Is it so long?

Gregers. It is indeed. Well, how goes it with you? You look well. You have put on flesh, and grown almost stout.

Hialmar. Well, "stout" is scarcely the word; but I daresay I look a little more of a man than I used to.

Gregers. Yes, you do; your outer man is in first-rate condition.

Hialmar [in a tone of gloom.] Ah, but the inner man! That is a very different matter, I can tell you! Of course you know of the terrible catastrophe that has befallen me and mine since last we met.

Gregers [more softly.] How are things going with your father now?

Hialmar. Don't let us talk of it, old fellow. Of course my poor unhappy father lives with me. He hasn't another soul in the world to care for him. But you can understand that this is a miserable subject for me. — Tell me, rather, how you have been getting on up at the works.

Gregers. I have had a delightfully lonely time of it — plenty of leisure to think and think about things. Come over here; we may as well make ourselves comfortable.

[He seats himself in an arm-chair by the fire and draws HIALMAR down into another alongside of it.]

Hialmar [sentimentally.] After all, Gregers, I thank you for inviting me to your father's table; for I take it as a sign that you have got over your feeling against me.

Gregers [surprised.] How could you imagine I had any feeling against you?

Hialmar. You had at first, you know.

Gregers. How at first?

Hialmar. After the great misfortune. It was natural enough that you should. Your father was within an ace of being drawn into that — well, that terrible business.

Gregers. Why should that give me any feeling against you? Who can have put that into your head?

Hialmar. I know it did, Gregers; your father told me so himself.

Gregers [starts.] My father! Oh indeed. H'm. — Was that why you never let me hear from you? — not a single word.

Hialmar. Yes.

Gregers. Not even when you made up your mind to become a photographer?

Hialmar. Your father said I had better not write to you at all, about anything.

Gregers [looking straight before him.] Well well, perhaps he was right. — But tell me now, Hialmar: are you pretty well satisfied with your present position?

Hialmar [with a little sigh.] Oh yes, I am; I have really no cause to complain. At first, as you may guess, I felt it a little strange. It was such a totally new state of things for me. But of course my whole circumstances were totally changed. Father's utter, irretrievable ruin, — the shame and disgrace of it, Gregers

Gregers [affected.] Yes, yes; I understand.

Hialmar. I couldn't think of remaining at college; there wasn't a shilling to spare; on the contrary, there were debts — mainly to your father I believe —

Gregers. H'm — -

Hialmar. In short, I thought it best to break, once for all, with my old surroundings and associations. It was your father that specially urged me to it; and since he interested himself so much in me

Gregers. My father did?

Hialmar. Yes, you surely knew that, didn't you? Where do you suppose I found the money to learn photography, and to furnish a studio and make a start? All that costs a pretty penny, I can tell you.

Gregers. And my father provided the money?

Hialmar. Yes, my dear fellow, didn't you know? I understood him to say he had written to you about it.

Gregers. Not a word about his part in the business. He must have forgotten it. Our correspondence has always been purely a business one. So it was my father that —!

Hialmar. Yes, certainly. He didn't wish it to be generally known; but he it was. And of course it was he, too, that put me in a position to marry. Don't you — don't you know about that either?

Gregers. No, I haven't heard a word of it. [Shakes him by the arm.] But, my dear Hialmar, I can't tell you what pleasure all this gives me — pleasure, and self-reproach. I have perhaps done my father injustice after all — in some things. This proves that he has a heart. It shows a sort of compunction —

Hialmar. Compunction —?

Gregers. Yes, yes — whatever you like to call it. Oh, I can't tell you how glad I am to hear this of father. — So you are a married man, Hialmar! That is further than I shall ever get. Well, I hope you are happy in your married life?

Hialmar. Yes, thoroughly happy. She is as good and capable a wife as any man could wish for. And she is by no means without culture.

Gregers [rather surprised.] No, of course not.

Hialmar. You see, life is itself an education. Her daily intercourse with me — And then we know one or two rather remarkable men, who come a good deal about us. I assure you, you would hardly know Gina again.

Gregers. Gina?

Hialmar. Yes; had you forgotten that her name was Gina?

Gregers. Whose name? I haven't the slightest idea —

Hialmar. Don't you remember that she used to be in service here?

Gregers [looks at him.] Is it Gina Hansen —?

Hialmar. Yes, of course it is Gina Hansen.

Gregers. — -who kept house for us during the last year of my mother's illness?

Hialmar. Yes, exactly. But, my dear friend, I'm quite sure your father told you that I was married.

Gregers [who has risen.] Oh yes, he mentioned it; but not that — [Walking about the room.] Stay — perhaps he did — now that I think of it. My father always writes such short letters. [Half seats himself on the arm of the chair.] Now, tell me, Hialmar — this is interesting — how did you come to know Gina — your wife?

Hialmar. The simplest thing in the world. You know Gina did not stay here long, everything was so much upset at that time, owing to your mother's illness and so forth, that Gina was not equal to it all; so she gave notice and left. That was the year before your mother died — or it may have been the same year.

Gregers. It was the same year. I was up at the works then. But afterwards —?

Hialmar. Well, Gina lived at home with her mother, Madam Hansen, an excellent hard-working woman, who kept a little eating-house. She had a room to let too; a very nice comfortable room.

Gregers. And I suppose you were lucky enough to secure it?

Hialmar. Yes; in fact, it was your father that recommended it to me. So it was there, you see, that I really came to know Gina.

Gregers. And then you got engaged?

Hialmar. Yes. It doesn't take young people long to fall in love —; h'm —

Gregers [rises and moves about a little.] Tell me: was it after your engagement — was it then that my father — I mean was it then that you began to take up photography?

Hialmar. Yes, precisely. I wanted to make a start, and to set up house as soon as possible; and your father and I agreed that this photography business was the readiest way. Gina thought so too. Oh, and there was another thing in its favour, by-the-bye: it happened, luckily, that Gina had learnt to retouch.

Gregers. That chimed in marvellously.

Hialmar [pleased, rises.] Yes, didn't it? Don't you think it was a marvellous piece of luck?

Gregers. Oh, unquestionably. My father seems to have been almost a kind of providence for you.

Hialmar [with emotion.] He did not forsake his old friend's son in the hour of his need. For he has a heart. you see.

Mrs. Sorby [enters, arm-in-arm with WERLE.] Nonsense, my dear Mr. Werle; you mustn't stop there any longer staring at all the lights. It's very bad for you.

Werle [lets go her arm and passes his hand over his eyes.] I daresay you are right.

[PETTERSEN and JENSEN carry round refreshment trays.]

Mrs. Sorby [to the Guests in the other room.] This way, if you please, gentlemen. Whoever wants a glass of punch must be so good as to come in here.

The Flabby Gentleman [comes up to MRS. SORBY.] Surely, it isn't possible that you have suspended our cherished right to smoke?

Mrs. Sorby. Yes. No smoking here, in Mr. Werle's sanctum, Chamberlain.

The Thin-haired Gentleman. When did you enact these stringent amendments on the cigar law, Mrs. Sorby?

Mrs. Sorby. After the last dinner, Chamberlain, when certain persons permitted themselves to overstep the mark.

The Thin-haired Gentleman. And may one never overstep the mark a little bit, Madame Bertha? Not the least little bit?

Mrs. Sorby. Not in any respect whatsoever, Mr. Balle.

[Most of the Guests have assembled in the study; servants hand round glasses of Punch.]

Werle [to HIALMAR, who is standing beside a table.] What are you studying so intently, Ekdal?

Hialmar. Only an album, Mr. Werle.

The Thin-haired Gentleman [who is wandering about.] Ah, photographs! They are quite in your line of course.

The Flabby Gentleman [in an arm-chair.] Haven't you brought any of your own with you?

Hialmar. No, I haven't.

The Flabby Gentleman. You ought to have; it's very good for the digestion to sit and look at pictures.

The Thin-haired Gentleman. And it contributes to the entertainment, you know.

The Short-sighted Gentleman. And all contributions are thankfully received.

Mrs. Sorby. The Chamberlains think that when one is invited out to dinner, one ought to exert oneself a little in return, Mr. Ekdal.

The Flabby Gentleman. Where one dines so well, that duty becomes a pleasure.

The Thin-haired Gentleman. And when it's a case of the struggle for existence, you know —

Mrs. Sorby. I quite agree with you!

[They continue the conversation, with laughter and joking.]

Gregers [softly.] You must join in, Hialmar.

Hialmar [writhing.] What am I to talk about?

The Flabby Gentleman. Don't you think, Mr. Werle, that Tokay may be considered one of the more wholesome sorts of wine?

Werle [by the fire.] I can answer for the Tokay you had to-day, at any rate; it's one of the very finest seasons. Of course you would notice that.

The Flabby Gentleman. Yes, it had a remarkably delicate flavour.

Hialmar [shyly.] Is there any difference between the seasons?

The Flabby Gentleman [laughs.] Come! That's good!

Werle [smiles.] It really doesn't pay to set fine wine before you.

The Thin-haired Gentleman. Tokay is like photographs, Mr. Ekdal: they both need sunshine. Am I not right?

Hialmar. Yes, light is important no doubt.

Mrs. Sorby. And it's exactly the same with Chamberlains — they, too, depend very much on sunshine,* as the saying is.

* The "sunshine" of Court favour.

The Thin-haired Gentleman. Oh fie! That's a very threadbare sarcasm!

The Short-sighted Gentleman. Mrs. Sorby is coming out —

The Flabby Gentleman. — and at our expense, too. [Holds up his finger reprovingly.] Oh, Madame Bertha, Madame Bertha!

Mrs. Sorby. Yes, and there's not the least doubt that the seasons differ greatly. The old vintages are the finest.

The Short-sighted Gentleman. Do you reckon me among the old vintages?

Mrs. Sorby. Oh, far from it.

The Thin-haired Gentleman. There now! But me, dear Mrs. Sorby —?

The Flabby Gentleman. Yes, and me? What vintage should you say that we belong to?

Mrs. Sorby. Why, to the sweet vintages, gentlemen.

[She sips a glass of punch. The gentlemen laugh and flirt with her.]

Werle. Mrs. Sorby can always find a loop-hole — when she wants to. Fill your glasses, gentlemen! Pettersen, will you see to it —! Gregers, suppose we have a glass together. [Gregers does not move.] Won't you join us, Ekdal? I found no opportunity of drinking with you at table.

[GRABERG, the Bookkeeper, looks in at the baize door.]

Graberg. Excuse me, sir, but I can't get out.

Werle. Have you been locked in again?

Graberg. Yes, and Flakstad has carried off the keys.

Werle. Well, you can pass out this way.

Graberg. But there's some one else —

Werle. All right; come through, both of you. Don't be afraid.

[GRABERG and OLD EKDAL come out of the office.]

Werle [involuntarily.] Ugh!

[The laughter and talk among the Guests cease. HIALMAR starts at the sight of his father, puts down his glass, and turns towards the fireplace.]

Ekdal [does not look up, but makes little bows to both sides as he passes, murmuring.] Beg pardon, come the wrong way. Door locked — door locked. Beg pardon.

[He and GRABERG go out by the back, to the right.]

Werle [between his teeth.] That idiot Graberg.

Gregers [open-mouthed and staring, to HIALMAR.] Why surely that wasn't —!

The Flabby Gentleman. What's the matter? Who was it?

Gregers. Oh, nobody, only the bookkeeper and some one with him.

The Short-sighted Gentleman [to HIALMAR.]

Did you know that man?

Hialmar. I don't know — I didn't notice —

The Flabby Gentleman. What the deuce has come over every one?

[He joins another group who are talking softly.]

Mrs. Sorby [whispers to the Servant.] Give him something to take with him; — something good, mind.

Pettersen [nods.] I'll see to it.

[Goes out.]

Gregers [softly and with emotion, to HIALMAR.] So that was really he!

Hialmar. Yes.

Gregers. And you could stand there and deny that you knew him!

Hialmar [whispers vehemently.] But how could I—!

Gregers. — acknowledge your own father?

Hialmar [with pain.] Oh, if you were in my place —

[The conversation amongst the Guests, which has been carried on in a low tone, now swells into constrained joviality.]

The Thin-haired Gentleman [approaching HIALMAR and GREGERS in a friendly manner.] Aha! Reviving old college memories, eh? Don't you smoke, Mr. Ekdal? May I give you a light? Oh, by-the-bye, we mustn't —

Hialmar. No, thank you, I won't —

The Flabby Gentleman. Haven't you a nice little poem you could recite to us, Mr. Ekdal? You used to recite so charmingly.

Hialmar. I am sorry I can't remember anything.

The Flabby Gentleman. Oh, that's a pity. Well, what shall we do, Balle?

[Both Gentlemen move away and pass into the other room.]

Hialmar [gloomily.] Gregers — I am going! When a man has felt the crushing hand of Fate, you see — Say good-bye to your father for me.

Gregers. Yes, yes. Are you going straight home?

Hialmar. Yes. Why?

Gregers. Oh, because I may perhaps look in on you later.

Hialmar. No, you mustn't do that. You must not come to my home. Mine is a melancholy abode, Gregers; especially after a splendid banquet like this. We can always arrange to meet somewhere in the town.

Mrs. Sorby [who has quietly approached.] Are you going, Ekdal?

Hialmar. Yes.

Mrs. Sorby. Remember me to Gina.

Hialmar. Thanks.

Mrs. Sorby. And say I am coming up to see her one of these days.

Hialmar. Yes, thank you. [To GREGERS.] Stay here; I will slip out unobserved.

[He saunters away, then into the other room, and so out to the right.]

Mrs. Sorby [softly to the Servant, who has come back.] Well, did you give the old man something?

Pettersen. Yes; I sent him off with a bottle of cognac.

Mrs. Sorby. Oh, you might have thought of something better than that.

Pettersen. Oh no, Mrs. Sorby; cognac is what he likes best in the world.

The Flabby Gentleman [in the doorway with a sheet of music in his hand.] Shall we play a duet, Mrs. Sorby?

Mrs. Sorby. Yes, suppose we do.

The Guests. Bravo, bravo!

[She goes with all the Guests through the back room, out to the right. GREGERS remains standing by the fire. WERLE is looking for Something on the writing-table, and appears to wish that GREGERS would go; as GREGERS does not move, WERLE goes towards the door.]

Gregers. Father, won't you stay a moment?

Werle [stops.] What is it?

Gregers. I must have a word with you.

Werle. Can it not wait till we are alone?

Gregers. No, it cannot; for perhaps we shall never be alone together.

Werle [drawing nearer.] What do you mean by that?

[During what follows, the pianoforte is faintly heard from the distant music-room.]

Gregers. How has that family been allowed to go so miserably to the wall?

Werle. You mean the Ekdals, I suppose.

Gregers. Yes, I mean the Ekdals. Lieutenant Ekdal was once so closely associated with you.

Werle. Much too closely; I have felt that to my cost for many a year. It is thanks to him that I—yes I— have had a kind of slur cast upon my reputation.

Gregers [softly.] Are you sure that he alone was to blame?

Werle. Who else do you suppose —?

Gregers. You and he acted together in that affair of the forests —

Werle. But was it not Ekdal that drew the map of the tracts we had bought — that fraudulent map! It was he who felled all that timber illegally on Government ground. In fact, the whole management was in his hands. I was quite in the dark as to what Lieutenant Ekdal was doing.

Gregers. Lieutenant Ekdal himself seems to have been very much in the dark as to what he was doing.

Werle. That may be. But the fact remains that he was found guilty and I acquitted.

Gregers. Yes, I know that nothing was proved against you.

Werle. Acquittal is acquittal. Why do you rake up these old miseries that turned my hair grey before its time? Is that the sort of thing you have been brooding over up there, all these years? I can assure you, Gregers, here in the town the whole story has been forgotten long ago — so far as I am concerned.

Gregers. But that unhappy Ekdal family —

Werle. What would you have had me do for the people? When Ekdal came out of prison he was a broken-down being, past all help. There are people in the world who dive to the bottom the moment they get a couple of slugs in their body, and never come to the surface again. You may take my word for it, Gregers, I have done all I could without positively laying myself open to all sorts of suspicion and gossip —

Gregers. Suspicion —? Oh, I see.

Werle. I have given Ekdal copying to do for the office, and I pay him far, far more for it than his work is worth —

Gregers [without looking at him.] H'm; that I don't doubt.

Werle. You laugh? Do you think I am not telling you the truth? Well, I certainly can't refer you to my books, for I never enter payments of that sort.

Gregers [smiles coldly.] No, there are certain payments it is best to keep no account of.

Werle [taken aback.] What do you mean by that?

Gregers [mustering up courage.] Have you entered what it cost you to have Hialmar Ekdal taught photography?

Werle. I? How "entered" it?

Gregers. I have learnt that it was you who paid for his training. And I have learnt, too, that it was you who enabled him to set up house so comfortably.

Werle. Well, and yet you talk as though I had done nothing for the Ekdals! I can assure you these people have cost me enough in all conscience.

Gregers. Have you entered any of these expenses in your books?

Werle. Why do you ask?

Gregers. Oh, I have my reasons. Now tell me: when you interested yourself so warmly in your old friend's son — it was just before his marriage, was it not?

Werle. Why, deuce take it — after all these years, how can I—?

Gregers. You wrote me a letter about that time — a business letter, of course; and in a postscript you mentioned — quite briefly — that Hialmar Ekdal had married a Miss Hansen.

Werle. Yes, that was quite right. That was her name.

Gregers. But you did not mention that this Miss Hansen was Gina Hansen — our former housekeeper.

Werle [with a forced laugh of derision.] No; to tell the truth, it didn't occur to me that you were so particularly interested in our former housekeeper.

Gregers. No more I was. But [lowers his voice] there were others in this house who were particularly interested in her.

Werle. What do you mean by that? [Flaring up.] You are not alluding to me, I hope?

Gregers [softly but firmly.] Yes, I am alluding to you.

Werle. And you dare —! You presume to —! How can that ungrateful hound — that photographer fellow — how dare he go making such insinuations!

Gregers. Hialmar has never breathed a word about this. I don't believe he has the faintest suspicion of such a thing.

Werle. Then where have you got it from? Who can have put such notions in your head?

Gregers. My poor unhappy mother told me; and that the very last time I saw her.

Werle. Your mother! I might have known as much! You and she — you always held together. It was she who turned you against me, from the first.

Gregers. No, it was all that she had to suffer and submit to, until she broke down and came to such a pitiful end.

Werle. Oh, she had nothing to suffer or submit to; not more than most people, at all events. But there's no getting on with morbid, overstrained creatures — that I have learnt to my cost. — And you could go on nursing such a suspicion — burrowing into all sorts of old rumours and slanders against your own father! I must say, Gregers, I really think that at your age you might find something more useful to do.

Gregers. Yes, it is high time.

Werle. Then perhaps your mind would be easier than it seems to be now. What can be your object in remaining up at the works, year out and year in, drudging away like a common clerk, and not drawing a farthing more than the ordinary monthly wage? It is downright folly.

Gregers. Ah, if I were only sure of that.

Werle. I understand you well enough. You want to be independent; you won't be beholden to me for anything. Well, now there happens to be an opportunity for you to become independent, your own master in everything.

Gregers. Indeed? In what way —?

Werle. When I wrote you insisting on your coming to town at once — h'm —

Gregers. Yes, what is it you really want of me? I have been waiting all day to know.

Werle. I want to propose that you should enter the firm, as partner.

Gregers. I! Join your firm? As partner?

Werle. Yes. It would not involve our being constantly together. You could take over the business here in town, and I should move up to the works.

Gregers. You would?

Werle. The fact is, I am not so fit for work as I once was. I am obliged to spare my eyes, Gregers; they have begun to trouble me.

Gregers. They have always been weak.

Werle. Not as they are now. And, besides, circumstances might possibly make it desirable for me to live up there — for a time, at any rate.

Gregers. That is certainly quite a new idea to me.

Werle. Listen, Gregers: there are many things that stand between us; but we are father and son after all. We ought surely to be able to come to some sort of understanding with each other.

Gregers. Outwardly, you mean, of course?

Werle. Well, even that would be something. Think it over, Gregers. Don't you think it ought to be possible? Eh?

Gregers [looking at him coldly.] There is something behind all this.

Werle. How so?

Gregers. You want to make use of me in some way.

Werle. In such a close relationship as ours, the one can always be useful to the other.

Gregers. Yes, so people say.

Werle. I want very much to have you at home with me for a time. I am a lonely man, Gregers; I have always felt lonely, all my life through; but most of all now that I am getting up in years. I feel the need of some one about me —

Gregers. You have Mrs. Sorby.

Werle. Yes, I have her; and she has become, I may say, almost indispensable to me. She is lively and even-tempered; she brightens up the house; and that is a very great thing for me.

Gregers. Well then, you have everything just as you wish it.

Werle. Yes, but I am afraid it can't last. A woman so situated may easily find herself in a false position, in the eyes of the world. For that matter it does a man no good, either.

Gregers. Oh, when a man gives such dinners as you give, he can risk a great deal.

Werle. Yes, but how about the woman, Gregers? I fear she won't accept the situation much longer; and even if she did — even if, out of attachment to me, she were to take her chance of gossip and scandal and all that —? Do you think, Gregers — you with your strong sense of justice —

Gregers [interrupts him.] Tell me in one word: are you thinking of marrying her?

Werle. Suppose I were thinking of it? What then?

Gregers. That's what I say: what then?

Werle. Should you be inflexibly opposed to it!

Gregers. — Not at all. Not by any means.

Werle. I was not sure whether your devotion to your mother's memory —

Gregers. I am not overstrained.

Werle. Well, whatever you may or may not be, at all events you have lifted a great weight from my mind. I am extremely pleased that I can reckon on your concurrence in this matter.

Gregers [looking intently at him.] Now I see the use you want to put me to.

Werle. Use to put you to? What an expression!

Gregers. Oh, don't let us be nice in our choice of words — not when we are alone together, at any rate. [With a short laugh.] Well well. So this is what made it absolutely essential that I should come to town in person. For the sake of Mrs. Sorby, we are to get up a pretence at family life in the house — a tableau of filial affection! That will be something new indeed.

Werle. How dare you speak in that tone!

Gregers. Was there ever any family life here? Never since I can remember. But now, forsooth, your plans demand something of the sort. No doubt it will have an excellent effect when it is reported that the son has hastened home, on the wings of filial piety, to the grey-haired father's wedding-feast. What will then remain of all the rumours as to the wrongs the poor dead mother had to submit to? Not a vestige. Her son annihilates them at one stroke.

Werle. Gregers — I believe there is no one in the world you detest as you do me.

Gregers [softly.] I have seen you at too close quarters.

Werle. You have seen me with your mother's eyes. [Lowers his voice a little.] But you should remember that her eyes were — clouded now and then.

Gregers [quivering.] I see what you are hinting at. But who was to blame for mother's unfortunate weakness? Why you, and all those —! The last of them was this woman that you palmed off upon Hialmar Ekdal, when you were — Ugh!

Werle [shrugs his shoulders.] Word for word as if it were your mother speaking!

Gregers [without heeding.] And there he is now, with his great, confiding, childlike mind, compassed about with all this treachery — living under the same roof with such a creature, and never dreaming that what he calls his home is built upon a lie! [Comes a step nearer.] When I look back upon your past, I seem to see a battle-field with shattered lives on every hand.

Werle. I begin to think the chasm that divides us is too wide.

Gregers [bowing, with self-command.] So I have observed; and therefore I take my hat and go.

Werle. You are going! Out of the house?

Gregers. Yes. For at last I see my mission in life.

Werle. What mission?

Gregers. You would only laugh if I told you.

Werle. A lonely man doesn't laugh so easily, Gregers.

Gregers [pointing towards the background.] Look, father, — the Chamberlains are playing blind-man's-buff with Mrs. Sorby. — Good-night and good-bye.

He goes out by the back to the right. Sounds of laughter and merriment from the Company, who are now visible in the outer room.]

Werle [muttering contemptuously after GREGERS.] Ha —! Poor wretch — and he says he is not overstrained!

Act 2

HIALMAR EKDAL'S studio, a good-sized room, evidently in the top storey of the building. On the right, a sloping roof of large panes of glass, half-covered by a blue curtain. In the right-hand corner, at the back, the entrance door; farther forward, on the same side, a door leading to the sitting-room. Two doors on the opposite side, and between them an iron stove. At the back, a wide double sliding-door. The studio is plainly but comfortably fitted up and furnished. Between the doors on the right, standing out a little from the wall, a sofa with a table and some chairs; on the table a lighted lamp with a shade; beside the stove an old arm-chair. Photographic instruments and apparatus of different kinds lying about the room. Against the back wall, to the left of the double door, stands a bookcase containing a few books, boxes, and bottles of chemicals, instruments, tools, and other objects. Photographs and small articles, such as camel's-hair pencils, paper, and so forth, lie on the table.

GINA EKDAL sits on a chair by the table, sewing. HEDVIG is sitting on the sofa, with her hands shading her eyes and her thumbs in her ears, reading a book.]

Gina [glances once or twice at HEDVIG, as if with secret anxiety; then says:] Hedvig!

[Hedvig does not hear.]

Gina [repeats more loudly.] Hedvig!

Hedvig [takes away her hands and looks up.] Yes, mother?

Gina. Hedvig dear, you mustn't sit reading any longer now.

Hedvig. Oh mother, mayn't I read a little more? Just a little bit?

Gina. No, no, you must put away your book now. Father doesn't like it; he never reads hisself in the evening.

Hedvig [shuts the book.] No, father doesn't care much about reading.

Gina [puts aside her sewing and takes up a lead pencil and a little account-book from the table.] Can you remember how much we paid for the butter to-day?

Hedvig. It was one crown sixty-five.

Gina. That's right. [Puts it down.] It's terrible what a lot of butter we get through in this house. Then there was the smoked sausage, and the cheese — let me see — [Writes] — and the ham — [Adds up.] Yes, that makes just —

Hedvig. And then the beer.

Gina. Yes, to be sure. [Writes.] How it do mount up! But we can't manage with no less.

Hedvig. And then you and I didn't need anything hot for dinner, as father was out.

Gina. No; that was so much to the good. And then I took eight crowns fifty for the photographs.

Hedvig. Really! So much as that?

Gina. Exactly eight crowns fifty.

[Silence. GINA takes up her sewing again, HEDVIG takes paper and pencil and begins to draw, shading her eyes with her left hand.]

Hedvig. Isn't it jolly to think that father is at Mr. Werle's big dinner-party?

Gina. You know he's not really Mr. Werle's guest. It was the son invited him. [After a pause.] We have nothing to do with that Mr. Werle.

Hedvig. I'm longing for father to come home. He promised to ask Mrs. Sorby for something nice for me.

Gina. Yes, there's plenty of good things going in that house, I can tell you.

Hedvig [goes on drawing.] And I believe I'm a little hungry too.

[OLD EKDAL, with the paper parcel under his arm and another parcel in his coat pocket, comes in by the entrance door.]

Gina. How late you are to-day, grandfather!

Ekdal. They had locked the office door. Had to wait in Graberg's room. And then they let me through — h'm.

Hedvig. Did you get some more copying to do, grandfather?

Ekdal. This whole packet. Just look.

Gina. That's capital.

Hedvig. And you have another parcel in your pocket.

Ekdal. Eh? Oh never mind, that's nothing. [Puts his stick away in a corner.] This work will keep me going a long time, Gina. [Opens one of the sliding-doors in the back wall a little.] Hush! [Peeps into the room for a moment, then pushes the door carefully to again.] Hee-hee! They're fast asleep, all the lot of them. And she's gone into the basket herself. Hee-hee!

Hedvig. Are you sure she isn't cold in that basket, grandfather?

Ekdal. Not a bit of it! Cold? With all that straw? [Goes towards the farther door on the left.] There are matches in here, I suppose.

Gina. The matches is on the drawers.

[EKDAL goes into his room.]

Hedvig. It's nice that grandfather has got all that copying.

Gina. Yes, poor old father; it means a bit of pocket-money for him.

Hedvig. And he won't be able to sit the whole forenoon down at that horrid Madam Eriksen's.

Gina. No more he won't.

[Short silence.]

Hedvig. Do you suppose they are still at the dinner-table?

Gina. Goodness knows; as like as not.

Hedvig. Think of all the delicious things father is having to eat! I'm certain he'll be in splendid spirits when he comes. Don't you think so, mother?

Gina. Yes; and if only we could tell him that we'd got the room let —

Hedvig. But we don't need that this evening.

Gina. Oh, we'd be none the worst of it, I can tell you. It's no use to us as it is.

Hedvig. I mean we don't need it this evening, for father will be in a good humour at any rate. It is best to keep the letting of the room for another time.

Gina [looks across at her.] You like having some good news to tell father when he comes home in the evening?

Hedvig. Yes; for then things are pleasanter somehow.

Gina [thinking to herself.] Yes, yes, there's something in that.

[OLD EKDAL comes in again and is going out by the foremost door to the left.]

Gina [half turning in her chair.] Do you want something out of the kitchen, grandfather?

Ekdal. Yes, yes, I do. Don't you trouble.

[Goes out.]

Gina. He's not poking away at the fire, is he? [Waits a moment.] Hedvig, go and see what he's about.

[EKDAL comes in again with a small jug of steaming hot water.]

Hedvig. Have you been getting some hot water, grandfather?

Ekdal. Yes, hot water. Want it for something. Want to write, and the ink has got as thick as porridge — h'm.

Gina. But you'd best have your supper, first, grandfather. It's laid in there.

Ekdal. Can't be bothered with supper, Gina. Very busy, I tell you. No one's to come to my room. No one — h'm.

[He goes into his room; GINA and HEDVIG look at each other.]

Gina [softly.] Can you imagine where he's got money from?

Hedvig. From Graberg, perhaps.

Gina. Not a bit of it. Graberg always sends the money to me.

Hedvig. Then he must have got a bottle on credit somewhere.

Gina. Poor grandfather, who'd give him credit?

HIALMAR EKDAL, in an overcoat and grey felt hat, comes in from the right.]

Gina [throws down her sewing and rises.] Why, Ekdal, Is that you already?

Hedvig [at the same time jumping up.] Fancy your coming so soon, father!

Hialmar [taking off his hat.] Yes, most of the people were coming away.

Hedvig. So early?

Hialmar. Yes, it was a dinner-party, you know.

[Is taking off his overcoat.]

Gina. Let me help you.

Hedvig. Me too.

[They draw off his coat; GINA hangs it up on the back wall.]

Hedvig. Were there many people there, father?

Hialmar. Oh no, not many. We were about twelve or fourteen at table.

Gina. And you had some talk with them all?

Hialmar. Oh yes, a little; but Gregers took me up most of the time.

Gina. Is Gregers as ugly as ever?

Hialmar. Well, he's not very much to look at. Hasn't the old man come home?

Hedvig. Yes, grandfather is in his room, writing.

Hialmar. Did he say anything?

Gina. No, what should he say?

Hialmar. Didn't he say anything about —? I heard something about his having been with Graberg. I'll go in and see him for a moment.

Gina. No, no, better not.

Hialmar. Why not? Did he say he didn't want me to go in?

Gina. I don't think he wants to see nobody this evening —

Hedvig [making signs.] H'm — h'm!

Gina [not noticing.] — he has been in to fetch hot water —

Hialmar. Aha! Then he's —

Gina. Yes, I suppose so.

Hialmar. Oh God! my poor old white-haired father! — Well, well; there let him sit and get all the enjoyment he can.

[OLD EKDAL, in an indoor coat and with a lighted pipe, comes from his room.]

Ekdal. Got home? Thought it was you I heard talking.

Hialmar. Yes, I have just come.

Ekdal. You didn't see me, did you?

Hialmar. No, but they told me you had passed through — so I thought I would follow you.

Ekdal. H'm, good of you, Hialmar. — Who were they, all those fellows?

Hialmar. — Oh, all sorts of people. There was Chamberlain Flor, and Chamberlain Balle, and Chamberlain Kaspersen, and Chamberlain — this, that, and the other — I don't know who all —

Ekdal [nodding.] Hear that, Gina! Chamberlains every one of them!

Gina. Yes, I hear as they're terrible genteel in that house nowadays.

Hedvig. Did the Chamberlains sing, father? Or did they read aloud?

Hialmar. No, they only talked nonsense. They wanted me to recite something for them; but I knew better than that.

Ekdal. You weren't to be persuaded, eh?

Gina. Oh, you might have done it.

Hialmar. No; one mustn't be at everybody's beck and call. [Walks about the room.] That's not my way, at any rate.

Ekdal. No, no; Hialmar's not to be had for the asking, he isn't.

Hialmar. I don't see why I should bother myself to entertain people on the rare occasions when I go into society. Let the others exert themselves. These fellows go from one great dinner-table to the next and gorge and guzzle day out and day in. It's for them to bestir themselves and do something in return for all the good feeding they get.

Gina. But you didn't say that?

Hialmar [humming.] Ho-ho-ho —; faith, I gave them a bit of my mind.

Ekdal. Not the Chamberlains?

Hialmar. Oh, why not? [Lightly.] After that, we had a little discussion about Tokay.

Ekdal. Tokay! There's a fine wine for you!

Hialmar [comes to a standstill.] It may be a fine wine. But of course you know the vintages differ; it all depends on how much sunshine the grapes have had.

Gina. Why, you know everything, Ekdal.

Ekdal. And did they dispute that?

Hialmar. They tried to; but they were requested to observe that it was just the same with Chamberlains — that with them, too, different batches were of different qualities.

Gina. What things you do think of!

Ekdal. Hee-hee! So they got that in their pipes too?

Hialmar. Right in their teeth.

Ekdal. Do you hear that, Gina? He said it right in the very teeth of all the Chamberlains.

Gina. Fancy —! Right in their teeth!

Hialmar. Yes, but I don't want it talked about. One doesn't speak of such things. The whole affair passed off quite amicably of course. They were nice, genial fellows; I didn't want to wound them — not I!

Ekdal. Right in their teeth, though —!

Hedvig [caressingly.] How nice it is to see you in a dress-coat! It suits you so well, father.

Hialmar. Yes, don't you think so? And this one really sits to perfection. It fits almost as if it had been made for me; — a little tight in the arm-holes perhaps; — help me, Hedvig [takes off the coat.] I think I'll put on my jacket. Where is my jacket, Gina?

Gina. Here it is. [Brings the jacket and helps him.]

Hialmar. That's it! Don't forget to send the coat back to Molvik first thing to-morrow morning.

Gina [laying it away.] I'll be sure and see to it.

Hialmar [stretching himself.] After all, there's a more homely feeling about this. A free-and-easy indoor costume suits my whole personality better. Don't you think so, Hedvig?

Hedvig. Yes, father.

Hialmar. When I loosen my necktie into a pair of flowing ends — like this?

Hedvig. Yes, that goes so well with your moustache and the sweep of your curls.

Hialmar. I should not call them curls exactly; I should rather say locks.

Hedvig. Yes, they are too big for curls.

Hialmar. Locks describes them better.

Hedvig [after a pause, twitching his jacket.] Father!

Hialmar. Well, what is it?

Hedvig. Oh, you know very well.

Hialmar. No, really I don't —

Hedvig [half laughing, half whispering.] Oh, yes, father; now don't tease me any longer!

Hialmar. Why, what do you mean?

Hedvig [shaking him.] Oh what nonsense; come, where are they, father? All the good things you promised me, you know?

Hialmar. Oh — if I haven't forgotten all about them!

Hedvig. Now you're only teasing me, father! Oh, it's too bad of you! Where have you put them?

Hialmar. No, I positively forgot to get anything. But wait a little! I have something else for you, Hedvig.

[Goes and searches in the pockets of the coat.]

Hedvig [skipping and clapping her hands.] Oh mother, mother!

Gina. There, you see; if you only give him time —

Hialmar [with a paper.] Look, here it is.

Hedvig. That? Why, that's only a paper.

Hialmar. That is the bill of fare, my dear; the whole bill of fare. Here you see: "Menu" — that means bill of fare.

Hedvig. Haven't you anything else?

Hialmar. I forgot the other things, I tell you. But you may take my word for it, these dainties are very unsatisfying. Sit down at the table and read the bill of fare, and then I'll describe to you how the dishes taste. Here you are, Hedvig.

Hedvig [gulping down her tears.] Thank you.

She seats herself, but does not read; GINA makes signs to her; HIALMAR notices it.]

Hialmar [pacing up and down the room.] It's monstrous what absurd things the father of a family is expected to think of; and if he forgets the smallest trifle, he is treated to sour faces at once. Well, well, one gets used to that too. [Stops near the stove, by the old man's chair.] Have you peeped in there this evening, father?

Ekdal. Yes, to be sure I have. She's gone into the basket.

Hialmar. Ah, she has gone into the basket. Then she's beginning to get used to it.

Ekdal. Yes; just as I prophesied. But you know there are still a few little things —

Hialmar. A few improvements, yes.

Ekdal. They've got to be made, you know.

Hialmar. Yes, let us have a talk about the improvements, father. Come, let us sit on the sofa.

Ekdal. All right. H'm — think I'll just fill my pipe first. Must clean it out, too. H'm.

[He goes into his room.]

Gina [smiling to HIALMAR.] His pipe!

Hialmar. Oh yes yes, Gina; let him alone — the poor shipwrecked old man. — Yes, these improvements — we had better get them out of hand to-morrow.

Gina. You'll hardly have time to-morrow, Ekdal.

Hedvig [interposing.] Oh yes he will, mother!

Gina. — for remember them prints that has to be retouched; they've sent for them time after time.

Hialmar. There now! those prints again! I shall get them finished all right! Have any new orders come in?

Gina. No, worse luck; to-morrow I have nothing but those two sittings, you know.

Hialmar. Nothing else? Oh no, if people won't set about things with a will —

Gina. But what more can I do? Don't I advertise in the papers as much as we can afford?

Hialmar. Yes, the papers, the papers; you see how much good they do. And I suppose no one has been to look at the room either?

Gina. No, not yet.

Hialmar. That was only to be expected. If people won't keep their eyes open — . Nothing can be done without a real effort, Gina!

Hedvig [going towards him.] Shall I fetch you the flute, father?

Hialmar. No; no flute for me; I want no pleasures in this world. [Pacing about.] Yes, indeed I will work to-morrow; you shall see if I don't. You may be sure I shall work as long as my strength holds out.

Gina. But my dear good Ekdal, I didn't mean it in that way.

Hedvig. Father, mayn't I bring in a bottle of beer?

Hialmar. No, certainly not. I require nothing, nothing — [Comes to a standstill.] Beer? Was it beer you were talking about?

Hedvig [cheerfully.] Yes, father; beautiful fresh beer.

Hialmar. Well — since you insist upon it, you may bring in a bottle.

Gina. Yes, do; and we'll be nice and cosy.

[HEDVIG runs towards the kitchen door.]

Hialmar [by the stove, stops her, looks at her, puts his arm round her neck and presses her to him.] Hedvig, Hedvig!

Hedvig [with tears of joy.] My dear, kind father!

Hialmar. No, don't call me that. Here have I been feasting at the rich man's table, — battening at the groaning board —! And I couldn't even —!

Gina [sitting at the table.] Oh, nonsense, nonsense, Ekdal.

Hialmar. It's not nonsense! And yet you mustn't be too hard upon me. You know that I love you for all that.

Hedvig [throwing her arms round him.] And we love you, oh, so dearly, father!

Hialmar. And if I am unreasonable once in a while, — why then — you must remember that I am a man beset by a host of cares. There, there! [Dries his eyes.] No beer at such a moment as this. Give me the flute.

[HEDVIG runs to the bookcase and fetches it.]

Hialmar. Thanks! That's right. With my flute in my hand and you two at my side — ah —!

[HEDVIG seats herself at the table near GINA; HIALMAR paces backwards and forwards, pipes up vigorously, and plays a Bohemian peasant-dance, but in a slow plaintive tempo, and with sentimental expression.]

Hialmar [breaking off the melody, holds out his left hand to GINA, and says with emotion:] Our roof may be poor and humble, Gina; but it is home. And with all my heart I say: here dwells my happiness.

[He begins to play again; almost immediately after, a knocking is heard at the entrance door.]

Gina [rising.] Hush, Ekdal, — I think there's some one at the door.

Hialmar [laying the flute on the bookcase.] There! Again!

[GINA goes and opens the door.]

Gregers Werle [in the passage.] Excuse me —

Gina [starting back slightly.] Oh!

Gregers. — does not Mr. Ekdal, the photographer, live here?

Gina. Yes, he does.

Hialmar [going towards the door.] Gregers! You here after all? Well, come in then.

Gregers [coming in.] I told you I would come and look you up.

Hialmar. But this evening —? Have you left the party?

Gregers. I have left both the party and my father's house. — Good evening, Mrs. Ekdal. I don't know whether you recognise me?

Gina. Oh yes; it's not difficult to know young Mr. Werle again.

Gregers. No, I am like my mother; and no doubt you remember her.

Hialmar. Left your father's house, did you say?

Gregers. Yes, I have gone to a hotel.

Hialmar. Indeed. Well, since you're here, take off your coat and sit down.

Gregers. Thanks.

[He takes off his overcoat. He is now dressed in a plain grey suit of a countrified cut.]

Hialmar. Here, on the sofa. Make yourself comfortable.

[GREGERS seats himself on the sofa; HIALMAR takes a chair at the table.]

Gregers [looking around him.] So these are your quarters, Hialmar — this is your home.

Hialmar. This is the studio, as you see —

Gina. But it's the largest of our rooms, so we generally sit here.

Hialmar. We used to live in a better place; but this flat has one great advantage: there are such capital outer rooms

Gina. And we have a room on the other side of the passage that we can let.

Gregers [to HIALMAR.] Ah — so you have lodgers too?

Hialmar. No, not yet. They're not so easy to find, you see; you have to keep your eyes open. [To HEDVIG.] What about that beer, eh?

[HEDVIG nods and goes out into the kitchen.]

Gregers. So that is your daughter?

Hialmar. Yes, that is Hedvig.

Gregers. And she is your only child?

Hialmar. Yes, the only one. She is the joy of our lives, and — [lowering his voice] — at the same time our deepest sorrow, Gregers.

Gregers. What do you mean?

Hialmar. She is in serious danger of losing her eyesight.

Gregers. Becoming blind?

Hialmar. Yes. Only the first symptoms have appeared as yet, and she may not feel it much for some time. But the doctor has warned us. It is coming, inexorably.

Gregers. What a terrible misfortune! How do you account for it?

Hialmar [sighs.] Hereditary, no doubt.

Gregers [starting.] Hereditary?

Gina. Ekdal's mother had weak eyes.

Hialmar. Yes, so my father says; I can't remember her.

Gregers. Poor child! And how does she take it?

Hialmar. Oh, you can imagine we haven't the heart to tell her of it. She dreams of no danger. Gay and careless and chirping like a little bird, she flutters onward into a life of endless night. [Overcome.] Oh, it is cruelly hard on me, Gregers.

[HEDVIG brings a tray with beer and glasses, which she sets upon the table.]

Hialmar [stroking her hair.] Thanks, thanks, Hedvig.

[HEDVIG puts her arm round his neck and whispers in his ear.]

HIALMAR. No, no bread and butter just now. [Looks up.] But perhaps you would like some, Gregers.

Gregers [with a gesture of refusal.] No, no thank you.

Hialmar [still melancholy.] Well, you can bring in a little all the same. If you have a crust, that is all I want. And plenty of butter on it, mind.

[HEDVIG nods gaily and goes out into the kitchen again.]

Gregers [who has been following her with his eyes.] She seems quite strong and healthy otherwise.

Gina. Yes. In other ways there's nothing amiss with her, thank goodness.

Gregers. She promises to be very like you, Mrs. Ekdal. How old is she now?

Gina. Hedvig is close on fourteen; her birthday is the day after to-morrow.

Gregers. She is pretty tall for her age, then.

Gina. Yes, she's shot up wonderful this last year.

Gregers. It makes one realise one's own age to see these young people growing up. — How long is it now since you were married?

Gina. We've been married — let me see — just on fifteen years.

Gregers. Is it so long as that?

Gina [becomes attentive; looks at him.] Yes, it is indeed.

Hialmar. Yes, so it is. Fifteen years all but a few months. [Changing his tone.] They must have been long years for you, up at the works, Gregers.

Gregers. They seemed long — while I was living them; now they are over, I hardly know how the time has gone.

[OLD EKDAL comes from his room without his pipe, but with his old-fashioned uniform cap on his head; his gait is somewhat unsteady.]

Ekdal. Come now, Hialmar, let's sit down and have a good talk about this — h'm — what was it again?

Hialmar [going towards him.] Father, we have a visitor here — Gregers Werle. — I don't know if you remember him.

Ekdal [looking at GREGERS, who has risen.] Werle? Is that the son? What does he want with me?

Hialmar. Nothing; it's me he has come to see.

Ekdal. Oh! Then there's nothing wrong?

Hialmar. No, no, of course not.

Ekdal [with a large gesture.] Not that I'm afraid, you know; but —

Gregers [goes over to him.] I bring you a greeting from your old hunting-grounds, Lieutenant Ekdal.

Ekdal. Hunting-grounds?

Gregers. Yes, up in Hoidal, about the works, you know.

Ekdal. Oh, up there. Yes, I knew all those places well in the old days.

Gregers. You were a great sportsman then.

Ekdal. So I was, I don't deny it. You're looking at my uniform cap. I don't ask anybody's leave to wear it in the house. So long as I don't go out in the streets with it —

[HEDVIG brings a plate of bread and butter, which she puts upon the table.]

Hialmar. Sit down, father, and have a glass of beer. Help yourself, Gregers.

[EKDAL mutters and stumbles over to the sofa. GREGERS seats himself on the chair nearest to him, HIALMAR on the other side of GREGERS. GINA sits a little way from the table, sewing; HEDVIG stands beside her father.]

Gregers. Can you remember, Lieutenant Ekdal, how Hialmar and I used to come up and visit you in the summer and at Christmas?

Ekdal. Did you? No, no, no; I don't remember it. But sure enough I've been a tidy bit of a sportsman in my day. I've shot bears too. I've shot nine of 'em, no less.

Gregers [looking sympathetically at him.] And now you never get any shooting?

Ekdal. Can't just say that, sir. Get a shot now and then perhaps. Of course not in the old way. For the woods you see — the woods, the woods —! [Drinks.] Are the woods fine up there now?

Gregers. Not so fine as in your time. They have been thinned a good deal.

Ekdal. Thinned? [More softly, and as if afraid.] It's dangerous work that. Bad things come of it. The woods revenge themselves.

Hialmar [filling up his glass.] Come — a little more, father.

Gregers. How can a man like you — such a man for the open air — live in the midst of a stuffy town, boxed within four walls?

Ekdal [laughs quietly and glances at HIALMAR.] Oh, it's not so bad here. Not at all so bad.

Gregers. But don't you miss all the things that used to be a part of your very being — the cool sweeping breezes, the free life in the woods and on the uplands, among beasts and birds —?

Ekdal [smiling.] Hialmar, shall we let him see it?

Hialmar [hastily and a little embarrassed.] Oh, no no, father; not this evening.

Gregers. What does he want to show me?

Hialmar. Oh, it's only something — you can see it another time.

Gregers [continues, to the old man.] You see I have been thinking, Lieutenant Ekdal, that you should come up with me to the works; I am sure to be going back soon. No doubt you could get some copying there too. And here, you have nothing on earth to interest you — nothing to liven you up.

Ekdal [stares in astonishment at him.] Have I nothing on earth to —!

Gregers. Of course you have Hialmar; but then he has his own family. And a man like you, who has always had such a passion for what is free and wild —

Ekdal [thumps the table.] Hialmar, he shall see it!

Hialmar. Oh, do you think it's worth while, father? It's all dark.

Ekdal. Nonsense; it's moonlight. [Rises.] He shall see it, I tell you. Let me pass! Come and help me, Hialmar.

Hedvig. Oh yes, do, father!

Hialmar [rising.] Very well then.

Gregers [to GINA.] What is it?

Gina. Oh, nothing so very wonderful, after all.

[EKDAL and HIALMAR have gone to the back wall and are each pushing back a side of the sliding door; HEDVIG helps the old man; GREGERS remains standing by the sofa; GINA sits still and sews. Through the open doorway a large, deep irregular garret is seen with odd nooks and corners; a couple of stove-pipes running through it, from rooms below. There are skylights through which clear moonbeams shine in on some parts of the great room; others lie in deep shadow.]

Ekdal [to GREGERS.] You may come close up if you like.

Gregers [going over to them.] Why, what is it?

Ekdal. Look for yourself. H'm.

Hialmar [somewhat embarrassed.] This belongs to father, you understand.

Gregers [at the door, looks into the garret.] Why, you keep poultry, Lieutenant Ekdal.

Ekdal. Should think we did keep poultry. They've gone to roost now. But you should just see our fowls by daylight, sir!

Hedvig. And there's a —

Ekdal. Sh — sh! don't say anything about it yet.

Gregers. And you have pigeons too, I see.

Ekdal. Oh yes, haven't we just got pigeons! They have their nest-boxes up there under the roof-tree; for pigeons like to roost high, you see.

Hialmar. They aren't all common pigeons.

Ekdal. Common! Should think not indeed! We have tumblers, and a pair of pouters, too. But come here! Can you see that hutch down there by the wall?

Gregers. Yes; what do you use it for?

Ekdal. That's where the rabbits sleep, sir.

Gregers. Dear me; so you have rabbits too?

Ekdal. Yes, you may take my word for it, we have rabbits! He wants to know if we have rabbits, Hialmar! H'm! But now comes the thing, let me tell you! Here we have it! Move away, Hedvig. Stand here; that's right, — and now look down there. — Don't you see a basket with straw in it?

Gregers. Yes. And I can see a fowl lying in the basket.

Ekdal. H'm — "a fowl"

Gregers. Isn't it a duck?

Ekdal [hurt.] Why, of course it's a duck.

Hialmar. But what kind of duck, do you think?

Hedvig. It's not just a common duck —

Ekdal. Sh!

Gregers. And it's not a Muscovy duck either.

Ekdal. No, Mr. — Werle; it's not a Muscovy duck; for it's a wild duck!

Gregers. Is it really? A wild duck?

Ekdal. Yes, that's what it is. That "fowl" as you call it — is the wild duck. It's our wild duck, sir.

Hedvig. My wild duck. It belongs to me.

Gregers. And can it live up here in the garret? Does it thrive?

Ekdal. Of course it has a trough of water to splash about in, you know.

Hialmar. Fresh water every other day.

Gina [turning towards HIALMAR.] But my dear Ekdal, it's getting icy cold here.

Ekdal. H'm, we had better shut up then. It's as well not to disturb their night's rest, too. Close up, Hedvig.

[HIALMAR and HEDVIG push the garret doors together.]

Ekdal. Another time you shall see her properly. [Seats himself in the arm-chair by the stove.] Oh, they're curious things, these wild ducks, I can tell you.

Gregers. How did you manage to catch it, Lieutenant Ekdal?

Ekdal. I didn't catch it. There's a certain man in this town whom we have to thank for it.

Gregers [starts slightly.] That man was not my father, was he?

Ekdal. You've hit it. Your father and no one else. H'm.

Hialmar. Strange that you should guess that, Gregers.

Gregers. You were telling me that you owed so many things to my father; and so I thought perhaps —

Gina. But we didn't get the duck from Mr. Werle himself —

Ekdal. It's Hakon Werle we have to thank for her, all the same, Gina. [To GREGERS.] He was shooting from a boat, you see, and he brought her down. But your father's sight is not very good now. H'm; she was only wounded.

Gregers. Ah! She got a couple of slugs in her body, I suppose.

Hialmar. Yes, two or three.

Hedvig. She was hit under the wing, so that she couldn't fly.

Gregers. And I suppose she dived to the bottom, eh?

Ekdal [sleepily, in a thick voice.] Of course. Always do that, wild ducks do. They shoot to the bottom as deep as they can get, sir — and bite themselves fast in the tangle and seaweed — and all the devil's own mess that grows down there. And they never come up again.

Gregers. But your wild duck came up again, Lieutenant Ekdal.

Ekdal. He had such an amazingly clever dog, your father had. And that dog — he dived in after the duck and fetched her up again.

Gregers [who has turned to HIALMAR.] And then she was sent to you here?

Hialmar. Not at once; at first your father took her home. But she wouldn't thrive there; so Pettersen was told to put an end to her —

Ekdal [half asleep.] H'm — yes — Pettersen — that ass —

Hialmar [speaking more softly.] That was how we got her, you see; for father knows Pettersen a little; and when he heard about the wild duck he got him to hand her over to us.

Gregers. And now she thrives as well as possible in the garret there?

Hialmar. Yes, wonderfully well. She has got fat. You see, she has lived in there so long now that she has forgotten her natural wild life; and it all depends on that.

Gregers. You are right there, Hialmar. Be sure you never let her get a glimpse of the sky and the sea — . But I mustn't stay any longer; I think your father is asleep.

Hialmar. Oh, as for that —

Gregers. But, by-the-bye — you said you had a room to let — a spare room?

Hialmar. Yes; what then? Do you know of anybody —?

Gregers. Can I have that room?

Hialmar. You?

Gina. Oh no, Mr. Werle, you —

Gregers. May I have the room? If so, I'll take possession first thing to-morrow morning.

Hialmar. Yes, with the greatest pleasure —

Gina. But, Mr. Werle, I'm sure it's not at all the sort of room for you.

Hialmar. Why, Gina! how can you say that?

Gina. Why, because the room's neither large enough nor light enough, and —

Gregers. That really doesn't matter, Mrs. Ekdal.

Hialmar. I call it quite a nice room, and not at all badly furnished either.

Gina. But remember the pair of them underneath.

Gregers. What pair?

Gina. Well, there's one as has been a tutor —

Hialmar. That's Molvik — Mr. Molvik, B.A.

Gina. And then there's a doctor, by the name of Relling.

Gregers. Relling? I know him a little; he practised for a time up in Hoidal.

Gina. They're a regular rackety pair, they are. As often as not, they're out on the loose in the evenings; and then they come home at all hours, and they're not always just —

Gregers. One soon gets used to that sort of thing. I daresay I shall be like the wild duck —

Gina. H'm; I think you ought to sleep upon it first, anyway.

Gregers. You seem very unwilling to have me in the house, Mrs. Ekdal.

Gina. Oh, no! What makes you think that?

Hialmar. Well, you really behave strangely about it,

Gina. [To GREGERS.] Then I suppose you intend to remain in the town for the present?

Gregers [putting on his overcoat.] Yes, now I intend to remain here.

Hialmar. And yet not at your father's? What do you propose to do, then?

Gregers. Ah, if I only knew that, Hialmar, I shouldn't be so badly off! But when one has the misfortune to be called Gregers —! "Gregers" — and then "Werle" after it; did you ever hear anything so hideous?

Hialmar. Oh, I don't think so at all.

Gregers. Ugh! Bah! I feel I should like to spit upon the fellow that answers to such a name. But when a man is once for all doomed to be Gregers — Werle in this world, as I am —

Hialmar [laughs.] Ha, ha! If you weren't Gregers Werle, what would you like to be?

Gregers. If I should choose, I should like best to be a clever dog.

Gina. A dog!

Hedvig [involuntarily.] Oh, no!

Gregers. Yes, an amazingly clever dog; one that goes to the bottom after wild ducks when they dive and bite themselves fast in tangle and sea-weed, down among the ooze.

Hialmar. Upon my word now, Gregers — I don't in the least know what you're driving at.

Gregers. Oh, well, you might not be much the wiser if you did. It's understood, then, that I move in early to-morrow morning. [To GINA.] I won't give you any trouble; I do everything for myself. [To HIALMAR.] We can talk about the rest to-morrow. — Good-night, Mrs. Ekdal. [Nods to HEDVIG.] Good-night.

Gina. Good-night, Mr. Werle.

Hedvig. Good-night.

Hialmar [who has lighted a candle.] Wait a moment, I must show you a light; the stairs are sure to be dark.

[GREGERS and HIALMAR go out by the passage door.]

Gina [looking straight before her, with her sewing in her lap.] Wasn't that queer-like talk about wanting to be a dog?

Hedvig. Do you know, mother — I believe he meant something quite different by that.

Gina. Why, what should he mean?

Hedvig. Oh, I don't know; but it seemed to me he meant something different from what he said — all the time.

Gina. Do you think so? Yes, it was sort of queer.

Hialmar [comes back.] The lamp was still burning. [Puts out the candle and sets it down.] Ah, now one can get a mouthful of food at last. [Begins to eat the bread and butter.] Well, you see, Gina — if only you keep your eyes open —

Gina. How, keep your eyes open —?

Hialmar. Why, haven't we at last had the luck to get the room let? And just think — to a person like Gregers — a good old friend.

Gina. Well, I don't know what to say about it.

Hedvig. Oh, mother, you'll see; it'll be such fun!

Hialmar. You're very strange. You were so bent upon getting the room let before; and now you don't like it.

Gina. Yes I do, Ekdal; if it had only been to some one else — But what do you suppose Mr. Werle will say?

Hialmar. Old Werle? It doesn't concern him.

116

Gina. But surely you can see that there's something amiss between them again, or the young man wouldn't be leaving home. You know very well those two can't get on with each other.

Hialmar. Very likely not, but —

Gina. And now Mr. Werle may fancy it's you that has egged him on —

Hialmar. Let him fancy so, then! Mr. Werle has done a great deal for me; far be it from me to deny it. But that doesn't make me everlastingly dependent upon him.

Gina. But, my dear Ekdal, maybe grandfather'll suffer for it. He may lose the little bit of work he gets from Graberg.

Hialmar. I could almost say: so much the better! Is it not humiliating for a man like me to see his grey-haired father treated as a pariah? But now I believe the fulness of time is at hand. [Takes a fresh piece of bread and butter.] As sure as I have a mission in life, I mean to fulfil it now!

Hedvig. Oh, yes, father, do!

Gina. Hush! Don't wake him!

Hialmar [more softly.] I will fulfil it, I say. The day shall come when — And that is why I say it's a good thing we have let the room; for that makes me more independent, The man who has a mission in life must be independent. [By the arm-chair, with emotion.] Poor old white-haired father! Rely on your Hialmar. He has broad shoulders — strong shoulders, at any rate. You shall yet wake up some fine day and — [To GINA.] Do you not believe it?

Gina [rising.] Yes, of course I do; but in the meantime suppose we see about getting him to bed.

Hialmar. Yes, come.

[They take hold of the old man carefully.]

117

Act 3

HIALMAR EKDAL'S studio. It is morning: the daylight shines through the large window in the slanting roof; the curtain is drawn back.

HIALMAR is sitting at the table, busy retouching a photograph; several others lie before him. Presently GINA, wearing her hat and cloak, enters by the passage door; she has a covered basket on her arm.]

Hialmar. Back already, Gina?

Gina. Oh, yes, one can't let the grass grow under one's feet.

[Sets her basket on a chair, and takes off her things.]

Hialmar. Did you look in at Gregers' room?

Gina. Yes, that I did. It's a rare sight, I can tell you; he's made a pretty mess to start off with.

Hialmar. How so?

Gina. He was determined to do everything for himself, he said; so he sets to work to light the stove, and what must he do but screw down the damper till the whole room is full of smoke. Ugh! There was a smell fit to —

Hialmar. Well, really!

Gina. But that's not the worst of it; for then he thinks he'll put out the fire, and goes and empties his water-jug into the stove, and so makes the whole floor one filthy puddle.

Hialmar. How annoying!

Gina. I've got the porter's wife to clear up after him, pig that he is! But the room won't be fit to live in till the afternoon.

Hialmar. What's he doing with himself in the meantime?

Gina. He said he was going out for a little while.

Hialmar. I looked in upon him, too, for a moment — after you had gone.

Gina. So I heard. You've asked him to lunch.

Hialmar. Just to a little bit of early lunch, you know. It's his first day — we can hardly do less. You've got something in the house, I suppose?

Gina. I shall have to find something or other.

Hialmar. And don't cut it too fine, for I fancy Relling and Molvik are coming up, too. I just happened to meet Relling on the stairs, you see; so I had to —

Gina. Oh, are we to have those two as well?

Hialmar. Good Lord — a couple more or less can't make any difference. Old Ekdal [opens his door and looks in]. I say, Hialmar — [Sees GINA.] Oh!

Gina. Do you want anything, grandfather?

Ekdal. Oh, no, it doesn't matter. H'm!

[Retires again.]

Gina [takes up the basket.] Be sure you see that he doesn't go out.

Hialmar. All right, all right. And, Gina, a little herring-salad wouldn't be a bad idea; Relling and Molvik were out on the loose again last night.

Gina. If only they don't come before I'm ready for them —

Hialmar. No, of course they won't; take your own time.

Gina. Very well; and meanwhile you can be working a bit.

Hialmar. Well, I am working! I am working as hard as I can!

Gina. Then you'll have that job off your hands, you see.

[She goes out to the kitchen with her basket. HIALMAR sits for a time pencilling away at the photograph, in an indolent and listless manner.]

Ekdal [peeps in, looks round the studio, and says softly:] Are you busy?

Hialmar. Yes, I'm toiling at these wretched pictures —

Ekdal. Well, well, never mind, — since you're so busy — h'm!

[He goes out again; the door stands open.]

Hialmar [continues for some time in silence then he lays down his brush and goes over to the door.] Are you busy, father?

Ekdal [in a grumbling tone, within.] If you're busy, I'm busy, too. H'm!

Hialmar. Oh, very well, then.

[Goes to his work again.]

Ekdal [presently, coming to the door again.] H'm; I say, Hialmar, I'm not so very busy, you know.

Hialmar. I thought you were writing.

Ekdal. Oh, devil take it! can't Graberg wait a day or two? After all, it's not a matter of life and death.

Hialmar. No; and you're not his slave either.

Ekdal. And about that other business in there —

Hialmar. Just what I was thinking of. Do you want to go in? Shall I open the door for you?

Ekdal. Well, it wouldn't be a bad notion.

Hialmar [rises.] Then we'd have that off our hands.

Ekdal. Yes, exactly. It's got to be ready first thing to-morrow. It is to-morrow, isn't it? H'm?

Hialmar. Yes, of course it's to-morrow.

[HIALMAR and EKDAL push aside each his half of the sliding door. The morning sun is shining in through the skylights; some doves are flying about; others sit cooing, upon the perches; the hens are heard clucking now and then, further back in the garret.]

Hialmar. There; now you can get to work, father.

Ekdal [goes in.] Aren't you coming, too?

Hialmar. Well, really, do you know —; I almost think — [Sees GINA at the kitchen door.] I? No; I haven't time; I must work. — But now for our new contrivance —

[He pulls a cord, a curtain slips down inside, the lower part consisting of a piece of old sailcloth, the upper part of a stretched fishing net. The floor of the garret is thus no longer visible.]

Hialmar [goes to the table.] So! Now, perhaps I can sit in peace for a little while.

Gina. Is he rampaging in there again?

Hialmar. Would you rather have had him slip down to Madam Eriksen's? [Seats himself.] Do you want anything? You know you said —

Gina. I only wanted to ask if you think we can lay the table for lunch here?

Hialmar. Yes; we have no early appointment, I suppose?

Gina. No, I expect no one to-day except those two sweethearts that are to be taken together.

Hialmar. Why the deuce couldn't they be taken together another day!

Gina. Don't you know, I told them to come in the afternoon, when you are having your nap.

Hialmar. Oh, that's capital. Very well, let us have lunch here then.

Gina. All right; but there's no hurry about laying the cloth; you can have the table for a good while yet.

Hialmar. Do you think I am not sticking at my work? I'm at it as hard as I can!

Gina. Then you'll be free later on, you know.

[Goes out into the kitchen again. Short pause.]

Ekdal [in the garret doorway, behind the net.] Hialmar!

Hialmar. Well?

Ekdal. Afraid we shall have to move the water-trough, after all.

Hialmar. What else have I been saying all along?

Ekdal. H'm — h'm — h'm.

121

[Goes away from the door again. HIALMAR goes on working a little; glances towards the garret and half rises. HEDVIG comes in from the kitchen.]

Hialmar [sits down again hurriedly.] What do you want?

Hedvig. I only wanted to come in beside you, father.

Hialmar [after a pause]. What makes you go prying around like that? Perhaps you are told off to watch me?

Hedvig. No, no.

Hialmar. What is your mother doing out there?

Hedvig. Oh, mother's in the middle of making the herring-salad. [Goes to the table]. Isn't there any little thing I could help you with, father?

Hialmar. Oh, no. It is right that I should bear the whole burden — so long as my strength holds out. Set your mind at rest, Hedvig; if only your father keeps his health —

Hedvig. Oh, no, father! You mustn't talk in that horrid way.

[She wanders about a little, stops by the doorway and looks into the garret.]

Hialmar. Tell me, what is he doing?

Hedvig. I think he's making a new path to the water-trough.

Hialmar. He can never manage that by himself! And here am I doomed to sit —!

Hedvig [goes to him.] Let me take the brush, father; I can do it, quite well.

Hialmar. Oh, nonsense; you will only hurt your eyes.

Hedvig. Not a bit. Give me the brush.

Hialmar [rising.] Well, it won't take more than a minute or two.

Hedvig. Pooh, what harm can it do then? [Takes the brush.] There! [Seats herself.] I can begin upon this one.

Hialmar. But mind you don't hurt your eyes! Do you hear? I won't be answerable; you do it on your own responsibility — understand that.

Hedvig [retouching.] Yes, yes, I understand.

Hialmar. You are quite clever at it, Hedvig. Only a minute or two, you know.

[He slips through by the edge of the curtain into the garret. HEDVIG sits at her work. HIALMAR and EKDAL are heard disputing inside.]

Hialmar [appears behind the net.] I say, Hedvig — give me those pincers that are lying on the shelf. And the chisel. [Turns away inside.] Now you shall see, father. Just let me show you first what I mean!

[HEDVIG has fetched the required tools from the shelf, and hands them to him through the net.]

Hialmar. Ah, thanks. I didn't come a moment too soon.

[Goes back from the curtain again; they are heard carpentering and talking inside. HEDVIG stands looking in at them. A moment later there is a knock at the passage door; she does not notice it.]

Gregers Werle [bareheaded, in indoor dress, enters and stops near the door.] H'm —!

Hedvig [turns and goes towards him.] Good morning. Please come in.

Gregers. Thank you. [Looking towards the garret.] You seem to have workpeople in the house.

Hedvig. No, it is only father and grandfather. I'll tell them you are here.

Gregers. No, no, don't do that; I would rather wait a little.

[Seats himself on the sofa.]

Hedvig. It looks so untidy here —

[Begins to clear away the photographs.]

Gregers. Oh, don't take them away. Are those prints that have to be finished off?

Hedvig. Yes, they are a few I was helping father with.

Gregers. Please don't let me disturb you.

Hedvig. Oh, no.

[She gathers the things to her and sits down to work; GREGERS looks at her, meanwhile, in silence.]

Gregers. Did the wild duck sleep well last night?

Hedvig. Yes, I think so, thanks.

Gregers [turning towards the garret.] It looks quite different by day from what it did last night in the moonlight.

Hedvig. Yes, it changes ever so much. It looks different in the morning and in the afternoon; and it's different on rainy days from what it is in fine weather.

Gregers. Have you noticed that?

Hedvig. Yes, how could I help it?

Gregers. Are you, too, fond of being in there with the wild duck?

Hedvig. Yes, when I can manage it —

Gregers. But I suppose you haven't much spare time; you go to school, no doubt.

Hedvig. No, not now; father is afraid of my hurting my eyes.

Gregers. Oh; then he reads with you himself?

Hedvig. Father has promised to read with me; but he has never had time yet.

Gregers. Then is there nobody else to give you a little help?

Hedvig. Yes, there is Mr. Molvik; but he is not always exactly — quite —

Gregers. Sober?

Hedvig. Yes, I suppose that's it!

Gregers. Why, then you must have any amount of time on your hands. And in there I suppose it is a sort world by itself?

Hedvig. Oh, yes, quite. And there are such lots of wonderful things.

Gregers. Indeed?

Hedvig. Yes, there are big cupboards full of books; and a great many of the books have pictures in them.

Gregers. Aha!

Hedvig. And there's an old bureau with drawers and flaps, and a big clock with figures that go out and in. But the clock isn't going now.

Gregers. So time has come to a standstill in there — in the wild duck's domain.

Hedvig. Yes. And then there's an old paint-box and things of that sort; and all the books.

Gregers. And you read the books, I suppose?

Hedvig. Oh, yes, when I get the chance. Most of them are English though, and I don't understand English. But then I look at the pictures. — There is one great big book called "Harrison's History of London."* It must be a hundred years old; and there are such heaps of pictures in it. At the beginning there is Death with an hour-glass and a woman. I think that is horrid. But then there are all the other pictures of churches, and castles, and streets, and great ships sailing on the sea.

* A New and Universal History of the Cities of London and Westminster, by Walter Harrison. London, 1775, folio.

Gregers. But tell me, where did all those wonderful things come from?

Hedvig. Oh, an old sea captain once lived here, and he brought them home with him. They used to call him "The Flying Dutchman." That was curious, because he wasn't a Dutchman at all.

Gregers. Was he not?

Hedvig. No. But at last he was drowned at sea; and so he left all those things behind him.

Gregers. Tell me now — when you are sitting in there looking at the pictures, don't you wish you could travel and see the real world for yourself?

Hedvig. Oh, no! I mean always to stay at home and help father and mother.

Gregers. To retouch photographs?

Hedvig. No, not only that. I should love above everything to learn to engrave pictures like those in the English books.

Gregers. H'm. What does your father say to that?

Hedvig. I don't think father likes it; father is strange about such things. Only think, he talks of my learning basket-making, and straw-plaiting! But I don't think that would be much good.

Gregers. Oh, no, I don't think so either.

Hedvig. But father was right in saying that if I had learnt basket-making I could have made the new basket for the wild duck.

Gregers. So you could; and it was you that ought to have done it, wasn't it?

Hedvig. Yes, for it's my wild duck.

Gregers. Of course it is.

Hedvig. Yes, it belongs to me. But I lend it to father and grandfather as often as they please.

Gregers. Indeed? What do they do with it?

Hedvig. Oh, they look after it, and build places for it, and so on.

Gregers. I see; for no doubt the wild duck is by far the most distinguished inhabitant of the garret?

Hedvig. Yes, indeed she is; for she is a real wild fowl, you know. And then she is so much to be pitied; she has no one to care for, poor thing.

Gregers. She has no family, as the rabbits have —

Hedvig. No. The hens too, many of them, were chickens together; but she has been taken right away from all her friends. And then there is so much that is strange about the wild duck. Nobody knows her, and nobody knows where she came from either.

Gregers. And she has been down in the depths of the sea.

Hedvig [with a quick glance at him, represses a smile and asks:] Why do you say "depths of the sea"?

Gregers. What else should I say?

Hedvig. You could say "the bottom of the sea."*

* Gregers here uses the old-fashioned expression "havsens bund," while Hedvig would have him use the more commonplace "havets bund" or "havbunden."

Gregers. Oh, mayn't I just as well say the depths of the sea?

Hedvig. Yes; but it sounds so strange to me when other people speak of the depths of the sea.

Gregers. Why so? Tell me why?

Hedvig. No, I won't; it's so stupid.

Gregers. Oh, no, I am sure it's not. Do tell me why you smiled.

Hedvig. Well, this is the reason: whenever I come to realise suddenly — in a flash — what is in there, it always seems to me that the whole room and everything in it should be called "the depths of the sea." But that is so stupid.

Gregers. You mustn't say that.

Hedvig. Oh, yes, for you know it is only a garret.

Gregers [looks fixedly at her.] Are you so sure of that?

Hedvig [astonished.] That it's a garret?

Gregers. Are you quite certain of it?

[HEDVIG is silent, and looks at him open-mouthed. GINA comes in from the kitchen with the table things.]

Gregers [rising.] I have come in upon you too early.

Gina. Oh, you must be somewhere; and we're nearly ready now, any way. Clear the table, Hedvig.

[HEDVIG clears away her things; she and GINA lay the cloth during what follows. GREGERS seats himself in the arm-chair, and turns over an album.]

Gregers. I hear you can retouch, Mrs. Ekdal.

Gina [with a side glance.] Yes, I can.

Gregers. That was exceedingly lucky.

Gina. How — lucky?

Gregers. Since Ekdal took to photography, I mean.

Hedvig. Mother can take photographs, too.

Gina. Oh, yes; I was bound to learn that.

Gregers. So it is really you that carry on the business, I suppose?

Gina. Yes, when Ekdal hasn't time himself —

Gregers. He is a great deal taken up with his old father, I daresay.

Gina. Yes; and then you can't expect a man like Ekdal to do nothing but take car-de-visits of Dick, Tom and Harry.

Gregers. I quite agree with you; but having once gone in for the thing —

Gina. You can surely understand, Mr. Werle, that Ekdal's not like one of your common photographers.

Gregers. Of course not; but still —

[A shot is fired within the garret.]

Gregers [starting up.] What's that?

Gina. Ugh! now they're firing again!

Gregers. Have they firearms in there?

Hedvig. They are out shooting.

Gregers. What! [At the door of the garret.] Are you shooting, Hialmar?

Hialmar [inside the net.] Are you there? I didn't know;

I was so taken up — [To HEDVIG.] Why did you not let us know? [Comes into the studio.]

Gregers. Do you go shooting in the garret?

Hialmar [showing a double-barrelled pistol.] Oh, only with this thing.

Gina. Yes, you and grandfather will do yourselves a mischief some day with that there pigstol.

Hialmar [with irritation.] I believe I have told you that this kind of firearm is called a pistol.

Gina. Oh, that doesn't make it much better, that I can see.

Gregers. So you have become a sportsman, too, Hialmar?

Hialmar. Only a little rabbit-shooting now and then. Mostly to please father, you understand.

Gina. Men are strange beings; they must always have something to pervert theirselves with.

Hialmar [snappishly.] Just so; we must always have something to divert ourselves with.

Gina. Yes, that's just what I say.

Hialmar. H'm. [To GREGERS.] You see the garret is fortunately so situated that no one can hear us shooting. [Lays the pistol on the top shelf of the bookcase.] Don't touch the pistol, Hedvig! One of the barrels is loaded; remember that.

Gregers [looking through the net.] You have a fowling-piece too, I see.

Hialmar. That is father's old gun. It's of no use now; something has gone wrong with the lock. But it's fun to have it all the same; for we can take it to pieces now and then, and clean and grease it, and screw it together again. — Of course, it's mostly father that fiddle-faddles with all that sort of thing.

Hedvig [beside GREGERS.] Now you can see the wild duck properly.

Gregers. I was just looking at her. One of her wings seems to me to droop a bit.

Hedvig. Well, no wonder; her wing was broken, you know.

Gregers. And she trails one foot a little. Isn't that so?

Hialmar. Perhaps a very little bit.

Hedvig. Yes, it was by that foot the dog took hold of her.

Hialmar. But otherwise she hasn't the least thing the matter with her; and that is simply marvellous for a creature that has a charge of shot in her body, and has been between a dog's teeth —

Gregers [with a glance at HEDVIG] — and that has lain in the depths of the sea — so long.

Hedvig [smiling.] Yes.

Gina [laying the table.] That blessed wild duck! What a lot of fuss you do make over her.

Hialmar. H'm; — will lunch soon be ready?

Gina. Yes, directly. Hedvig, you must come and help me now.

[GINA and HEDVIG go out into the kitchen.]

Hialmar [in a low voice.] I think you had better not stand there looking in at father; he doesn't like it. [GREGERS moves away from the garret door.] Besides, I may as well shut up before the others come. [Claps his hands to drive the fowls back.] Shh — shh, in with you! [Draws up the curtain and pulls the doors together.] All the contrivances are my own invention. It's really quite amusing to have things of this sort to potter with, and to put to rights when they get out of order. And it's absolutely necessary, too; for Gina objects to having rabbits and fowls in the studio.

Gregers. To be sure; and I suppose the studio is your wife's special department?

Hialmar. As a rule, I leave the everyday details of business to her; for then I can take refuge in the parlour and give my mind to more important things.

Gregers. What things may they be, Hialmar?

Hialmar. I wonder you have not asked that question sooner. But perhaps you haven't heard of the invention?

Gregers. The invention? No.

Hialmar. Really? Have you not? Oh, no, out there in the wilds —

Gregers. So you have invented something, have you?

Hialmar. It is not quite completed yet; but I am working at it. You can easily imagine that when I resolved to devote myself to photography, it wasn't simply with the idea of taking likenesses of all sorts of commonplace people.

Gregers. No; your wife was saying the same thing just now.

Hialmar. I swore that if I consecrated my powers to this handicraft, I would so exalt it that it should become both an art and a science. And to that end I determined to make this great invention.

Gregers. And what is the nature of the invention? What purpose does it serve?

Hialmar. Oh, my dear fellow, you mustn't ask for details yet. It takes time, you see. And you must not think that my motive is vanity. It is not for my own sake that I am working. Oh, no; it is my life's mission that stands before me night and day.

Gregers. What is your life's mission?

Hialmar. Do you forget the old man with the silver hair?

Gregers. Your poor father? Well, but what can you do for him?

Hialmar. I can raise up his self-respect from the dead, by restoring the name of Ekdal to honour and dignity.

Gregers. Then that is your life's mission?

Hialmar. Yes. I will rescue the shipwrecked man. For shipwrecked he was, by the very first blast of the storm. Even while those terrible investigations were going on, he was no longer himself. That pistol there — the one we use to shoot rabbits with — has played its part in the tragedy of the house of Ekdal.

Gregers. The pistol? Indeed?

Hialmar. When the sentence of imprisonment was passed — he had the pistol in his hand —

Gregers. Had he —?

Hialmar. Yes; but he dared not use it. His courage failed him. So broken, so demoralised was he even then! Oh, can you understand it? He, a soldier; he, who had shot nine bears, and who was descended from two lieutenant-colonels — one after the other, of course. Can you understand it, Gregers?

Gregers. Yes, I understand it well enough.

Hialmar. I cannot. And once more the pistol played a part in the history of our house. When he had put on the grey clothes and was under lock and key — oh, that was a terrible time for me, I can tell you. I kept the blinds drawn down over both my windows. When I peeped out, I saw the sun shining as if nothing had happened. I could not understand it. I saw people going along the street, laughing and talking about indifferent things. I could not understand it. It seemed to me that the whole of existence must be at a standstill — as if under an eclipse.

Gregers. I felt that, too, when my mother died.

Hialmar. It was in such an hour that Hialmar Ekdal pointed the pistol at his own breast.

Gregers. You, too, thought of —!

Hialmar. Yes.

Gregers. But you did not fire?

Hialmar. No. At the decisive moment I won the victory over myself. I remained in life. But I can assure you it takes some courage to choose life under circumstances like those.

Gregers. Well, that depends on how you look at it.

Hialmar. Yes, indeed, it takes courage. But I am glad I was firm: for now I shall soon perfect my invention; and Dr. Relling thinks, as I do myself, that father may be allowed to wear his uniform again. I will demand that as my sole reward.

Gregers. So that is what he meant about his uniform —?

Hialmar. Yes, that is what he most yearns for. You can't think how my heart bleeds for him. Every time we celebrate any little family festival — Gina's and my wedding-day, or whatever it may be — in comes the old man in the lieutenant's uniform of happier days. But if he only hears a knock at the door — for he daren't show himself to strangers, you know — he hurries back to his room again as fast as his old legs can carry him. Oh, it's heart-rending for a son to see such things!

Gregers. How long do you think it will take you to finish your invention?

Hialmar. Come now, you mustn't expect me to enter into particulars like that. An invention is not a thing completely under one's own control. It depends largely on inspiration — on intuition — and it is almost impossible to predict when the inspiration may come.

Gregers. But it's advancing?

Hialmar. Yes, certainly, it is advancing. I turn it over in my mind every day; I am full of it. Every afternoon, when I have had my dinner, I shut myself up in the parlour, where I can ponder undisturbed. But I can't be goaded to it; it's not a bit of good; Relling says so, too.

Gregers. And you don't think that all that business in the garret draws you off and distracts you too much?

Hialmar. No, no, no; quite the contrary. You mustn't say that. I cannot be everlastingly absorbed in the same laborious train of thought. I must have something alongside of it to fill up the time of waiting. The inspiration, the intuition, you see — when it comes, it comes, and there's an end of it.

Gregers. My dear Hialmar, I almost think you have something of the wild duck in you.

Hialmar. Something of the wild duck? How do you mean?

Gregers. You have dived down and bitten yourself fast in the undergrowth.

Hialmar. Are you alluding to the well-nigh fatal shot that has broken my father's wing — and mine, too?

Gregers. Not exactly to that. I don't say that your wing has been broken; but you have strayed into a poisonous marsh, Hialmar; an insidious disease has taken hold of you, and you have sunk down to die in the dark.

Hialmar. I? To die in the dark? Look here, Gregers, you must really leave off talking such nonsense.

Gregers. Don't be afraid; I shall find a way to help you up again. I, too, have a mission in life now; I found it yesterday.

Hialmar. That's all very well; but you will please leave me out of it. I can assure you that — apart from my very natural melancholy, of course — I am as contented as any one can wish to be.

Gregers. Your contentment is an effect of the marsh poison.

Hialmar. Now, my dear Gregers, pray do not go on about disease and poison; I am not used to that sort of talk. In my house nobody ever speaks to me about unpleasant things.

Gregers. Ah, that I can easily believe.

Hialmar. It's not good for me, you see. And there are no marsh poisons here, as you express it. The poor photographer's roof is lowly, I know — and my circumstances are narrow. But I am an inventor, and I am the bread-winner of a family. That exalts me above my mean surroundings. — Ah, here comes lunch!

GINA and HEDVIG bring bottles of ale, a decanter of brandy, glasses, etc. At the same time, RELLING and MOLVIK enter from the passage; they are both without hat or overcoat. MOLVIK is dressed in black.]

Gina [placing the things upon the table.] Ah, you two have come in the nick of time.

Relling. Molvik got it into his head that he could smell herring-salad, and then there was no holding him. — Good morning again, Ekdal.

Hialmar. Gregers, let me introduce you to Mr. Molvik. Doctor — Oh, you know Relling, don't you?

Gregers. Yes, slightly.

Relling. Oh, Mr. Werle, junior! Yes, we two have had one or two little skirmishes up at the Hoidal works. You've just moved in?

Gregers. I moved in this morning.

Relling. Molvik and I live right under you; so you haven't far to go for the doctor and the clergyman, if you should need anything in that line.

Gregers. Thanks, it's not quite unlikely; for yesterday we were thirteen at table.

Hialmar. Oh, come now, don't let us get upon unpleasant subjects again!

Relling. You may make your mind easy, Ekdal; I'll be hanged if the finger of fate points to you.

Hialmar. I should hope not, for the sake of my family. But let us sit down now, and eat and drink and be merry.

Gregers. Shall we not wait for your father?

Hialmar. No, his lunch will be taken in to him later. Come along!

[The men seat themselves at table, and eat and drink. GINA and HEDVIG go in and out and wait upon them.]

Relling. Molvik was frightfully screwed yesterday, Mrs. Ekdal.

Gina. Really? Yesterday again?

Relling. Didn't you hear him when I brought him home last night?

Gina. No, I can't say I did.

Relling. That was a good thing, for Molvik was disgusting last night.

Gina. Is that true, Molvik?

Molvik. Let us draw a veil over last night's proceedings. That sort of thing is totally foreign to my better self.

Relling [to GREGERS.] It comes over him like a sort of possession, and then I have to go out on the loose with him. Mr. Molvik is daemonic, you see.

Gregers. Daemonic?

Relling. Molvik is daemonic, yes.

Gregers. H'm.

Relling. And daemonic natures are not made to walk straight through the world; they must meander a little now and then. — Well, so you still stick up there at those horrible grimy works?

Gregers. I have stuck there until now.

Relling. And did you ever manage to collect that claim you went about presenting?

Gregers. Claim? [Understands him.] Ah, I see.

Hialmar. Have you been presenting claims, Gregers?

Gregers. Oh, nonsense.

Relling. Faith, but he has, though! He went round to all the cotters' cabins presenting something he called "the claim of the ideal."

Gregers. I was young then.

Relling. You're right; you were very young. And as for the claim of the ideal — you never got it honoured while I was up there.

Gregers. Nor since either.

Relling. Ah, then you've learnt to knock a little discount off, I expect.

Gregers. Never, when I have a true man to deal with.

Hialmar. No, I should think not, indeed. A little butter, Gina.

Relling. And a slice of bacon for Molvik.

Molvik. Ugh; not bacon!

[A knock at the garret door.]

Hialmar. Open the door, Hedvig; father wants to come out.

[HEDVIG goes over and opens the door a little way; EKDAL enters with a fresh rabbit-skin; she closes the door after him.]

Ekdal. Good morning, gentlemen! Good sport to-day. Shot a big one.

Hialmar. And you've gone and skinned it without waiting for me —!

Ekdal. Salted it, too. It's good tender meat, is rabbit; it's sweet; it tastes like sugar. Good appetite to you, gentlemen!

[Goes into his room.]

Molvik [rising.] Excuse me —; I can't —; I must get downstairs immediately —

Relling. Drink some soda water, man!

Molvik [hurrying away.] Ugh — ugh!

[Goes out by the passage door.]

Relling [to HIALMAR.] Let us drain a glass to the old hunter.

Hialmar [clinks glasses with him.] To the undaunted sportsman who has looked death in the face!

Relling. To the grey-haired — [Drinks.] By-the-bye, is his hair grey or white?

Hialmar. Something between the two, I fancy; for that matter, he has very few hairs left of any colour.

Relling. Well, well, one can get through the world with a wig. After all, you are a happy man, Ekdal; you have your noble mission to labour for —

Hialmar. And I do labour, I can tell you.

Relling. And then you have your excellent wife, shuffling quietly in and out in her felt slippers, with that see-saw walk of hers, and making everything cosy and comfortable about you —

Hialmar. Yes, Gina — [nods to her] — you were a good helpmate on the path of life.

Gina. Oh, don't sit there cricketising me.

Relling. And your Hedvig, too, Ekdal!

Hialmar [affected.] The child, yes! The child before everything! Hedvig, come here to me. [Strokes her hair.] What day is it to-morrow, eh?

Hedvig [shaking him.] Oh, no, you're not to say anything, father.

Hialmar. It cuts me to the heart when I think what a poor affair it will be; only a little festivity in the garret —

Hedvig. Oh, but that's just what I like!

Relling. Just you wait till the wonderful invention sees the light, Hedvig!

Hialmar. Yes, indeed — then you shall see —! Hedvig, I have resolved to make your future secure. You shall live in comfort all your days. I will demand — something or other — on your behalf. That shall be the poor inventor's sole reward.

Hedvig [whispering, with her arms round his neck.] Oh, you dear, kind father!

Relling [to GREGERS.] Come now, don't you find it pleasant, for once in a way, to sit at a well-spread table in a happy family circle?

Hialmar. Ah, yes, I really prize these social hours.

Gregers. For my part, I don't thrive in marsh vapours.

Relling. Marsh vapours?

Hialmar. Oh, don't begin with that stuff again!

Gina. Goodness knows there's no vapours in this house, Mr. Werle; I give the place a good airing every blessed day.

Gregers [leaves the table.] No airing you can give will drive out the taint I mean.

Hialmar. Taint!

Gina. Yes, what do you say to that, Ekdal!

Relling. Excuse me — may it not be you yourself that have brought the taint from those mines up there?

Gregers. It is like you to call what I bring into this house a taint.

Relling [goes up to him.] Look here, Mr. Werle, junior: I have a strong suspicion that you are still carrying about that "claim of the ideal" large as life, in your coat-tail pocket.

Gregers. I carry it in my breast.

Relling. Well, wherever you carry it, I advise you not to come dunning us with it here, so long as I am on the premises.

Gregers. And if I do so none the less?

Relling. Then you'll go head-foremost down the stairs; now I've warned you.

Hialmar [rising.] Oh, but Relling —!

Gregers. Yes, you may turn me out —

Gina [interposing between them.] We can't have that,

Relling. But I must say, Mr. Werle, it ill becomes you to talk about vapours and taints, after all the mess you made with your stove.

[A knock at the passage door.]

Hedvig. Mother, there's somebody knocking.

Hialmar. There now, we're going to have a whole lot of people!

Gina. I'll go [Goes over and opens the door, starts, and draws back.] Oh — oh, dear!

[WERLE, in a fur coat, advances one step into the room.]

Werle. Excuse me; but I think my son is staying here.

Gina [with a gulp.] Yes.

Hialmar [approaching him.] Won't you do us the honour to —?

Werle. Thank you, I merely wish to speak to my son.

Gregers. What is it? Here I am.

Werle. I want a few words with you, in your room.

Gregers. In my room? Very well — [About to go.

Gina. No, no, your room's not in a fit state —

Werle. Well then, out in the passage here; I want to have a few words with you alone.

Hialmar. You can have them here, sir. Come into the parlour, Relling.

[HIALMAR and RELLING go off to the right. GINA takes HEDVIG with her into the kitchen.]

Gregers [after a short pause.] Well, now we are alone.

Werle. From something you let fall last evening, and from your coming to lodge with the Ekdals, I can't help inferring that you intend to make yourself unpleasant to me, in one way or another.

Gregers. I intend to open Hialmar Ekdal's eyes. He shall see his position as it really is — that is all.

Werle. Is that the mission in life you spoke of yesterday?

Gregers. Yes. You have left me no other.

Werle. Is it I, then, that have crippled your mind, Gregers?

Gregers. You have crippled my whole life. I am not thinking of all that about mother — But it's thanks to you that I am continually haunted and harassed by a guilty conscience.

Werle. Indeed! It is your conscience that troubles you, is it?

Gregers. I ought to have taken a stand against you when the trap was set for Lieutenant Ekdal. I ought to have cautioned him; for I had a misgiving as to what was in the wind.

Werle. Yes, that was the time to have spoken.

Gregers. I did not dare to, I was so cowed and spiritless. I was mortally afraid of you — not only then, but long afterwards.

Werle. You have got over that fear now, it appears.

Gregers. Yes, fortunately. The wrong done to old Ekdal, both by me and by — others, can never be undone; but Hialmar I can rescue from all the falsehood and deception that are bringing him to ruin.

Werle. Do you think that will be doing him a kindness?

Gregers. I have not the least doubt of it.

Werle. You think our worthy photographer is the sort of man to appreciate such friendly offices?

Gregers. Yes, I do.

Werle. H'm — we shall see.

Gregers. Besides, if I am to go on living, I must try to find some cure for my sick conscience.

Werle. It will never be sound. Your conscience has been sickly from childhood. That is a legacy from your mother, Gregers — the only one she left you.

Gregers [with a scornful half-smile.] Have you not yet forgiven her for the mistake you made in supposing she would bring you a fortune?

Werle. Don't let us wander from the point. — Then you hold to your purpose of setting young Ekdal upon what you imagine to be the right scent?

Gregers. Yes, that is my fixed resolve.

Werle. Well, in that case I might have spared myself this visit; for, of course, it is useless to ask whether you will return home with me?

Gregers. Quite useless.

Werle. And I suppose you won't enter the firm either?

Gregers. No.

Werle. Very good. But as I am thinking of marrying again, your share in the property will fall to you at once.*

* By Norwegian law, before a widower can marry again, a certain proportion of his property must be settled on his children by his former marriage.

Gregers [quickly.] No, I do not want that.

Werle. You don't want it?

Gregers. No, I dare not take it, for conscience' sake.

Werle [after a pause.] Are you going up to the works again?

Gregers. No; I consider myself released from your service.

Werle. But what are you going to do?

Gregers. Only to fulfil my mission; nothing more.

Werle. Well but afterwards? What are you going to live upon?

Gregers. I have laid by a little out of my salary.

Werle. How long will that last?

Gregers. I think it will last my time.

Werle. What do you mean?

Gregers. I shall answer no more questions.

Werle. Good-bye then, Gregers.

Gregers. Good-bye.

[WERLE goes.]

Hialmar [peeping in.] He's gone, isn't he?

Gregers. Yes.

HIALMAR and RELLING enter; also GINA and HEDVIG from the kitchen.]

Relling. That luncheon-party was a failure.

Gregers. Put on your coat, Hialmar; I want you to come for a long walk with me.

Hialmar. With pleasure. What was it your father wanted? Had it anything to do with me?

Gregers. Come along. We must have a talk. I'll go and put on my overcoat.

[Goes out by the passage door.]

Gina. You shouldn't go out with him, Ekdal.

Relling. No, don't you do it. Stay where you are.

Hialmar [gets his hat and overcoat.] Oh, nonsense! When a friend of my youth feels impelled to open his mind to me in private —

Relling. But devil take it — don't you see that the fellow's mad, cracked, demented!

Gina. There, what did I tell you! His mother before him had crazy fits like that sometimes.

Hialmar. The more need for a friend's watchful eye. [To GINA.] Be sure you have dinner ready in good time. Good-bye for the present.

[Goes out by the passage door.]

Relling. It's a thousand pities the fellow didn't go to hell through one of the Hoidal mines.

Gina. Good Lord! what makes you say that?

Relling [muttering.] Oh, I have my own reasons.

Gina. Do you think young Werle is really mad?

Relling. No, worse luck; he's no madder than most other people. But one disease he has certainly got in his system.

Gina. What is it that's the matter with him?

Relling. Well, I'll tell you, Mrs. Ekdal. He is suffering from an acute attack of integrity.

Gina. Integrity?

Hedvig. Is that a kind of disease?

Relling. Yes, it's a national disease; but it only appears sporadically. [Nods to GINA.] Thanks for your hospitality.

[He goes out by the passage door.]

Gina [moving restlessly to and fro.] Ugh, that Gregers Werle — he was always a wretched creature.

Hedvig [standing by the table, and looking searchingly at her.] I think all this is very strange.

Act 4

HIALMAR EKDAL'S studio. A photograph has just been taken; a camera with the cloth over it, a pedestal, two chairs, a folding table, etc., are standing out in the room. Afternoon light; the sun is going down; a little later it begins to grow dusk.

GINA stands in the passage doorway, with a little box and a wet glass plate in her hand, and is speaking to somebody outside.]

Gina. Yes, certainly. When I make a promise I keep it. The first dozen shall be ready on Monday. Good afternoon.

[Someone is heard going downstairs. GINA shuts the door, slips the plate into the box, and puts it into the covered camera.]

Hedvig [comes in from the kitchen.] Are they gone?

Gina [tidying up.] Yes, thank goodness, I've got rid of them at last.

Hedvig. But can you imagine why father hasn't come home yet?

Gina. Are you sure he's not down in Relling's room?

Hedvig. No, he's not; I ran down the kitchen stair just now and asked.

Gina. And his dinner standing and getting cold, too.

Hedvig. Yes, I can't understand it. Father's always so careful to be home to dinner!

Gina. Oh, he'll be here directly, you'll see.

Hedvig. I wish he would come; everything seems so queer to-day.

Gina [calls out.] Here he is!

[HIALMAR EKDAL comes in at the passage door.]

Hedvig [going to him.] Father! Oh, what a time we've been waiting for you!

Gina [glancing sidelong at him.] You've been out a long time, Ekdal.

Hialmar [without looking at her.] Rather long, yes.

[He takes off his overcoat; GINA and HEDVIG go to help him; he motions them away.]

Gina. Perhaps you've had dinner with Werle?

Hialmar [hanging up his coat.] No.

Gina [going towards the kitchen door.] Then I'll bring some in for you.

Hialmar. No; let the dinner alone. I want nothing to eat.

Hedvig [going nearer to him.] Are you not well, father?

Hialmar. Well? Oh, yes, well enough. We have had a tiring walk, Gregers and I.

Gina. You didn't ought to have gone so far, Ekdal; you're not used to it.

Hialmar. H'm; there's many a thing a man must get used to in this world. [Wanders about the room.] Has any one been here whilst I was out?

Gina. Nobody but the two sweethearts.

Hialmar. No new orders?

Gina. No, not to-day.

Hedvig. There will be some to-morrow, father, you'll see.

Hialmar. I hope there will; for to-morrow I am going to set to work in real earnest.

Hedvig. To-morrow! Don't you remember what day it is to-morrow?

Hialmar. Oh, yes, by-the-bye — . Well, the day after, then. Henceforth I mean to do everything myself; I shall take all the work into my own hands.

Gina. Why, what can be the good of that, Ekdal? It'll only make your life a burden to you. I can manage the photography all right; and you can go on working at your invention.

Hedvig. And think of the wild duck, father, — and all the hens and rabbits and —!

Hialmar. Don't talk to me of all that trash! From to-morrow I will never set foot in the garret again.

Hedvig. Oh, but father, you promised that we should have a little party —

Hialmar. H'm, true. Well, then, from the day after to-morrow. I should almost like to wring that cursed wild duck's neck!

Hedvig [shrieks.] The wild duck!

Gina. Well I never!

Hedvig [shaking him.] Oh, no, father; you know it's my wild duck!

Hialmar. That is why I don't do it. I haven't the heart to — for your sake, Hedvig. But in my inmost soul I feel that I ought to do it. I ought not to tolerate under my roof a creature that has been through those hands.

Gina. Why, good gracious, even if grandfather did get it from that poor creature, Pettersen —

Hialmar [wandering about.] There are certain claims — what shall I call them? — let me say claims of the ideal — certain obligations, which a man cannot disregard without injury to his soul.

Hedvig [going after him.] But think of the wild duck, — the poor wild duck!

Hialmar [stops.] I tell you I will spare it — for your sake. Not a hair of its head shall be — I mean, it shall be spared. There are greater problems than that to be dealt with. But you should go out a little now, Hedvig, as usual; it is getting dusk enough for you now.

Hedvig. No, I don't care about going out now.

Hialmar. Yes, do; it seems to me your eyes are blinking a great deal; all these vapours in here are bad for you. The air is heavy under this roof.

Hedvig. Very well, then, I'll run down the kitchen stair and go for a little walk. My cloak and hat? — oh, they're in my own room. Father — be sure you don't do the wild duck any harm whilst I'm out.

Hialmar. Not a feather of its head shall be touched. [Draws her to him.] You and I, Hedvig — we two —! Well, go along.

[HEDVIG nods to her parents and goes out through the kitchen.]

Hialmar [walks about without looking up.] Gina.

Gina. Yes?

Hialmar. From to-morrow — or, say, from the day after to-morrow — I should like to keep the household account-book myself.

Gina. Do you want to keep the accounts too, now?

Hialmar. Yes; or to check the receipts at any rate.

Gina. Lord help us! that's soon done.

Hialmar. One would hardly think so; at any rate you seem to make the money go a very long way. [Stops and looks at her.] How do you manage it?

Gina. It's because me and Hedvig, we need so little.

Hialmar. Is it the case that father is very liberally paid for the copying he does for Mr. Werle?

Gina. I don't know as he gets anything out of the way. I don't know the rates for that sort of work.

Hialmar. Well, what does he get, about? Let me hear!

Gina. Oh, it varies; I daresay it'll come to about as much as he costs us, with a little pocket-money over.

Hialmar. As much as he costs us! And you have never told me this before!

Gina. No, how could I tell you? It pleased you so much to think he got everything from you.

Hialmar. And he gets it from Mr. Werle.

Gina. Oh, well, he has plenty and to spare, he has.

Hialmar. Light the lamp for me, please!

Gina [lighting the lamp.] And, of course, we don't know as it's Mr. Werle himself; it may be Graberg —

Hialmar. Why attempt such an evasion?

Gina. I don't know; I only thought —

Hialmar. H'm!

Gina. It wasn't me that got grandfather that copying. It was Bertha, when she used to come about us.

Hialmar. It seems to me your voice is trembling.

Gina [putting the lamp-shade on.] Is it?

Hialmar. And your hands are shaking, are they not?

Gina [firmly.] Come right out with it, Ekdal. What has he been saying about me?

Hialmar. Is it true — can it be true that — that there was an — an understanding between you and Mr. Werle, while you were in service there?

Gina. That's not true. Not at that time. Mr. Werle did come after me, that's a fact. And his wife thought there was something in it, and then she made such a hocus-pocus and hurly-burly, and she hustled me and bustled me about so that I left her service.

Hialmar. But afterwards, then?

Gina. Well, then I went home. And mother — well, she wasn't the woman you took her for, Ekdal; she kept on worrying and worrying at me about one thing and another — for Mr. Werle was a widower by that time.

Hialmar. Well, and then?

Gina. I suppose you've got to know it. He gave me no peace until he'd had his way.

Hialmar [striking his hands together.] And this is the mother of my child! How could you hide this from me?

Gina. Yes, it was wrong of me; I ought certainly to have told you long ago.

Hialmar. You should have told me at the very first; — then I should have known the sort of woman you were.

Gina. But would you have married me all the same?

Hialmar. How can you dream that I would?

Gina. That's just why I didn't dare tell you anything, then. For I'd come to care for you so much, you see; and I couldn't go and make myself utterly miserable —

Hialmar [walks about.] And this is my Hedvig's mother. And to know that all I see before me — [kicks at a chair] — all that I call my home — I owe to a favoured predecessor! Oh, that scoundrel Werle!

Gina. Do you repent of the fourteen — the fifteen years we've lived together?

Hialmar [placing himself in front of her.] Have you not every day, every hour, repented of the spider's-web of deceit you have spun around me? Answer me that! How could you help writhing with penitence and remorse? Gina Oh, my dear Ekdal, I've had all I could do to look after the house and get through the day's work —

Hialmar. Then you never think of reviewing your past?

Gina. No; Heaven knows I'd almost forgotten those old stories.

Hialmar. Oh, this dull, callous contentment! To me there is something revolting about it. Think of it — never so much as a twinge of remorse!

Gina. But tell me, Ekdal — what would have become of you if you hadn't had a wife like me?

Hialmar. Like you —!

Gina. Yes; for you know I've always been a bit more practical and wide-awake than you. Of course I'm a year or two older.

Hialmar. What would have become of me!

Gina. You'd got into all sorts of bad ways when first you met me; that you can't deny.

Hialmar. "Bad ways" do you call them? Little do you know what a man goes through when he is in grief and despair — especially a man of my fiery temperament.

Gina. Well, well, that may be so. And I've no reason to crow over you, neither; for you turned a moral of a husband, that you did, as soon as ever you had a house and home of your own. — And now we'd got everything so nice and cosy about us; and me and Hedvig was just thinking we'd soon be able to let ourselves go a bit, in the way of both food and clothes.

Hialmar. In the swamp of deceit, yes.

Gina. I wish to goodness that detestable thing had never set his foot inside our doors!

Hialmar. And I, too, thought my home such a pleasant one. That was a delusion. Where shall I now find the elasticity of spirit to bring my invention into the world of reality? Perhaps it will die with me; and then it will be your past, Gina, that will have killed it.

Gina [nearly crying.] You mustn't say such things, Ekdal. Me, that has only wanted to do the best I could for you, all my days!

Hialmar. I ask you, what becomes of the breadwinner's dream? When I used to lie in there on the sofa and brood over my invention, I had a clear enough presentiment that it would sap my vitality to the last drop. I felt even then that the day when I held the patent in my hand — that day — would bring my — release. And then it was my dream that you should live on after me, the dead inventor's well-to-do widow.

Gina [drying her tears.] No, you mustn't talk like that, Ekdal. May the Lord never let me see the day I am left a widow!

Hialmar. Oh, the whole dream has vanished. It is all over now. All over!

GREGERS WERLE opens the passage door cautiously and looks in.]

Gregers. May I come in?

Hialmar. Yes, come in.

Gregers [comes forward, his face beaming with satisfaction, and holds out both his hands to them.] Well, dear friends —! [Looks from one to the other, and whispers to HIALMAR.] Have you not done it yet?

Hialmar [aloud.] It is done.

Gregers. It is?

Hialmar. I have passed through the bitterest moments of my life.

Gregers. But also, I trust, the most ennobling.

Hialmar. Well, at any rate, we have got through it for the present.

Gina. God forgive you, Mr. Werle.

Gregers [in great surprise.] But I don't understand this.

Hialmar. What don't you understand?

Gregers. After so great a crisis — a crisis that is to be the starting-point of an entirely new life — of a communion founded on truth, and free from all taint of deception —

Hialmar. Yes, yes, I know; I know that quite well.

Gregers. I confidently expected, when I entered the room, to find the light of transfiguration shining upon me from both husband and wife. And now I see nothing but dulness, oppression, gloom —

146

Gina. Oh, is that it?

[Takes off the lamp-shade.]

Gregers. You will not understand me, Mrs. Ekdal. Ah, well, you, I suppose, need time to — . But you, Hialmar? Surely you feel a new consecration after the great crisis.

Hialmar. Yes, of course I do. That is — in a sort of way.

Gregers. For surely nothing in the world can compare with the joy of forgiving one who has erred, and raising her up to oneself in love.

Hialmar. Do you think a man can so easily throw off the bitter cup I have drained?

Gregers. No, not a common man, perhaps. But a man like you —!

Hialmar. Good God! I know that well enough. But you must keep me up to it, Gregers. It takes time, you know.

Gregers. You have much of the wild duck in you, Hialmar.

[RELLING has come in at the passage door.]

Relling. Oho! is the wild duck to the fore again?

Hialmar. Yes; Mr. Werle's wing-broken victim.

Relling. Mr. Werle's —? So it's him you are talking about?

Hialmar. Him and — ourselves.

Relling [in an undertone to GREGERS.] May the devil fly away with you!

Hialmar. What is that you are saying?

Relling. Only uttering a heartfelt wish that this quacksalver would take himself off. If he stays here, he is quite equal to making an utter mess of life, for both of you.

Gregers. These two will not make a mess of life, Mr. Relling. Of course I won't speak of Hialmar — him we know. But she, too, in her innermost heart, has certainly something loyal and sincere —

Gina [almost crying.] You might have let me alone for what I was, then.

Relling [to GREGERS.] Is it rude to ask what you really want in this house?

Gregers. To lay the foundations of a true marriage.

Relling. So you don't think Ekdal's marriage is good enough as it is?

Gregers. No doubt it is as good a marriage as most others, worse luck. But a true marriage it has yet to become.

Hialmar. You have never had eyes for the claims of the ideal, Relling.

Relling. Rubbish, my boy! — but excuse me, Mr. Werle: how many — in round numbers — how many true marriages have you seen in the course of your life?

Gregers. Scarcely a single one.

Relling. Nor I either.

Gregers. But I have seen innumerable marriages of the opposite kind. And it has been my fate to see at close quarters what ruin such a marriage can work in two human souls.

Hialmar. A man's whole moral basis may give away beneath his feet; that is the terrible part of it.

Relling. Well, I can't say I've ever been exactly married, so I don't pretend to speak with authority. But this I know, that the child enters into the marriage problem. And you must leave the child in peace.

Hialmar. Oh — Hedvig! my poor Hedvig!

Relling. Yes, you must be good enough to keep Hedvig outside of all this. You two are grown-up people; you are free, in God's name, to make what mess and muddle you please of your life. But you must deal cautiously with Hedvig, I tell you; else you may do her a great injury.

Hialmar. An injury!

Relling. Yes, or she may do herself an injury — and perhaps others, too.

Gina. How can you know that, Relling?

Hialmar. Her sight is in no immediate danger, is it?

Relling. I am not talking about her sight. Hedvig is at a critical age. She may be getting all sorts of mischief into her head.

Gina. That's true — I've noticed it already! She's taken to carrying on with the fire, out in the kitchen. She calls it playing at house-on-fire. I'm often scared for fear she really sets fire to the house.

Relling. You see; I thought as much.

Gregers [to RELLING.] But how do you account for that?

Relling [sullenly.] Her constitution's changing, sir.

Hialmar. So long as the child has me —! So long as I am above ground —!

[A knock at the door.]

Gina. Hush, Ekdal; there's some one in the passage. [Calls out.] Come in!

[MRS. SORBY, in walking dress, comes in.]

Mrs. Sorby. Good evening.

Gina [going towards her.] Is it really you, Bertha?

Mrs. Sorby. Yes, of course it is. But I'm disturbing you, I'm afraid?

Hialmar. No, not at all; an emissary from that house —

Mrs. Sorby [to GINA.] To tell the truth, I hoped your men-folk would be out at this time. I just ran up to have a little chat with you, and to say good-bye.

Gina. Good-bye? Are you going away, then?

Mrs. Sorby. Yes, to-morrow morning, — up to Hoidal. Mr. Werle started this afternoon. [Lightly to GREGERS.] He asked me to say good-bye for him.

Gina. Only fancy —!

Hialmar. So Mr. Werle has gone? And now you are going after him?

Mrs. Sorby. Yes, what do you say to that, Ekdal?

Hialmar. I say: beware!

Gregers. I must explain the situation. My father and Mrs. Sorby are going to be married.

Hialmar. Going to be married!

Gina. Oh, Bertha! So it's come to that at last!

Relling [his voice quivering a little.] This is surely not true?

Mrs. Sorby. Yes, my dear Relling, it's true enough.

Relling. You are going to marry again?

Mrs. Sorby. Yes, it looks like it. Werle has got a special licence, and we are going to be married quite quietly, up at the works.

Gregers. Then I must wish you all happiness, like a dutiful stepson.

Mrs. Sorby. Thank you very much — if you mean what you say. I certainly hope it will lead to happiness, both for Werle and for me.

Relling. You have every reason to hope that. Mr. Werle never gets drunk — so far as I know; and I don't suppose he's in the habit of thrashing his wives, like the late lamented horse-doctor.

Mrs. Sorby. Come now, let Sorby rest in peace. He had his good points, too.

Relling. Mr. Werle has better ones, I have no doubt. Mrs. Sorby. He hasn't frittered away all that was good in him, at any rate. The man who does that must take the consequences.

Relling. I shall go out with Molvik this evening.

Mrs. Sorby. You mustn't do that, Relling. Don't do it — for my sake.

Relling. There's nothing else for it. [To HIALMAR.] If you're going with us, come along.

Gina. No, thank you. Ekdal doesn't go in for that sort of dissertation.

Hialmar [half aloud, in vexation.] Oh, do hold your tongue!

Relling. Good-bye, Mrs. — Werle.

[Goes out through the passage door.]

Gregers [to MRS. SORBY.] You seem to know Dr. Relling pretty intimately.

Mrs. Sorby. Yes, we have known each other for many years. At one time it seemed as if things might have gone further between us.

Gregers. It was surely lucky for you that they did not.

Mrs. Sorby. You may well say that. But I have always been wary of acting on impulse. A woman can't afford absolutely to throw herself away.

Gregers. Are you not in the least afraid that I may let my father know about this old friendship?

Mrs. Sorby. Why, of course, I have told him all about it myself.

Gregers. Indeed?

Mrs. Sorby. Your father knows every single thing that can, with any truth, be said about me. I have told him all; it was the first thing I did when I saw what was in his mind.

Gregers. Then you have been franker than most people, I think.

Mrs. Sorby. I have always been frank. We women find that the best policy.

Hialmar. What do you say to that, Gina?

Gina. Oh, we're not all alike, us women aren't. Some are made one way, some another.

Mrs. Sorby. Well, for my part, Gina, I believe it's wisest to do as I've done. And Werle has no secrets either, on his side. That's really the great bond between us, you see. Now he can talk to me as openly as a child. He has never had the chance to do that before. Fancy a man like him, full of health and vigour, passing his whole youth and the best years of his life in listening to nothing but penitential sermons! And very often the sermons had for their text the most imaginary offences — at least so I understand.

Gina. That's true enough.

Gregers. If you ladies are going to follow up this topic, I had better withdraw.

Mrs. Sorby. You can stay as far as that's concerned. I shan't say a word more. But I wanted you to know that I had done nothing secretly or in an underhand way. I may seem to have come in for a great piece of luck; and so I have, in a sense. But after all, I don't think I am getting any more than I am giving. I shall stand by him always, and I can tend and care for him as no one else can, now that he is getting helpless.

Hialmar. Getting helpless?

Gregers [to MRS. SORBY.] Hush, don't speak of that here.

Mrs. Sorby. There is no disguising it any longer, however much he would like to. He is going blind.

Hialmar [starts.] Going blind? That's strange. He, too, going blind!

Gina. Lots of people do.

Mrs. Sorby. And you can imagine what that means to a business man. Well, I shall try as well as I can to make my eyes take the place of his. But I mustn't stay any longer; I have heaps of things to do. — Oh, by-the-bye, Ekdal, I was to tell you that if there is anything Werle can do for you, you must just apply to Graberg.

Gregers. That offer I am sure Hialmar Ekdal will decline with thanks.

Mrs. Sorby. Indeed? I don't think he used to be so —

Gina. No, Bertha, Ekdal doesn't need anything from Mr. Werle now.

Hialmar [slowly, and with emphasis.] Will you present my compliments to your future husband, and say that I intend very shortly to call upon Mr. Graberg —

Gregers. What! You don't really mean that?

Hialmar. To call upon Mr. Graberg, I say, and obtain an account of the sum I owe his principal. I will pay that debt of honour — ha ha ha! a debt of honour, let us call it! In any case, I will pay the whole with five per cent. interest.

Gina. But, my dear Ekdal, God knows we haven't got the money to do it.

Hialmar. Be good enough to tell your future husband that I am working assiduously at my invention. Please tell him that what sustains me in this laborious task is the wish to free myself from a torturing burden of debt. That is my reason for proceeding with the invention. The entire profits shall be devoted to releasing me from my pecuniary obligations to your future husband.

Mrs. Sorby. Something has happened here.

151

Hialmar. Yes, you are right.

Mrs. Sorby. Well, good-bye. I had something else to speak to you about, Gina; but it must keep till another time. Good-bye.

[HIALMAR and GREGERS bow silently. GINA follows MRS. SORBY to the door.]

Hialmar. Not beyond the threshold, Gina!

[MRS. SORBY goes; GINA shuts the door after her.]

Hialmar. There now, Gregers; I have got that burden of debt off my mind.

Gregers. You soon will, at all events.

Hialmar. I think my attitude may be called correct.

Gregers. You are the man I have always taken you for.

Hialmar. In certain cases, it is impossible to disregard the claim of the ideal. Yet, as the breadwinner of a family, I cannot but writhe and groan under it. I can tell you it is no joke for a man without capital to attempt the repayment of a long-standing obligation, over which, so to speak, the dust of oblivion had gathered. But it cannot be helped: the Man in me demands his rights.

Gregers [laying his hand on HIALMAR'S shoulder.] My dear Hialmar — was it not a good thing I came?

Hialmar. Yes.

Gregers. Are you not glad to have had your true position made clear to you?

Hialmar [somewhat impatiently.] Yes, of course I am. But there is one thing that is revolting to my sense of justice.

Gregers. And what is that?

Hialmar. It is that — but I don't know, whether I ought to express myself so unreservedly about your father.

Gregers. Say what you please, so far as I am concerned.

Hialmar. Well, then, is it not exasperating to think that it is not I, but he, who will realise the true marriage?

Gregers. How can you say such a thing?

Hialmar. Because it is clearly the case. Isn't the marriage between your father and Mrs. Sorby founded upon complete confidence, upon entire and unreserved candour on both sides? They hide nothing from each other, they keep no secrets in the background; their relation is based, if I may put it so, on mutual confession and absolution.

Gregers. Well, what then?

Hialmar. Well, is not that the whole thing? Did you not yourself say that this was precisely the difficulty that had to be overcome in order to found a true marriage?

Gregers. But this is a totally different matter, Hialmar.

You surely don't compare either yourself or your wife with those two —? Oh, you understand me well enough.

Hialmar. Say what you like, there is something in all this that hurts and offends my sense of justice. It really looks as if there were no just providence to rule the world.

Gina. Oh, no, Ekdal; for God's sake don't say such things.

Gregers. H'm; don't let us get upon those questions.

Hialmar. And yet, after all, I cannot but recognise the guiding finger of fate. He is going blind.

Gina. Oh, you can't be sure of that.

Hialmar. There is no doubt about it. At all events there ought not to be; for in that very fact lies the righteous retribution. He has hoodwinked a confiding fellow creature in days gone by —

Gregers. I fear he has hoodwinked many.

Hialmar. And now comes inexorable, mysterious Fate, and demands Werle's own eyes.

Gina. Oh, how dare you say such dreadful things! You make me quite scared.

Hialmar. It is profitable, now and then, to plunge deep into the night side of existence.

HEDVIG, in her hat and cloak, comes in by the passage door. She is pleasurably excited and out of breath.]

Gina. Are you back already?

Hedvig. Yes, I didn't care to go any farther. It was a good thing, too; for I've just met some one at the door.

Hialmar. It must have been that Mrs. Sorby.

Hedvig. Yes.

Hialmar [walks up and down.] I hope you have seen her for the last time.

[Silence. HEDVIG, discouraged, looks first at one and then at the other, trying to divine their frame of mind.]

Hedvig [approaching, coaxingly.] Father.

Hialmar. Well — what is it, Hedvig?

Hedvig. Mrs. Sorby had something with her for me,

Hialmar [stops.] For you?

Hedvig. Yes. Something for to-morrow.

Gina. Bertha has always given you some little thing on your birthday.

Hialmar. What is it?

Hedvig. Oh, you mustn't see it now. Mother is to give it to me to-morrow morning before I'm up.

Hialmar. What is all this hocus-pocus that I am to be in the dark about!

Hedvig [quickly.] Oh, no, you may see it if you like. It's a big letter.

[Takes the letter out of her cloak pocket.]

Hialmar. A letter, too?

Hedvig. Yes, it is only a letter. The rest will come afterwards, I suppose. But fancy — a letter! I've never had a letter before. And there's "Miss" written upon it. [Reads.] "Miss Hedvig Ekdal." Only fancy — that's me!

Hialmar. Let me see that letter.

Hedvig [hands it to him.] There it is.

Hialmar. That is Mr. Werle's hand.

Gina. Are you sure of that, Ekdal?

Hialmar. Look for yourself.

Gina. Oh, what do I know about such-like things?

Hialmar. Hedvig, may I open the letter — and read it?

Hedvig. Yes, of course you may, if you want to.

Gina. No, not to-night, Ekdal; it's to be kept till to-morrow.

Hedvig [softly.] Oh, can't you let him read it! It's sure to be something good; and then father will be glad, and everything will be nice again.

Hialmar. I may open it then?

Hedvig. Yes, do, father. I'm so anxious to know what it is.

Hialmar. Well and good. [Opens the letter, takes out a paper, reads it through, and appears bewildered.] What is this —!

Gina. What does it say?

Hedvig. Oh, yes, father — tell us!

Hialmar. Be quiet. [Reads it through again; he has turned pale, but says with self-control:] It is a deed of gift, Hedvig.

Hedvig. Is it? What sort of gift am I to have?

Hialmar. Read for yourself.

[HEDVIG goes over and reads for a time by the lamp.]

Hialmar [half-aloud, clenching his hands.] The eyes! The eyes — and then that letter!

Hedvig [leaves off reading.] Yes, but it seems to me that it's grandfather that's to have it.

Hialmar [takes letter from her.] Gina — can you understand this?

Gina. I know nothing whatever about it; tell me what's the matter.

Hialmar. Mr. Werle writes to Hedvig that her old grandfather need not trouble himself any longer with the copying, but that he can henceforth draw on the office for a hundred crowns a month

Gregers. Aha!

Hedvig. A hundred crowns, mother! I read that.

Gina. What a good thing for grandfather!

Hialmar. — a hundred crowns a month so long as he needs it — that means, of course, so long as he lives.

Gina. Well, so he's provided for, poor dear.

Hialmar. But there is more to come. You didn't read that, Hedvig. Afterwards this gift is to pass on to you.

Hedvig. To me! The whole of it?

Hialmar. He says that the same amount is assured to you for the whole of your life. Do you hear that, Gina?

Gina. Yes, I hear.

Hedvig. Fancy — all that money for me! [Shakes him.] Father, father, aren't you glad —?

Hialmar [eluding her.] Glad! [Walks about.] Oh what vistas — what perspectives open up before me! It is Hedvig, Hedvig that he showers these benefactions upon!

Gina. Yes, because it's Hedvig's birthday —

Hedvig. And you'll get it all the same, father! You know quite well I shall give all the money to you and mother.

Hialmar. To mother, yes! There we have it.

Gregers. Hialmar, this is a trap he is setting for you.

Hialmar. Do you think it's another trap?

Gregers. When he was here this morning he said: Hialmar Ekdal is not the man you imagine him to be.

Hialmar. Not the man —!

Gregers. That you shall see, he said.

Hialmar. He meant you should see that I would let myself be bought off —!

Hedvig. Oh mother, what does all this mean?

Gina. Go and take off your things.

[HEDVIG goes out by the kitchen door, half-crying.]

Gregers. Yes, Hialmar — now is the time to show who was right, he or I.

Hialmar [slowly tears the paper across, lays both pieces on the table, and says:] Here is my answer.

Gregers. Just what I expected.

Hialmar [goes over to GINA, who stands by the stove, and says in a low voice:] Now please make a clean breast of it. If the connection between you and him was quite over when you — came to care for me, as you call it — why did he place us in a position to marry?

Gina. I suppose he thought as he could come and go in our house.

Hialmar. Only that? Was not he afraid of a possible contingency?

Gina. I don't know what you mean.

Hialmar. I want to know whether — your child has the right to live under my roof.

Gina [draws herself up; her eyes flash.] You ask that!

Hialmar. You shall answer me this one question: Does Hedvig belong to me — or —? Well!

156

Gina [looking at him with cold defiance.] I don't know.

Hialmar [quivering a little.] You don't know!

Gina. How should I know. A creature like me —

Hialmar [quietly turning away from her.] Then I have nothing more to do in this house.

Gregers. Take care, Hialmar! Think what you are doing!

Hialmar [puts on his overcoat.] In this case, there is nothing for a man like me to think twice about.

Gregers. Yes indeed, there are endless things to be considered. You three must be together if you are to attain the true frame of mind for self-sacrifice and forgiveness.

Hialmar. I don't want to attain it. Never, never! My hat! [Takes his hat.] My home has fallen in ruins about me. [Bursts into tears.] Gregers, I have no child!

Hedvig [who has opened the kitchen door.] What is that you're saying? [Coming to him.] Father, father!

Gina. There, you see!

Hialmar. Don't come near me, Hedvig! Keep far away. I cannot bear to see you. Oh! those eyes —! Good-bye.

[Makes for the door.]

Hedvig [clinging close to him and screaming loudly.] No! no! Don't leave me!

Gina [cries out.] Look at the child, Ekdal! Look at the child!

Hialmar. I will not! I cannot! I must get out — away from all this!

[He tears himself away from HEDVIG, and goes out by the passage door.]

Hedvig [with despairing eyes.] He is going away from us, mother! He is going away from us! He will never come back again!

Gina. Don't cry, Hedvig. Father's sure to come back again.

Hedvig [throws herself sobbing on the sofa.] No, no, he'll never come home to us any more.

Gregers. Do you believe I meant all for the best, Mrs. Ekdal?

Gina. Yes, I daresay you did; but God forgive you, all the same.

Hedvig [lying on the sofa.] Oh, this will kill me! What have I done to him? Mother, you must fetch him home again!

Gina. Yes yes yes; only be quiet, and I'll go out and look for him. [Puts on her outdoor things.] Perhaps he's gone in to Relling's. But you mustn't lie there and cry. Promise me!

Hedvig [weeping convulsively.] Yes, I'll stop, I'll stop; if only father comes back!

Gregers [to GINA, who is going.] After all, had you not better leave him to fight out his bitter fight to the end?

Gina. Oh, he can do that afterwards. First of all, we must get the child quieted.

[Goes out by the passage door.]

Hedvig [sits up and dries her tears.] Now you must tell me what all this means. Why doesn't father want me any more?

Gregers. You mustn't ask that till you are a big girl — quite grown-up.

Hedvig [sobs.] But I can't go on being as miserable as this till I'm grown-up. — I think I know what it is. — Perhaps I'm not really father's child.

Gregers [uneasily.] How could that be?

Hedvig. Mother might have found me. And perhaps father has just got to know it; I've read of such things.

Gregers. Well, but if it were so —

Hedvig. I think he might be just as fond of me for all that. Yes, fonder almost. We got the wild duck in a present, you know, and I love it so dearly all the same.

Gregers [turning the conversation.] Ah, the wild duck, by-the-bye! Let us talk about the wild duck a little, Hedvig.

Hedvig. The poor wild duck! He doesn't want to see it any more either. Only think, he wanted to wring its neck!

Gregers. Oh, he won't do that.

Hedvig. No; but he said he would like to. And I think it was horrid of father to say it; for I pray for the wild duck every night, and ask that it may be preserved from death and all that is evil.

Gregers [looking at her.] Do you say your prayers every night?

Hedvig. Yes.

Gregers. Who taught you to do that?

Hedvig. I myself; one time when father was very ill, and had leeches on his neck, and said that death was staring him in the face.

Gregers. Well?

Hedvig. Then I prayed for him as I lay in bed; and since then I have always kept it up.

Gregers. And now you pray for the wild duck too?

Hedvig. I thought it was best to bring in the wild duck; for she was so weakly at first.

Gregers. Do you pray in the morning, too?

Hedvig. No, of course not.

Gregers. Why not in the morning as well?

Hedvig. In the morning it's light, you know, and there's nothing in particular to be afraid of.

Gregers. And your father was going to wring the neck of the wild duck that you love so dearly?

Hedvig. No; he said he ought to wring its neck, but he would spare it for my sake; and that was kind of father.

Gregers [coming a little nearer.] But suppose you were to sacrifice the wild duck of your own free will for his sake.

Hedvig [rising.] The wild duck!

Gregers. Suppose you were to make a free-will offering, for his sake, of the dearest treasure you have in the world!

Hedvig. Do you think that would do any good?

Gregers. Try it, Hedvig.

Hedvig [softly, with flashing eyes.] Yes, I will try it.

Gregers. Have you really the courage for it, do you think?

Hedvig. I'll ask grandfather to shoot the wild duck for me.

Gregers. Yes, do. — But not a word to your mother about it.

Hedvig. Why not?

Gregers. She doesn't understand us.

Hedvig. The wild duck! I'll try it to-morrow morning.

[GINA comes in by the passage door.]

Hedvig [going towards her.] Did you find him, mother?

Gina. No, but I heard as he had called and taken Relling with him.

Gregers. Are you sure of that?

Gina. Yes, the porter's wife said so. Molvik went with them,too, she said.

Gregers. This evening, when his mind so sorely needs to wrestle in solitude —!

Gina [takes off her things.] Yes, men are strange creatures, so they are. The Lord only knows where Relling has dragged him to! I ran over to Madam Eriksen's, but they weren't there.

Hedvig [struggling to keep back her tears.] Oh, if he should never come home any more!

Gregers. He will come home again. I shall have news to give him to-morrow; and then you shall see how he comes home. You may rely upon that, Hedvig, and sleep in peace. Good-night.

[He goes out by the passage door.]

Hedvig [throws herself sobbing on GINA'S neck.] Mother, mother!

Gina [pats her shoulder and sighs.] Ah yes; Relling was right, he was. That's what comes of it when crazy creatures go about presenting the claims of the — what-you-may-call-it.

Act 5

HIALMAR EKDAL'S studio. Cold, grey morning light. Wet snow lies upon the large panes of the sloping roof-window.

GINA comes from the kitchen with an apron and bib on, and carrying a dusting-brush and a duster; she goes towards the sitting-room door. At the same moment HEDVIG comes hurriedly in from the passage.]

Gina [stops.] Well?

Hedvig. Oh, mother, I almost think he's down at Relling's —

Gina. There, you see!

Hedvig. — because the porter's wife says she could hear that Relling had two people with him when he came home last night.

Gina. That's just what I thought.

Hedvig. But it's no use his being there, if he won't come up to us.

Gina. I'll go down and speak to him at all events.

OLD EKDAL, in dressing-gown and slippers, and with a lighted pipe, appears at the door of his room.]

Ekdal. Hialmar — Isn't Hialmar at home?

Gina. No, he's gone out.

Ekdal. So early? And in such a tearing snowstorm? Well well; just as he pleases; I can take my morning walk alone.

[He slides the garret door aside; HEDVIG helps him; he goes in; she closes it after him.]

Hedvig [in an undertone.] Only think, mother, when poor grandfather hears that father is going to leave us.

Gina. Oh, nonsense; grandfather mustn't hear anything about it. It was a heaven's mercy he wasn't at home yesterday in all that hurly-burly.

Hedvig. Yes, but —

[GREGERS comes in by the passage door.]

Gregers. Well, have you any news of him?

Gina. They say he's down at Relling's.

Gregers. At Relling's! Has he really been out with those creatures?

Gina. Yes, like enough.

162

Gregers. When he ought to have been yearning for solitude, to collect and clear his thoughts —

Gina. Yes, you may well say so.

[RELLING enters from the passage.]

Hedvig [going to him.] Is father in your room?

Gina [at the same time.] Is he there?

Relling. Yes, to be sure he is.

Hedvig. And you never let us know!

Relling. Yes; I'm a brute. But in the first place I had to look after the other brute; I mean our daemonic friend, of course; and then I fell so dead asleep that —

Gina. What does Ekdal say to-day?

Relling. He says nothing whatever.

Hedvig. Doesn't he speak?

Relling. Not a blessed word.

Gregers. No no,; I can understand that very well.

Gina. But what's he doing then?

Relling. He's lying on the sofa, snoring.

Gina. Oh is he? Yes, Ekdal's a rare one to snore.

Hedvig. Asleep? Can he sleep?

Relling. Well, it certainly looks like it.

Gregers. No wonder, after the spiritual conflict that has rent him —

Gina. And then he's never been used to gadding about out of doors at night.

Hedvig. Perhaps it's a good thing that he's getting sleep, mother.

Gina. Of course it is; and we must take care we don't wake him up too early. Thank you, Relling. I must get the house cleaned up a bit now, and then — Come and help me, Hedvig.

[GINA and HEDVIG go into the sitting-room.]

Gregers [turning to RELLING.] What is your explanation of the spiritual tumult that is now going on in Hialmar Ekdal?

Relling. Devil a bit of a spiritual tumult have I noticed in him.

Gregers. What! Not at such a crisis, when his whole life has been placed on a new foundation —? How can you think that such an individuality as Hialmar's —?

Relling. Oh, individuality — he! If he ever had any tendency to the abnormal developments you call individuality, I can assure you it was rooted out of him while he was still in his teens.

Gregers. That would be strange indeed, — considering the loving care with which he was brought up.

Relling. By those two high-flown, hysterical maiden aunts, you mean?

Gregers. Let me tell you that they were women who never forgot the claim of the ideal — but of course you will only jeer at me again.

Relling. No, I'm in no humour for that. I know all about those ladies; for he has ladled out no end of rhetoric on the subject of his "two soul-mothers." But I don't think he has much to thank them for. Ekdal's misfortune is that in his own circle he has always been looked upon as a shining light —

Gregers. Not without reason, surely. Look at the depth of his mind!

Relling. I have never discovered it. That his father believed in it I don't so much wonder; the old lieutenant has been an ass all his days.

Gregers. He has had a child-like mind all his days; that is what you cannot understand.

Relling. Well, so be it. But then, when our dear, sweet Hialmar went to college, he at once passed for the great light of the future amongst his comrades too. He was handsome, the rascal — red and white — a shop-girl's dream of manly beauty; and with his superficially emotional temperament, and his sympathetic voice, and his talent for declaiming other people's verses and other people's thoughts —

Gregers [indignantly.] Is it Hialmar Ekdal you are talking about in this strain?

Relling. Yes, with your permission; I am simply giving you an inside view of the idol you are grovelling before.

Gregers. I should hardly have thought I was quite stone blind.

Relling. Yes you are — or not far from it. You are a sick man, too, you see.

Gregers. You are right there.

Relling. Yes. Yours is a complicated case. First of all, there is that plaguy integrity-fever; and then — what's worse — you are always in a delirium of hero-worship; you must always have something to adore, outside yourself.

Gregers. Yes, I must certainly seek it outside myself.

Relling. But you make such shocking mistakes about every new phoenix you think you have discovered. Here again you have come to a cotter's cabin with your claim of the ideal; and the people of the house are insolvent.

Gregers. If you don't think better than that of Hialmar Ekdal, what pleasure can you find in being everlastingly with him?

Relling. Well, you see, I'm supposed to be a sort of a doctor — save the mark! I can't but give a hand to the poor sick folk who live under the same roof with me.

Gregers. Oh, indeed! Hialmar Ekdal is sick too, is he!

Relling. Most people are, worse luck.

Gregers. And what remedy are you applying in Hialmar's case?

Relling. My usual one. I am cultivating the life-illusion* in him.

* "Livslognen," literally "the life-lie."

Gregers. Life-illusion? I didn't catch what you said.

Relling. Yes, I said illusion. For illusion, you know, is the stimulating principle.

Gregers. May I ask with what illusion Hialmar is inoculated?

Relling. No, thank you; I don't betray professional secrets to quacksalvers. You would probably go and muddle his case still more than you have already. But my method is infallible. I have applied it to Molvik as well. I have made him "daemonic." That's the blister I have to put on his neck.

Gregers. Is he not really daemonic then?

Relling. What the devil do you mean by daemonic! It's only a piece of gibberish I've invented to keep up a spark of life in him. But for that, the poor harmless creature would have succumbed to self-contempt and despair many a long year ago. And then the old lieutenant! But he has hit upon his own cure, you see.

Gregers. Lieutenant Ekdal? What of him?

Relling. Just think of the old bear-hunter shutting himself up in that dark garret to shoot rabbits! I tell you there is not a happier sportsman in the world than that old man pottering about in there among all that rubbish. The four or five withered Christmas-trees he has saved up are the same to him as the whole great fresh Hoidal forest; the cock and the hens are big game-birds in the fir-tops; and the rabbits that flop about the garret floor are the bears he has to battle with — the mighty hunter of the mountains!

Gregers. Poor unfortunate old man! Yes; he has indeed had to narrow the ideals of his youth.

Relling. While I think of it, Mr. Werle, junior — don't use that foreign word: ideals. We have the excellent native word: lies.

Gregers. Do you think the two things are related?

Relling. Yes, just about as closely as typhus and putrid fever.

Gregers. Dr. Relling, I shall not give up the struggle until I have rescued Hialmar from your clutches!

Relling. So much the worse for him. Rob the average man of his life-illusion, and you rob him of his happiness at the same stroke. [To HEDVIG, who comes in from the sitting-room.] Well, little wild-duck-mother, I'm just going down to see whether papa is still lying meditating upon that wonderful invention of his.

[Goes out by passage door.]

Gregers [approaches HEDVIG.] I can see by your face that you have not yet done it.

Hedvig. What? Oh, that about the wild duck! No.

Gregers. I suppose your courage failed when the time came.

Hedvig. No, that wasn't it. But when I awoke this morning and remembered what we had been talking about, it seemed so strange.

Gregers. Strange?

Hedvig. Yes, I don't know — Yesterday evening, at the moment, I thought there was something so delightful about it; but since I have slept and thought of it again, it somehow doesn't seem worth while.

Gregers. Ah, I thought you could not have grown up quite unharmed in this house.

Hedvig. I don't care about that, if only father would come up —

Gregers. Oh, if only your eyes had been opened to that which gives life its value — if you possessed the true, joyous, fearless spirit of sacrifice, you would soon see how he would come up to you. — But I believe in you still, Hedvig. [

[He goes out by the passage door. HEDVIG wanders about the room for a time; she is on the point of going into the kitchen when a knock is heard at the garret door. HEDVIG goes over and opens it a little; old EKDAL comes out; she pushes the door to again.]

Ekdal. H'm, it's not much fun to take one's morning walk alone.

Hedvig. Wouldn't you like to go shooting, grandfather?

Ekdal. It's not the weather for it to-day. It's so dark there, you can scarcely see where you're going.

Hedvig. Do you never want to shoot anything besides the rabbits?

Ekdal. Do you think the rabbits aren't good enough?

166

Hedvig. Yes, but what about the wild duck?

Ekdal. Ho-ho! are you afraid I shall shoot your wild duck? Never in the world. Never.

Hedvig. No, I suppose you couldn't; they say it's very difficult to shoot wild ducks.

Ekdal. Couldn't! Should rather think I could.

Hedvig. How would you set about it, grandfather? — I don't mean with my wild duck, but with others?

Ekdal. I should take care to shoot them in the breast, you know; that's the surest place. And then you must shoot against the feathers, you see — not the way of the feathers.

Hedvig. Do they die then, grandfather?

Ekdal. Yes, they die right enough — when you shoot properly. — Well, I must go and brush up a bit. H'm — understand — h'm.

[Goes into his room.] [

[HEDVIG waits a little, glances towards the sitting-room door, goes over to the book-case, stands on tip-toe, takes the double-barrelled pistol down from the shelf, and looks at it. GINA, with brush and duster, comes from the sitting-room. HEDVIG hastily lays down the pistol, unobserved.]

Gina. Don't stand raking amongst father's things, Hedvig.

Hedvig [goes away from the bookcase.] I was only going to tidy up a little.

Gina. You'd better go into the kitchen, and see if the coffee's keeping hot; I'll take his breakfast on a tray, when I go down to him.

[HEDVIG goes out. GINA begins to sweep and clean up the studio. Presently the passage door is opened with hesitation, and HIALMAR EKDAL looks in. He has on his overcoat, but not his hat; he is unwashed, and his hair is dishevelled and unkempt. His eyes are dull and heavy.]

Gina [standing with the brush in her hand, and looking at him.] Oh, there now, Ekdal — so you've come after all?

Hialmar [comes in and answers in a toneless voice.] I come only to depart again immediately.

Gina. Yes, yes, I suppose so. But, Lord help us! what a sight you are!

Hialmar. A sight?

Gina. And your nice winter coat too! Well, that's done for.

Hedvig [at the kitchen door.] Mother, hadn't I better —? [Sees HIALMAR, gives a loud scream of joy, and runs to him.] Oh, father, father!

Hialmar [turns away and makes a gesture of repulsion]. Away, away, away! [To GINA.] Keep her away from me, I say!

Gina [in a low tone.] Go into the sitting-room, Hedvig.

[HEDVIG does so without a word.]

Hialmar [fussily pulls out the table-drawer.] I must have my books with me. Where are my books?

Gina. Which books?

Hialmar. My scientific books, of course; the technical magazines I require for my invention.

Gina [searches in the bookcase.] Is it these here paper-covered ones?

Hialmar. Yes, of course.

Gina [lays a heap of magazines on the table.] Shan't I get Hedvig to cut them for you?

Hialmar. I don't require to have them cut for me.

[Short silence.]

Gina. Then you're still set on leaving us, Ekdal?

Hialmar [rummaging amongst the books.] Yes, that is a matter of course, I should think.

Gina. Well, well.

Hialmar [vehemently.] How can I live here, to be stabbed to the heart every hour of the day?

Gina. God forgive you for thinking such vile things of me.

Hialmar. Prove —!

Gina. I think it's you as has got to prove.

Hialmar. After a past like yours? There are certain claims — I may almost call them claims of the ideal —

Gina. But what about grandfather? What's to become of him, poor dear?

Hialmar. I know my duty; my helpless father will come with me. I am going out into the town to make arrangements — H'm — [hesitatingly] — has any one found my hat on the stairs?

Gina. No. Have you lost your hat?

Hialmar. Of course I had it on when I came in last night; there's no doubt about that; but I couldn't find it this morning.

Gina. Lord help us! where have you been to with those two ne'er-do-weels?

Hialmar. Oh, don't bother me about trifles. Do you suppose I am in the mood to remember details?

Gina. If only you haven't caught cold, Ekdal ——

[Goes out into the kitchen.]

Hialmar [talks to himself in a low tone of irritation, whilst he empties the table-drawer.] You're a scoundrel, Relling! — You're a low fellow! — Ah, you shameless tempter! — I wish I could get some one to stick a knife into you!

[He lays some old letters on one side, finds the torn document of yesterday, takes it up and looks at the pieces; puts it down hurriedly as GINA enters.]

Gina [sets a tray with coffee, etc., on the table.] Here's a drop of something hot, if you'd fancy it. And there's some bread and butter and a snack of salt meat.

Hialmar [glancing at the tray.] Salt meat? Never under this roof! It's true I have not had a mouthful of solid food for nearly twenty-four hours; but no matter. — My memoranda! The commencement of my autobiography! What has become of my diary, and all my important papers? [Opens the sitting-room door but draws back.] She is there too!

Gina. Good Lord! the child must be somewhere!

Hialmar. Come out.

[He makes room, HEDVIG comes, scared, into the studio.]

Hialmar [With his hand upon the door-handle, says to GINA:] In these, the last moments I spend in my former home, I wish to be spared from interlopers ——

[Goes into the room.]

Hedvig [with a bound towards her mother, asks softly, trembling.] Does that mean me?

Gina. Stay out in the kitchen, Hedvig; or, no — you'd best go into your own room. [Speaks to HIALMAR as she goes in to him.] Wait a bit, Ekdal; don't rummage so in the drawers; I know where everything is.

Hedvig [stands a moment immovable, in terror and perplexity, biting her lips to keep back the tears; then she clenches her hands convulsively, and says softly:] The wild duck.

[She steals over and takes the pistol from the shelf, opens the garret door a little way, creeps in, and draws the door to after her. HIALMAR and GINA can be heard disputing in the sitting-room.]

Hialmar [comes in with some manuscript books and old loose papers, which he lays upon the table.] That portmanteau is of no use! There are a thousand and one things I must drag with me.

Gina [following with the portmanteau.] Why not leave all the rest for the present, and only take a shirt and a pair of woollen drawers with you?

Hialmar. Whew! — all these exhausting preparations —!

[Pulls off his overcoat and throws it upon the sofa.]

Gina. And there's the coffee getting cold.

Hialmar. H'm.

[Drinks a mouthful without thinking of it, and then another.]

Gina [dusting the backs of the chairs.] A nice job you'll have to find such another big garret for the rabbits.

Hialmar. What! Am I to drag all those rabbits with me too?

Gina. You don't suppose grandfather can get on without his rabbits.

Hialmar. He must just get used to doing without them. Have not I to sacrifice very much greater things than rabbits!

Gina [dusting the bookcase.] Shall I put the flute in the portmanteau for you?

Hialmar. No. No flute for me. But give me the pistol!

Gina. Do you want to take the pigstol with you?

Hialmar. Yes. My loaded pistol.

Gina [searching for it.] It's gone. He must have taken it in with him.

Hialmar. Is he in the garret?

Gina. Yes, of course he's in the garret.

Hialmar. H'm — poor lonely old man.

[He takes a piece of bread and butter, eats it, and finishes his cup of coffee.]

Gina. If we hadn't have let that room, you could have moved in there.

Hialmar. And continued to live under the same roof with —! Never, — never!

Gina. But couldn't you put up with the sitting-room for a day or two? You could have it all to yourself.

Hialmar. Never within these walls!

Gina. Well then, down with Relling and Molvik.

Hialmar. Don't mention those wretches' names to me! The very thought of them almost takes away my appetite. — Oh no, I must go out into the storm and the snow-drift, — go from house to house and seek shelter for my father and myself.

Gina. But you've got no hat, Ekdal! You've been and lost your hat, you know.

Hialmar. Oh those two brutes, those slaves of all the vices! A hat must be procured. [Takes another piece of bread and butter.] Some arrangements must be made. For I have no mind to throw away my life, either.

[Looks for something on the tray.]

Gina. What are you looking for?

Hialmar. Butter.

Gina. I'll get some at once.

[Goes out into the kitchen.]

Hialmar [calls after her.] Oh it doesn't matter; dry bread is good enough for me.

Gina [brings a dish of butter.] Look here; this is fresh churned.

[She pours out another cup of coffee for him; he seats himself on the sofa, spreads more butter on the already buttered bread, and eats and drinks awhile in silence.]

Hialmar. Could I, without being subject to intrusion — intrusion of any sort — could I live in the sitting-room there for a day or two?

Gina. Yes, to be sure you could, if you only would.

Hialmar. For I see no possibility of getting all father's things out in such a hurry.

Gina. And, besides, you've surely got to tell him first as you don't mean to live with us others no more.

Hialmar [pushes away his coffee cup.] Yes, there is that too; I shall have to lay bare the whole tangled story to him — I must turn matters over; I must have breathing-time; I cannot take all these burdens on my shoulders in a single day.

Gina. No, especially in such horrible weather as it is outside.

Hialmar [touching WERLE'S letter.] I see that paper is still lying about here.

Gina. Yes, I haven't touched it.

Hialmar. So far as I am concerned it is mere waste paper —

Gina. Well, I have certainly no notion of making any use of it.

171

Hialmar. — but we had better not let it get lost all the same; — in all the upset when I move, it might easily —

Gina. I'll take good care of it, Ekdal.

Hialmar. The donation is in the first instance made to father, and it rests with him to accept or decline it.

Gina [sighs.] Yes, poor old father —

Hialmar. To make quite safe — Where shall I find some gum?

Gina [goes to the bookcase.] Here's the gum-pot.

Hialmar. And a brush?

Gina. The brush is here too.

[Brings him the things.]

Hialmar [takes a pair of scissors.] Just a strip of paper at the back — [Clips and gums.] Far be it from me to lay hands upon what it not my own — and least of all upon what belongs to a destitute old man — and to — the other as well. — There now. Let it lie there for a time; and when it is dry, take it away. I wish never to see that document again. Never! [GREGERS WERLE enters from the passage.]

Gregers [somewhat surprised.] What, — are you sitting here, Hialmar?

Hialmar [rises hurriedly.] I had sunk down from fatigue.

Gregers. You have been having breakfast, I see.

Hialmar. The body sometimes makes its claims felt too.

Gregers. What have you decided to do?

Hialmar. For a man like me, there is only one course possible. I am just putting my most important things together. But it takes time, you know.

Gina [with a touch of impatience.] Am I to get the room ready for you, or am I to pack your portmanteau?

Hialmar [after a glance of annoyance at GREGERS.] Pack — and get the room ready!

Gina [takes the portmanteau.] Very well; then I'll put in the shirt and the other things.

[Goes into the sitting-room and draws the door to after her.]

Gregers [after a short silence.] I never dreamed that this would be the end of it. Do you really feel it a necessity to leave house and home?

172

Hialmar [wanders about restlessly.] What would you have me do? — I am not fitted to bear unhappiness, Gregers. I must feel secure and at peace in my surroundings.

Gregers. But can you not feel that here? Just try it. I should have thought you had firm ground to build upon now — if only you start afresh. And, remember, you have your invention to live for.

Hialmar. Oh don't talk about my invention. It's perhaps still in the dim distance.

Gregers. Indeed!

Hialmar. Why, great heavens, what would you have me invent? Other people have invented almost everything already. It becomes more and more difficult every day —

Gregers. And you have devoted so much labour to it.

Hialmar. It was that blackguard Relling that urged me to it.

Gregers. Relling?

Hialmar. Yes, it was he that first made me realise my aptitude for making some notable discovery in photography.

Gregers. Aha — it was Relling!

Hialmar. Oh, I have been so truly happy over it! Not so much for the sake of the invention itself, as because Hedvig believed in it — believed in it with a child's whole eagerness of faith. — At least, I have been fool enough to go and imagine that she believed in it.

Gregers. Can you really think Hedvig has been false towards you?

Hialmar. I can think anything now. It is Hedvig that stands in my way. She will blot out the sunlight from my whole life.

Gregers. Hedvig! Is it Hedvig you are talking of? How should she blot out your sunlight?

Hialmar [without answering.] How unutterably I have loved that child! How unutterably happy I have felt every time I came home to my humble room, and she flew to meet me, with her sweet little blinking eyes. Oh, confiding fool that I have been! I loved her unutterably; — and I yielded myself up to the dream, the delusion, that she loved me unutterably in return.

Gregers. Do you call that a delusion?

Hialmar. How should I know? I can get nothing out of Gina; and besides, she is totally blind to the ideal side of these complications. But to you I feel impelled to open my mind, Gregers. I cannot shake off this frightful doubt — perhaps Hedvig has never really and honestly loved me.

Gregers. What would you say if she were to give you a proof of her love? [Listens.] What's that? I thought I heard the wild duck —?

Hialmar. It's the wild duck quacking. Father's in the garret.

173

Gregers. Is he? [His face lights up with joy.] I say you may yet have proof that your poor misunderstood Hedvig loves you!

Hialmar. Oh, what proof can she give me? I dare not believe in any assurance from that quarter.

Gregers. Hedvig does not know what deceit means.

Hialmar. Oh Gregers, that is just what I cannot be sure of. Who knows what Gina and that Mrs. Sorby may many a time have sat here whispering and tattling about? And Hedvig usually has her ears open, I can tell you. Perhaps the deed of gift was not such a surprise to her, after all. In fact, I'm not sure but that I noticed something of the sort.

Gregers. What spirit is this that has taken possession of you?

Hialmar. I have had my eyes opened. Just you notice; — you'll see, the deed of gift is only a beginning. Mrs. Sorby has always been a good deal taken up with Hedvig; and now she has the power to do whatever she likes for the child. They can take her from me whenever they please.

Gregers. Hedvig will never, never leave you.

Hialmar. Don't be so sure of that. If only they beckon to her and throw out a golden bait —! And oh! I have loved her so unspeakably! I would have counted it my highest happiness to take her tenderly by the hand and lead her, as one leads a timid child through a great dark empty room! — I am cruelly certain now that the poor photographer in his humble attic has never really and truly been anything to her. She has only cunningly contrived to keep on a good footing with him until the time came.

Gregers. You don't believe that yourself, Hialmar.

Hialmar. That is just the terrible part of it — I don't know what to believe, — I never can know it. But can you really doubt that it must be as I say? Ho-ho, you have far too much faith in the claim of the ideal, my good Gregers! If those others came, with the glamour of wealth about them, and called to the child:— "Leave him: come to us: here life awaits you —!"

Gregers [quickly.] Well, what then?

Hialmar. If I then asked her: Hedvig, are you willing to renounce that life for me? [Laughs scornfully.] No thank you! You would soon hear what answer I should get.

[A pistol shot is heard from within the garret.]

Gregers [loudly and joyfully.] Hialmar!

Hialmar. There now; he must needs go shooting too.

Gina [comes in.] Oh Ekdal, I can hear grandfather blazing away in the garret by himself.

Hialmar. I'll look in —

Gregers [eagerly, with emotion.] Wait a moment! Do you know what that was?

Hialmar. Yes, of course I know.

Gregers. No you don't know. But I do. That was the proof!

Hialmar. What proof?

Gregers. It was a child's free-will offering. She has got your father to shoot the wild duck.

Hialmar. To shoot the wild duck!

Gina. Oh, think of that —!

Hialmar. What was that for?

Gregers. She wanted to sacrifice to you her most cherished possession; for then she thought you would surely come to love her again.

Hialmar [tenderly, with emotion.] Oh, poor child!

Gina. What things she does think of!

Gregers. She only wanted your love again, Hialmar. She could not live without it.

Gina [struggling with her tears.] There, you can see for yourself, Ekdal.

Hialmar. Gina, where is she?

Gina [sniffs.] Poor dear, she's sitting out in the kitchen, I dare say.

Hialmar [goes over, tears open the kitchen door, and says:] Hedvig, come, come in to me! [Looks around.] No, she's not here.

Gina. Then she must be in her own little room.

Hialmar [without.] No, she's not here either. [Comes in.] She must have gone out.

Gina. Yes, you wouldn't have her anywheres in the house.

Hialmar. Oh, if she would only come home quickly, so that I can tell her — Everything will come right now, Gregers; now I believe we can begin life afresh.

Gregers [quietly.] I knew it; I knew the child would make amends.

OLD EKDAL appears at the door of his room; he is in full uniform, and is busy buckling on his sword.]

Hialmar [astonished.] Father! Are you there?

Gina. Have you been firing in your room?

Ekdal [resentfully, approaching.] So you go shooting alone, do you, Hialmar?

Hialmar [excited and confused.] Then it wasn't you that fired that shot in the garret?

175

Ekdal. Me that fired? H'm.

Gregers [calls out to HIALMAR.] She has shot the wild duck herself!

Hialmar. What can it mean? [Hastens to the garret door, tears it aside, looks in and calls loudly:] Hedvig!

Gina [runs to the door.] Good God, what's that!

Hialmar [goes in.] She's lying on the floor!

Gregers. Hedvig! lying on the floor!

[Goes in to HIALMAR]

Gina [at the same time.] Hedvig! [Inside the garret] No, no, no!

Ekdal. Ho-ho! does she go shooting, too, now?

[HIALMAR, GINA and GREGERS carry HEDVIG into the studio; in her dangling right hand she holds the pistol fast clasped in her fingers.]

Hialmar [distracted.] The pistol has gone off. She has wounded herself. Call for help! Help!

Gina [runs into the passage and calls down.] Relling! Relling! Doctor Relling; come up as quick as you can!

[HIALMAR and GREGERS lay HEDVIG down on the sofa.]

Ekdal [quietly.] The woods avenge themselves.

Hialmar [on his knees beside HEDVIG.] She'll soon come to now. She's coming to —; yes, yes, yes.

Gina [who has come in again.] Where has she hurt herself? I can't see anything —

[RELLING comes hurriedly, and immediately after him MOLVIK; the latter without his waistcoat and necktie, and with his coat open.]

Relling. What's the matter here?

Gina. They say Hedvig has shot herself.

Hialmar. Come and help us!

Relling. Shot herself!

[He pushes the table aside and begins to examine her.]

Hialmar [kneeling and looking anxiously up at him.] It can't be dangerous? Speak, Relling! She is scarcely bleeding at all. It can't be dangerous?

Relling. How did it happen?

Hialmar. Oh, we don't know —

Gina. She wanted to shoot the wild duck.

Relling. The wild duck?

Hialmar. The pistol must have gone off.

Relling. H'm. Indeed.

Ekdal. The woods avenge themselves. But I'm not afraid, all the same.

[Goes into the garret and closes the door after him.]

Hialmar. Well, Relling, — why don't you say something?

Relling. The ball has entered the breast.

Hialmar. Yes, but she's coming to!

Relling. Surely you can see that Hedvig is dead.

Gina [bursts into tears.] Oh my child, my child —

Gregers [huskily.] In the depths of the sea —

Hialmar [jumps up.] No, no, she must live! Oh, for God's sake, Relling — only a moment — only just till I can tell her how unspeakably I loved her all the time!

Relling. The bullet has gone through her heart. Internal hemorrhage. Death must have been instantaneous.

Hialmar. And I! I hunted her from me like an animal! And she crept terrified into the garret and died for love of me! [Sobbing.] I can never atone to her! I can never tell her —! [Clenches his hands and cries, upwards.] O thou above —! If thou be indeed! Why hast thou done this thing to me?

Gina. Hush, hush, you mustn't go on that awful way. We had no right to keep her, I suppose.

Molvik. The child is not dead, but sleepeth.

Relling. Bosh.

Hialmar [becomes calm, goes over to the sofa, folds his arms, and looks at HEDVIG.] There she lies so stiff and still.

Relling [tries to loosen the pistol.] She's holding it so tight, so tight.

Gina. No, no, Relling, don't break her fingers; let the pigstol be.

Hialmar. She shall take it with her.

Gina. Yes, let her. But the child mustn't lie here for a show. She shall go to her own room, so she shall. Help me, Ekdal.

[HIALMAR and GINA take HEDVIG between them.]

Hialmar [as they are carrying her.] Oh, Gina, Gina, can you survive this!

Gina. We must help each other to bear it. For now at least she belongs to both of us.

Molvik [stretches out his arms and mumbles.] Blessed be the Lord; to earth thou shalt return; to earth thou shalt return —

Relling [whispers.] Hold your tongue, you fool; you're drunk.

[HIALMAR and GINA carry the body out through the kitchen door. RELLING shuts it after them. MOLVIK slinks out into the passage.]

Relling [goes over to GREGERS and says:] No one shall ever convince me that the pistol went off by accident.

Gregers [who has stood terrified, with convulsive twitchings.] Who can say how the dreadful thing happened?

Relling. The powder has burnt the body of her dress. She must have pressed the pistol right against her breast and fired.

Gregers. Hedvig has not died in vain. Did you not see how sorrow set free what is noble in him?

Relling. Most people are ennobled by the actual presence of death. But how long do you suppose this nobility will last in him?

Gregers. Why should it not endure and increase throughout his life?

Relling. Before a year is over, little Hedvig will be nothing to him but a pretty theme for declamation.

Gregers. How dare you say that of Hialmar Ekdal?

Relling. We will talk of this again, when the grass has first withered on her grave. Then you'll hear him spouting about "the child too early torn from her father's heart;" then you'll see him steep himself in a syrup of sentiment and self-admiration and self-pity. Just you wait!

Gregers. If you are right and I am wrong, then life is not worth living.

Relling. Oh, life would be quite tolerable, after all, if only we could be rid of the confounded duns that keep on pestering us, in our poverty, with the claim of the ideal.

Gregers [looking straight before him.] In that case, I am glad that my destiny is what is.

Relling. May I inquire, — what is your destiny?

Gregers [going.] To be the thirteenth at table.

Relling. The devil it is.

Hedda Gabler

Henrik Ibsen

Translated by Edmund Gosse and William Archer

With an introduction by William Archer

Table of Contents

Introduction

Characters

Act First

Act Second

Act Third

Act Fourth

Introduction

From Munich, on June 29, 1890, Ibsen wrote to the Swedish poet, Count Carl Soilsky: "Our intention has all along been to spend the summer in the Tyrol again. But circumstances are against our doing so. I am at present engaged upon a new dramatic work, which for several reasons has made very slow progress, and I do not leave Munich until I can take with me the completed first draft. There is little or no prospect of my being able to complete it in July." Ibsen did not leave Munich at all that season. On October 30 he wrote: "At present I am utterly engrossed in a new play. Not one leisure hour have I had for several months." Three weeks later (November 20) he wrote to his French translator, Count Prozor: "My new play is finished; the manuscript went off to Copenhagen the day before yesterday. . . . It produces a curious feeling of emptiness to be thus suddenly separated from a work which has occupied one's time and thoughts for several months, to the exclusion of all else. But it is a good thing, too, to have done with it. The constant intercourse with the fictitious personages was beginning to make me quite nervous." To the same correspondent he wrote on December 4: "The title of the play is *Hedda Gabler*. My intention in giving it this name was to indicate that Hedda, as a personality, is to be regarded rather as her father's daughter than as her husband's wife. It was not my desire to deal in this play with so-called problems. What I principally wanted to do was to depict human beings, human emotions, and human destinies, upon a groundwork of certain of the social conditions and principles of the present day."

So far we read the history of the play in the official "Correspondence."[1] Some interesting glimpses into the poet's moods during the period between the completion of *The Lady from the Sea* and the publication of *Hedda Gabler* are to be found in the series of letters to Fraulein Emilie Bardach, of Vienna, published by Dr. George Brandes.[2] This young lady Ibsen met at Gossensass in the Tyrol in the autumn of 1889. The record of their brief friendship belongs to the history of *The Master Builder* rather than to that of *Hedda Gabler*, but the allusions to his work in his letters to her during the winter of 1889 demand some examination.

So early as October 7, 1889, he writes to her: "A new poem begins to dawn in me. I will execute it this winter, and try to transfer to it the bright atmosphere of the summer. But I feel that it will end in sadness — such is my nature." Was this "dawning" poem *Hedda Gabler*? Or was it rather *The Master Builder* that was germinating in his mind? Who shall say? The latter hypothesis seems the more probable, for it is hard to believe that at any stage in the incubation of *Hedda Gabler* he can have conceived it as even beginning in gaiety. A week later, however, he appears to have made up his mind that the time had not come for the poetic utilisation of his recent experiences. He writes on October 15: "Here I sit as usual at my writing-table. Now I would fain work, but am unable to. My fancy, indeed, is very active. But it always wanders awayours. I cannot repress my summer memories — nor do I wish to. I live through my experience again and again and yet again. To transmute it all into a poem, I find, in the meantime, impossible." Clearly, then, he felt that his imagination ought to have been engaged on some theme having no relation to his summer experiences — the theme, no doubt, of *Hedda Gabler*. In his next letter, dated October 29, he writes: "Do not be troubled because I cannot, in the meantime, create (*dichten*). In reality I am for ever creating, or, at any rate, dreaming of something which, when in the fulness of time it ripens, will reveal itself as a creation (*Dichtung*)." On November 19 he says: "I am very busily occupied with preparations for my new poem. I sit almost the whole day at my writing-table. Go out only in the evening for a little while." The five following letters contain no allusion to the play; but on September 18, 1890, he wrote: "My wife and son are at present at Riva, on the Lake of Garda, and will probably remain there until the middle of October, or even longer. Thus I am quite alone here, and cannot get away. The new play on which I am at present engaged will probably not be ready until November, though I sit at my writing-table daily, and almost the whole day long."

Here ends the history of *Hedda Gabler*, so far as the poet's letters carry us. Its hard clear outlines, and perhaps somewhat bleak atmosphere, seem to have resulted from a sort of reaction against the sentimental "dreamery" begotten of his Gossensass experiences. He sought refuge in the chill materialism of Hedda from the ardent transcendentalism of Hilda, whom he already heard knocking at the door. He was not yet in the mood to deal with her on the plane of poetry.[3]

Hedda Gabler was published in Copenhagen on December 16, 1890. This was the first of Ibsen's plays to be translated from proof-sheets and published in England and America almost simultaneously with its first appearance in Scandinavia. The earliest theatrical performance took place at the Residenz Theater, Munich, on the last day of January 1891, in the presence of the poet, Frau Conrad–Ramlo playing the title-part. The Lessing Theater, Berlin, followed suit on February 10. Not till February 25 was the play seen in Copenhagen, with Fru Hennings as Hedda. On the following night it was given for the first time in Christiania, the Norwegian Hedda being Froken Constance Bruun. It was this production which the poet saw when he visited the Christiania Theater for the first time after his return to Norway, August 28, 1891. It would take pages to give even the baldest list of the productions and revivals of *Hedda Gabler* in Scandinavia and Germany, where it has always ranked among Ibsen's most popular works. The admirable production of the play by Miss Elizabeth Robins and Miss Marion Lea, at the Vaudeville Theatre, London, April 20, 1891, may rank as the second great step towards the popularisation of Ibsen in England, the first being the Charrington–Achurch production of *A Doll's House* in 1889. Miss Robins afterwards repeated her fine performance of Hedda many times, in London, in the English provinces, and in New York. The character has also been acted in London by Eleonora Duse, and as I write (March, 5, 1907) by Mrs. Patrick Campbell, at the Court Theatre. In Australia and America, Hedda has frequently been acted by Miss Nance O'Neill and other actresses — quite recently by a Russian actress, Madame Alla Nazimova, who (playing in English) seems to have made a notable success both in this part and in Nora. The first French Hedda Gabler was Mlle. Marthe Brandes, who played the part at the Vaudeville Theatre, Paris, on December 17, 1891, the performance being introduced by a lecture by M. Jules Lemaitre. In Holland, in Italy, in Russia, the play has been acted times without number. In short (as might easily have been foretold) it has rivalled *A Doll's House* in world-wide popularity.

It has been suggested,[4] I think without sufficient ground, that Ibsen deliberately conceived *Hedda Gabler* as an "international" play, and that the scene is really the "west end" of any European city. To me it seems quite clear that Ibsen had Christiania in mind, and the Christiania of a somewhat earlier period than the 'nineties. The electric cars, telephones, and other conspicuous factors in the life of a modern capital are notably absent from the play. There is no electric light in Secretary Falk's villa. It is still the habit for ladies to return on foot from evening parties, with gallant swains escorting them. This "suburbanism," which so distressed the London critics of 1891, was characteristic of the Christiania Ibsen himself had known in the 'sixties — the Christiania of *Love's Comedy* — rather than of the greatly extended and modernised city of the end of the century. Moreover Lovborg's allusions to the fiord, and the suggested picture of Sheriff Elvsted, his family and his avocations are all distinctively Norwegian. The truth seems to be very simple — the environment and the subsidiary personages are all thoroughly national, but Hedda herself is an "international" type, a product of civilisation by no means peculiar to Norway.

We cannot point to any individual model or models who "sat to" Ibsen for the character of Hedda.[5] The late Grant Allen declared that Hedda was "nothing more nor less than the girl we take down to dinner in London nineteen times out of twenty"; in which case Ibsen must have suffered from a superfluity of models, rather than from any difficulty in finding one. But the fact is that in this, as in all other instances, the word "model" must be taken in a very different sense from that in which it is commonly used in painting. Ibsen undoubtedly used models for this trait and that, but never for a whole figure. If his characters can be called portraits at all, they are composite portraits. Even when it seems pretty clear that the initial impulse towards the creation of a particular character came from some individual, the original figure is entirely transmuted in the process of harmonisation with the dramatic scheme. We need not, therefore, look for a definite prototype of Hedda; but Dr. Brandes shows that two of that lady's exploits were probably suggested by the anecdotic history of the day.

Ibsen had no doubt heard how the wife of a well-known Norwegian composer, in a fit of raging jealousy excited by her husband's prolonged absence from home, burnt the manuscript of a symphony which he had just finished. The circumstances under which Hedda burns Lovborg's manuscript are, of course, entirely different and infinitely more dramatic; but here we have merely another instance of the dramatisation or "poetisation" of the raw material of life. Again, a still more painful incident probably came to his knowledge about the same time. A beautiful and very intellectual woman was married to a well-known man who had been addicted to drink, but had entirely conquered the vice. One day a mad whim seized her to put his self-mastery and her power over him to the test. As it happened to be his birthday, she rolled into his study a small keg of brandy, and then withdrew. She returned some time after wards to find that he had broached the keg, and lay insensible on the floor. In this anecdote we cannot but recognise the germ, not only of Hedda's temptation of Lovborg, but of a large part of her character.

"Thus," says Dr. Brandes, "out of small and scattered traits of reality Ibsen fashioned his close-knit and profoundly thought-out works of art."

For the character of Eilert Lovborg, again, Ibsen seem unquestionably to have borrowed several traits from a definite original. A young Danish man of letters, whom Dr. Brandes calls Holm, was an enthusiastic admirer of Ibsen, and came to be on very friendly terms with him. One day Ibsen was astonished to receive, in Munich, a parcel addressed from Berlin by this young man, containing, without a word of explanation, a packet of his (Ibsen's) letters, and a photograph which he had presented to Holm. Ibsen brooded and brooded over the incident, and at last came to the conclusion that the young man had intended to return her letters and photograph to a young lady to whom he was known to be attached, and had in a fit of aberration mixed up the two objects of his worship. Some time after, Holm appeared at Ibsen's rooms. He talked quite rationally, but professed to have no knowledge whatever of the letter-incident, though he admitted the truth of Ibsen's conjecture that the "belle dame sans merci" had demanded the return of her letters and portrait. Ibsen was determined to get at the root of the mystery; and a little inquiry into his young friend's habits revealed the fact that he broke his fast on a bottle of port wine, consumed a bottle of Rhine wine at lunch, of Burgundy at dinner, and finished off the evening with one or two more bottles of port. Then he heard, too, how, in the course of a night's carouse, Holm had lost the manuscript of a book; and in these traits he saw the outline of the figure of Eilert Lovborg.

Some time elapsed, and again Ibsen received a postal packet from Holm. This one contained his will, in which Ibsen figured as his residuary legatee. But many other legatees were mentioned in the instrument — all of them ladies, such as Fraulein Alma Rothbart, of Bremen, and Fraulein Elise Kraushaar, of Berlin. The bequests to these meritorious spinsters were so generous that their sum considerably exceeded the amount of the testator's property. Ibsen gently but firmly declined the proffered inheritance; but Holm's will no doubt suggested to him the figure of that red-haired "Mademoiselle Diana," who is heard of but not seen in *Hedda Gabler*, and enabled him to add some further traits to the portraiture of Lovborg. When the play appeared, Holm recognised himself with glee in the character of the bibulous man of letters, and thereafter adopted "Eilert Lovborg" as his pseudonym. I do not, therefore, see why Dr. Brandes should suppress his real name; but I willingly imitate him in erring on the side of discretion. The poor fellow died several years ago.

Some critics have been greatly troubled as to the precise meaning of Hedda's fantastic vision of Lovborg "with vine-leaves in his hair." Surely this is a very obvious image or symbol of the beautiful, the ideal, aspect of bacchic elation and revelry. Antique art, or I am much mistaken, shows us many figures of Dionysus himself and his followers with vine-leaves entwined their hair. To Ibsen's mind, at any rate, the image had long been familiar. In *Peer Gynt* (Act iv. sc. 8), when Peer, having carried off Anitra, finds himself in a particularly festive mood, he cries: "Were there vine-leaves around, I would garland my brow." Again, in *Emperor and Galilean* (Pt. ii. Act 1) where Julian, in the procession of Dionysus, impersonates the god himself, it is directed that he shall wear a wreath of vine-leaves. Professor Dietrichson relates that among the young artists whose society Ibsen frequented during his first years in Rome, it was customary, at their little festivals, for the revellers to deck themselves in this fashion. But the image is so obvious that there is no need to trace it to any personal experience. The attempt to place Hedda's vine-leaves among Ibsen's obscurities is an example of the firm resolution not to understand which animated the criticism of the 'nineties.

Dr. Brandes has dealt very severely with the character of Eilert Lovborg, alleging that we cannot believe in the genius attributed to him. But where is he described as a genius? The poet represents him as a very able student of sociology; but that is quite a different thing from attributing to him such genius as must necessarily shine forth in every word he utters. Dr. Brandes, indeed, declines to believe even in his ability as a sociologist, on the ground that it is idle to write about the social development of the future. "To our prosaic minds," he says, "it may seem as if the most sensible utterance on the subject is that of the fool of the play: 'The future! Good heavens, we know nothing of the future.'" The best retort to this criticism is that which Eilert himself makes: "There's a thing or two to be said about it all the same." The intelligent forecasting of the future (as Mr. H. G. Wells has shown) is not only clearly distinguishable from fantastic Utopianism, but is indispensable to any large staTesmanship or enlightened social activity. With very real and very great respect for Dr. Brandes, I cannot think that he has been fortunate in his treatment of Lovborg's character. It has been represented as an absurdity that he would think of reading abstracts from his new book to a man like Tesman, whom he despises. But though Tesman is a ninny, he is, as Hedda says, a "specialist"— he is a competent, plodding student of his subject. Lovborg may quite naturally wish to see how his new method, or his excursion into a new field, strikes the average scholar of the Tesman type. He is, in fact, "trying it on the dog"— neither an unreasonable nor an unusual proceeding. There is, no doubt, a certain improbability in the way in which Lovborg is represented as carrying his manuscript around, and especially in Mrs. Elvsted's production of his rough draft from her pocket; but these are mechanical trifles, on which only a niggling criticism would dream of laying stress.

Of all Ibsen's works, *Hedda Gabler* is the most detached, the most objective — a character-study pure and simple. It is impossible — or so it seems to me — to extract any sort of general idea from it. One cannot even call it a satire, unless one is prepared to apply that term to the record of a "case" in a work of criminology. Reverting to Dumas's dictum that a play should contain "a painting, a judgment, an ideal," we may say the *Hedda Gabler* fulfils only the first of these requirements. The poet does not even pass judgment on his heroine: he simply paints her full-length portrait with scientific impassivity. But what a portrait! How searching in insight, how brilliant in colouring, how rich in detail! Grant Allen's remark, above quoted, was, of course, a whimsical exaggeration; the Hedda type is not so common as all that, else the world would quickly come to an end. But particular traits and tendencies of the Hedda type are very common in modern life, and not only among women. Hyperaesthesia lies at the root of her tragedy. With a keenly critical, relentlessly solvent intelligence, she combines a morbid shrinking from all the gross and prosaic detail of the sensual life. She has nothing to take her out of herself — not a single intellectual interest or moral enthusiasm. She cherishes, in a languid way, a petty social ambition; and even that she finds obstructed and baffled. At the same time she learns that another woman has had the courage to love and venture all, where she, in her cowardice, only hankered and refrained. Her malign egoism rises up uncontrolled, and calls to its aid her quick and subtle intellect. She ruins the other woman's happiness, but in doing so incurs a danger from which her sense of personal dignity revolts. Life has no such charm for her that she cares to purchase it at the cost of squalid humiliation and self-contempt. The good and the bad in her alike impel her to have done with it all; and a pistol-shot ends what is surely one of the most poignant character-tragedies in literature. Ibsen's brain never worked at higher pressure than in the conception and adjustment of those "crowded hours" in which Hedda, tangled in the web of Will and Circumstance, struggles on till she is too weary to struggle any more.

It may not be superfluous to note that the "a" in "Gabler" should be sounded long and full, like the "a" in "Garden"— *not* like the "a" in "gable" or in "gabble."

W. A.

[1]Letters 214, 216, 217, 219.

[2]In the Ibsen volume of *Die Literatur* (Berlin).

[3]Dr. Julius Elias (*Neue deutsche Rundschau*, December 1906, p. 1462) makes the curious assertion that the character of Thea Elvsted was in part borrowed from this "Gossensasser Hildetypus." It is hard to see how even Gibes' ingenuity could distil from the same flower two such different essences as Thea and Hilda.

[4]See article by Herman Bang in *Neue deutsche Rundschau*, December 1906, p. 1495.

[5]Dr. Brahm (*Neue deutsche Rundschau*, December 1906, P. 1422) says that after the first performance of *Hedda Gabler* in Berlin Ibsen confided to him that the character had been suggested by a German lady whom he met in Munich, and who did not shoot, but poisoned herself. Nothing more seems to be known of this lady. See, too, an article by Julius Elias in the same magazine, p. 1460.

Characters

*George Tesman.**

Hedda Tesman, his wife.

Miss Juliana Tesman, his aunt.

Mrs. Elvsted.

*Judge** Brack.*

Eilert Lovborg.

Berta, servant at the Tesmans.

The scene of the action is Tesman's villa, in the west end of

Christiania.

* Tesman, whose Christian name in the original is "Jorgen," is described as "stipendiat i kulturhistorie"— that is to say, the holder of a scholarship for purposes of research into the History of Civilisation.

** In the original "Assessor."

Act First

A spacious, handsome, and tastefully furnished drawing room, decorated in dark colours. In the back, a wide doorway with curtains drawn back, leading into a smaller room decorated in the same style as the drawing-room. In the right-hand wall of the front room, a folding door leading out to the hall. In the opposite wall, on the left, a glass door, also with curtains drawn back. Through the panes can be seen part of a verandah outside, and trees covered with autumn foliage. An oval table, with a cover on it, and surrounded by chairs, stands well forward. In front, by the wall on the right, a wide stove of dark porcelain, a high-backed arm-chair, a cushioned foot-rest, and two footstools. A settee, with a small round table in front of it, fills the upper right-hand corner. In front, on the left, a little way from the wall, a sofa. Further back than the glass door, a piano. On either side of the doorway at the back a whatnot with terra-cotta and majolica ornaments. — Against the back wall of the inner room a sofa, with a table, and one or two chairs. Over the sofa hangs the portrait of a handsome elderly man in a General's uniform. Over the table a hanging lamp, with an opal glass shade. — A number of bouquets are arranged about the drawing-room, in vases and glasses. Others lie upon the tables. The floors in both rooms are covered with thick carpets. — Morning light. The sun shines in through the glass door.

Miss Juliana Tesman, with her bonnet on a carrying a parasol, comes in from the hall, followed by *Berta*, who carries a bouquet wrapped in paper. *Miss Tesman* is a comely and pleasant-looking lady of about sixty-five. She is nicely but simply dressed in a grey walking-costume. *Berta* is a middle-aged woman of plain and rather countrified appearance.

Miss Tesman. [Stops close to the door, listens, and says softly:] Upon my word, I don't believe they are stirring yet!

Berta. [Also softly.] I told you so, Miss. Remember how late the steamboat got in last night. And then, when they got home! — good Lord, what a lot the young mistress had to unpack before she could get to bed.

Miss Tesman. Well well — let them have their sleep out. But let us see that they get a good breath of the fresh morning air when they do appear.

She goes to the glass door and throws it open.

Berta. [Beside the table, at a loss what to do with the bouquet in her hand.] I declare there isn't a bit of room left. I think I'll put it down here, Miss. [She places it on the piano.

Miss Tesman. So you've got a new mistress now, my dear Berta. Heaven knows it was a wrench to me to part with you.

Berta. [On the point of weeping.] And do you think it wasn't hard for me, too, Miss? After all the blessed years I've been with you and Miss Rina.[6]

Miss Tesman. We must make the best of it, Berta. There was nothing else to be done. George can't do without you, you see-he absolutely can't. He has had you to look after him ever since he was a little boy.

Berta. Ah but, Miss Julia, I can't help thinking of Miss Rina lying helpless at home there, poor thing. And with only that new girl too! She'll never learn to take proper care of an invalid.

Miss Tesman. Oh, I shall manage to train her. And of course, you know, I shall take most of it upon myself. You needn't be uneasy about my poor sister, my dear Berta.

Berta. Well, but there's another thing, Miss. I'm so mortally afraid I shan't be able to suit the young mistress.

Miss Tesman. Oh well — just at first there may be one or two things —

Berta. Most like she'll be terrible grand in her ways.

Miss Tesman. Well, you can't wonder at that — General Gabler's daughter! Think of the sort of life she was accustomed to in her father's time. Don't you remember how we used to see her riding down the road along with the General? In that long black habit — and with feathers in her hat?

Berta. Yes, indeed — I remember well enough! — But, good Lord, I should never have dreamt in those days that she and Master George would make a match of it.

Miss Tesman. Nor I. — But by-the-bye, Berta — while I think of it: in future you mustn't say Master George. You must say Dr. Tesman.

Berta. Yes, the young mistress spoke of that too — last night — the moment they set foot in the house. Is it true then, Miss?

Miss Tesman. Yes, indeed it is. Only think, Berta — some foreign university has made him a doctor — while he has been abroad, you understand. I hadn't heard a word about it, until he told me himself upon the pier.

Berta. Well well, he's clever enough for anything, he is. But I didn't think he'd have gone in for doctoring people.

Miss Tesman. No no, it's not that sort of doctor he is. [Nods significantly.] But let me tell you, we may have to call him something still grander before long.

Berta. You don't day so! What can that be, Miss?

Miss Tesman. [Smiling.] H'm — wouldn't you like to know! [With emotion.] Ah, dear dear — if my poor brother could only look up from his grave now, and see what his little boy has grown into! [Looks around.] But bless me, Berta — why have you done this? Taken the chintz covers off all the furniture.

Berta. The mistress told me to. She can't abide covers on the chairs, she says.

Miss Tesman. Are they going to make this their everyday sitting-room then?

Berta. Yes, that's what I understood — from the mistress. Master George — the doctor — he said nothing.

George Tesman comes from the right into the inner room, humming to himself, and carrying an unstrapped empty portmanteau. He is a middle-sized, young-looking man of thirty-three, rather stout, with a round, open, cheerful face, fair hair and beard. He wears spectacles, and is somewhat carelessly dressed in comfortable indoor clothes.

Miss Tesman. Good morning, good morning, George.

190

Tesman. [In the doorway between the rooms.] Aunt Julia! Dear Aunt Julia! [Goes up to her and shakes hands warmly.] Come all this way — so early! Eh?

Miss Tesman. Why, of course I had to come and see how you were getting on.

Tesman. In spite of your having had no proper night's rest?

Miss Tesman. Oh, that makes no difference to me.

Tesman. Well, I suppose you got home all right from the pier? Eh?

Miss Tesman. Yes, quite safely, thank goodness. Judge Brack was good enough to see me right to my door.

Tesman. We were so sorry we couldn't give you a seat in the carriage. But you saw what a pile of boxes Hedda had to bring with her.

Miss Tesman. Yes, she had certainly plenty of boxes.

Berta. [To *Tesman.*] Shall I go in and see if there's anything I can do for the mistress?

Tesman. No thank you, Berta — you needn't. She said she would ring if she wanted anything.

Berta. [Going towards the right.] Very well.

Tesman. But look here — take this portmanteau with you.

Berta. [Taking it.] I'll put it in the attic.

She goes out by the hall door.

Tesman. Fancy, Auntie — I had the whole of that portmanteau chock full of copies of the documents. You wouldn't believe how much I have picked up from all the archives I have been examining — curious old details that no one has had any idea of —

Miss Tesman. Yes, you don't seem to have wasted you time on your wedding trip, George.

Tesman. No, that I haven't. But do take off your bonnet, Auntie. Look here! Let me untie the strings — eh?

Miss Tesman. [While he does so.] Well well — this is just as if you were still at home with us.

Tesman. [With the bonnet in his hand, looks at it from all sides.] Why, what a gorgeous bonnet you've been investing in!

Miss Tesman. I bought it on Hedda's account.

Tesman. On Hedda's account? Eh?

Miss Tesman. Yes, so that Hedda needn't be ashamed of me if we happened to go out together.

Tesman. [Patting her cheek.] You always think of everything, Aunt Julia. [Lays the bonnet on a chair beside the table.] And now, look here — suppose we sit comfortably on the sofa and have a little chat, till Hedda comes.

They seat themselves. She places her parasol in the corner of the sofa.

Miss Tesman. [Takes both his hands and looks at him.] What a delight it is to have you again, as large as life, before my very eyes, George! My George — my poor brother's own boy!

Tesman. And it's a delight for me, too, to see you again, Aunt Julia! You, who have been father and mother in one to me.

Miss Tesman. Oh yes, I know you will always keep a place in your heart for your old aunts.

Tesman. And what about Aunt Rina? No improvement — eh?

Miss Tesman. Oh, no — we can scarcely look for any improvement in her case, poor thing. There she lies, helpless, as she has lain for all these years. But heaven grant I may not lose her yet awhile! For if I did, I don't know what I should make of my life, George — especially now that I haven't you to look after any more.

Tesman. [Patting her back.] There there there —!

Miss Tesman. [Suddenly changing her tone.] And to think that here are you a married man, George! — And that you should be the one to carry off Hedda Gabler — the beautiful Hedda Gabler! Only think of it — she, that was so beset with admirers!

Tesman. [Hums a little and smiles complacently.] Yes, I fancy I have several good friends about town who would like to stand in my shoes — eh?

Miss Tesman. And then this fine long wedding-tour you have had! More than five — nearly six months —

Tesman. Well, for me it has been a sort of tour of research as well. I have had to do so much grubbing among old records — and to read no end of books too, Auntie.

Miss Tesman. Oh yes, I suppose so. [More confidentially, and lowering her voice a little.] But listen now, George — have you nothing — nothing special to tell me?

Tesman. As to our journey?

Miss Tesman. Yes.

Tesman. No, I don't know of anything except what I have told you in my letters. I had a doctor's degree conferred on me — but that I told you yesterday.

Miss Tesman. Yes, yes, you did. But what I mean is — haven't you any — any — expectations —?

Tesman. Expectations?

Miss Tesman. Why you know, George — I'm your old auntie!

Tesman. Why, of course I have expectations.

Miss Tesman. Ah!

Tesman. I have every expectation of being a professor one of these days.

Miss Tesman. Oh yes, a professor —

Tesman. Indeed, I may say I am certain of it. But my dear Auntie — you know all about that already!

Miss Tesman. [Laughing to herself.] Yes, of course I do. You are quite right there. [Changing the subject.] But we were talking about your journey. It must have cost a great deal of money, George?

Tesman.

Well, you see — my handsome travelling-scholarship went a good way.

Miss Tesman. But I can't understand how you can have made it go far enough for two.

Tesman. No, that's not easy to understand — eh?

Miss Tesman. And especially travelling with a lady — they tell me that makes it ever so much more expensive.

Tesman. Yes, of course — it makes it a little more expensive. But Hedda had to have this trip, Auntie! She really had to. Nothing else would have done.

Miss Tesman. No no, I suppose not. A wedding-tour seems to be quite indispensable nowadays. — But tell me now — have you gone thoroughly over the house yet?

Tesman. Yes, you may be sure I have. I have been afoot ever since daylight.

Miss Tesman. And what do you think of it all?

Tesman. I'm delighted! Quite delighted! Only I can't think what we are to do with the two empty rooms between this inner parlour and Hedda's bedroom.

Miss Tesman. [Laughing.] Oh my dear George, I daresay you may find some use for them — in the course of time.

Tesman. Why of course you are quite right, Aunt Julia! You mean as my library increases — eh?

Miss Tesman. Yes, quite so, my dear boy. It was your library I was thinking of.

Tesman. I am specially pleased on Hedda's account. Often and often, before we were engaged, she said that she would never care to live anywhere but in Secretary Falk's villa.[7]

Miss Tesman. Yes, it was lucky that this very house should come into the market, just after you had started.

193

Tesman. Yes, Aunt Julia, the luck was on our side, wasn't it — eh?

Miss Tesman. But the expense, my dear George! You will find it very expensive, all this.

Tesman. [Looks at her, a little cast down.] Yes, I suppose I shall, Aunt!

Miss Tesman. Oh, frightfully!

Tesman. How much do you think? In round numbers? — Eh?

Miss Tesman. Oh, I can't even guess until all the accounts come in.

Tesman. Well, fortunately, Judge Brack has secured the most favourable terms for me, so he said in a letter to Hedda.

Miss Tesman. Yes, don't be uneasy, my dear boy. — Besides, I have given security for the furniture and all the carpets.

Tesman. Security? You? My dear Aunt Julia — what sort of security could you give?

Miss Tesman. I have given a mortgage on our annuity.

Tesman. [Jumps up.] What! On your — and Aunt Rina's annuity!

Miss Tesman. Yes, I knew of no other plan, you see.

Tesman. [Placing himself before her.] Have you gone out of your senses, Auntie? Your annuity — it's all that you and Aunt Rina have to live upon.

Miss Tesman. Well well — don't get so excited about it. It's only a matter of form you know — Judge Brack assured me of that. It was he that was kind enough to arrange the whole affair for me. A mere matter of form, he said.

Tesman. Yes, that may be all very well. But nevertheless —

Miss Tesman. You will have your own salary to depend upon now. And, good heavens, even if we did have to pay up a little —! To eke things out a bit at the start —! Why, it would be nothing but a pleasure to us.

Tesman. Oh Auntie — will you never be tired of making sacrifices for me!

Miss Tesman. [Rises and lays her hand on his shoulders.] Have I any other happiness in this world except to smooth your way for you, my dear boy. You, who have had neither father nor mother to depend on. And now we have reached the goal, George! Things have looked black enough for us, sometimes; but, thank heaven, now you have nothing to fear.

Tesman. Yes, it is really marvellous how every thing has turned out for the best.

Miss Tesman. And the people who opposed you — who wanted to bar the way for you — now you have them at your feet. They have fallen, George. Your most dangerous rival — his fall was the worst. — And now he has to lie on the bed he has made for himself — poor misguided creature.

Tesman. Have you heard anything of Eilert? Since I went away, I mean.

Miss Tesman. Only that he is said to have published a new book.

Tesman. What! Eilert Lovborg! Recently — eh?

Miss Tesman. Yes, so they say. Heaven knows whether it can be worth anything! Ah, when your new book appears — that will be another story, George! What is it to be about?

Tesman. It will deal with the domestic industries of Brabant during the Middle Ages.

Miss Tesman. Fancy — to be able to write on such a subject as that!

Tesman. However, it may be some time before the book is ready. I have all these collections to arrange first, you see.

Miss Tesman. Yes, collecting and arranging — no one can beat you at that. There you are my poor brother's own son.

Tesman. I am looking forward eagerly to setting to work at it; especially now that I have my own delightful home to work in.

Miss Tesman. And, most of all, now that you have got the wife of your heart, my dear George.

Tesman. [Embracing her.] Oh yes, yes, Aunt Julia! Hedda — she is the best part of it all! I believe I hear her coming — eh?

Hedda enters from the left through the inner room. Her face and figure show refinement and distinction. Her complexion is pale and opaque. Her steel-grey eyes express a cold, unruffled repose. Her hair is of an agreeable brown, but not particularly abundant. She is dressed in a tasteful, somewhat loose-fitting morning gown.

Miss Tesman. [Going to meet *Hedda*.] Good morning, my dear Hedda! Good morning, and a hearty welcome!

Hedda. [Holds out her hand.] Good morning, dear Miss Tesman! So early a call! That is kind of you.

Miss Tesman. [With some embarrassment.] Well — has the bride slept well in her new home?

Hedda. Oh yes, thanks. Passably.

Tesman. [Laughing.] Passably! Come, that's good, Hedda! You were sleeping like a stone when I got up.

Hedda. Fortunately. Of course one has always to accustom one's self to new surroundings, Miss Tesman — little by little. [Looking towards the left.] Oh, there the servant has gone and opened the veranda door, and let in a whole flood of sunshine.

Miss Tesman. [Going towards the door.] Well, then we will shut it.

Hedda. No no, not that! Tesman, please draw the curtains. That will give a softer light.

Tesman. [At the door.] All right — all right. — There now, Hedda, now you have both shade and fresh air.

Hedda. Yes, fresh air we certainly must have, with all these stacks of flowers —. But — won't you sit down, Miss Tesman?

Miss Tesman. No, thank you. Now that I have seen that everything is all right here — thank heaven! — I must be getting home again. My sister is lying longing for me, poor thing.

Tesman. Give her my very best love, Auntie; and say I shall look in and see her later in the day.

Miss Tesman. Yes, yes, I'll be sure to tell her. But by-the-bye, George —[Feeling in her dress pocket]— I had almost forgotten — I have something for you here.

Tesman. What is it, Auntie? Eh?

Miss Tesman. [Produces a flat parcel wrapped in newspaper and hands it to him.] Look here, my dear boy.

Tesman. [Opening the parcel.] Well, I declare! — Have you really saved them for me, Aunt Julia! Hedda! isn't this touching — eh?

Hedda. [Beside the whatnot on the right.] Well, what is it?

Tesman. My old morning-shoes! My slippers.

Hedda. Indeed. I remember you often spoke of them while we were abroad.

Tesman. Yes, I missed them terribly. [Goes up to her.] Now you shall see them, Hedda!

Hedda. [Going towards the stove.] Thanks, I really don't care about it.

Tesman. [Following her.] Only think — ill as she was, Aunt Rina embroidered these for me. Oh you can't think how many associations cling to them.

Hedda. [At the table.] Scarcely for me.

Miss Tesman. Of course not for Hedda, George.

Tesman. Well, but now that she belongs to the family, I thought —

Hedda. [Interrupting.] We shall never get on with this servant, Tesman.

Miss Tesman. Not get on with Berta?

Tesman. Why, dear, what puts that in your head? Eh?

Hedda. [Pointing.] Look there! She has left her old bonnet lying about on a chair.

Tesman. [In consternation, drops the slippers on the floor.] Why, Hedda —

Hedda. Just fancy, if any one should come in and see it!

Tesman. But Hedda — that's Aunt Julia's bonnet.

Hedda. Is it!

Miss Tesman. [Taking up the bonnet.] Yes, indeed it's mine. And, what's more, it's not old, Madam Hedda.

Hedda. I really did not look closely at it, Miss Tesman.

Miss Tesman. [Trying on the bonnet.] Let me tell you it's the first time I have worn it — the very first time.

Tesman. And a very nice bonnet it is too — quite a beauty!

Miss Tesman. Oh, it's no such great things, George. [Looks around her.] My parasol —? Ah, here. [Takes it.] For this is mine too —[mutters] — not Berta's.

Tesman. A new bonnet and a new parasol! Only think, Hedda.

Hedda. Very handsome indeed.

Tesman. Yes, isn't it? Eh? But Auntie, take a good look at Hedda before you go! See how handsome she is!

Miss Tesman. Oh, my dear boy, there's nothing new in that. Hedda was always lovely.

She nods and goes toward the right.

Tesman. [Following.] Yes, but have you noticed what splendid condition she is in? How she has filled out on the journey?

Hedda. [Crossing the room.] Oh, do be quiet —!

Miss Tesman. [Who has stopped and turned.] Filled out?

Tesman. Of course you don't notice it so much now that she has that dress on. But I, who can see —

Hedda. [At the glass door, impatiently.] Oh, you can't see anything.

Tesman. It must be the mountain air in the Tyrol —

Hedda. [Curtly, interrupting.] I am exactly as I was when I started.

Tesman. So you insist; but I'm quite certain you are not. Don't you agree with me, Auntie?

Miss Tesman. [Who has been gazing at her with folded hands.] Hedda is lovely — lovely — lovely. [Goes up to her, takes her head between both hands, draws it downwards, and kisses her hair.] God bless and preserve Hedda Tesman — for George's sake.

Hedda. [Gently freeing herself.] Oh —! Let me go.

Miss Tesman. [In quiet emotion.] I shall not let a day pass without coming to see you.

Tesman. No you won't, will you, Auntie? Eh?

Miss Tesman. Good-bye — good-bye!

She goes out by the hall door. *Tesman* accompanies her. The door remains half open. *Tesman* can be heard repeating his message to Aunt Rina and his thanks for the slippers.

In the meantime, *Hedda* walks about the room, raising her arms and clenching her hands as if in desperation. Then she flings back the curtains from the glass door, and stands there looking out.

Presently, *Tesman* returns and closes the door behind him.

Tesman. [Picks up the slippers from the floor.] What are you looking at, Hedda?

Hedda. [Once more calm and mistress of herself.] I am only looking at the leaves. They are so yellow — so withered.

Tesman. [Wraps up the slippers and lays them on the table.] Well, you see, we are well into September now.

Hedda. [Again restless.] Yes, to think of it! — already in-in September.

Tesman. Don't you think Aunt Julia's manner was strange, dear? Almost solemn? Can you imagine what was the matter with her? Eh?

Hedda. I scarcely know her, you see. Is she not often like that?

Tesman. No, not as she was today.

Hedda. [Leaving the glass door.] Do you think she was annoyed about the bonnet?

Tesman. Oh, scarcely at all. Perhaps a little, just at the moment —

Hedda. But what an idea, to pitch her bonnet about in the drawing-room! No one does that sort of thing.

Tesman. Well you may be sure Aunt Julia won't do it again.

Hedda. In any case, I shall manage to make my peace with her.

Tesman. Yes, my dear, good Hedda, if you only would.

Hedda. When you call this afternoon, you might invite her to spend the evening here.

Tesman. Yes, that I will. And there's one thing more you could do that would delight her heart.

Hedda. What is it?

Tesman. If you could only prevail on yourself to say *du*[8] to her. For my sake, Hedda? Eh?

Hedda. No, no, Tesman — you really mustn't ask that of me. I have told you so already. I shall try to call her "Aunt"; and you must be satisfied with that.

Tesman. Well well. Only I think now that you belong to the family, you —

Hedda. H'm — I can't in the least see why —

She goes up towards the middle doorway.

Tesman. [After a pause.] Is there anything the matter with you, Hedda? Eh?

Hedda. I'm only looking at my old piano. It doesn't go at all well with all the other things.

Tesman. The first time I draw my salary, we'll see about exchanging it.

Hedda. No, no — no exchanging. I don't want to part with it. Suppose we put it there in the inner room, and then get another here in its place. When it's convenient, I mean.

Tesman. [A little taken aback.] Yes — of course we could do that.

Hedda. [Takes up the bouquet from the piano.] These flowers were not here last night when we arrived.

Tesman. Aunt Julia must have brought them for you.

Hedda. [Examining the bouquet.] A visiting-card. [Takes it out and reads:] "Shall return later in the day." Can you guess whose card it is?

Tesman. No. Whose? Eh?

Hedda. The name is "Mrs. Elvsted."

Tesman. Is it really? Sheriff Elvsted's wife? Miss Rysing that was.

Hedda. Exactly. The girl with the irritating hair, that she was always showing off. An old flame of yours I've been told.

Tesman. [Laughing.] Oh, that didn't last long; and it was before I met you, Hedda. But fancy her being in town!

Hedda. It's odd that she should call upon us. I have scarcely seen her since we left school.

Tesman. I haven't see her either for — heaven knows how long. I wonder how she can endure to live in such an out-of-the way hole — eh?

Hedda. [After a moment's thought, says suddenly.] Tell me, Tesman — isn't it somewhere near there that he — that — Eilert Lovborg is living?

Tesman. Yes, he is somewhere in that part of the country.

Berta enters by the hall door.

Berta. That lady, ma'am, that brought some flowers a little while ago, is here again. [Pointing.] The flowers you have in your hand, ma'am.

Hedda. Ah, is she? Well, please show her in.

Berta opens the door for *Mrs. Elvsted*, and goes out herself. — *Mrs. Elvsted* is a woman of fragile figure, with pretty, soft features. Her eyes are light blue, large, round, and somewhat prominent, with a startled, inquiring expression. Her hair is remarkably light, almost flaxen, and unusually abundant and wavy. She is a couple of years younger than *Hedda*. She wears a dark visiting dress, tasteful, but not quite in the latest fashion.

Hedda. [Receives her warmly.] How do you do, my dear Mrs. Elvsted? It's delightful to see you again.

Mrs. Elvsted. [Nervously, struggling for self-control.] Yes, it's a very long time since we met.

Tesman. [Gives her his hand.] And we too — eh?

Hedda. Thanks for your lovely flowers —

Mrs. Elvsted. Oh, not at all —. I would have come straight here yesterday afternoon; but I heard that you were away —

Tesman. Have you just come to town? Eh?

Mrs. Elvsted. I arrived yesterday, about midday. Oh, I was quite in despair when I heard that you were not at home.

Hedda. In despair! How so?

Tesman. Why, my dear Mrs. Rysing — I mean Mrs. Elvsted —

Hedda. I hope that you are not in any trouble?

Mrs. Elvsted. Yes, I am. And I don't know another living creature here that I can turn to.

Hedda. [Laying the bouquet on the table.] Come — let us sit here on the sofa —

Mrs. Elvsted. Oh, I am too restless to sit down.

Hedda. Oh no, you're not. Come here.

She draws *Mrs. Elvsted* down upon the sofa and sits at her side.

Tesman. Well? What is it, Mrs. Elvsted —?

Hedda. Has anything particular happened to you at home?

Mrs. Elvsted. Yes — and no. Oh — I am so anxious you should not misunderstand me —

Hedda. Then your best plan is to tell us the whole story, Mrs. Elvsted.

Tesman. I suppose that's what you have come for — eh?

Mrs. Elvsted. Yes, yes — of course it is. Well then, I must tell you — if you don't already know — that Eilert Lovborg is in town, too.

Hedda. Lovborg —!

Tesman. What! Has Eilert Lovborg come back? Fancy that, Hedda!

Hedda. Well well — I hear it.

Mrs. Elvsted. He has been here a week already. Just fancy — a whole week! In this terrible town, alone! With so many temptations on all sides.

Hedda. But, my dear Mrs. Elvsted — how does he concern you so much?

Mrs. Elvsted. [Looks at her with a startled air, and says rapidly.] He was the children's tutor.

Hedda. Your children's?

Mrs. Elvsted. My husband's. I have none.

Hedda. Your step-children's, then?

Mrs. Elvsted. Yes.

Tesman. [Somewhat hesitatingly.] Then was he — I don't know how to express it — was he — regular enough in his habits to be fit for the post? Eh?

Mrs. Elvsted. For the last two years his conduct has been irreproachable.

Tesman. Has it indeed? Fancy that, Hedda!

Hedda. I hear it.

Mrs. Elvsted. Perfectly irreproachable, I assure you! In every respect. But all the same — now that I know he is here — in this great town — and with a large sum of money in his hands — I can't help being in mortal fear for him.

Tesman. Why did he not remain where he was? With you and your husband? Eh?

Mrs. Elvsted. After his book was published he was too restless and unsettled to remain with us.

Tesman. Yes, by-the-bye, Aunt Julia told me he had published a new book.

Mrs. Elvsted. Yes, a big book, dealing with the march of civilisation — in broad outline, as it were. It came out about a fortnight ago. And since it has sold so well, and been so much read — and made such a sensation —

Tesman. Has it indeed? It must be something he has had lying by since his better days.

Mrs. Elvsted. Long ago, you mean?

Tesman. Yes.

Mrs. Elvsted. No, he has written it all since he has been with us — within the last year.

Tesman. Isn't that good news, Hedda? Think of that.

Mrs. Elvsted. Ah yes, if only it would last!

Hedda. Have you seen him here in town?

Mrs. Elvsted. No, not yet. I have had the greatest difficulty in finding out his address. But this morning I discovered it at last.

Hedda. [Looks searchingly at her.] Do you know, it seems to me a little odd of your husband — h'm —

Mrs. Elvsted. [Starting nervously.] Of my husband! What?

Hedda. That he should send you to town on such an errand — that he does not come himself and look after his friend.

Mrs. Elvsted. Oh no, no — my husband has no time. And besides, *i* — *i* had some shopping to do.

Hedda. [With a slight smile.] Ah, that is a different matter.

Mrs. Elvsted. [Rising quickly and uneasily.] And now I beg and implore you, Mr. Tesman — receive Eilert Lovborg kindly if he comes to you! And that he is sure to do. You see you were such great friends in the old days. And then you are interested in the same studies — the same branch of science — so far as I can understand.

Tesman. We used to be at any rate.

Mrs. Elvsted. That is why I beg so earnestly that you — you too — will keep a sharp eye upon him. Oh, you will promise me that, Mr. Tesman — won't you?

Tesman. With the greatest of pleasure, Mrs. Rysing —

Hedda. Elvsted.

Tesman. I assure you I shall do all I possibly can for Eilert. You may rely upon me.

Mrs. Elvsted. Oh, how very, very kind of you! [Presses his hands.] Thanks, thanks, thanks! [Frightened.] You see, my husband is so very fond of him!

Hedda. [Rising.] You ought to write to him, Tesman. Perhaps he may not care to come to you of his own accord.

Tesman. Well, perhaps it would be the right thing to do, Hedda? Eh?

Hedda. And the sooner the better. Why not at once?

Mrs. Elvsted. [Imploringly.] Oh, if you only would!

Tesman. I'll write this moment. Have you his address, Mrs. — Mrs. Elvsted.

Mrs. Elvsted. Yes. [Takes a slip of paper from her pocket, and hands it to him.] Here it is.

Tesman. Good, good. Then I'll go in — [Looks about him.] By-the-bye — my slippers? Oh, here. [Takes the packet and is about to go.

Hedda. Be sure you write him a cordial, friendly letter. And a good long one too.

Tesman. Yes, I will.

Mrs. Elvsted. But please, please don't say a word to show that I have suggested it.

Tesman. No, how could you think I would? Eh?

He goes out to the right, through the inner room.

Hedda. [Goes up to *Mrs. Elvsted*, smiles, and says in a low voice.] There! We have killed two birds with one stone.

Mrs. Elvsted. What do you mean?

Hedda. Could you not see that I wanted him to go?

Mrs. Elvsted. Yes, to write the letter —

Hedda. And that I might speak to you alone.

Mrs. Elvsted. [Confused.] About the same thing?

Hedda. Precisely.

Mrs. Elvsted. [Apprehensively.] But there is nothing more, Mrs. Tesman! Absolutely nothing!

Hedda. Oh yes, but there is. There is a great deal more — I can see that. Sit here — and we'll have a cosy, confidential chat.

She forces *Mrs. Elvsted* to sit in the easy-chair beside the stove, and seats herself on one of the footstools.

Mrs. Elvsted. [Anxiously, looking at her watch.] But, my dear Mrs. Tesman — I was really on the point of going.

Hedda. Oh, you can't be in such a hurry. — Well? Now tell me something about your life at home.

Mrs. Elvsted. Oh, that is just what I care least to speak about.

Hedda. But to me, dear —? Why, weren't we schoolfellows?

Mrs. Elvsted. Yes, but you were in the class above me. Oh, how dreadfully afraid of you I was then!

Hedda. Afraid of me?

Mrs. Elvsted. Yes, dreadfully. For when we met on the stairs you used always to pull my hair.

Hedda. Did I, really?

Mrs. Elvsted. Yes, and once you said you would burn it off my head.

Hedda. Oh that was all nonsense, of course.

Mrs. Elvsted. Yes, but I was so silly in those days. — And since then, too — we have drifted so far — far apart from each other. Our circles have been so entirely different.

Hedda. Well then, we must try to drift together again. Now listen. At school we said du[9] to each other; and we called each other by our Christian names —

Mrs. Elvsted. No, I am sure you must be mistaken.

Hedda. No, not at all! I can remember quite distinctly. So now we are going to renew our old friendship. [Draws the footstool closer to *Mrs. Elvsted.*] There now! [Kisses her cheek.] You must say du to me and call me Hedda.

Mrs. Elvsted. [Presses and pats her hands.] Oh, how good and kind you are! I am not used to such kindness.

Hedda. There, there, there! And I shall say du to you, as in the old days, and call you my dear Thora.

Mrs. Elvsted. My name is Thea.[10]

Hedda. Why, of course! I meant Thea. [Looks at her compassionately.] So you are not accustomed to goodness and kindness, Thea? Not in your own home?

Mrs. Elvsted. Oh, if I only had a home! But I haven't any; I have never had a home.

Hedda. [Looks at her for a moment.] I almost suspected as much.

Mrs. Elvsted. [Gazing helplessly before her.] Yes — yes — yes.

Hedda. I don't quite remember — was it not as housekeeper that you first went to Mr. Elvsted's?

Mrs. Elvsted. I really went as governess. But his wife — his late wife — was an invalid — and rarely left her room. So I had to look after the housekeeping as well.

Hedda. And then — at last — you became mistress of the house.

Mrs. Elvsted. [Sadly.] Yes, I did.

Hedda. Let me see — about how long ago was that?

Mrs. Elvsted. My marriage?

Hedda. Yes.

Mrs. Elvsted. Five years ago.

Hedda. To be sure; it must be that.

Mrs. Elvsted. Oh those five years —! Or at all events the last two or three of them! Oh, if you[1] could only imagine —

Hedda. [Giving her a little slap on the hand.] De? Fie, Thea!

Mrs. Elvsted. Yes, yes, I will try —. Well, if — you could only imagine and understand —

Hedda. [Lightly.] Eilert Lovborg has been in your neighbourhood about three years, hasn't he?

Mrs. Elvsted. [Looks at here doubtfully.] Eilert Lovborg? Yes — he has.

Hedda. Had you known him before, in town here?

Mrs. Elvsted. Scarcely at all. I mean — I knew him by name of course.

Hedda. But you saw a good deal of him in the country?

Mrs. Elvsted. Yes, he came to us every day. You see, he gave the children lessons; for in the long run I couldn't manage it all myself.

Hedda. No, that's clear. — And your husband —? I suppose he is often away from home?

Mrs. Elvsted. Yes. Being sheriff, you know, he has to travel about a good deal in his district.

Hedda. [Leaning against the arm of the chair.] Thea — my poor, sweet Thea — now you must tell me everything — exactly as it stands.

Mrs. Elvsted. Well, then you must question me.

Hedda. What sort of a man is your husband, Thea? I mean — you know — in everyday life. Is he kind to you?

Mrs. Elvsted. [Evasively.] I am sure he means well in everything.

Hedda. I should think he must be altogether too old for you. There is at least twenty years' difference between you, is there not?

Mrs. Elvsted. [Irritably.] Yes, that is true, too. Everything about him is repellent to me! We have not a thought in common. We have no single point of sympathy — he and I.

Hedda. But is he not fond of you all the same? In his own way?

Mrs. Elvsted. Oh I really don't know. I think he regards me simply as a useful property. And then it doesn't cost much to keep me. I am not expensive.

Hedda. That is stupid of you.

Mrs. Elvsted. [Shakes her head.] It cannot be otherwise — not with him. I don't think he really cares for any one but himself — and perhaps a little for the children.

Hedda. And for Eilert Lovborg, Thea?

Mrs. Elvsted. [Looking at her.] For Eilert Lovborg? What puts that into your head?

Hedda. Well, my dear — I should say, when he sends you after him all the way to town —— [Smiling almost imperceptibly.] And besides, you said so yourself, to Tesman.

Mrs. Elvsted. [With a little nervous twitch.] Did I? Yes, I suppose I did. [Vehemently, but not loudly.] No — I may just as well make a clean breast of it at once! For it must all come out in any case.

Hedda. Why, my dear Thea —?

Mrs. Elvsted. Well, to make a long story short: My husband did not know that I was coming.

Hedda. What! Your husband didn't know it!

Mrs. Elvsted. No, of course not. For that matter, he was away from home himself — he was travelling. Oh, I could bear it no longer, Hedda! I couldn't indeed — so utterly alone as I should have been in future.

Hedda. Well? And then?

Mrs. Elvsted. So I put together some of my things — what I needed most — as quietly as possible. And then I left the house.

Hedda. Without a word?

Mrs. Elvsted. Yes — and took the train to town.

Hedda. Why, my dear, good Thea — to think of you daring to do it!

Mrs. Elvsted. [Rises and moves about the room.] What else could I possibly do?

Hedda. But what do you think your husband will say when you go home again?

Mrs. Elvsted. [At the table, looks at her.] Back to him?

Hedda. Of course.

Mrs. Elvsted. I shall never go back to him again.

Hedda. [Rising and going towards her.] Then you have left your home — for good and all?

Mrs. Elvsted. Yes. There was nothing else to be done.

Hedda. But then — to take flight so openly.

Mrs. Elvsted. Oh, it's impossible to keep things of that sort secret.

Hedda. But what do you think people will say of you, Thea?

Mrs. Elvsted. They may say what they like, for aught *I* care. [Seats herself wearily and sadly on the sofa.] I have done nothing but what I had to do.

Hedda. [After a short silence.] And what are your plans now? What do you think of doing.

Mrs. Elvsted. I don't know yet. I only know this, that I must live here, where Eilert Lovborg is — if I am to live at all.

Hedda. [Takes a chair from the table, seats herself beside her, and strokes her hands.] My dear Thea — how did this — this friendship — between you and Eilert Lovborg come about?

Mrs. Elvsted. Oh it grew up gradually. I gained a sort of influence over him.

Hedda. Indeed?

Mrs. Elvsted. He gave up his old habits. Not because I asked him to, for I never dared do that. But of course he saw how repulsive they were to me; and so he dropped them.

Hedda. [Concealing an involuntary smile of scorn.] Then you have reclaimed him — as the saying goes — my little Thea.

Mrs. Elvsted. So he says himself, at any rate. And he, on his side, has made a real human being of me — taught me to think, and to understand so many things.

Hedda. Did he give you lessons too, then?

Mrs. Elvsted. No, not exactly lessons. But he talked to me — talked about such an infinity of things. And then came the lovely, happy time when I began to share in his work — when he allowed me to help him!

Hedda. Oh he did, did he?

Mrs. Elvsted. Yes! He never wrote anything without my assistance.

Hedda. You were two good comrades, in fact?

Mrs. Elvsted. [Eagerly.] Comrades! Yes, fancy, Hedda — that is the very word he used! — Oh, I ought to feel perfectly happy; and yet I cannot; for I don't know how long it will last.

Hedda. Are you no surer of him than that?

Mrs. Elvsted. [Gloomily.] A woman's shadow stands between Eilert Lovborg and me.

Hedda. [Looks at her anxiously.] Who can that be?

Mrs. Elvsted. I don't know. Some one he knew in his — in his past. Some one he has never been able wholly to forget.

Hedda. What has he told you — about this?

Mrs. Elvsted. He has only once — quite vaguely — alluded to it.

Hedda. Well! And what did he say?

Mrs. Elvsted. He said that when they parted, she threatened to shoot him with a pistol.

Hedda. [With cold composure.] Oh nonsense! No one does that sort of thing here.

Mrs. Elvsted. No. And that is why I think it must have been that red-haired singing-woman whom he once —

Hedda. Yes, very likely.

Mrs. Elvsted. For I remember they used to say of her that she carried loaded firearms.

Hedda. Oh — then of course it must have been she.

Mrs. Elvsted. [Wringing her hands.] And now just fancy, Hedda — I hear that this singing-woman — that she is in town again! Oh, I don't know what to do —

Hedda. [Glancing towards the inner room.] Hush! Here comes Tesman. [Rises and whispers.] Thea — all this must remain between you and me.

Mrs. Elvsted. [Springing up.] Oh yes — yes! For heaven's sake —!

George Tesman, with a letter in his hand, comes from the right through the inner room.

Tesman. There now — the epistle is finished.

Hedda. That's right. And now Mrs. Elvsted is just going. Wait a moment — I'll go with you to the garden gate.

Tesman. Do you think Berta could post the letter, Hedda dear?

Hedda. [Takes it.] I will tell her to.

Berta enters from the hall.

Berta. Judge Brack wishes to know if Mrs. Tesman will receive him.

Hedda. Yes, ask Judge Brack to come in. And look here — put this letter in the post.

Berta. [Taking the letter.] Yes, ma'am.

She opens the door for *Judge Brack* and goes out herself. Brack is a main of forty-five; thick set, but well-built and elastic in his movements. His face is roundish with an aristocratic profile. His hair is short, still almost black, and carefully dressed. His eyebrows thick. His moustaches are also thick, with short-cut ends. He wears a well-cut walking-suit, a little too youthful for his age. He uses an eye-glass, which he now and then lets drop.

Judge Brack. [With his hat in his hand, bowing.] May one venture to call so early in the day?

Hedda. Of course one may.

Tesman. [Presses his hand.] You are welcome at any time. [Introducing him.] Judge Brack — Miss Rysing —

Hedda. Oh —!

Brack. [Bowing.] Ah — delighted —

Hedda. [Looks at him and laughs.] It's nice to have a look at you by daylight, Judge!

Brack. So you find me — altered?

Hedda. A little younger, I think.

Brack. Thank you so much.

Tesman. But what do you think of Hedda — eh? Doesn't she look flourishing? She has actually —

Hedda. Oh, do leave me alone. You haven't thanked Judge Brack for all the trouble he has taken —

Brack. Oh, nonsense — it was a pleasure to me —

Hedda. Yes, you are a friend indeed. But here stands Thea all impatience to be off — so *au revoir* Judge. I shall be back again presently.

Mutual salutations. *Mrs. Elvsted* and *Hedda* go out by the hall door.

Brack. Well — is your wife tolerably satisfied —

Tesman. Yes, we can't thank you sufficiently. Of course she talks of a little re-arrangement here and there; and one or two things are still wanting. We shall have to buy some additional trifles.

Brack. Indeed!

Tesman. But we won't trouble you about these things. Hedda say she herself will look after what is wanting. — Shan't we sit down? Eh?

Brack. Thanks, for a moment. [Seats himself beside the table.] There is something I wanted to speak to about, my dear Tesman.

Tesman. Indeed? Ah, I understand! [Seating himself.] I suppose it's the serious part of the frolic that is coming now. Eh?

Brack. Oh, the money question is not so very pressing; though, for that matter, I wish we had gone a little more economically to work.

Tesman. But that would never have done, you know! Think of Hedda, my dear fellow! You, who know her so well —! I couldn't possibly ask her to put up with a shabby style of living!

Brack. No, no — that is just the difficulty.

Tesman. And then — fortunately — it can't be long before I receive my appointment.

Brack. Well, you see — such things are often apt to hang fire for a long time.

Tesman. Have you heard anything definite? Eh?

Brack. Nothing exactly definite —. [Interrupting himself.] But by-the-bye — I have one piece of news for you.

Tesman. Well?

Brack. Your old friend, Eilert Lovborg, has returned to town.

Tesman. I know that already.

Brack. Indeed! How did you learn it?

Tesman. From that lady who went out with Hedda.

Brack. Really? What was her name? I didn't quite catch it.

Tesman. Mrs. Elvsted.

Brack. Aha — Sheriff Elvsted's wife? Of course — he has been living up in their regions.

Tesman. And fancy — I'm delighted to hear that he is quite a reformed character.

Brack. So they say.

Tesman. And then he has published a new book — eh?

Brack. Yes, indeed he has.

Tesman. And I hear it has made some sensation!

Brack. Quite an unusual sensation.

Tesman. Fancy — isn't that good news! A man of such extraordinary talents —. I felt so grieved to think that he had gone irretrievably to ruin.

Brack. That was what everybody thought.

Tesman. But I cannot imagine what he will take to now! How in the world will he be able to make his living? Eh?

During the last words, *Hedda* has entered by the hall door.

Hedda. [To *Brack*, laughing with a touch of scorn.] Tesman is for ever worrying about how people are to make their living.

Tesman. Well you see, dear — we were talking about poor Eilert Lovborg.

Hedda. [Glancing at him rapidly.] Oh, indeed? [Sets herself in the arm-chair beside the stove and asks indifferently:] What is the matter with him?

Tesman. Well — no doubt he has run through all his property long ago; and he can scarcely write a new book every year — eh? So I really can't see what is to become of him.

Brack. Perhaps I can give you some information on that point.

Tesman. Indeed!

Brack. You must remember that his relations have a good deal of influence.

Tesman. Oh, his relations, unfortunately, have entirely washed their hands of him.

Brack. At one time they called him the hope of the family.

Tesman. At one time, yes! But he has put an end to all that.

Hedda. Who knows? [With a slight smile.] I hear they have reclaimed him up at Sheriff Elvsted's —

Brack. And then this book that he has published —

Tesman. Well well, I hope to goodness they may find something for him to do. I have just written to him. I asked him to come and see us this evening, Hedda dear.

Brack. But my dear fellow, you are booked for my bachelor's party this evening. You promised on the pier last night.

Hedda. Had you forgotten, Tesman?

Tesman. Yes, I had utterly forgotten.

Brack. But it doesn't matter, for you may be sure he won't come.

Tesman. What makes you think that? Eh?

Brack. [With a little hesitation, rising and resting his hands on the back of his chair.] My dear Tesman — and you too, Mrs. Tesman — I think I ought not to keep you in the dark about something that — that —

Tesman. That concerns Eilert —?

Brack. Both you and him.

Tesman. Well, my dear Judge, out with it.

Brack. You must be prepared to find your appointment deferred longer than you desired or expected.

Tesman. [Jumping up uneasily.] Is there some hitch about it? Eh?

Brack. The nomination may perhaps be made conditional on the result of a competition —

Tesman. Competition! Think of that, Hedda!

Hedda. [Leans further back in the chair.] Aha — aha!

Tesman. But who can my competitor be? Surely not —?

Brack. Yes, precisely — Eilert Lovborg.

Tesman. [Clasping his hands.] No, no — it's quite impossible! Eh?

Brack. H'm — that is what it may come to, all the same.

Tesman. Well but, Judge Brack — it would show the most incredible lack of consideration for me. [Gesticulates with his arms.] For — just think — I'm a married man! We have married on the strength of these prospects, Hedda and I; and run deep into debt; and borrowed money from Aunt Julia too. Good heavens, they had as good as promised me the appointment. Eh?

Brack. Well, well, well — no doubt you will get it in the end; only after a contest.

Hedda. [Immovable in her arm-chair.] Fancy, Tesman, there will be a sort of sporting interest in that.

Tesman. Why, my dearest Hedda, how can you be so indifferent about it?

Hedda. [As before.] I am not at all indifferent. I am most eager to see who wins.

Brack. In any case, Mrs. Tesman, it is best that you should know how matters stand. I mean — before you set about the little purchases I hear you are threatening.

Hedda. This can make no difference.

Brack. Indeed! Then I have no more to say. Good-bye! [To *Tesman*.] I shall look in on my way back from my afternoon walk, and take you home with me.

Tesman. Oh yes, yes — your news has quite upset me.

Hedda. [Reclining, holds out her hand.] Good-bye, Judge; and be sure you call in the afternoon.

Brack. Many thanks. Good-bye, good-bye!

Tesman. [Accompanying him to the door.] Good-bye my dear Judge! You must really excuse me —— [*Judge Brack* goes out by the hall door.

Tesman. [Crosses the room.] Oh Hedda — one should never rush into adventures. Eh?

Hedda. [Looks at him, smiling.] Do you do that?

Tesman. Yes, dear — there is no denying — it was adventurous to go and marry and set up house upon mere expectations.

Hedda. Perhaps you are right there.

Tesman. Well — at all events, we have our delightful home, Hedda! Fancy, the home we both dreamed of — the home we were in love with, I may almost say. Eh?

Hedda. [Rising slowly and wearily.] It was part of our compact that we were to go into society — to keep open house.

Tesman. Yes, if you only knew how I had been looking forward to it! Fancy — to see you as hostess — in a select circle! Eh? Well, well, well — for the present we shall have to get on without society, Hedda — only to invite Aunt Julia now and then. — Oh, I intended you to lead such an utterly different life, dear —!

Hedda. Of course I cannot have my man in livery just yet.

Tesman. Oh, no, unfortunately. It would be out of the question for us to keep a footman, you know.

Hedda. And the saddle-horse I was to have had —

Tesman. [Aghast.] The saddle-horse!

Hedda. — I suppose I must not think of that now.

Tesman. Good heavens, no! — that's as clear as daylight!

Hedda. [Goes up the room.] Well, I shall have one thing at least to kill time with in the meanwhile.

Tesman. [Beaming.] Oh thank heaven for that! What is it, Hedda. Eh?

Hedda. [In the middle doorway, looks at him with covert scorn.] My pistols, George.

Tesman. [In alarm.] Your pistols!

Hedda. [With cold eyes.] General Gabler's pistols.

She goes out through the inner room, to the left.

Tesman. [Rushes up to the middle doorway and calls after her:] No, for heaven's sake, Hedda darling — don't touch those dangerous things! For my sake Hedda! Eh?

[6]Pronounce *Reena*.

[7]In the original "Statsradinde Falks villa"— showing that it had belonged to the widow of a cabinet minister.

[8]*Du* equals thou: Tesman means, "If you could persuade yourself to *tutoyer* her."

[9]See previous note.

[10]Pronounce *Tora* and *Taya*.

[11]Mrs. Elvsted here uses the formal pronoun *De*, whereupon Hedda rebukes her. In her next speech Mrs. Elvsted says *du*.

Act Second

The room at the *Tesmans'* as in the first Act, except that the piano has been removed, and an elegant little writing-table with the book-shelves put in its place. A smaller table stands near the sofa on the left. Most of the bouquets have been taken away. *Mrs. Elvsted's* bouquet is upon the large table in front. — It is afternoon.

Hedda, dressed to receive callers, is alone in the room. She stands by the open glass door, loading a revolver. The fellow to it lies in an open pistol-case on the writing-table.

Hedda. [Looks down the garden, and calls:] So you are here again, Judge!

Brack. [Is heard calling from a distance.] As you see, Mrs. Tesman!

Hedda. [Raises the pistol and points.] Now I'll shoot you, Judge Brack!

Brack. [Calling unseen.] No, no, no! Don't stand aiming at me!

Hedda. This is what comes of sneaking in by the back way.[12] [She fires.

Brack. [Nearer.] Are you out of your senses —!

Hedda. Dear me — did I happen to hit you?

Brack. [Still outside.] I wish you would let these pranks alone!

Hedda. Come in then, Judge.

Judge Brack, dressed as though for a men's party, enters by the glass door. He carries a light overcoat over his arm.

Brack. What the deuce — haven't you tired of that sport, yet? What are you shooting at?

Hedda. Oh, I am only firing in the air.

Brack. [Gently takes the pistol out of her hand.] Allow me, madam! [Looks at it.] Ah — I know this pistol well! [Looks around.] Where is the case? Ah, here it is. [Lays the pistol in it, and shuts it.] Now we won't play at that game any more today.

Hedda. Then what in heaven's name would you have me do with myself?

Brack. Have you had no visitors?

Hedda. [Closing the glass door.] Not one. I suppose all our set are still out of town.

Brack. And is Tesman not at home either?

Hedda. [At the writing-table, putting the pistol-case in a drawer which she shuts.] No. He rushed off to his aunt's directly after lunch; he didn't expect you so early.

Brack. H'm — how stupid of me not to have thought of that!

Hedda. [Turning her head to look at him.] Why stupid?

Brack. Because if I had thought of it I should have come a little — earlier.

Hedda. [Crossing the room.] Then you would have found no one to receive you; for I have been in my room changing my dress ever since lunch.

Brack. And is there no sort of little chink that we could hold a parley through?

Hedda. You have forgotten to arrange one.

Brack. That was another piece of stupidity.

Hedda. Well, we must just settle down here — and wait. Tesman is not likely to be back for some time yet.

Brack. Never mind; I shall not be impatient.

Hedda seats herself in the corner of the sofa. *Brack* lays his overcoat over the back of the nearest chair, and sits down, but keeps his hat in his hand. A short silence. They look at each other.

Hedda. Well?

Brack. [In the same tone.] Well?

Hedda. I spoke first.

Brack. [Bending a little forward.] Come, let us have a cosy little chat, Mrs. Hedda.[13]

Hedda. [Leaning further back in the sofa.] Does it not seem like a whole eternity since our last talk? Of course I don't count those few words yesterday evening and this morning.

Brack. You mean since out last confidential talk? Our last *tete-a-tete*?

Hedda. Well yes — since you put it so.

Brack. Not a day passed but I have wished that you were home again.

Hedda. And I have done nothing but wish the same thing.

Brack. You? Really, Mrs. Hedda? And I thought you had been enjoying your tour so much!

Hedda. Oh yes, you may be sure of that!

Brack. But Tesman's letters spoke of nothing but happiness.

Hedda. Oh, Tesman! You see, he thinks nothing is so delightful as grubbing in libraries and making copies of old parchments, or whatever you call them.

Brack. [With a smile of malice.] Well, that is his vocation in life — or part of it at any rate.

Hedda. Yes, of course; and no doubt when it's your vocation —. But *I*! Oh, my dear Mr. Brack, how mortally bored I have been.

Brack. [Sympathetically.] Do you really say so? In downright earnest?

Hedda. Yes, you can surely understand it —! To go for six whole months without meeting a soul that knew anything of our circle, or could talk about things we were interested in.

Brack. Yes, yes — I too should feel that a deprivation.

Hedda. And then, what I found most intolerable of all —

Brack. Well?

Hedda. — was being everlastingly in the company of — one and the same person —

Brack. [With a nod of assent.] Morning, noon, and night, yes — at all possible times and seasons.

Hedda. I said "everlastingly."

Brack. Just so. But I should have thought, with our excellent Tesman, one could —

Hedda. Tesman is — a specialist, my dear Judge.

Brack. Undeniable.

Hedda. And specialists are not at all amusing to travel with. Not in the long run at any rate.

Brack. Not even — the specialist one happens to love?

Hedda. Faugh — don't use that sickening word!

Brack. [Taken aback.] What do you say, Mrs. Hedda?

Hedda. [Half laughing, half irritated.] You should just try it! To hear of nothing but the history of civilisation, morning, noon, and night —

Brack. Everlastingly.

Hedda. Yes yes yes! And then all this about the domestic industry of the middle ages —! That's the most disgusting part of it!

Brack. [Looks searchingly at her.] But tell me — in that case, how am I to understand your —? H'm —

Hedda. My accepting George Tesman, you mean?

Brack. Well, let us put it so.

Hedda. Good heavens, do you see anything so wonderful in that?

Brack. Yes and no — Mrs. Hedda.

Hedda. I had positively danced myself tired, my dear Judge. My day was done —— [With a slight shudder.] Oh no — I won't say that; nor think it either!

Brack. You have assuredly no reason to.

Hedda. Oh, reasons —— [Watching him closely.] And George Tesman — after all, you must admit that he is correctness itself.

Brack. His correctness and respectability are beyond all question.

Hedda. And I don't see anything absolutely ridiculous about him. — Do you?

Brack. Ridiculous? N— no — I shouldn't exactly say so —

Hedda. Well — and his powers of research, at all events, are untiring. — I see no reason why he should not one day come to the front, after all.

Brack. [Looks at her hesitatingly.] I thought that you, like every one else, expected him to attain the highest distinction.

Hedda. [With an expression of fatigue.] Yes, so I did. — And then, since he was bent, at all hazards, on being allowed to provide for me — I really don't know why I should not have accepted his offer?

Brack. No — if you look at it in that light —

Hedda. It was more than my other adorers were prepared to do for me, my dear Judge.

Brack. [Laughing.] Well, I can't answer for all the rest; but as for myself, you know quite well that I have always entertained a — a certain respect for the marriage tie — for marriage as an institution, Mrs. Hedda.

Hedda. [Jestingly.] Oh, I assure you I have never cherished any hopes with respect to you.

Brack. All I require is a pleasant and intimate interior, where I can make myself useful in every way, and am free to come and go as — as a trusted friend —

Hedda. Of the master of the house, do you mean?

Brack. [Bowing.] Frankly — of the mistress first of all; but of course of the master too, in the second place. Such a triangular friendship — if I may call it so — is really a great convenience for all the parties, let me tell you.

Hedda. Yes, I have many a time longed for some one to make a third on our travels. Oh — those railway-carriage *tete-a-tetes* —!

Brack. Fortunately your wedding journey is over now.

Hedda. [Shaking her head.] Not by a long — long way. I have only arrived at a station on the line.

Brack. Well, then the passengers jump out and move about a little, Mrs. Hedda.

Hedda. I never jump out.

Brack. Really?

Hedda. No — because there is always some one standing by to —

Brack. [Laughing.] To look at your ankles, do you mean?

Hedda. Precisely.

Brack. Well but, dear me —

Hedda. [With a gesture of repulsion.] I won't have it. I would rather keep my seat where I happen to be — and continue the *tete-a-tete*.

Brack. But suppose a third person were to jump in and join the couple.

Hedda. Ah — that is quite another matter!

Brack. A trusted, sympathetic friend —

Hedda. — with a fund of conversation on all sorts of lively topics —

Brack. — and not the least bit of a specialist!

Hedda. [With an audible sigh.] Yes, that would be a relief indeed.

Brack. [Hears the front door open, and glances in that direction.] The triangle is completed.

Hedda. [Half aloud.] And on goes the train.

George Tesman, in a grey walking-suit, with a soft felt hat, enters from the hall. He has a number of unbound books under his arm and in his pockets.

Tesman. [Goes up to the table beside the corner settee.] Ouf — what a load for a warm day — all these books. [Lays them on the table.] I'm positively perspiring, Hedda. Hallo — are you there already, my dear Judge? Eh? Berta didn't tell me.

Brack. [Rising.] I came in through the garden.

Hedda. What books have you got there?

Tesman. [Stands looking them through.] Some new books on my special subjects — quite indispensable to me.

Hedda. Your special subjects?

Brack. Yes, books on his special subjects, Mrs. Tesman.

Brack and *Hedda* exchange a confidential smile.

Hedda. Do you need still more books on your special subjects?

Tesman. Yes, my dear Hedda, one can never have too many of them. Of course one must keep up with all that is written and published.

Hedda. Yes, I suppose one must.

Tesman. [Searching among his books.] And look here — I have got hold of Eilert Lovborg's new book too. [Offering it to her.] Perhaps you would like to glance through it, Hedda? Eh?

Hedda. No, thank you. Or rather — afterwards perhaps.

Tesman. I looked into it a little on the way home.

Brack. Well, what do you think of it — as a specialist?

Tesman. I think it shows quite remarkable soundness of judgment. He never wrote like that before. [Putting the books together.] Now I shall take all these into my study. I'm longing to cut the leaves —! And then I must change my clothes. [To *Brack*.] I suppose we needn't start just yet? Eh?

Brack. Oh, dear no — there is not the slightest hurry.

Tesman. Well then, I will take my time. [Is going with his books, but stops in the doorway and turns.] By-the-bye, Hedda — Aunt Julia is not coming this evening.

Hedda. Not coming? Is it that affair of the bonnet that keeps her away?

Tesman. Oh, not at all. How could you think such a thing of Aunt Julia? Just fancy —! The fact is, Aunt Rina is very ill.

Hedda. She always is.

Tesman. Yes, but today she is much worse than usual, poor dear.

Hedda. Oh, then it's only natural that her sister should remain with her. I must bear my disappointment.

Tesman. And you can't imagine, dear, how delighted Aunt Julia seemed to be — because you had come home looking so flourishing!

Hedda. [Half aloud, rising.] Oh, those everlasting Aunts!

Tesman. What?

Hedda. [Going to the glass door.] Nothing.

Tesman. Oh, all right. [He goes through the inner room, out to the right.

Brack. What bonnet were you talking about?

Hedda. Oh, it was a little episode with Miss Tesman this morning. She had laid down her bonnet on the chair there —[Looks at him and smiles.]— and I pretended to think it was the servant's.

Brack. [Shaking his head.] Now my dear Mrs. Hedda, how could you do such a thing? To the excellent old lady, too!

Hedda. [Nervously crossing the room.] Well, you see — these impulses come over me all of a sudden; and I cannot resist them. [Throws herself down in the easy-chair by the stove.] Oh, I don't know how to explain it.

Brack. [Behind the easy-chair.] You are not really happy — that is at the bottom of it.

Hedda. [Looking straight before her.] I know of no reason why I should be — happy. Perhaps you can give me one?

Brack. Well-amongst other things, because you have got exactly the home you had set your heart on.

Hedda. [Looks up at him and laughs.] Do you too believe in that legend?

Brack. Is there nothing in it, then?

Hedda. Oh yes, there is something in it.

Brack. Well?

Hedda. There is this in it, that I made use of Tesman to see me home from evening parties last summer —

Brack. I, unfortunately, had to go quite a different way.

Hedda. That's true. I know you were going a different way last summer.

Brack. [Laughing.] Oh fie, Mrs. Hedda! Well, then — you and Tesman —?

Hedda. Well, we happened to pass here one evening; Tesman, poor fellow, was writhing in the agony of having to find conversation; so I took pity on the learned man —

Brack. [Smiles doubtfully.] You took pity? H'm —

Hedda. Yes, I really did. And so — to help him out of his torment — I happened to say, in pure thoughtlessness, that I should like to live in this villa.

Brack. No more than that?

Hedda. Not that evening.

Brack. But afterwards?

Hedda. Yes, my thoughtlessness had consequences, my dear Judge.

Brack. Unfortunately that too often happens, Mrs. Hedda.

Hedda. Thanks! So you see it was this enthusiasm for Secretary Falk's villa that first constituted a bond of sympathy between George Tesman and me. From that came our engagement and our marriage, and our wedding journey, and all the rest of it. Well, well, my dear Judge — as you make your bed so you must lie, I could almost say.

Brack. This is exquisite! And you really cared not a rap about it all the time?

Hedda. No, heaven knows I didn't.

Brack. But now? Now that we have made it so homelike for you?

Hedda. Uh — the rooms all seem to smell of lavender and dried rose-leaves. — But perhaps it's Aunt Julia that has brought that scent with her.

Brack. [Laughing.] No, I think it must be a legacy from the late Mrs. Secretary Falk.

Hedda. Yes, there is an odour of mortality about it. It reminds me of a bouquet — the day after the ball. [Clasps her hands behind her head, leans back in her chair and looks at him.] Oh, my dear Judge — you cannot imagine how horribly I shall bore myself here.

Brack. Why should not you, too, find some sort of vocation in life, Mrs. Hedda?

Hedda. A vocation — that should attract me?

Brack. If possible, of course.

Hedda. Heaven knows what sort of a vocation that could be. I often wonder whether —— [Breaking off.] But that would never do either.

Brack. Who can tell? Let me hear what it is.

Hedda. Whether I might not get Tesman to go into politics, I mean.

Brack. [Laughing.] Tesman? No really now, political life is not the thing for him — not at all in his line.

Hedda. No, I daresay not. — But if I could get him into it all the same?

Brack. Why — what satisfaction could you find in that? If he is not fitted for that sort of thing, why should you want to drive him into it?

Hedda. Because I am bored, I tell you! [After a pause.] So you think it quite out of the question that Tesman should ever get into the ministry?

Brack. H'm — you see, my dear Mrs. Hedda — to get into the ministry, he would have to be a tolerably rich man.

Hedda. [Rising impatiently.] Yes, there we have it! It is this genteel poverty I have managed to drop into —! [Crosses the room.] That is what makes life so pitiable! So utterly ludicrous! — For that's what it is.

Brack. Now *I* should say the fault lay elsewhere.

Hedda. Where, then?

Brack. You have never gone through any really stimulating experience.

Hedda. Anything serious, you mean?

Brack. Yes, you may call it so. But now you may perhaps have one in store.

Hedda. [Tossing her head.] Oh, you're thinking of the annoyances about this wretched professorship! But that must be Tesman's own affair. I assure you I shall not waste a thought upon it.

Brack. No, no, I daresay not. But suppose now that what people call — in elegant language — a solemn responsibility were to come upon you? [Smiling.] A new responsibility, Mrs. Hedda?

Hedda. [Angrily.] Be quiet! Nothing of that sort will ever happen!

Brack. [Warily.] We will speak of this again a year hence — at the very outside.

Hedda. [Curtly.] I have no turn for anything of the sort, Judge Brack. No responsibilities for me!

Brack. Are you so unlike the generality of women as to have no turn for duties which —?

Hedda. [Beside the glass door.] Oh, be quiet, I tell you! — I often think there is only one thing in the world I have any turn for.

Brack. [Drawing near to her.] And what is that, if I may ask?

Hedda. [Stands looking out.] Boring myself to death. Now you know it. [Turns, looks towards the inner room, and laughs.] Yes, as I thought! Here comes the Professor.

Brack. [Softly, in a tone of warning.] Come, come, come, Mrs. Hedda!

George Tesman, dressed for the party, with his gloves and hat in his hand, enters from the right through the inner room.

Tesman. Hedda, has no message come from Eilert Lovborg? Eh?

Hedda. No.

Tesman. Then you'll see he'll be here presently.

Brack. Do you really think he will come?

Tesman. Yes, I am almost sure of it. For what you were telling us this morning must have been a mere floating rumour.

Brack. You think so?

Tesman. At any rate, Aunt Julia said she did not believe for a moment that he would ever stand in my way again. Fancy that!

Brack. Well then, that's all right.

Tesman. [Placing his hat and gloves on a chair on the right.] Yes, but you must really let me wait for him as long as possible.

Brack. We have plenty of time yet. None of my guests will arrive before seven or half-past.

Tesman. Then meanwhile we can keep Hedda company, and see what happens. Eh?

Hedda. [Placing *Brack's* hat and overcoat upon the corner settee.] And at the worst Mr. Lovborg can remain here with me.

Brack. [Offering to take his things.] Oh, allow me, Mrs. Tesman! — What do you mean by "At the worst"?

Hedda. If he won't go with you and Tesman.

Tesman. [Looks dubiously at her.] But, Hedda dear — do you think it would quite do for him to remain here with you? Eh? Remember, Aunt Julia can't come.

Hedda. No, but Mrs. Elvsted is coming. We three can have a cup of tea together.

Tesman. Oh yes, that will be all right.

Brack. [Smiling.] And that would perhaps be the safest plan for him.

Hedda. Why so?

Brack. Well, you know, Mrs. Tesman, how you used to gird at my little bachelor parties. You declared they were adapted only for men of the strictest principles.

Hedda. But no doubt Mr. Lovborg's principles are strict enough now. A converted sinner —— [*Berta* appears at the hall door.

Berta. There's a gentleman asking if you are at home, ma'am —

Hedda. Well, show him in.

Tesman. [Softly.] I'm sure it is he! Fancy that!

Eilert Lovborg enters from the hall. He is slim and lean; of the same age as *Tesman*, but looks older and somewhat worn-out. His hair and beard are of a blackish brown, his face long and pale, but with patches of colour on the cheeks. He is dressed in a well-cut black visiting suit, quite new. He has dark gloves and a silk hat. He stops near the door, and makes a rapid bow, seeming somewhat embarrassed.

Tesman. [Goes up to him and shakes him warmly by the hand.] Well, my dear Eilert — so at last we meet again!

Eilert Lovborg. [Speaks in a subdued voice.] Thanks for your letter, Tesman. [Approaching *Hedda.*] Will you too shake hands with me, Mrs. Tesman?

Hedda. [Taking his hand.] I am glad to see you, Mr. Lovborg. [With a motion of her hand.] I don't know whether you two gentlemen —?

Lovborg. [Bowing slightly.] Judge Brack, I think.

Brack. [Doing likewise.] Oh yes — in the old days —

Tesman. [To *Lovborg*, with his hands on his shoulders.] And now you must make yourself entirely at home, Eilert! Mustn't he, Hedda? — For I hear you are going to settle in town again? Eh?

Lovborg. Yes, I am.

Tesman. Quite right, quite right. Let me tell you, I have got hold of your new book; but I haven't had time to read it yet.

Lovborg. You may spare yourself the trouble.

Tesman. Why so?

Lovborg. Because there is very little in it.

Tesman. Just fancy — how can you say so?

Brack. But it has been very much praised, I hear.

Lovborg. That was what I wanted; so I put nothing into the book but what every one would agree with.

Brack. Very wise of you.

Tesman. Well but, my dear Eilert —!

Lovborg. For now I mean to win myself a position again — to make a fresh start.

Tesman. [A little embarrassed.] Ah, that is what you wish to do? Eh?

Lovborg. [Smiling, lays down his hat, and draws a packet wrapped in paper, from his coat pocket.] But when this one appears, George Tesman, you will have to read it. For this is the real book — the book I have put my true self into.

Tesman. Indeed? And what is it?

Lovborg. It is the continuation.

Tesman. The continuation? Of what?

Lovborg. Of the book.

226

Tesman. Of the new book?

Lovborg. Of course.

Tesman. Why, my dear Eilert — does it not come down to our own days?

Lovborg. Yes, it does; and this one deals with the future.

Tesman. With the future! But, good heavens, we know nothing of the future!

Lovborg. No; but there is a thing or two to be said about it all the same. [Opens the packet.] Look here —

Tesman. Why, that's not your handwriting.

Lovborg. I dictated it. [Turning over the pages.] It falls into two sections. The first deals with the civilising forces of the future. And here is the second —[running through the pages towards the end]— forecasting the probable line of development.

Tesman. How odd now! I should never have thought of writing anything of that sort.

Hedda. [At the glass door, drumming on the pane.] H'm —. I daresay not.

Lovborg. [Replacing the manuscript in its paper and laying the packet on the table.] I brought it, thinking I might read you a little of it this evening.

Tesman. That was very good of you, Eilert. But this evening —? [Looking back at *Brack.*] I don't see how we can manage it —

Lovborg. Well then, some other time. There is no hurry.

Brack. I must tell you, Mr. Lovborg — there is a little gathering at my house this evening — mainly in honour of Tesman, you know —

Lovborg. [Looking for his hat.] Oh — then I won't detain you —

Brack. No, but listen — will you not do me the favour of joining us?

Lovborg. [Curtly and decidedly.] No, I can't — thank you very much.

Brack. Oh, nonsense — do! We shall be quite a select little circle. And I assure you we shall have a "lively time," as Mrs. Hed — as Mrs. Tesman says.

Lovborg. I have no doubt of it. But nevertheless —

Brack. And then you might bring your manuscript with you, and read it to Tesman at my house. I could give you a room to yourselves.

Tesman. Yes, think of that, Eilert — why shouldn't you? Eh?

Hedda. [Interposing.] But, Tesman, if Mr. Lovborg would really rather not! I am sure Mr. Lovborg is much more inclined to remain here and have supper with me.

Lovborg. [Looking at her.] With you, Mrs. Tesman?

Hedda. And with Mrs. Elvsted.

Lovborg. Ah —— [Lightly.] I saw her for a moment this morning.

Hedda. Did you? Well, she is coming this evening. So you see you are almost bound to remain, Mr. Lovborg, or she will have no one to see her home.

Lovborg. That's true. Many thanks, Mrs. Tesman — in that case I will remain.

Hedda. Then I have one or two orders to give the servant —

She goes to the hall door and rings. *Berta* enters. *Hedda* talks to her in a whisper, and points towards the inner room. *Berta* nods and goes out again.

Tesman. [At the same time, to *Lovborg*.] Tell me, Eilert — is it this new subject — the future — that you are going to lecture about?

Lovborg. Yes.

Tesman. They told me at the bookseller's that you are going to deliver a course of lectures this autumn.

Lovborg. That is my intention. I hope you won't take it ill, Tesman.

Tesman. Oh no, not in the least! But —?

Lovborg. I can quite understand that it must be very disagreeable to you.

Tesman. [Cast down.] Oh, I can't expect you, out of consideration for me, to —

Lovborg. But I shall wait till you have received your appointment.

Tesman. Will you wait? Yes but — yes but — are you not going to compete with me? Eh?

Lovborg. No; it is only the moral victory I care for.

Tesman. Why, bless me — then Aunt Julia was right after all! Oh yes — I knew it! Hedda! Just fancy — Eilert Lovborg is not going to stand in our way!

Hedda. [Curtly.] Our way? Pray leave me out of the question.

She goes up towards the inner room, where *Berta* is placing a tray with decanters and glasses on the table. *Hedda* nods approval, and comes forward again. *Berta* goes out.

Tesman. [At the same time.] And you, Judge Brack — what do you say to this? Eh?

Brack. Well, I say that a moral victory — h'm — may be all very fine —

Tesman. Yes, certainly. But all the same —

Hedda. [Looking at *Tesman* with a cold smile.] You stand there looking as if you were thunderstruck —

Tesman. Yes — so I am — I almost think —

Brack. Don't you see, Mrs. Tesman, a thunderstorm has just passed over?

Hedda. [Pointing towards the room.] Will you not take a glass of cold punch, gentlemen?

Brack. [Looking at his watch.] A stirrup-cup? Yes, it wouldn't come amiss.

Tesman. A capital idea, Hedda! Just the thing! Now that the weight has been taken off my mind —

Hedda. Will you not join them, Mr. Lovborg?

Lovborg. [With a gesture of refusal.] No, thank you. Nothing for me.

Brack. Why bless me — cold punch is surely not poison.

Lovborg. Perhaps not for everyone.

Hedda. I will deep Mr. Lovborg company in the meantime.

Tesman. Yes, yes, Hedda dear, do.

He and *Brack* go into the inner room, seat themselves, drink punch, smoke cigarettes, and carry on a lively conversation during what follows. *Eilert Lovborg* remains standing beside the stove. *Hedda* goes to the writing-table.

Hedda. [Raising he voice a little.] Do you care to look at some photographs, Mr. Lovborg? You know Tesman and I made a tour in they Tyrol on our way home?

She takes up an album, and places it on the table beside the sofa, in the further corner of which she seats herself. *Eilert Lovborg* approaches, stops, and looks at her. Then he takes a chair and seats himself to her left.

Hedda. [Opening the album.] Do you see this range of mountains, Mr. Lovborg? It's the Ortler group. Tesman has written the name underneath. Here it is: "The Ortler group near Meran."

Lovborg. [Who has never taken his eyes off her, says softly and slowly:] Hedda — Gabler!

Hedda. [Glancing hastily at him.] Ah! Hush!

Lovborg. [Repeats softly.] Hedda Gabler!

Hedda. [Looking at the album.] That was my name in the old days — when we two knew each other.

Lovborg. And I must teach myself never to say Hedda Gabler again — never, as long as I live.

Hedda. [Still turning over the pages.] Yes, you must. And I think you ought to practise in time. The sooner the better, I should say.

Lovborg. [In a tone of indignation.] Hedda Gabler married? And married to — George Tesman!

Hedda. Yes — so the world goes.

Lovborg. Oh, Hedda, Hedda — how could you[14] throw yourself away!

Hedda. [Looks sharply at him.] What? I can't allow this!

Lovborg. What do you mean?

Tesman comes into the room and goes towards the sofa.

Hedda. [Hears him coming and says in an indifferent tone.] And this is a view from the Val d'Ampezzo, Mr. Lovborg. Just look at these peaks! [Looks affectionately up at *Tesman*.] What's the name of these curious peaks, dear?

Tesman. Let me see. Oh, those are the Dolomites.

Hedda. Yes, that's it! — Those are the Dolomites, Mr. Lovborg.

Tesman. Hedda, dear — I only wanted to ask whether I shouldn't bring you a little punch after all? For yourself at any rate — eh?

Hedda. Yes, do, please; and perhaps a few biscuits.

Tesman. No cigarettes?

Hedda. No.

Tesman. Very well.

He goes into the inner room and out to the right. *Brack* sits in the inner room, and keeps an eye from time to time on *Hedda* and *Lovborg*.

Lovborg. [Softly, as before.] Answer me, Hedda — how could you go and do this?

Hedda. [Apparently absorbed in the album.] If you continue to say *du* to me I won't talk to you.

Lovborg. May I not say *du* even when we are alone?

Hedda. No. You may think it; but you mustn't say it.

Lovborg. Ah, I understand. It is an offence against George Tesman, whom you[15] — love.

Hedda. [Glances at him and smiles.] Love? What an idea!

Lovborg. You don't love him then!

Hedda. But I won't hear of any sort of unfaithfulness! Remember that.

Lovborg. Hedda — answer me one thing —

Hedda. Hush! [*Tesman* enters with a small tray from the inner room.

Tesman. Here you are! Isn't this tempting? [He puts the tray on the table.

Hedda. Why do you bring it yourself?

Tesman. [Filling the glasses.] Because I think it's such fun to wait upon you, Hedda.

Hedda. But you have poured out two glasses. Mr. Lovborg said he wouldn't have any —

Tesman. No, but Mrs. Elvsted will soon be here, won't she?

Hedda. Yes, by-the-bye — Mrs. Elvsted —

Tesman. Had you forgotten her? Eh?

Hedda. We were so absorbed in these photographs. [Shows him a picture.] Do you remember this little village?

Tesman. Oh, it's that one just below the Brenner Pass. It was there we passed the night —

Hedda. — and met that lively party of tourists.

Tesman. Yes, that was the place. Fancy — if we could only have had you with us, Eilert! Eh?

He returns to the inner room and sits beside *Brack*.

Lovborg. Answer me one thing, Hedda —

Hedda. Well?

Lovborg. Was there no love in your friendship for me either? Not a spark — not a tinge of love in it?

Hedda. I wonder if there was? To me it seems as though we were two good comrades — two thoroughly intimate friends. [Smilingly.] You especially were frankness itself.

Lovborg. It was you that made me so.

Hedda. As I look back upon it all, I think there was really something beautiful, something fascinating — something daring — in-in that secret intimacy — that comradeship which no living creature so much as dreamed of.

Lovborg. Yes, yes, Hedda! Was there not? — When I used to come to your father's in the afternoon — and the General sat over at the window reading his papers — with his back towards us —

Hedda. And we two on the corner sofa —

Lovborg. Always with the same illustrated paper before us —

Hedda. For want of an album, yes.

Lovborg. Yes, Hedda, and when I made my confessions to you — told you about myself, things that at that time no one else knew! There I would sit and tell you of my escapades — my days and nights of devilment. Oh, Hedda — what was the power in you that forced me to confess these things?

Hedda. Do you think it was any power in me?

Lovborg. How else can I explain it? And all those — those roundabout questions you used to put to me —

Hedda. Which you understood so particularly well —

Lovborg. How could you sit and question me like that? Question me quite frankly —

Hedda. In roundabout terms, please observe.

Lovborg. Yes, but frankly nevertheless. Cross-question me about — all that sort of thing?

Hedda. And how could you answer, Mr. Lovborg?

Lovborg. Yes, that is just what I can't understand — in looking back upon it. But tell me now, Hedda — was there not love at the bottom of our friendship? On your side, did you not feel as though you might purge my stains away — if I made you my confessor? Was it not so?

Hedda. No, not quite.

Lovborg. What was you motive, then?

Hedda. Do think it quite incomprehensible that a young girl — when it can be done — without any one knowing —

Lovborg. Well?

Hedda. — should be glad to have a peep, now and then, into a world which —?

Lovborg. Which —?

Hedda. — which she is forbidden to know anything about?

Lovborg. So that was it?

Hedda. Partly. Partly — I almost think.

Lovborg. Comradeship in the thirst for life. But why should not that, at any rate, have continued?

Hedda. The fault was yours.

Lovborg. It was you that broke with me.

Hedda. Yes, when our friendship threatened to develop into something more serious. Shame upon you, Eilert Lovborg! How could you think of wronging your — your frank comrade.

Lovborg. [Clenches his hands.] Oh, why did you not carry out your threat? Why did you not shoot me down?

Hedda. Because I have such a dread of scandal.

Lovborg. Yes, Hedda, you are a coward at heart.

Hedda. A terrible coward. [Changing her tone.] But it was a lucky thing for you. And now you have found ample consolation at the Elvsteds'.

Lovborg. I know what Thea has confided to you.

Hedda. And perhaps you have confided to her something about us?

Lovborg. Not a word. She is too stupid to understand anything of that sort.

Hedda. Stupid?

Lovborg. She is stupid about matters of that sort.

Hedda. And I am cowardly. [Bends over towards him, without looking him in the face, and says more softly:] But now I will confide something to you.

Lovborg. [Eagerly.] Well?

Hedda. The fact that I dared not shoot you down —

Lovborg. Yes!

Hedda. — that was not my arrant cowardice — that evening.

Lovborg. [Looks at her a moment, understands, and whispers passionately.] Oh, Hedda! Hedda Gabler! Now I begin to see a hidden reason beneath our comradeship! You[16] and I—! After all, then, it was your craving for life —

Hedda. [Softly, with a sharp glance.] Take care! Believe nothing of the sort!

Twilight has begun to fall. The hall door is opened from without by *Berta.*

Hedda. [Closes the album with a bang and calls smilingly:] Ah, at last! My darling Thea — come along!

Mrs. Elvsted enters from the hall. She is in evening dress. The door is closed behind her.

Hedda. [On the sofa, stretches out her arms towards her.] My sweet Thea — you can't think how I have been longing for you!

Mrs. Elvsted, in passing, exchanges slight salutations with the gentlemen in the inner room, then goes up to the table and gives *Hedda* her hand. *Eilert Lovborg* has risen. He and *Mrs. Elvsted* greet each other with a silent nod.

Mrs. Elvsted. Ought I to go in and talk to your husband for a moment?

Hedda. Oh, not at all. Leave those two alone. They will soon be going.

Mrs. Elvsted. Are they going out?

Hedda. Yes, to a supper-party.

Mrs. Elvsted. [Quickly, to *Lovborg*.] Not you?

Lovborg. No.

Hedda. Mr. Lovborg remains with us.

Mrs. Elvsted. [Takes a chair and is about to seat herself at his side.] Oh, how nice it is here!

Hedda. No, thank you, my little Thea! Not there! You'll be good enough to come over here to me. I will sit between you.

Mrs. Elvsted. Yes, just as you please.

She goes round the table and seats herself on the sofa on *Hedda's* right. *Lovborg* re-seats himself on his chair.

Lovborg. [After a short pause, to *Hedda*.] Is not she lovely to look at?

Hedda. [Lightly stroking her hair.] Only to look at!

Lovborg. Yes. For we two — she and I— we are two real comrades. We have absolute faith in each other; so we can sit and talk with perfect frankness —

Hedda. Not round about, Mr. Lovborg?

Lovborg. Well —

Mrs. Elvsted. [Softly clinging close to *Hedda*.] Oh, how happy I am, Hedda! For only think, he says I have inspired him too.

Hedda. [Looks at her with a smile.] Ah! Does he say that, dear?

Lovborg. And then she is so brave, Mrs. Tesman!

Mrs. Elvsted. Good heavens — am I brave?

Lovborg. Exceedingly — where your comrade is concerned.

Hedda. Exceedingly — where your comrade is concerned.

Hedda. Ah, yes — courage! If one only had that!

Lovborg. What then? What do you mean?

Hedda. Then life would perhaps be liveable, after all. [With a sudden change of tone.] But now, my dearest Thea, you really must have a glass of cold punch.

Mrs. Elvsted. No, thanks — I never take anything of that kind.

Hedda. Well then, you, Mr. Lovborg.

Lovborg. Nor I, thank you.

Mrs. Elvsted. No, he doesn't either.

Hedda. [Looks fixedly at him.] But if I say you shall?

Lovborg. It would be of no use.

Hedda. [Laughing.] Then I, poor creature, have no sort of power over you?

Lovborg. Not in that respect.

Hedda. But seriously, I think you ought to — for your own sake.

Mrs. Elvsted. Why, Hedda —!

Lovborg. How so?

Hedda. Or rather on account of other people.

Lovborg. Indeed?

Hedda. Otherwise people might be apt to suspect that — in your heart of hearts — you did not feel quite secure — quite confident in yourself.

Mrs. Elvsted. [Softly.] Oh please, Hedda —!

Lovborg. People may suspect what they like — for the present.

Mrs. Elvsted. [Joyfully.] Yes, let them!

Hedda. I saw it plainly in Judge Brack's face a moment ago.

Lovborg. What did you see?

Hedda. His contemptuous smile, when you dared not go with them into the inner room.

Lovborg. Dared not? Of course I preferred to stop here and talk to you.

Mrs. Elvsted. What could be more natural, Hedda?

Hedda. But the Judge could not guess that. And I say, too, the way he smiled and glanced at Tesman when you dared not accept his invitation to this wretched little supper-party of his.

Lovborg. Dared not! Do you say I dared not?

Hedda. I don't say so. But that was how Judge Brack understood it.

Lovborg. Well, let him.

Hedda. Then you are not going with them?

Lovborg. I will stay here with you and Thea.

Mrs. Elvsted. Yes, Hedda — how can you doubt that?

Hedda. [Smiles and nods approvingly to *Lovborg*.] Firm as a rock! Faithful to your principles, now and for ever! Ah, that is how a man should be! [Turns to *Mrs. Elvsted* and caresses her.] Well now, what did I tell you, when you came to us this morning in such a state of distraction —

Lovborg. [Surprised.] Distraction!

Mrs. Elvsted. [Terrified.] Hedda — oh Hedda —!

Hedda. You can see for yourself! You haven't the slightest reason to be in such mortal terror — — [Interrupting herself.] There! Now we can all three enjoy ourselves!

Lovborg. [Who has given a start.] Ah — what is all this, Mrs. Tesman?

Mrs. Elvsted. Oh my God, Hedda! What are you saying? What are you doing?

Hedda. Don't get excited! That horrid Judge Brack is sitting watching you.

Lovborg. So she was in mortal terror! On my account!

Mrs. Elvsted. [Softly and piteously.] Oh, Hedda — now you have ruined everything!

Lovborg. [Looks fixedly at her for a moment. His face is distorted.] So that was my comrade's frank confidence in me?

Mrs. Elvsted. [Imploringly.] Oh, my dearest friend — only let me tell you —

Lovborg. [Takes one of the glasses of punch, raises it to his lips, and says in a low, husky voice.] Your health, Thea!

He empties the glass, puts it down, and takes the second.

Mrs. Elvsted. [Softly.] Oh, Hedda, Hedda — how could you do this?

Hedda. I do it? *I*? Are you crazy?

Lovborg. Here's to your health too, Mrs. Tesman. Thanks for the truth. Hurrah for the truth!

He empties the glass and is about to re-fill it.

Hedda. [Lays her hand on his arm.] Come, come — no more for the present. Remember you are going out to supper.

Mrs. Elvsted. No, no, no!

Hedda. Hush! They are sitting watching you.

Lovborg. [Putting down the glass.] Now, Thea — tell me the truth —

Mrs. Elvsted. Yes.

Lovborg. Did your husband know that you had come after me?

Mrs. Elvsted. [Wringing her hands.] Oh, Hedda — do you hear what his is asking?

Lovborg. Was it arranged between you and him that you were to come to town and look after me? Perhaps it was the Sheriff himself that urged you to come? Aha, my dear — no doubt he wanted my help in his office! Or was it at the card-table that he missed me?

Mrs. Elvsted. [Softly, in agony.] Oh, Lovborg, Lovborg —!

Lovborg. [Seizes a glass and is on the point of filling it.] Here's a glass for the old Sheriff too!

Hedda. [Preventing him.] No more just now. Remember, you have to read your manuscript to Tesman.

Lovborg. [Calmly, putting down the glass.] It was stupid of me all this. Thea — to take it in this way, I mean. Don't be angry with me, my dear, dear comrade. You shall see — both you and the others — that if I was fallen once — now I have risen again! Thanks to you, Thea.

Mrs. Elvsted. [Radiant with joy.] Oh, heaven be praised —!

Brack has in the meantime looked at his watch. He and *Tesman* rise and come into the drawing-room.

Brack. [Takes his hat and overcoat.] Well, Mrs. Tesman, our time has come.

Hedda. I suppose it has.

Lovborg. [Rising.] Mine too, Judge Brack.

Mrs. Elvsted. [Softly and imploringly.] Oh, Lovborg, don't do it!

Hedda. [Pinching her arm.] They can hear you!

Mrs. Elvsted. [With a suppressed shriek.] Ow!

Lovborg. [To *Brack*.] You were good enough to invite me.

Judge Brack. Well, are you coming after all?

Lovborg. Yes, many thanks.

Brack. I'm delighted —

Lovborg. [To *Tesman*, putting the parcel of MS. in his pocket.] I should like to show you one or two things before I send it to the printers.

Tesman. Fancy — that will be delightful. But, Hedda dear, how is Mrs. Elvsted to get home? Eh?

Hedda. Oh, that can be managed somehow.

Lovborg. [Looking towards the ladies.] Mrs. Elvsted? Of course, I'll come again and fetch her. [Approaching.] At ten or thereabouts, Mrs. Tesman? Will that do?

Hedda. Certainly. That will do capitally.

Tesman. Well, then, that's all right. But you must not expect me so early, Hedda.

Hedda. Oh, you may stop as long — as long as every you please.

Mrs. Elvsted. [Trying to conceal her anxiety.] Well then, Mr. Lovborg — I shall remain here until you come.

Lovborg. [With his hat in his hand.] Pray do, Mrs. Elvsted.

Brack. And now off goes the excursion train, gentlemen! I hope we shall have a lively time, as a certain fair lady puts it.

Hedda. Ah, if only the fair lady could be present unseen —!

Brack. Why unseen?

Hedda. In order to hear a little of your liveliness at first hand, Judge Brack.

Brack. [Laughing.] I should not advise the fair lady to try it.

Tesman. [Also laughing.] Come, you're a nice one Hedda! Fancy that!

Brack. Well, good-bye, good-bye, ladies.

Lovborg. [Bowing.] About ten o'clock, then,

Brack, Lovborg, and *Tesman* go out by the hall door. At the same time, *Berta* enters from the inner room with a lighted lamp, which she places on the drawing-room table; she goes out by the way she came.

Mrs. Elvsted. [Who has risen and is wandering restlessly about the room.] Hedda — Hedda — what will come of all this?

Hedda. At ten o'clock — he will be here. I can see him already — with vine-leaves in his hair — flushed and fearless —

Mrs. Elvsted. Oh, I hope he may.

Hedda. And then, you see — then he will have regained control over himself. Then he will be a free man for all his days.

Mrs. Elvsted. Oh God! — if he would only come as you see him now!

Hedda. He will come as I see him — so, and not otherwise! [Rises and approaches *thea.*] You may doubt him as long as you please; *I* believe in him. And now we will try —

Mrs. Elvsted. You have some hidden motive in this, Hedda!

Hedda. Yes, I have. I want for once in my life to have power to mould a human destiny.

Mrs. Elvsted. Have you not the power?

Hedda. I have not — and have never had it.

Mrs. Elvsted. Not your husband's?

Hedda. Do you think that is worth the trouble? Oh, if you could only understand how poor I am. And fate has made you so rich! [Clasps her passionately in her arms.] I think I must burn your hair off after all.

Mrs. Elvsted. Let me go! Let me go! I am afraid of you, Hedda!

Berta. [In the middle doorway.] Tea is laid in the dining-room, ma'am.

Hedda. Very well. We are coming

Mrs. Elvsted. No, no, no! I would rather go home alone! At once!

Hedda. Nonsense! First you shall have a cup of tea, you little stupid. And then — at ten o'clock — Eilert Lovborg will be here — with vine-leaves in his hair.

She drags *Mrs. Elvsted* almost by force to the middle doorway.

[12] "Bagveje" means both "back ways" and "underhand courses."

[13]As this form of address is contrary to English usage, and as the note of familiarity would be lacking in "Mrs. Tesman," Brack may, in stage representation, say "Miss Hedda," thus ignoring her marriage and reverting to the form of address no doubt customarry between them of old.

[14]He uses the familiar *du*.

[15]From this point onward Lovborg use the formal *De*.

[16]In this speech he once more says *du*. Hedda addresses him throughout as *De*.

Act Third

The room at the *Tesmans'*. The curtains are drawn over the middle doorway, and also over the glass door. The lamp, half turned down, and with a shade over it, is burning on the table. In the stove, the door of which stands open, there has been a fire, which is now nearly burnt out.

Mrs. Elvsted, wrapped in a large shawl, and with her feet upon a foot-rest, sits close to the stove, sunk back in the arm-chair. *Hedda*, fully dressed, lies sleeping upon the sofa, with a sofa-blanket over her.

Mrs. Elvsted. [After a pause, suddenly sits up in her chair, and listens eagerly. Then she sinks back again wearily, moaning to herself.] Not yet! — Oh God — oh God — not yet!

Berta slips cautiously in by the hall door. She has a letter in her hand.

Mrs. Elvsted. [Turns and whispers eagerly.] Well — has any one come?

Berta. [Softly.] Yes, a girl has just brought this letter.

Mrs. Elvsted. [Quickly, holding out her hand.] A letter! Give it to me!

Berta. No, it's for Dr. Tesman, ma'am.

Mrs. Elvsted. Oh, indeed.

Berta. It was Miss Tesman's servant that brought it. I'll lay it here on the table.

Mrs. Elvsted. Yes, do.

Berta. [Laying down the letter.] I think I had better put out the lamp. It's smoking.

Mrs. Elvsted. Yes, put it out. It must soon be daylight now.

Berta. [Putting out the lamp.] It is daylight already, ma'am.

Mrs. Elvsted. Yes, broad day! And no one come back yet —!

Berta. Lord bless you, ma'am — I guessed how it would be.

Mrs. Elvsted. You guessed?

Berta. Yes, when I saw that a certain person had come back to town — and that he went off with them. For we've heard enough about that gentleman before now.

Mrs. Elvsted. Don't speak so loud. You will waken Mrs. Tesman.

Berta. [Looks towards the sofa and sighs.] No, no — let her sleep, poor thing. Shan't I put some wood on the fire?

Mrs. Elvsted. Thanks, not for me.

Berta. Oh, very well. [She goes softly out by the hall door.

Hedda. [Is wakened by the shutting of the door, and looks up.] What's that —?

Mrs. Elvsted. It was only the servant.

Hedda. [Looking about her.] Oh, we're here —! Yes, now I remember. [Sits erect upon the sofa, stretches herself, and rubs her eyes.] What o'clock is it, Thea?

Mrs. Elvsted. [Looks at her watch.] It's past seven.

Hedda. When did Tesman come home?

Mrs. Elvsted. He has not come.

Hedda. Not come home yet?

Mrs. Elvsted. [Rising.] No one has come.

Hedda. Think of our watching and waiting here till four in the morning —

Mrs. Elvsted. [Wringing her hands.] And how I watched and waited for him!

Hedda. [Yawns, and says with her hand before her mouth.] Well well — we might have spared ourselves the trouble.

Mrs. Elvsted. Did you get a little sleep?

Hedda. Oh yes; I believe I have slept pretty well. Have you not?

Mrs. Elvsted. Not for a moment. I couldn't, Hedda! — not to save my life.

Hedda. [Rises and goes towards her.] There there there! There's nothing to be so alarmed about. I understand quite well what has happened.

Mrs. Elvsted. Well, what do you think? Won't you tell me?

Hedda. Why, of course it has been a very late affair at Judge Brack's —

Mrs. Elvsted. Yes, yes — that is clear enough. But all the same —

Hedda. And then, you see, Tesman hasn't cared to come home and ring us up in the middle of the night. [Laughing.] Perhaps he wasn't inclined to show himself either — immediately after a jollification.

Mrs. Elvsted. But in that case — where can he have gone?

Hedda. Of course he has gone to his Aunts' and slept there. They have his old room ready for him.

Mrs. Elvsted. No, he can't be with them for a letter has just come for him from Miss Tesman. There it lies.

Hedda. Indeed? [Looks at the address.] Why yes, it's addressed in Aunt Julia's hand. Well then, he has remained at Judge Brack's. And as for Eilert Lovborg — he is sitting, with vine leaves in his hair, reading his manuscript.

Mrs. Elvsted. Oh, Hedda, you are just saying things you don't believe a bit.

Hedda. You really are a little blockhead, Thea.

Mrs. Elvsted. Oh yes, I suppose I am.

Hedda. And how mortally tired you look.

Mrs. Elvsted. Yes, I am mortally tired.

Hedda. Well then, you must do as I tell you. You must go into my room and lie down for a little while.

Mrs. Elvsted. Oh no, no — I shouldn't be able to sleep.

Hedda. I am sure you would.

Mrs. Elvsted. Well, but you husband is certain to come soon now; and then I want to know at once —

Hedda. I shall take care to let you know when he comes.

Mrs. Elvsted. Do you promise me, Hedda?

Hedda. Yes, rely upon me. Just you go in and have a sleep in the meantime.

Mrs. Elvsted. Thanks; then I'll try. [She goes off to the inner room.

Hedda goes up to the glass door and draws back the curtains. The broad daylight streams into the room. Then she takes a little hand-glass from the writing-table, looks at herself in it, and arranges her hair. Next she goes to the hall door and presses the bell-button.

Berta presently appears at the hall door.

Berta. Did you want anything, ma'am?

Hedda. Yes; you must put some more wood in the stove. I am shivering.

Berta. Bless me — I'll make up the fire at once. [She rakes the embers together and lays a piece of wood upon them; then stops and listens.] That was a ring at the front door, ma'am.

Hedda. Then go to the door. I will look after the fire.

Berta. It'll soon burn up. [She goes out by the hall door.

Hedda kneels on the foot-rest and lays some more pieces of wood in the stove.

After a short pause, *George Tesman* enters from the hall. He steals on tiptoe towards the middle doorway and is about to slip through the curtains.

Hedda. [At the stove, without looking up.] Good morning.

Tesman. [Turns.] Hedda! [Approaching her.] Good heavens — are you up so early? Eh?

Hedda. Yes, I am up very early this morning.

Tesman. And I never doubted you were still sound asleep! Fancy that, Hedda!

Hedda. Don't speak so loud. Mrs. Elvsted is resting in my room.

Tesman. Has Mrs. Elvsted been here all night?

Hedda. Yes, since no one came to fetch her.

Tesman. Ah, to be sure.

Hedda. [Closes the door of the stove and rises.] Well, did you enjoy yourselves at Judge Brack's?

Tesman. Have you been anxious about me? Eh?

Hedda. No, I should never think of being anxious. But I asked if you had enjoyed yourself.

Tesman. Oh yes — for once in a way. Especially the beginning of the evening; for then Eilert read me part of his book. We arrived more than an hour too early — fancy that! And Brack had all sorts of arrangements to make — so Eilert read to me.

Hedda. [Seating herself by the table on the right.] Well? Tell me then —

Tesman. [Sitting on a footstool near the stove.] Oh, Hedda, you can't conceive what a book that is going to be! I believe it is one of the most remarkable things that have ever been written. Fancy that!

Hedda. Yes yes; I don't care about that —

Tesman. I must make a confession to you, Hedda. When he had finished reading — a horrid feeling came over me.

Hedda. A horrid feeling?

Tesman. I felt jealous of Eilert for having had it in him to write such a book. Only think, Hedda!

Hedda. Yes, yes, I am thinking!

Tesman. And then how pitiful to think that he — with all his gifts — should be irreclaimable, after all.

Hedda. I suppose you mean that he has more courage than the rest?

Tesman. No, not at all — I mean that he is incapable of taking his pleasure in moderation.

Hedda. And what came of it all — in the end?

Tesman. Well, to tell the truth, I think it might best be described as an orgie, Hedda.

Hedda. Had he vine-leaves in his hair?

Tesman. Vine-leaves? No, I saw nothing of the sort. But he made a long, rambling speech in honour of the woman who had inspired him in his work — that was the phrase he used.

Hedda. Did he name her?

Tesman. No, he didn't; but I can't help thinking he meant Mrs. Elvsted. You may be sure he did.

Hedda. Well — where did you part from him?

Tesman. On the way to town. We broke up — the last of us at any rate — all together; and Brack came with us to get a breath of fresh air. And then, you see, we agreed to take Eilert home; for he had had far more than was good for him.

Hedda. I daresay.

Tesman. But now comes the strange part of it, Hedda; or, I should rather say, the melancholy part of it. I declare I am almost ashamed — on Eilert's account — to tell you —

Hedda. Oh, go on —!

Tesman. Well, as we were getting near town, you see, I happened to drop a little behind the others. Only for a minute or two — fancy that!

Hedda. Yes yes yes, but —?

Tesman. And then, as I hurried after them — what do you think I found by the wayside? Eh?

Hedda. Oh, how should I know!

Tesman. You mustn't speak of it to a soul, Hedda! Do you hear! Promise me, for Eilert's sake. [Draws a parcel, wrapped in paper, from his coat pocket.] Fancy, dear — I found this.

Hedda. Is not that the parcel he had with him yesterday?

Tesman. Yes, it is the whole of his precious, irreplaceable manuscript! And he had gone and lost it, and knew nothing about it. Only fancy, Hedda! So deplorably —

Hedda. But why did you not give him back the parcel at once?

Tesman. I didn't dare to — in the state he was then in —

Hedda. Did you not tell any of the others that you had found it?

Tesman. Oh, far from it! You can surely understand that, for Eilert's sake, I wouldn't do that.

Hedda. So no one knows that Eilert Lovborg's manuscript is in your possession?

Tesman. No. And no one must know it.

Hedda. Then what did you say to him afterwards?

Tesman. I didn't talk to him again at all; for when we got in among the streets, he and two or three of the others gave us the slip and disappeared. Fancy that!

Hedda. Indeed! They must have taken him home then.

Tesman. Yes, so it would appear. And Brack, too, left us.

Hedda. And what have you been doing with yourself since?

Tesman. Well, I and some of the others went home with one of the party, a jolly fellow, and took our morning coffee with him; or perhaps I should rather call it our night coffee — eh? But now, when I have rested a little, and given Eilert, poor fellow, time to have his sleep out, I must take this back to him.

Hedda. [Holds out her hand for the packet.] No — don't give it to him! Not in such a hurry, I mean. Let me read it first.

Tesman. No, my dearest Hedda, I mustn't, I really mustn't.

Hedda. You must not?

Tesman. No — for you can imagine what a state of despair he will be in when he wakens and misses the manuscript. He has no copy of it, you must know! He told me so.

Hedda. [Looking searchingly at him.] Can such a thing not be reproduced? Written over again?

Tesman. No, I don't think that would be possible. For the inspiration, you see —

Hedda. Yes, yes — I suppose it depends on that —[Lightly.] But, by-the-bye — here is a letter for you.

Tesman. Fancy —!

Hedda. [Handing it to him.] It came early this morning.

Tesman. It's from Aunt Julia! What can it be? [He lays the packet on the other footstool, opens the letter, runs his eye through it, and jumps up.] Oh, Hedda — she says that poor Aunt Rina is dying!

Hedda. Well, we were prepared for that.

Tesman. And that if I want to see her again, I must make haste. I'll run in to them at once.

Hedda. [Suppressing a smile.] Will you run?

Tesman. Oh, my dearest Hedda — if you could only make up your mind to come with me! Just think!

Hedda. [Rises and says wearily, repelling the idea.] No, no don't ask me. I will not look upon sickness and death. I loathe all sorts of ugliness.

Tesman. Well, well, then —! [Bustling around.] My hat —? My overcoat —? Oh, in the hall —. I do hope I mayn't come too late, Hedda! Eh?

Hedda. Oh, if you run —— [Berta appears at the hall door.

Berta. Judge Brack is at the door, and wishes to know if he may come in.

Tesman. At this time! No, I can't possibly see him.

Hedda. But I can. [To Berta.] Ask Judge Brack to come in. [Berta goes out.

Hedda. [Quickly, whispering.] The parcel, Tesman!

She snatches it up from the stool.

Tesman. Yes, give it to me!

Hedda. No, no, I will keep it till you come back.

She goes to the writing-table and places it in the bookcase. Tesman stands in a flurry of haste, and cannot get his gloves on.

Judge Brack enters from the hall.

Hedda. [Nodding to him.] You are an early bird, I must say.

Brack. Yes, don't you think so! [To Tesman.] Are you on the move, too?

Tesman. Yes, I must rush of to my aunts'. Fancy — the invalid one is lying at death's door, poor creature.

Brack. Dear me, is she indeed? Then on no account let me detain you. At such a critical moment —

Tesman. Yes, I must really rush —— Good-bye! Good-bye!

He hastens out by the hall door.

Hedda. [Approaching.] You seem to have made a particularly lively night of it at your rooms, Judge Brack.

Brack. I assure you I have not had my clothes off, Mrs. Hedda.

Hedda. Not you, either?

Brack. No, as you may see. But what has Tesman been telling you of the night's adventures?

Hedda. Oh, some tiresome story. Only that they went and had coffee somewhere or other.

Brack. I have heard about that coffee-party already. Eilert Lovborg was not with them, I fancy?

Hedda. No, they had taken him home before that.

Brack. Tesman too?

Hedda. No, but some of the others, he said.

Brack. [Smiling.] George Tesman is really an ingenuous creature, Mrs. Hedda.

Hedda. Yes, heaven knows he is. Then is there something behind all this?

Brack. Yes, perhaps there may be.

Hedda. Well then, sit down, my dear Judge, and tell your story in comfort.

She seats herself to the left of the table. *Brack* sits near her, at the long side of the table.

Hedda. Now then?

Brack. I had special reasons for keeping track of my guests — last night.

Hedda. Of Eilert Lovborg among the rest, perhaps?

Brack. Frankly, yes.

Hedda. Now you make me really curious —

Brack. Do you know where he and one or two of the others finished the night, Mrs. Hedda?

Hedda. If it is not quite unmentionable, tell me.

Brack. Oh no, it's not at all unmentionable. Well, they put in an appearance at a particularly animated soiree.

Hedda. Of the lively kind?

Brack. Of the very liveliest —

Hedda. Tell me more of this, Judge Brack —

Brack. Lovborg, as well as the others, had been invited in advance. I knew all about it. But he had declined the invitation; for now, as you know, he has become a new man.

Hedda. Up at the Elvsteds', yes. But he went after all, then?

Brack. Well, you see, Mrs. Hedda — unhappily the spirit moved him at my rooms last evening —

Hedda. Yes, I hear he found inspiration.

Brack. Pretty violent inspiration. Well, I fancy that altered his purpose; for we menfolk are unfortunately not always so firm in our principles as we ought to be.

Hedda. Oh, I am sure you are an exception, Judge Brack. But as to Lovborg —?

Brack. To make a long story short — he landed at last in Mademoiselle Diana's rooms.

Hedda. Mademoiselle Diana's?

Brack. It was Mademoiselle Diana that was giving the soiree, to a select circle of her admirers and her lady friends.

Hedda. Is she a red-haired woman?

Brack. Precisely.

Hedda. A sort of a — singer?

Brack. Oh yes — in her leisure moments. And moreover a mighty huntress — of men — Mrs. Hedda. You have no doubt heard of her. Eilert Lovborg was one of her most enthusiastic protectors — in the days of his glory.

Hedda. And how did all this end?

Brack. Far from amicably, it appears. After a most tender meeting, they seem to have come to blows —

Hedda. Lovborg and she?

Brack. Yes. He accused her or her friends of having robbed him. He declared that his pocket-book had disappeared — and other things as well. In short, he seems to have made a furious disturbance.

Hedda. And what came of it all?

Brack. It came to a general scrimmage, in which the ladies as well as the gentlemen took part. Fortunately the police at last appeared on the scene.

Hedda. The police too?

Brack. Yes. I fancy it will prove a costly frolic for Eilert Lovborg, crazy being that he is.

Hedda. How so?

Brack. He seems to have made a violent resistance — to have hit one of the constables on the head and torn the coat off his back. So they had to march him off to the police-station with the rest.

Hedda. How have you learnt all this?

Brack. From the police themselves.

Hedda. [Gazing straight before her.] So that is what happened. Then he had no vine-leaves in his hair.

Brack. Vine-leaves, Mrs. Hedda?

Hedda. [Changing her tone.] But tell me now, Judge — what is your real reason for tracking out Eilert Lovborg's movements so carefully?

Brack. In the first place, it could not be entirely indifferent to me if it should appear in the police-court that he came straight from my house.

Hedda. Will the matter come into court then?

Brack. Of course. However, I should scarcely have troubled so much about that. But I thought that, as a friend of the family, it was my duty to supply you and Tesman with a full account of his nocturnal exploits.

Hedda. Why so, Judge Brack?

Brack. Why, because I have a shrewd suspicion that he intends to use you as a sort of blind.

Hedda. Oh, how can you think such a thing!

Brack. Good heavens, Mrs. Hedda — we have eyes in our head. Mark my words! This Mrs. Elvsted will be in no hurry to leave town again.

Hedda. Well, even if there should be anything between them, I suppose there are plenty of other places where they could meet.

Brack. Not a single home. Henceforth, as before, every respectable house will be closed against Eilert Lovborg.

Hedda. And so ought mine to be, you mean?

Brack. Yes. I confess it would be more than painful to me if this personage were to be made free of your house. How superfluous, how intrusive, he would be, if he were to force his way into —

Hedda. — into the triangle?

Brack. Precisely. It would simply mean that I should find myself homeless.

Hedda. [Looks at him with a smile.] So you want to be the one cock in the basket[17] — that is your aim.

Brack. [Nods slowly and lowers his voice.] Yes, that is my aim. And for that I will fight — with every weapon I can command.

Hedda. [Her smile vanishing.] I see you are a dangerous person — when it comes to the point.

Brack. Do you think so?

Hedda. I am beginning to think so. And I am exceedingly glad to think — that you have no sort of hold over me.

Brack. [Laughing equivocally.] Well well, Mrs. Hedda — perhaps you are right there. If I had, who knows what I might be capable of?

Hedda. Come come now, Judge Brack! That sounds almost like a threat.

Brack. [Rising.] Oh, not at all! The triangle, you know, ought, if possible, to be spontaneously constructed.

Hedda. There I agree with you.

Brack. Well, now I have said all I had to say; and I had better be getting back to town. Good-bye, Mrs. Hedda. [He goes towards the glass door.

Hedda. [Rising.] Are you going through the garden?

Brack. Yes, it's a short cut for me.

Hedda. And then it is a back way, too.

Brack. Quite so. I have no objection to back ways. They may be piquant enough at times.

Hedda. When there is ball practice going on, you mean?

Brack. [In the doorway, laughing to her.] Oh, people don't shoot their tame poultry, I fancy.

Hedda. [Also laughing.] Oh no, when there is only one cock in the basket —

They exchange laughing nods of farewell. He goes. She closes the door behind him.

Hedda, who has become quite serious, stands for a moment looking out. Presently she goes and peeps through the curtain over the middle doorway. Then she goes to the writing-table, takes *Lovborg's* packet out of the bookcase, and is on the point of looking through its contents. *Berta* is heard speaking loudly in the hall. *Hedda* turns and listens. Then she hastily locks up the packet in the drawer, and lays the key on the inkstand.

Eilert Lovborg, with his greatcoat on and his hat in his hand, tears open the hall door. He looks somewhat confused and irritated.

Lovborg. [Looking towards the hall.] and I tell you I must and will come in! There!

He closes the door, turns, sees *Hedda*, at once regains his self-control, and bows.

Hedda. [At the writing-table.] Well, Mr Lovborg, this is rather a late hour to call for Thea.

Lovborg. You mean rather an early hour to call on you. Pray pardon me.

Hedda. How do you know that she is still here?

Lovborg. They told me at her lodgings that she had been out all night.

Hedda. [Going to the oval table.] Did you notice anything about the people of the house when they said that?

Lovborg. [Looks inquiringly at her.] Notice anything about them?

Hedda. I mean, did they seem to think it odd?

Lovborg. [Suddenly understanding.] Oh yes, of course! I am dragging her down with me! However, I didn't notice anything. — I suppose Tesman is not up yet.

Hedda. No — I think not —

Lovborg. When did he come home?

Hedda. Very late.

Lovborg. Did he tell you anything?

Hedda. Yes, I gathered that you had had an exceedingly jolly evening at Judge Brack's.

Lovborg. Nothing more?

Hedda. I don't think so. However, I was so dreadfully sleepy —

Mrs. Elvsted enters through the curtains of the middle doorway.

Mrs. Elvsted. [Going towards him.] Ah, Lovborg! At last —!

Lovborg. Yes, at last. And too late!

Mrs. Elvsted. [Looks anxiously at him.] What is too late?

Lovborg. Everything is too late now. It is all over with me.

Mrs. Elvsted. Oh no, no — don't say that!

Lovborg. You will say the same when you hear —

Mrs. Elvsted. I won't hear anything!

Hedda. Perhaps you would prefer to talk to her alone? If so, I will leave you.

Lovborg. No, stay — you too. I beg you to stay.

Mrs. Elvsted. Yes, but I won't hear anything, I tell you.

Lovborg. It is not last night's adventures that I want to talk about.

Mrs. Elvsted. What is it then —?

Lovborg. I want to say that now our ways must part.

Mrs. Elvsted. Part!

Hedda. [Involuntarily.] I knew it!

Lovborg. You can be of no more service to me, Thea.

Mrs. Elvsted. How can you stand there and say that! No more service to you! Am I not to help you now, as before? Are we not to go on working together?

Lovborg. Henceforward I shall do no work.

Mrs. Elvsted. [Despairingly.] Then what am I to do with my life?

Lovborg. You must try to live your life as if you had never know me.

Mrs. Elvsted. But you know I cannot do that!

Lovborg. Try if you cannot, Thea. You must go home again —

Mrs. Elvsted. [In vehement protest.] Never in this world! Where you are, there will I be also! I will not let myself be driven away like this! I will remain here! I will be with you when the book appears.

Hedda. [Half aloud, in suspense.] Ah yes — the book!

Lovborg. [Looks at her.] My book and Thea's; for that is what it is.

Mrs. Elvsted. Yes, I feel that it is. And that is why I have a right to be with you when it appears! I will see with my own eyes how respect and honour pour in upon you afresh. And the happiness — the happiness — oh, I must share it with you!

Lovborg. Thea — our book will never appear.

Hedda. Ah!

Mrs. Elvsted. Never appear!

Lovborg. Can never appear.

Mrs. Elvsted. [In agonised foreboding.] Lovborg — what have you done with the manuscript?

Hedda. [Looks anxiously at him.] Yes, the manuscript —?

Mrs. Elvsted. Where is it?

Lovborg. The manuscript —. Well then — I have torn the manuscript into a thousand pieces.

Mrs. Elvsted. [Shrieks.] Oh no, no —!

Hedda. [Involuntarily.] But that's not —

Lovborg. [Looks at her.] Not true, you think?

Hedda. [Collecting herself.] Oh well, of course — since you say so. But it sounded so improbable —

Lovborg. It is true, all the same.

Mrs. Elvsted. [Wringing her hands.] Oh God — oh God, Hedda — torn his own work to pieces!

Lovborg. I have torn my own life to pieces. So why should I not tear my life-work too —?

Mrs. Elvsted. And you did this last night?

Lovborg. Yes, I tell you! Tore it into a thousand pieces — and scattered them on the fiord — far out. There there is cool sea-water at any rate — let them drift upon it — drift with the current and the wind. And then presently they will sink — deeper and deeper — as I shall, Thea.

Mrs. Elvsted. Do you know, Lovborg, that what you have done with the book — I shall think of it to my dying day as though you had killed a little child.

Lovborg. Yes, you are right. It is a sort of child-murder.

Mrs. Elvsted. How could you, then —! Did not the child belong to me too?

Hedda. [Almost inaudibly.] Ah, the child —

Mrs. Elvsted. [Breathing heavily.] It is all over then. Well well, now I will go, Hedda.

Hedda. But you are not going away from town?

Mrs. Elvsted. Oh, I don't know what I shall do. I see nothing but darkness before me. [She goes out by the hall door.

Hedda. [Stands waiting for a moment.] So you are not going to see her home, Mr. Lovborg?

Lovborg. I? Through the streets? Would you have people see her walking with me?

Hedda. Of course I don't know what else may have happened last night. But is it so utterly irretrievable?

Lovborg. It will not end with last night — I know that perfectly well. And the thing is that now I have no taste for that sort of life either. I won't begin it anew. She has broken my courage and my power of braving life out.

Hedda. [Looking straight before her.] So that pretty little fool has had her fingers in a man's destiny. [Looks at him.] But all the same, how could you treat her so heartlessly.

Lovborg. Oh, don't say that I was heartless!

Hedda. To go and destroy what has filled her whole soul for months and years! You do not call that heartless!

Lovborg. To you I can tell the truth, Hedda.

Hedda. The truth?

Lovborg. First promise me — give me your word — that what I now confide in you Thea shall never know.

Hedda. I give you my word.

Lovborg. Good. Then let me tell you that what I said just now was untrue.

Hedda. About the manuscript?

Lovborg. Yes. I have not torn it to pieces — nor thrown it into the fiord.

Hedda. No, no —. But — where is it then?

Lovborg. I have destroyed it none the less — utterly destroyed it, Hedda!

Hedda. I don't understand.

Lovborg. Thea said that what I had done seemed to her like a child-murder.

Hedda. Yes, so she said.

Lovborg. But to kill his child — that is not the worst thing a father can do to it.

Hedda. Not the worst?

Lovborg. Suppose now, Hedda, that a man — in the small hours of the morning — came home to his child's mother after a night of riot and debauchery, and said: "Listen — I have been here and there — in this place and in that. And I have taken our child with — to this place and to that. And I have lost the child — utterly lost it. The devil knows into what hands it may have fallen — who may have had their clutches on it."

Hedda. Well — but when all is said and done, you know — this was only a book —

Lovborg. Thea's pure soul was in that book.

Hedda. Yes, so I understand.

Lovborg. And you can understand, too, that for her and me together no future is possible.

Hedda. What path do you mean to take then?

Lovborg. None. I will only try to make an end of it all — the sooner the better.

Hedda. [A step nearer him.] Eilert Lovborg — listen to me. — Will you not try to — to do it beautifully?

Lovborg. Beautifully? [Smiling.] With vine-leaves in my hair, as you used to dream in the old days —?

Hedda. No, no. I have lost my faith in the vine-leaves. But beautifully nevertheless! For once in a way! — Good-bye! You must go now — and do not come here any more.

Lovborg. Good-bye, Mrs. Tesman. And give George Tesman my love.

He is on the point of going.

Hedda. No, wait! I must give you a memento to take with you.

She goes to the writing-table and opens the drawer and the pistol-case; then returns to *Lovborg* with one of the pistols.

Lovborg. [Looks at her.] This? Is this the memento?

Hedda. [Nodding slowly.] Do you recognise it? It was aimed at you once.

Lovborg. You should have used it then.

Hedda. Take it — and do you use it now.

Lovborg. [Puts the pistol in his breast pocket.] Thanks!

Hedda. And beautifully, Eilert Lovborg. Promise me that!

Lovborg. Good-bye, Hedda Gabler. [He goes out by the hall door.

Hedda listens for a moment at the door. Then she goes up to the writing-table, takes out the packet of manuscript, peeps under the cover, draws a few of the sheets half out, and looks at them. Next she goes over and seats herself in the arm-chair beside the stove, with the packet in her lap. Presently she opens the stove door, and then the packet.

Hedda. [Throws one of the quires into the fire and whispers to herself.] Now I am burning your child, Thea! — Burning it, curly-locks! [Throwing one or two more quires into the stove.] Your child and Eilert Lovborg's. [Throws the rest in.] I am burning — I am burning your child.

[17] "Enest hane i kurven" — a proverbial saying.

Act Fourth

The same rooms at the *Tesmans'*. It is evening. The drawing-room is in darkness. The back room is light by the hanging lamp over the table. The curtains over the glass door are drawn close.

Hedda, dressed in black, walks to and fro in the dark room. Then she goes into the back room and disappears for a moment to the left. She is heard to strike a few chords on the piano. Presently she comes in sight again, and returns to the drawing-room.

Berta enters from the right, through the inner room, with a lighted lamp, which she places on the table in front of the corner settee in the drawing-room. Her eyes are red with weeping, and she has black ribbons in her cap. She goes quietly and circumspectly out to the right. *Hedda* goes up to the glass door, lifts the curtain a little aside, and looks out into the darkness.

Shortly afterwards, *Miss Tesman*, in mourning, with a bonnet and veil on, comes in from the hall. *Hedda* goes towards her and holds out her hand.

Miss Tesman. Yes, Hedda, here I am, in mourning and forlorn; for now my poor sister has at last found peace.

Hedda. I have heard the news already, as you see. Tesman sent me a card.

Miss Tesman. Yes, he promised me he would. But nevertheless I thought that to Hedda — here in the house of life — I ought myself to bring the tidings of death.

Hedda. That was very kind of you.

Miss Tesman. Ah, Rina ought not to have left us just now. This is not the time for Hedda's house to be a house of mourning.

Hedda. [Changing the subject.] She died quite peacefully, did she not, Miss Tesman?

Miss Tesman. Oh, her end was so calm, so beautiful. And then she had the unspeakable happiness of seeing George once more — and bidding him good-bye. — Has he not come home yet?

Hedda. No. He wrote that he might be detained. But won't you sit down?

Miss Tesman. No thank you, my dear, dear Hedda. I should like to, but I have so much to do. I must prepare my dear one for her rest as well as I can. She shall go to her grave looking her best.

Hedda. Can I not help you in any way?

Miss Tesman. Oh, you must not think of it! Hedda Tesman must have no hand in such mournful work. Nor let her thought dwell on it either — not at this time.

Hedda. One is not always mistress of one's thoughts —

Miss Tesman. [Continuing.] Ah yes, it is the way of the world. At home we shall be sewing a shroud; and here there will soon be sewing too, I suppose — but of another sort, thank God!

George Tesman enters by the hall door.

Hedda. Ah, you have come at last!

Tesman. You here, Aunt Julia? With Hedda? Fancy that!

Miss Tesman. I was just going, my dear boy. Well, have you done all you promised?

Tesman. No; I'm really afraid I have forgotten half of it. I must come to you again tomorrow. To-day my brain is all in a whirl. I can't keep my thoughts together.

Miss Tesman. Why, my dear George, you mustn't take it in this way.

Tesman. Mustn't —? How do you mean?

Miss Tesman. Even in your sorrow you must rejoice, as I do — rejoice that she is at rest.

Tesman. Oh yes, yes — you are thinking of Aunt Rina.

Hedda. You will feel lonely now, Miss Tesman.

Miss Tesman. Just at first, yes. But that will not last very long, I hope. I daresay I shall soon find an occupant for Rina's little room.

Tesman. Indeed? Who do you think will take it? Eh?

Miss Tesman. Oh, there's always some poor invalid or other in want of nursing, unfortunately.

Hedda. Would you really take such a burden upon you again?

Miss Tesman. A burden! Heaven forgive you, child — it has been no burden to me.

Hedda. But suppose you had a total stranger on your hands —

Miss Tesman. Oh, one soon makes friends with sick folk; and it's such an absolute necessity for me to have some one to live for. Well, heaven be praised, there may soon be something in this house, too, to keep an old aunt busy.

Hedda. Oh, don't trouble about anything here.

Tesman. Yes, just fancy what a nice time we three might have together, if —?

Hedda. If —?

Tesman. [Uneasily.] Oh nothing. It will all come right. Let us hope so — eh?

Miss Tesman. Well well, I daresay you two want to talk to each other. [Smiling.] And perhaps Hedda may have something to tell you too, George. Good-bye! I must go home to Rina. [Turning at the door.] How strange it is to think that now Rina is with me and with my poor brother as well!

Tesman. Yes, fancy that, Aunt Julia! Eh?

Miss Tesman goes out by the hall door.

Hedda. [Follows *Tesman* coldly and searchingly with her eyes.] I almost believe your Aunt Rina's death affects you more than it does your Aunt Julia.

Tesman. Oh, it's not that alone. It's Eilert I am so terribly uneasy about.

Hedda. [Quickly.] Is there anything new about him?

Tesman. I looked in at his rooms this afternoon, intending to tell him the manuscript was in safe keeping.

Hedda. Well, did you find him?

Tesman. No. He wasn't at home. But afterwards I met Mrs. Elvsted, and she told me that he had been here early this morning.

Hedda. Yes, directly after you had gone.

Tesman. And he said that he had torn his manuscript to pieces — eh?

Hedda. Yes, so he declared.

Tesman. Why, good heavens, he must have been completely out of his mind! And I suppose you thought it best not to give it back to him, Hedda?

Hedda. No, he did not get it.

Tesman. But of course you told him that we had it?

Hedda. No. [Quickly.] Did you tell Mrs. Elvsted?

Tesman. No; I thought I had better not. But you ought to have told him. Fancy, if, in desperation, he should go and do himself some injury! Let me have the manuscript, Hedda! I will take it to him at once. Where is it?

Hedda. [Cold and immovable, leaning on the arm-chair.] I have not got it.

Tesman. Have not got it? What in the world do you mean?

Hedda. I have burnt it — every line of it.

Tesman. [With a violent movement of terror.] Burnt! Burnt Eilert's manuscript!

Hedda. Don't scream so. The servant might hear you.

Tesman. Burnt! Why, good God —! No, no, no! It's impossible!

Hedda. It is so, nevertheless.

Tesman. Do you know what you have done, Hedda? It's unlawful appropriation of lost property. Fancy that! Just ask Judge Brack, and he'll tell you what it is.

Hedda. I advise you not to speak of it — either to Judge Brack or to anyone else.

Tesman. But how could you do anything so unheard-of? What put it into your head? What possessed you? Answer me that — eh?

Hedda. [Suppressing an almost imperceptible smile.] I did it for your sake, George.

Tesman. For my sake!

Hedda. This morning, when you told me about what he had read to you —

Tesman. Yes yes — what then?

Hedda. You acknowledged that you envied him his work.

Tesman. Oh, of course I didn't mean that literally.

Hedda. No matter — I could not bear the idea that any one should throw you into the shade.

Tesman. [In an outburst of mingled doubt and joy.] Hedda! Oh, is this true? But — but — I never knew you show your love like that before. Fancy that!

Hedda. Well, I may as well tell you that — just at this time —— [Impatiently breaking off.] No, no; you can ask Aunt Julia. She well tell you, fast enough.

Tesman. Oh, I almost think I understand you, Hedda! [Clasps his hands together.] Great heavens! do you really mean it! Eh?

Hedda. Don't shout so. The servant might hear.

Tesman. [Laughing in irrepressible glee.] The servant! Why, how absurd you are, Hedda. It's only my old Berta! Why, I'll tell Berta myself.

Hedda. [Clenching her hands together in desperation.] Oh, it is killing me, — it is killing me, all this!

Tesman. What is, Hedda? Eh?

Hedda. [Coldly, controlling herself.] All this — absurdity — George.

Tesman. Absurdity! Do you see anything absurd in my being overjoyed at the news! But after all — perhaps I had better not say anything to Berta.

Hedda. Oh — why not that too?

Tesman. No, no, not yet! But I must certainly tell Aunt Julia. And then that you have begun to call me George too! Fancy that! Oh, Aunt Julia will be so happy — so happy!

Hedda. When she hears that I have burnt Eilert Lovborg's manuscript — for your sake?

Tesman. No, by-the-bye — that affair of the manuscript — of course nobody must know about that. But that you love me so much,[18] Hedda — Aunt Julia must really share my joy in that! I wonder, now, whether this sort of thing is usual in young wives? Eh?

Hedda. I think you had better ask Aunt Julia that question too.

Tesman. I will indeed, some time or other. [Looks uneasy and downcast again.] And yet the manuscript — the manuscript! Good God! it is terrible to think what will become of poor Eilert now.

Mrs. Elvsted, dressed as in the first Act, with hat and cloak, enters by the hall door.

Mrs. Elvsted. [Greets them hurriedly, and says in evident agitation.] Oh, dear Hedda, forgive my coming again.

Hedda. What is the matter with you, Thea?

Tesman. Something about Eilert Lovborg again — eh?

Mrs. Elvsted. Yes! I am dreadfully afraid some misfortune has happened to him.

Hedda. [Seized her arm.] Ah — do you think so?

Tesman. Why, good Lord — what makes you think that, Mrs. Elvsted?

Mrs. Elvsted. I heard them talking of him at my boarding-house — just as I came in. Oh, the most incredible rumours are afloat about him today.

Tesman. Yes, fancy, so I heard too! And I can bear witness that he went straight home to bed last night. Fancy that!

Hedda. Well, what did they say at the boarding-house?

Mrs. Elvsted. Oh, I couldn't make out anything clearly. Either they knew nothing definite, or else —. They stopped talking when the saw me; and I did not dare to ask.

Tesman. [Moving about uneasily.] We must hope — we must hope that you misunderstood them, Mrs. Elvsted.

Mrs. Elvsted. No, no; I am sure it was of him they were talking. And I heard something about the hospital or —

Tesman. The hospital?

Hedda. No — surely that cannot be!

Mrs. Elvsted. Oh, I was in such mortal terror! I went to his lodgings and asked for him there.

Hedda. You could make up your mind to that, Thea!

Mrs. Elvsted. What else could I do? I really could bear the suspense no longer.

Tesman. But you didn't find him either — eh?

Mrs. Elvsted. No. And the people knew nothing about him. He hadn't been home since yesterday afternoon, they said.

Tesman. Yesterday! Fancy, how could they say that?

Mrs. Elvsted. Oh, I am sure something terrible must have happened to him.

Tesman. Hedda dear — how would it be if I were to go and make inquiries —?

Hedda. No, no — don't you mix yourself up in this affair.

Judge Brack, with his hat in his hand, enters by the hall door, which *Berta* opens, and closes behind him. He looks grave and bows in silence.

Tesman. Oh, is that you, my dear Judge? Eh?

Brack. Yes. It was imperative I should see you this evening.

Tesman. I can see you have heard the news about Aunt Rina?

Brack. Yes, that among other things.

Tesman. Isn't it sad — eh?

Brack. Well, my dear Tesman, that depends on how you look at it.

Tesman. [Looks doubtfully at him.] Has anything else happened?

Brack. Yes.

Hedda. [In suspense.] Anything sad, Judge Brack?

Brack. That, too, depends on how you look at it, Mrs. Tesman.

Mrs. Elvsted. [Unable to restrain her anxiety.] Oh! it is something about Eilert Lovborg!

Brack. [With a glance at her.] What makes you think that, Madam? Perhaps you have already heard something —?

Mrs. Elvsted. [In confusion.] No, nothing at all, but —

Tesman. Oh, for heaven's sake, tell us!

Brack. [Shrugging his shoulders.] Well, I regret to say Eilert Lovborg has been taken to the hospital. He is lying at the point of death.

Mrs. Elvsted. [Shrieks.] Oh God! oh God —!

Tesman. To the hospital! And at the point of death!

Hedda. [Involuntarily.] So soon then —

Mrs. Elvsted. [Wailing.] And we parted in anger, Hedda!

Hedda. [Whispers.] Thea — Thea — be careful!

Mrs. Elvsted. [Not heeding her.] I must go to him! I must see him alive!

Brack. It is useless, Madam. No one will be admitted.

Mrs. Elvsted. Oh, at least tell me what has happened to him? What is it?

Tesman. You don't mean to say that he has himself —— Eh?

Hedda. Yes, I am sure he has.

Brack. [Keeping his eyes fixed upon her.] Unfortunately you have guessed quite correctly, Mrs. Tesman.

Mrs. Elvsted. Oh, how horrible!

Tesman. Himself, then! Fancy that!

Hedda. Shot himself!

Brack. Rightly guessed again, Mrs. Tesman.

Mrs. Elvsted. [With an effort at self-control.] When did it happen, Mr. Brack?

Brack. This afternoon — between three and four.

Tesman. But, good Lord, where did he do it? Eh?

Brack. [With some hesitation.] Where? Well — I suppose at his lodgings.

Mrs. Elvsted. No, that cannot be; for I was there between six and seven.

Brack. Well then, somewhere else. I don't know exactly. I only know that he was found —. He had shot himself — in the breast.

Mrs. Elvsted. Oh, how terrible! That he should die like that!

Hedda. [To *Brack*.] Was it in the breast?

Brack. Yes — as I told you.

Hedda. Not in the temple?

Brack. In the breast, Mrs. Tesman.

Hedda. Well, well — the breast is a good place, too.

265

Brack. How do you mean, Mrs. Tesman?

Hedda. [Evasively.] Oh, nothing — nothing.

Tesman. And the wound is dangerous, you say — eh?

Brack. Absolutely mortal. The end has probably come by this time.

Mrs. Elvsted. Yes, yes, I feel it. The end! The end! Oh, Hedda —!

Tesman. But tell me, how have you learnt all this?

Brack. [Curtly.] Through one of the police. A man I had some business with.

Hedda. [In a clear voice.] At last a deed worth doing!

Tesman. [Terrified.] Good heavens, Hedda! what are you saying?

Hedda. I say there is beauty in this.

Brack. H'm, Mrs. Tesman —

Mrs. Elvsted. Oh, Hedda, how can you talk of beauty in such an act!

Hedda. Eilert Lovborg has himself made up his account with life. He has had the courage to do — the one right thing.

Mrs. Elvsted. No, you must never think that was how it happened! It must have been in delirium that he did it.

Tesman. In despair!

Hedda. That he did not. I am certain of that.

Mrs. Elvsted. Yes, yes! In delirium! Just as when he tore up our manuscript.

Brack. [Starting.] The manuscript? Has he torn that up?

Mrs. Elvsted. Yes, last night.

Tesman. [Whispers softly.] Oh, Hedda, we shall never get over this.

Brack. H'm, very extraordinary.

Tesman. [Moving about the room.] To think of Eilert going out of the world in this way! And not leaving behind him the book that would have immortalised his name —

Mrs. Elvsted. Oh, if only it could be put together again!

Tesman. Yes, if it only could! I don't know what I would not give —

Mrs. Elvsted. Perhaps it can, Mr. Tesman.

Tesman. What do you mean?

Mrs. Elvsted. [Searches in the pocket of her dress.] Look here. I have kept all the loose notes he used to dictate from.

Hedda. [A step forward.] Ah —!

Tesman. You have kept them, Mrs. Elvsted! Eh?

Mrs. Elvsted. Yes, I have them here. I put them in my pocket when I left home. Here they still are —

Tesman. Oh, do let me see them!

Mrs. Elvsted. [Hands him a bundle of papers.] But they are in such disorder — all mixed up.

Tesman. Fancy, if we could make something out of them, after all! Perhaps if we two put our heads together —

Mrs. Elvsted. Oh yes, at least let us try —

Tesman. We will manage it! We must! I will dedicate my life to this task.

Hedda. You, George? Your life?

Tesman. Yes, or rather all the time I can spare. My own collections must wait in the meantime. Hedda — you understand, eh? I owe this to Eilert's memory.

Hedda. Perhaps.

Tesman. And so, my dear Mrs. Elvsted, we will give our whole minds to it. There is no use in brooding over what can't be undone — eh? We must try to control our grief as much as possible, and —

Mrs. Elvsted. Yes, yes, Mr. Tesman, I will do the best I can.

Tesman. Well then, come here. I can't rest until we have looked through the notes. Where shall we sit? Here? No, in there, in the back room. Excuse me, my dear Judge. Come with me, Mrs. Elvsted.

Mrs. Elvsted. Oh, if only it were possible!

Tesman and *Mrs. Elvsted* go into the back room. She takes off her hat and cloak. They both sit at the table under the hanging lamp, and are soon deep in an eager examination of the papers. *Hedda* crosses to the stove and sits in the arm-chair. Presently *Brack* goes up to her.

Hedda. [In a low voice.] Oh, what a sense of freedom it gives one, this act of Eilert Lovborg's.

Brack. Freedom, Mrs. Hedda? Well, of course, it is a release for him —

Hedda. I mean for me. It gives me a sense of freedom to know that a deed of deliberate courage is still possible in this world — a deed of spontaneous beauty.

Brack. [Smiling.] H'm — my dear Mrs. Hedda —

Hedda. Oh, I know what you are going to say. For you are a kind of specialist too, like — you know!

Brack. [Looking hard at her.] Eilert Lovborg was more to you than perhaps you are willing to admit to yourself. Am I wrong?

Hedda. I don't answer such questions. I only know that Eilert Lovborg has had the courage to live his life after his own fashion. And then — the last great act, with its beauty! Ah! that he should have the will and the strength to turn away from the banquet of life — so early.

Brack. I am sorry, Mrs. Hedda — but I fear I must dispel an amiable illusion.

Hedda. Illusion?

Brack. Which could not have lasted long in any case.

Hedda. What do you mean?

Brack. Eilert Lovborg did not shoot himself — voluntarily.

Hedda. Not voluntarily?

Brack. No. The thing did not happen exactly as I told it.

Hedda. [In suspense.] Have you concealed something? What is it?

Brack. For poor Mrs. Elvsted's sake I idealised the facts a little.

Hedda. What are the facts?

Brack. First, that he is already dead.

Hedda. At the hospital?

Brack. Yes — without regaining consciousness.

Hedda. What more have you concealed?

Brack. This — the event did not happen at his lodgings.

Hedda. Oh, that can make no difference.

Brack. Perhaps it may. For I must tell you — Eilert Lovborg was found shot in-in Mademoiselle Diana's boudoir.

Hedda. [Makes a motion as if to rise, but sinks back again.] That is impossible, Judge Brack! He cannot have been there again today.

Brack. He was there this afternoon. He went there, he said, to demand the return of something which they had taken from him. Talked wildly about a lost child —

Hedda. Ah — so that is why —

Brack. I thought probably he meant his manuscript; but now I hear he destroyed that himself. So I suppose it must have been his pocket-book.

Hedda. Yes, no doubt. And there — there he was found?

Brack. Yes, there. With a pistol in his breast-pocket, discharged. The ball had lodged in a vital part.

Hedda. In the breast — yes?

Brack. No — in the bowels.

Hedda. [Looks up at him with an expression of loathing.] That too! Oh, what curse is it that makes everything I touch turn ludicrous and mean?

Brack. There is one point more, Mrs. Hedda — another disagreeable feature in the affair.

Hedda. And what is that?

Brack. The pistol he carried —

Hedda. [Breathless.] Well? What of it?

Brack. He must have stolen it.

Hedda. [Leaps up.] Stolen it! That is not true! He did not steal it!

Brack. No other explanation is possible. He must have stolen it —. Hush!

Tesman and *Mrs. Elvsted* have risen from the table in the back-room, and come into the drawing-room.

Tesman. [With the papers in both his hands.] Hedda, dear, it is almost impossible to see under that lamp. Think of that!

Hedda. Yes, I am thinking.

Tesman. Would you mind our sitting at you writing-table — eh?

Hedda. If you like. [Quickly.] No, wait! Let me clear it first!

Tesman. Oh, you needn't trouble, Hedda. There is plenty of room.

269

Hedda. No no, let me clear it, I say! I will take these things in and put them on the piano. There!

She has drawn out an object, covered with sheet music, from under the bookcase, places several other pieces of music upon it, and carries the whole into the inner room, to the left. *Tesman* lays the scraps of paper on the writing-table, and moves the lamp there from the corner table. He and Mrs. Elvsted sit down and proceed with their work. *Hedda* returns.

Hedda. [Behind Mrs. Elvsted's chair, gently ruffling her hair.] Well, my sweet Thea — how goes it with Eilert Lovborg's monument?

Mrs. Elvsted. [Looks dispiritedly up at her.] Oh, it will be terribly hard to put in order.

Tesman. We must manage it. I am determined. And arranging other people's papers is just the work for me.

Hedda goes over to the stove, and seats herself on one of the footstools. *Brack* stands over her, leaning on the arm-chair.

Hedda. [Whispers.] What did you say about the pistol?

Brack. [Softly.] That he must have stolen it.

Hedda. Why stolen it?

Brack. Because every other explanation ought to be impossible, Mrs. Hedda.

Hedda. Indeed?

Brack. [Glances at her.] Of course Eilert Lovborg was here this morning. Was he not?

Hedda. Yes.

Brack. Were you alone with him?

Hedda. Part of the time.

Brack. Did you not leave the room whilst he was here?

Hedda. No.

Brack. Try to recollect. Were you not out of the room a moment?

Hedda. Yes, perhaps just a moment — out in the hall.

Brack. And where was you pistol-case during that time?

Hedda. I had it locked up in —

Brack. Well, Mrs. Hedda?

Hedda. The case stood there on the writing-table.

Brack. Have you looked since, to see whether both the pistols are there?

Hedda. No.

Brack. Well, you need not. I saw the pistol found in Lovborg's pocket, and I knew it at once as the one I had seen yesterday — and before, too.

Hedda. Have you it with you?

Brack. No; the police have it.

Hedda. What will the police do with it?

Brack. Search till they find the owner.

Hedda. Do you think they will succeed?

Brack. [Bends over her and whispers.] No, Hedda Gabler — not so long as I say nothing.

Hedda. [Looks frightened at him.] And if you do not say nothing — what then?

Brack. [Shrugs his shoulders.] There is always the possibility that the pistol was stolen.

Hedda. [Firmly.] Death rather than that.

Brack. [Smiling.] People say such things — but they don't do them.

Hedda. [Without replying.] And supposing the pistol was not stolen, and the owner is discovered? What then?

Brack. Well, Hedda — then comes the scandal!

Hedda. The scandal!

Brack. Yes, the scandal — of which you are so mortally afraid. You will, of course, be brought before the court — both you and Mademoiselle Diana. She will have to explain how the thing happened — whether it was an accidental shot or murder. Did the pistol go off as he was trying to take it out of his pocket, to threaten her with? Or did she tear the pistol out of his hand, shoot him, and push it back into his pocket? That would be quite like her; for she is an able-bodied young person, this same Mademoiselle Diana.

Hedda. But *I* have nothing to do with all this repulsive business.

Brack. No. But you will have to answer the question: Why did you give Eilert the pistol? And what conclusions will people draw from the fact that you did give it to him?

Hedda. [Lets her head sink.] That is true. I did not think of that.

Brack. Well, fortunately, there is no danger, so long as I say nothing.

Hedda. [Looks up at him.] So I am in your power, Judge Brack. You have me at your beck and call, from this time forward.

Brack. [Whispers softly.] Dearest Hedda — believe me — I shall not abuse my advantage.

Hedda. I am in your power none the less. Subject to your will and your demands. A slave, a slave then! [Rises impetuously.] No, I cannot endure the thought of that! Never!

Brack. [Looks half-mockingly at her.] People generally get used to the inevitable.

Hedda. [Returns his look.] Yes, perhaps. [She crosses to the writing-table. Suppressing an involuntary smile, she imitates *Tesman's* intonations.] Well? Are you getting on, George? Eh?

Tesman. Heaven knows, dear. In any case it will be the work of months.

Hedda. [As before.] Fancy that! [Passes her hands softly through Mrs. Elvsted's hair.] Doesn't it seem strange to you, Thea? Here are you sitting with Tesman — just as you used to sit with Eilert Lovborg?

Mrs. Elvsted. Ah, if I could only inspire your husband in the same way!

Hedda. Oh, that will come too — in time.

Tesman. Yes, do you know, Hedda — I really think I begin to feel something of the sort. But won't you go and sit with Brack again?

Hedda. Is there nothing I can do to help you two?

Tesman. No, nothing in the world. [Turning his head.] I trust to you to keep Hedda company, my dear Brack.

Brack. [With a glance at *Hedda*.] With the very greatest of pleasure.

Hedda. Thanks. But I am tired this evening. I will go in and lie down a little on the sofa.

Tesman. Yes, do dear — eh?

Hedda goes into the back room and draws the curtains. A short pause. Suddenly she is heard playing a wild dance on the piano.

Mrs. Elvsted. [Starts from her chair.] Oh — what is that?

Tesman. [Runs to the doorway.] Why, my dearest Hedda — don't play dance-music to-night! Just think of Aunt Rina! And of Eilert too!

Hedda. [Puts her head out between the curtains.] And of Aunt Julia. And of all the rest of them. — After this, I will be quiet. [Closes the curtains again.]

Tesman. [At the writing-table.] It's not good for her to see us at this distressing work. I'll tell you what, Mrs. Elvsted — you shall take the empty room at Aunt Julia's, and then I will come over in the evenings, and we can sit and work there — eh?

Hedda. [In the inner room.] I hear what you are saying, Tesman. But how am

I to get through the evenings out here? Tesman.

[Turning over the papers.] Oh, I daresay Judge Brack will be so kind as to look in now and then, even though I am out.

Brack. [In the arm-chair, calls out gaily.] Every blessed evening, with all the pleasure in life, Mrs. Tesman! We shall get on capitally together, we two!

Hedda. [Speaking loud and clear.] Yes, don't you flatter yourself we will, Judge Brack? Now that you are the one cock in the basket —

A shot is heard within. *Tesman, mrs. Elvsted*, and *Brack* leap to their feet.

Tesman. Oh, now she is playing with those pistols again.

He throws back the curtains and runs in, followed by *Mrs. Elvsted. Hedda* lies stretched on the sofa, lifeless. Confusion and cries. *Berta* enters in alarm from the right.

Tesman. [Shrieks to *Brack*.] Shot herself! Shot herself in the temple! Fancy that!

Brack. [Half-fainting in the arm-chair.] Good God! — people don't do such things.

[18] Literally, "That you burn for me."

An Enemy of the People
A play in five acts

Henrik Ibsen

Translated by R. Farquharson Sharp

Table of Contents

Dramatis Personae

ACT I

ACT II

ACT III

ACT IV

ACT V

Dramatis Personae

Dr Thomas Stockmann, Medical Officer of the Municipal Baths.

Mrs. Stockmann, his wife.

Petra [their daughter] a teacher.

Ejlif & Morten [their sons, aged 13 and 10 respectively].

Peter Stockmann [the Doctor's elder brother], Mayor of the

Town and Chief Constable, Chairman of the Baths' Committee, etc.

Morten Kiil, a tanner [Mrs. Stockmann's adoptive father].

Hovstad, editor of the "People's Messenger."

Billing, sub-editor.

Captain Horster.

Aslaksen, a printer.

Men of various conditions and occupations, a few women, and a troop of schoolboys — the audience at a public meeting.

The action takes place in a coastal town in southern Norway,

ACT I

[SCENE. — DR. STOCKMANN'S sitting-room. It is evening. The room is plainly but neatly appointed and furnished. In the right-hand wall are two doors; the farther leads out to the hall, the nearer to the doctor's study. In the left-hand wall, opposite the door leading to the hall, is a door leading to the other rooms occupied by the family. In the middle of the same wall stands the stove, and, further forward, a couch with a looking-glass hanging over it and an oval table in front of it. On the table, a lighted lamp, with a lampshade. At the back of the room, an open door leads to the dining-room. BILLING is seen sitting at the dining table, on which a lamp is burning. He has a napkin tucked under his chin, and MRS. STOCKMANN is standing by the table handing him a large plate-full of roast beef. The other places at the table are empty, and the table somewhat in disorder, evidently a meal having recently been finished.]

Mrs Stockmann. You see, if you come an hour late, Mr. Billing, you have to put up with cold meat.

Billing [as he eats]. It is uncommonly good, thank you — remarkably good.

Mrs Stockmann. My husband makes such a point of having his meals punctually, you know.

Billing. That doesn't affect me a bit. Indeed, I almost think I enjoy a meal all the better when I can sit down and eat all by myself, and undisturbed.

Mrs Stockmann. Oh well, as long as you are enjoying it —. [Turns to the hall door, listening.] I expect that is Mr. Hovstad coming too.

Billing. Very likely.

[PETER STOCKMANN comes in. He wears an overcoat and his official hat, and carries a stick.]

Peter Stockmann. Good evening, Katherine.

Mrs Stockmann [coming forward into the sitting-room]. Ah, good evening — is it you? How good of you to come up and see us!

Peter Stockmann. I happened to be passing, and so —[looks into the dining-room]. But you have company with you, I see.

Mrs Stockmann [a little embarrassed]. Oh, no — it was quite by chance he came in. [Hurriedly.] Won't you come in and have something, too?

Peter Stockmann. I! No, thank you. Good gracious — hot meat at night! Not with my digestion,

Mrs Stockmann. Oh, but just once in a way —

Peter Stockmann. No, no, my dear lady; I stick to my tea and bread and butter. It is much more wholesome in the long run — and a little more economical, too.

Mrs Stockmann [smiling]. Now you mustn't think that Thomas and I are spendthrifts.

Peter Stockmann. Not you, my dear; I would never think that of you. [Points to the Doctor's study.] Is he not at home?

Mrs Stockmann. No, he went out for a little turn after supper — he and the boys.

Peter Stockmann. I doubt if that is a wise thing to do. [Listens.] I fancy I hear him coming now.

Mrs Stockmann. No, I don't think it is he. [A knock is heard at the door.] Come in! [HOVSTAD comes in from the hall.] Oh, it is you, Mr. Hovstad!

Hovstad. Yes, I hope you will forgive me, but I was delayed at the printers. Good evening, Mr. Mayor.

Peter Stockmann [bowing a little distantly]. Good evening. You have come on business, no doubt.

Hovstad. Partly. It's about an article for the paper.

Peter Stockmann. So I imagined. I hear my brother has become a prolific contributor to the "People's Messenger."

Hovstad. Yes, he is good enough to write in the "People's Messenger" when he has any home truths to tell.

Mrs Stockmann [to HOVSTAD]. But won't you —? [Points to the dining-room.]

Peter Stockmann. Quite so, quite so. I don't blame him in the least, as a writer, for addressing himself to the quarters where he will find the readiest sympathy. And, besides that, I personally have no reason to bear any ill will to your paper, Mr. Hovstad.

Hovstad. I quite agree with you.

Peter Stockmann. Taking one thing with another, there is an excellent spirit of toleration in the town — an admirable municipal spirit. And it all springs from the fact of our having a great common interest to unite us — an interest that is in an equally high degree the concern of every right-minded citizen

Hovstad. The Baths, yes.

Peter Stockmann. Exactly —— our fine, new, handsome Baths. Mark my words, Mr. Hovstad — the Baths will become the focus of our municipal life! Not a doubt of it!

Mrs Stockmann. That is just what Thomas says.

Peter Stockmann. Think how extraordinarily the place has developed within the last year or two! Money has been flowing in, and there is some life and some business doing in the town. Houses and landed property are rising in value every day.

Hovstad. And unemployment is diminishing,

Peter Stockmann. Yes, that is another thing. The burden on the poor rates has been lightened, to the great relief of the propertied classes; and that relief will be even greater if only we get a really good summer this year, and lots of visitors — plenty of invalids, who will make the Baths talked about.

Hovstad. And there is a good prospect of that, I hear.

Peter Stockmann. It looks very promising. Inquiries about apartments and that sort of thing are reaching us, every day.

Hovstad. Well, the doctor's article will come in very suitably.

Peter Stockmann. Has he been writing something just lately?

Hovstad. This is something he wrote in the winter; a recommendation of the Baths — an account of the excellent sanitary conditions here. But I held the article over, temporarily.

Peter Stockmann. Ah — some little difficulty about it, I suppose?

Hovstad. No, not at all; I thought it would be better to wait until the spring, because it is just at this time that people begin to think seriously about their summer quarters.

Peter Stockmann. Quite right; you were perfectly right, Mr. Hovstad.

Hovstad. Yes, Thomas is really indefatigable when it is a question of the Baths.

Peter Stockmann. Well remember, he is the Medical Officer to the Baths.

Hovstad. Yes, and what is more, they owe their existence to him.

Peter Stockmann. To him? Indeed! It is true I have heard from time to time that some people are of that opinion. At the same time I must say I imagined that I took a modest part in the enterprise,

Mrs Stockmann. Yes, that is what Thomas is always saying.

Hovstad. But who denies it, Mr. Stockmann? You set the thing going and made a practical concern of it; we all know that. I only meant that the idea of it came first from the doctor.

Peter Stockmann. Oh, ideas yes! My brother has had plenty of them in his time — unfortunately. But when it is a question of putting an idea into practical shape, you have to apply to a man of different mettle. Mr. Hovstad. And I certainly should have thought that in this house at least . . .

Mrs Stockmann. My dear Peter —

Hovstad. How can you think that —?

Mrs Stockmann. Won't you go in and have something, Mr. Hovstad? My husband is sure to be back directly.

Hovstad. Thank you, perhaps just a morsel. [Goes into the dining-room.]

Peter Stockmann [lowering his voice a little]. It is a curious thing that these farmers' sons never seem to lose their want of tact.

Mrs Stockmann. Surely it is not worth bothering about! Cannot you and Thomas share the credit as brothers?

Peter Stockmann. I should have thought so; but apparently some people are not satisfied with a share.

Mrs Stockmann. What nonsense! You and Thomas get on so capitally together. [Listens.] There he is at last, I think. [Goes out and opens the door leading to the hall.]

Dr Stockmann [laughing and talking outside]. Look here — here is another guest for you, Katherine. Isn't that jolly! Come in, Captain Horster; hang your coat up on this peg. Ah, you don't wear an overcoat. Just think, Katherine; I met him in the street and could hardly persuade him to come up! [CAPTAIN HORSTER comes into the room and greets MRS. STOCKMANN. He is followed by DR. STOCKMANN.] Come along in, boys. They are ravenously hungry again, you know. Come along, Captain Horster; you must have a slice of beef. [Pushes HORSTER into the dining-room. EJLIF and MORTEN go in after them.]

Mrs Stockmann. But, Thomas, don't you see —?

Dr Stockmann [turning in the doorway]. Oh, is it you, Peter? [Shakes hands with him.] Now that is very delightful.

Peter Stockmann. Unfortunately I must go in a moment —

Dr Stockmann. Rubbish! There is some toddy just coming in. You haven't forgotten the toddy, Katherine?

Mrs Stockmann. Of course not; the water is boiling now. [Goes into the dining-room.]

Peter Stockmann. Toddy too!

Dr Stockmann. Yes, sit down and we will have it comfortably.

Peter Stockmann. Thanks, I never care about an evening's drinking.

Dr Stockmann. But this isn't an evening's drinking.

Peter Stockmann. It seems to me —. [Looks towards the dining-room.] It is extraordinary how they can put away all that food.

Dr Stockmann [rubbing his hands]. Yes, isn't it splendid to see young people eat? They have always got an appetite, you know! That's as it should be. Lots of food — to build up their strength! They are the people who are going to stir up the fermenting forces of the future, Peter.

Peter Stockmann. May I ask what they will find here to "stir up," as you put it?

Dr Stockmann. Ah, you must ask the young people that — when the times comes. We shan't be able to see it, of course. That stands to reason — two old fogies, like us.

Peter Stockmann. Really, really! I must say that is an extremely odd expression to —

Dr Stockmann. Oh, you mustn't take me too literally, Peter. I am so heartily happy and contented, you know. I think it is such an extraordinary piece of good fortune to be in the middle of all this growing, germinating life. It is a splendid time to live in! It is as if a whole new world were being created around one.

Peter Stockmann. Do you really think so?

Dr Stockmann. Ah, naturally you can't appreciate it as keenly as I. You have lived all your life in these surroundings, and your impressions have been blunted. But I, who have been buried all these years in my little corner up north, almost without ever seeing a stranger who might bring new ideas with him — well, in my case it has just the same effect as if I had been transported into the middle of a crowded city.

Peter Stockmann. Oh, a city —!

Dr Stockmann. I know, I know; it is all cramped enough here, compared with many other places. But there is life here — there is promise — there are innumerable things to work for and fight for; and that is the main thing. [Calls.] Katherine, hasn't the postman been here?

Mrs Stockmann [from the dining-room]. No.

Dr Stockmann. And then to be comfortably off, Peter! That is something one learns to value, when one has been on the brink of starvation, as we have.

Peter Stockmann. Oh, surely —

Dr Stockmann. Indeed I can assure you we have often been very hard put to it, up there. And now to be able to live like a lord! Today, for instance, we had roast beef for dinner — and, what is more, for supper too. Won't you come and have a little bit? Or let me show it you, at any rate? Come here —

Peter Stockmann. No, no — not for worlds!

Dr Stockmann. Well, but just come here then. Do you see, we have got a table-cover?

Peter Stockmann. Yes, I noticed it.

Dr Stockmann. And we have got a lamp-shade too. Do you see? All out of Katherine's savings! It makes the room so cosy. Don't you think so? Just stand here for a moment — no, no, not there — just here, that's it! Look now, when you get the light on it altogether. I really think it looks very nice, doesn't it?

Peter Stockmann. Oh, if you can afford luxuries of this kind —

Dr Stockmann. Yes, I can afford it now. Katherine tells me I earn almost as much as we spend.

Peter Stockmann. Almost — yes!

Dr Stockmann. But a scientific man must live in a little bit of style. I am quite sure an ordinary civil servant spends more in a year than I do.

Peter Stockmann. I daresay. A civil servant — a man in a well-paid position . . .

Dr Stockmann. Well, any ordinary merchant, then! A man in that position spends two or three times as much as —

Peter Stockmann. It just depends on circumstances.

Dr Stockmann. At all events I assure you I don't waste money unprofitably. But I can't find it in my heart to deny myself the pleasure of entertaining my friends. I need that sort of thing, you know. I have lived for so long shut out of it all, that it is a necessity of life to me to mix with young, eager, ambitious men, men of liberal and active minds; and that describes every one of those fellows who are enjoying their supper in there. I wish you knew more of Hovstad.

Peter Stockmann. By the way, Hovstad was telling me he was going to print another article of yours.

Dr Stockmann. An article of mine?

Peter Stockmann. Yes, about the Baths. An article you wrote in the winter.

Dr Stockmann. Oh, that one! No, I don't intend that to appear just for the present.

Peter Stockmann. Why not? It seems to me that this would be the most opportune moment.

Dr Stockmann. Yes, very likely — under normal conditions. [Crosses the room.]

Peter Stockmann [following him with his eyes]. Is there anything abnormal about the present conditions?

Dr Stockmann [standing still]. To tell you the truth, Peter, I can't say just at this moment — at all events not tonight. There may be much that is very abnormal about the present conditions — and it is possible there may be nothing abnormal about them at all. It is quite possible it may be merely my imagination.

Peter Stockmann. I must say it all sounds most mysterious. Is there something going on that I am to be kept in ignorance of? I should have imagined that I, as Chairman of the governing body of the Baths —

Dr Stockmann. And I should have imagined that I—. Oh, come, don't let us fly out at one another, Peter.

Peter Stockmann. Heaven forbid! I am not in the habit of flying out at people, as you call it. But I am entitled to request most emphatically that all arrangements shall be made in a businesslike manner, through the proper channels, and shall be dealt with by the legally constituted authorities. I can allow no going behind our backs by any roundabout means.

Dr Stockmann. Have I ever at any time tried to go behind your backs?

Peter Stockmann. You have an ingrained tendency to take your own way, at all events; and, that is almost equally inadmissible in a well ordered community, The individual ought undoubtedly to acquiesce in subordinating himself to the community — or, to speak more accurately, to the authorities who have the care of the community's welfare.

Dr Stockmann. Very likely. But what the deuce has all this got to do with me?

Peter Stockmann. That is exactly what you never appear to be willing to learn, my dear Thomas. But, mark my words, some day you will have to suffer for it — sooner or later. Now I have told you. Good-bye.

Dr Stockmann. Have you taken leave of your senses? You are on the wrong scent altogether.

Peter Stockmann. I am not usually that. You must excuse me now if I— [calls into the dining-room]. Good night, Katherine. Good night, gentlemen. [Goes out.]

Mrs Stockmann [coming from the dining-room]. Has he gone?

Dr Stockmann. Yes, and in such a bad temper.

Mrs Stockmann. But, dear Thomas, what have you been doing to him again?

Dr Stockmann. Nothing at all. And, anyhow, he can't oblige me to make my report before the proper time.

Mrs Stockmann. What have you got to make a report to him about?

Dr Stockmann. Hm! Leave that to me, Katherine. It is an extraordinary thing that the postman doesn't come.

[HOVSTAD, BILLING and HORSTER have got up from the table and come into the sitting-room. EJLIF and MORTEN come in after them.]

Billing [stretching himself]. Ah! — one feels a new man after a meal like that.

Hovstad. The mayor wasn't in a very sweet temper tonight, then.

Dr Stockmann. It is his stomach; he has wretched digestion.

Hovstad. I rather think it was us two of the "People's Messenger" that he couldn't digest.

Mrs Stockmann. I thought you came out of it pretty well with him.

Hovstad. Oh yes; but it isn't anything more than a sort of truce.

Billing. That is just what it is! That word sums up the situation.

Dr Stockmann. We must remember that Peter is a lonely man, poor chap. He has no home comforts of any kind; nothing but everlasting business. And all that infernal weak tea wash that he pours into himself! Now then, my boys, bring chairs up to the table. Aren't we going to have that toddy, Katherine?

Mrs Stockmann [going into the dining-room]. I am just getting it.

Dr Stockmann. Sit down here on the couch beside me, Captain Horster. We so seldom see you. Please sit down, my friends. [They sit down at the table. MRS. STOCKMANN brings a tray, with a spirit-lamp, glasses, bottles, etc., upon it.]

Mrs Stockmann. There you are! This is arrack, and this is rum, and this one is the brandy. Now every one must help themselves.

Dr Stockmann [taking a glass]. We will. [They all mix themselves some toddy.] And let us have the cigars. Ejlif, you know where the box is. And you, Morten, can fetch my pipe. [The two boys go into the room on the right.] I have a suspicion that Ejlif pockets a cigar now and then! — but I take no notice of it. [Calls out.] And my smoking-cap too, Morten. Katherine, you can tell him where I left it. Ah, he has got it. [The boys bring the various things.] Now, my friends. I stick to my pipe, you know. This one has seen plenty of bad weather with me up north. [Touches glasses with them.] Your good health! Ah, it is good to be sitting snug and warm here,

Mrs Stockmann [who sits knitting]. Do you sail soon, Captain Horster?

Horster. I expect to be ready to sail next week.

Mrs Stockmann. I suppose you are going to America?

Horster. Yes, that is the plan.

Mrs Stockmann. Then you won't be able to take part in the coming election?

Horster. Is there going to be an election?

Billing. Didn't you know?

Horster. No, I don't mix myself up with those things.

Billing. But do you not take an interest in public affairs?

Horster. No, I don't know anything about politics.

Billing. All the same, one ought to vote, at any rate.

Horster. Even if one doesn't know anything about what is going on?

Billing. Doesn't know! What do you mean by that? A community is like a ship; everyone ought to be prepared to take the helm.

Horster. Maybe that is all very well on shore; but on board ship it wouldn't work.

Hovstad. It is astonishing how little most sailors care about what goes on on shore.

Billing. Very extraordinary.

Dr Stockmann. Sailors are like birds of passage; they feel equally at home in any latitude. And that is only an additional reason for our being all the more keen, Hovstad. Is there to be anything of public interest in tomorrow's "Messenger"?

Hovstad. Nothing about municipal affairs. But the day after tomorrow I was thinking of printing your article —

Dr Stockmann. Ah, devil take it — my article! Look here, that must wait a bit.

Hovstad. Really? We had just got convenient space for it, and I thought it was just the opportune moment —

Dr Stockmann. Yes, yes, very likely you are right; but it must wait all the same. I will explain to you later. [PETRA comes in from the hall, in hat and cloak and with a bundle of exercise books under her arm.]

Petra. Good evening.

Dr Stockmann. Good evening, Petra; come along.

[Mutual greetings; PETRA takes off her things and puts them down on a chair by the door.]

Petra. And you have all been sitting here enjoying yourselves, while I have been out slaving!

Dr Stockmann. Well, come and enjoy yourself too!

Billing. May I mix a glass for you?

Petra [coming to the table]. Thanks, I would rather do it; you always mix it too strong. But I forgot, father — I have a letter for you. [Goes to the chair where she has laid her things.]

Dr Stockmann. A letter? From whom?

Petra [looking in her coat pocket]. The postman gave it to me just as I was going out.

Dr Stockmann [getting up and going to her]. And you only give to me now!

Petra. I really had not time to run up again. There it is!

Dr Stockmann [seizing the letter]. Let's see, let's see, child! [Looks at the address.] Yes, that's all right!

Mrs Stockmann. Is it the one you have been expecting go anxiously, Thomas?

Dr Stockmann. Yes, it is. I must go to my room now and — Where shall I get a light, Katherine? Is there no lamp in my room again?

Mrs Stockmann. Yes, your lamp is already lit on your desk.

Dr Stockmann. Good, good. Excuse me for a moment — [Goes into his study.]

Petra. What do you suppose it is, mother?

Mrs Stockmann. I don't know; for the last day or two he has always been asking if the postman has not been,

Billing. Probably some country patient.

Petra. Poor old dad! — he will overwork himself soon. [Mixes a glass for herself.] There, that will taste good!

Hovstad. Have you been teaching in the evening school again today?

Petra [sipping from her glass]. Two hours.

Billing. And four hours of school in the morning?

Petra. Five hours.

Mrs Stockmann. And you have still got exercises to correct, I see.

Petra. A whole heap, yes.

Horster. You are pretty full up with work too, it seems to me.

Petra. Yes — but that is good. One is so delightfully tired after it.

Billing. Do you like that?

Petra. Yes, because one sleeps so well then.

Morten. You must be dreadfully wicked, Petra.

Petra. Wicked?

Morten. Yes, because you work so much. Mr. Rorlund says work is a punishment for our sins.

Ejlif. Pooh, what a duffer, you are, to believe a thing like that!

Mrs Stockmann. Come, come, Ejlif!

Billing [laughing]. That's capital!

Hovstad. Don't you want to work as hard as that, Morten?

Morten. No, indeed I don't.

Hovstad. What do you want to be, then?

Morten. I should like best to be a Viking,

Ejlif. You would have to be a pagan then.

Morten. Well, I could become a pagan, couldn't I?

Billing. I agree with you, Morten! My sentiments, exactly.

Mrs Stockmann [signalling to him]. I am sure that is not true, Mr. Billing.

Billing. Yes, I swear it is! I am a pagan, and I am proud of it. Believe me, before long we shall all be pagans.

Morten. And then shall be allowed to do anything we like?

Billing. Well, you'll see, Morten.

Mrs Stockmann. You must go to your room now, boys; I am sure you have some lessons to learn for tomorrow.

Ejlif. I should like so much to stay a little longer —

Mrs Stockmann. No, no; away you go, both of you, [The boys say good night and go into the room on the left.]

Hovstad. Do you really think it can do the boys any harm to hear such things?

Mrs Stockmann. I don't know; but I don't like it.

Petra. But you know, mother, I think you really are wrong about it.

Mrs Stockmann. Maybe, but I don't like it — not in our own home.

Petra. There is so much falsehood both at home and at school. At home one must not speak, and at school we have to stand and tell lies to the children.

Horster. Tell lies?

Petra. Yes, don't you suppose we have to teach them all sorts of things that we don't believe?

Billing. That is perfectly true.

Petra. If only I had the means, I would start a school of my own; and it would be conducted on very different lines.

Billing. Oh, bother the means —!

Horster. Well if you are thinking of that, Miss Stockmann, I shall be delighted to provide you with a schoolroom. The great big old house my father left me is standing almost empty; there is an immense dining-room downstairs —

Petra [laughing]. Thank you very much; but I am afraid nothing will come of it.

Hovstad. No, Miss Petra is much more likely to take to journalism, I expect. By the way, have you had time to do anything with that English story you promised to translate for us?

Petra. No, not yet, but you shall have it in good time.

[DR. STOCKMANN comes in from his room with an open letter in his hand.]

Dr Stockmann [waving the letter]. Well, now the town will have something new to talk about, I can tell you!

Billing. Something new?

Mrs Stockmann. What is this?

Dr Stockmann. A great discovery, Katherine.

Hovstad. Really?

Mrs Stockmann. A discovery of yours?

Dr Stockmann. A discovery of mine. [Walks up and down.] Just let them come saying, as usual, that it is all fancy and a crazy man's imagination! But they will be careful what they say this time, I can tell you!

Petra. But, father, tell us what it is.

Dr Stockmann. Yes, yes — only give me time, and you shall know all about it. If only I had Peter here now! It just shows how we men can go about forming our judgments, when in reality we are as blind as any moles —

Hovstad. What are you driving at, Doctor?

Dr Stockmann [standing still by the table]. Isn't it the universal opinion that our town is a healthy spot?

Hovstad. Certainly.

Dr Stockmann. Quite an unusually healthy spot, in fact — a place that deserves to be recommended in the warmest possible manner either for invalids or for people who are well —

Mrs Stockmann. Yes, but my dear Thomas —

Dr Stockmann. And we have been recommending it and praising it — I have written and written, both in the "Messenger" and in pamphlets . . .

Hovstad. Well, what then?

Dr Stockmann. And the Baths — we have called them the "main artery of the town's life-blood," the "nerve-centre of our town," and the devil knows what else —

Billing. "The town's pulsating heart" was the expression I once used on an important occasion.

Dr Stockmann. Quite so. Well, do you know what they really are, these great, splendid, much praised Baths, that have cost so much money — do you know what they are?

Hovstad. No, what are they?

Mrs Stockmann. Yes, what are they?

Dr Stockmann. The whole place is a pest-house!

Petra. The Baths, father?

Mrs Stockmann [at the same time], Our Baths?

Hovstad. But, Doctor —

Billing. Absolutely incredible!

Dr Stockmann. The whole Bath establishment is a whited, poisoned sepulchre, I tell you — the gravest possible danger to the public health! All the nastiness up at Molledal, all that stinking filth, is infecting the water in the conduit-pipes leading to the reservoir; and the same cursed, filthy poison oozes out on the shore too —

Horster. Where the bathing-place is?

Dr Stockmann. Just there.

Hovstad. How do you come to be so certain of all this, Doctor?

Dr Stockmann. I have investigated the matter most conscientiously. For a long time past I have suspected something of the kind. Last year we had some very strange cases of illness among the visitors — typhoid cases, and cases of gastric fever —

Mrs Stockmann. Yes, that is quite true.

Dr Stockmann. At the time, we supposed the visitors had been infected before they came; but later on, in the winter, I began to have a different opinion; and so I set myself to examine the water, as well as I could.

Mrs Stockmann. Then that is what you have been so busy with?

Dr Stockmann. Indeed I have been busy, Katherine. But here I had none of the necessary scientific apparatus; so I sent samples, both of the drinking-water and of the sea-water, up to the University, to have an accurate analysis made by a chemist.

Hovstad. And have you got that?

Dr Stockmann [showing him the letter]. Here it is! It proves the presence of decomposing organic matter in the water — it is full of infusoria. The water is absolutely dangerous to use, either internally or externally.

Mrs Stockmann. What a mercy you discovered it in time.

Dr Stockmann. You may well say so.

Hovstad. And what do you propose to do now, Doctor?

Dr Stockmann. To see the matter put right, naturally.

Hovstad. Can that be done?

Dr Stockmann. It must be done. Otherwise the Baths will be absolutely useless and wasted. But we need not anticipate that; I have a very clear idea what we shall have to do.

Mrs Stockmann. But why have you kept this all so secret, dear?

Dr Stockmann. Do you suppose I was going to run about the town gossiping about it, before I had absolute proof? No, thank you. I am not such a fool.

Petra. Still, you might have told us —

Dr Stockmann. Not a living soul. But tomorrow you may run around to the old Badger —

Mrs Stockmann. Oh, Thomas! Thomas!

Dr Stockmann. Well, to your grandfather, then. The old boy will have something to be astonished at! I know he thinks I am cracked — and there are lots of other people who think so too, I have noticed. But now these good folks shall see — they shall just see! [Walks about, rubbing his hands.] There will be a nice upset in the town, Katherine; you can't imagine what it will be. All the conduit-pipes will have to be relaid.

Hovstad [getting up]. All the conduit-pipes —?

Dr Stockmann. Yes, of course. The intake is too low down; it will have to be lifted to a position much higher up.

Petra. Then you were right after all.

Dr Stockmann. Ah, you remember, Petra — I wrote opposing the plans before the work was begun. But at that time no one would listen to me. Well, I am going to let them have it now. Of course I have prepared a report for the Baths Committee; I have had it ready for a week, and was only waiting for this to come. [Shows the letter.] Now it shall go off at once. [Goes into his room and comes back with some papers.] Look at that! Four closely written sheets! — and the letter shall go with them. Give me a bit of paper, Katherine — something to wrap them up in. That will do! Now give it to-to-[stamps his foot]— what the deuce is her name? — give it to the maid, and tell her to take it at once to the Mayor.

[Mrs. Stockmann takes the packet and goes out through the dining-room.]

Petra. What do you think Uncle Peter will say, father?

Dr Stockmann. What is there for him to say? I should think he would be very glad that such an important truth has been brought to light.

Hovstad. Will you let me print a short note about your discovery in the "Messenger?"

Dr Stockmann. I shall be very much obliged if you will.

Hovstad. It is very desirable that the public should be informed of it without delay.

Dr Stockmann. Certainly.

Mrs Stockmann [coming back]. She has just gone with it.

Billing. Upon my soul, Doctor, you are going to be the foremost man in the town!

Dr Stockmann [walking about happily]. Nonsense! As a matter of fact I have done nothing more than my duty. I have only made a lucky find — that's all. Still, all the same . . .

Billing. Hovstad, don't you think the town ought to give Dr. Stockmann some sort of testimonial?

Hovstad. I will suggest it, anyway.

Billing. And I will speak to Aslaksen about it.

Dr Stockmann. No, my good friends, don't let us have any of that nonsense. I won't hear anything of the kind. And if the Baths Committee should think of voting me an increase of salary, I will not accept it. Do you hear, Katherine? — I won't accept it.

Mrs Stockmann. You are quite right, Thomas.

Petra [lifting her glass]. Your health, father!

Hovstad and Billing. Your health, Doctor! Good health!

Horster [touches glasses with DR. STOCKMANN]. I hope it will bring you nothing but good luck.

Dr Stockmann. Thank you, thank you, my dear fellows! I feel tremendously happy! It is a splendid thing for a man to be able to feel that he has done a service to his native town and to his fellow-citizens. Hurrah, Katherine! [He puts his arms round her and whirls her round and round, while she protests with laughing cries. They all laugh, clap their hands, and cheer the DOCTOR. The boys put their heads in at the door to see what is going on.]

ACT II

[SCENE — The same. The door into the dining room is shut. It is morning. MRS. STOCKMANN, with a sealed letter in her hand, comes in from the dining room, goes to the door of the DOCTOR'S study, and peeps in.]

Mrs Stockmann. Are you in, Thomas?

Dr Stockmann [from within his room]. Yes, I have just come in. [Comes into the room.] What is it?

Mrs Stockmann. A letter from your brother.

Dr Stockmann. Aha, let us see! [Opens the letter and reads:] "I return herewith the manuscript you sent me" [reads on in a low murmur] H'm! —

Mrs Stockmann. What does he say?

Dr Stockmann [putting the papers in his pocket]. Oh, he only writes that he will come up here himself about midday.

Mrs Stockmann. Well, try and remember to be at home this time.

Dr Stockmann. That will be all right; I have got through all my morning visits.

Mrs Stockmann. I am extremely curious to know how he takes it.

Dr Stockmann. You will see he won't like it's having been I, and not he, that made the discovery.

Mrs Stockmann. Aren't you a little nervous about that?

Dr Stockmann. Oh, he really will be pleased enough, you know. But, at the same time, Peter is so confoundedly afraid of anyone's doing any service to the town except himself.

Mrs Stockmann. I will tell you what, Thomas — you should be good natured, and share the credit of this with him. Couldn't you make out that it was he who set you on the scent of this discovery?

Dr Stockmann. I am quite willing. If only I can get the thing set right. I—

[MORTEN KIIL puts his head in through the door leading from the hall, looks around in an enquiring manner, and chuckles.]

Morten Kiil [slyly]. Is it — is it true?

Mrs Stockmann [going to the door]. Father! — is it you?

Dr Stockmann. Ah, Mr. Kiil — good morning, good morning!

Mrs Stockmann. But come along in.

Morten Kiil. If it is true, I will; if not, I am off.

Dr Stockmann. If what is true?

Morten Kiil. This tale about the water supply, is it true?

Dr Stockmann. Certainly it is true, but how did you come to hear it?

Morten Kiil [coming in]. Petra ran in on her way to the school —

Dr Stockmann. Did she?

Morten Kiil. Yes; and she declares that — I thought she was only making a fool of me — but it isn't like Petra to do that.

Dr Stockmann. Of course not. How could you imagine such a thing!

Morten Kiil. Oh well, it is better never to trust anybody; you may find you have been made a fool of before you know where you are. But it is really true, all the same?

Dr Stockmann. You can depend upon it that it is true. Won't you sit down? [Settles him on the couch.] Isn't it a real bit of luck for the town —

Morten Kiil [suppressing his laughter]. A bit of luck for the town?

Dr Stockmann. Yes, that I made the discovery in good time.

Morten Kiil [as before]. Yes, yes, Yes! — But I should never have thought you the sort of man to pull your own brother's leg like this!

Dr Stockmann. Pull his leg!

Mrs Stockmann. Really, father dear —

Morten Kiil [resting his hands and his chin on the handle of his stick and winking slyly at the DOCTOR]. Let me see, what was the story? Some kind of beast that had got into the water-pipes, wasn't it?

Dr Stockmann. Infusoria — yes.

Morten Kiil. And a lot of these beasts had got in, according to Petra — a tremendous lot.

Dr Stockmann. Certainly; hundreds of thousands of them, probably.

Morten Kiil. But no one can see them — isn't that so?

Dr Stockmann. Yes; you can't see them,

Morten Kiil [with a quiet chuckle]. Damn — it's the finest story I have ever heard!

Dr Stockmann. What do you mean?

Morten Kiil. But you will never get the Mayor to believe a thing like that.

Dr Stockmann. We shall see.

Morten Kiil. Do you think he will be fool enough to —?

Dr Stockmann. I hope the whole town will be fools enough.

Morten Kiil. The whole town! Well, it wouldn't be a bad thing. It would just serve them right, and teach them a lesson. They think themselves so much cleverer than we old fellows. They hounded me out of the council; they did, I tell you — they hounded me out. Now they shall pay for it. You pull their legs too, Thomas!

Dr Stockmann. Really, I—

Morten Kiil. You pull their legs! [Gets up.] If you can work it so that the Mayor and his friends all swallow the same bait, I will give ten pounds to a charity — like a shot!

Dr Stockmann. That is very kind of you.

Morten Kiil. Yes, I haven't got much money to throw away, I can tell you; but, if you can work this, I will give five pounds to a charity at Christmas.

[HOVSTAD comes in by the hall door.]

Hovstad. Good morning! [Stops.] Oh, I beg your pardon

Dr Stockmann. Not at all; come in.

Morten Kiil [with another chuckle]. Oho! — is he in this too?

Hovstad. What do you mean?

Dr Stockmann. Certainly he is.

Morten Kiil. I might have known it! It must get into the papers. You know how to do it, Thomas! Set your wits to work. Now I must go.

Dr Stockmann. Won't you stay a little while?

Morten Kiil. No, I must be off now. You keep up this game for all it is worth; you won't repent it, I'm damned if you will!

[He goes out; MRS. STOCKMANN follows him into the hall.]

Dr Stockmann [laughing]. Just imagine — the old chap doesn't believe a word of all this about the water supply.

Hovstad. Oh that was it, then?

Dr Stockmann. Yes, that was what we were talking about. Perhaps it is the same thing that brings you here?

Hovstad. Yes, it is, Can you spare me a few minutes, Doctor?

Dr Stockmann. As long as you like, my dear fellow.

Hovstad. Have you heard from the Mayor yet?

Dr Stockmann. Not yet. He is coming here later.

Hovstad. I have given the matter a great deal of thought since last night.

Dr Stockmann. Well?

Hovstad. From your point of view, as a doctor and a man of science, this affair of the water supply is an isolated matter. I mean, you do not realise that it involves a great many other things.

Dr Stockmann. How, do you mean? — Let us sit down, my dear fellow. No, sit here on the couch. [HOVSTAD Sits down on the couch, DR. STOCKMANN On a chair on the other side of the table.] Now then. You mean that —?

Hovstad. You said yesterday that the pollution of the water was due to impurities in the soil.

Dr Stockmann. Yes, unquestionably it is due to that poisonous morass up at Molledal.

Hovstad. Begging your pardon, Doctor, I fancy it is due to quite another morass altogether.

Dr Stockmann. What morass?

Hovstad. The morass that the whole life of our town is built on and is rotting in.

Dr Stockmann. What the deuce are you driving at, Hovstad?

Hovstad. The whole of the town's interests have, little by little, got into the hands of a pack of officials.

Dr Stockmann. Oh, come! — they are not all officials.

Hovstad. No, but those that are not officials are at any rate the officials' friends and adherents; it is the wealthy folk, the old families in the town, that have got us entirely in their hands.

Dr Stockmann. Yes, but after all they are men of ability and knowledge.

Hovstad. Did they show any ability or knowledge when they laid the conduit pipes where they are now?

Dr Stockmann. No, of course that was a great piece of stupidity on their part. But that is going to be set right now.

Hovstad. Do you think that will be all such plain sailing?

Dr Stockmann. Plain sailing or no, it has got to be done, anyway.

Hovstad. Yes, provided the press takes up the question.

Dr Stockmann. I don't think that will be necessary, my dear fellow, I am certain my brother —

Hovstad. Excuse me, doctor; I feel bound to tell you I am inclined to take the matter up.

Dr Stockmann. In the paper?

Hovstad. Yes. When I took over the "People's Messenger" my idea was to break up this ring of self-opinionated old fossils who had got hold of all the influence.

Dr Stockmann. But you know you told me yourself what the result had been; you nearly ruined your paper.

Hovstad. Yes, at the time we were obliged to climb down a peg or two, it is quite true — because there was a danger of the whole project of the Baths coming to nothing if they failed us. But now the scheme has been carried through, and we can dispense with these grand gentlemen.

Dr Stockmann. Dispense with them, yes; but, we owe them a great debt of gratitude.

Hovstad. That shall be recognised ungrudgingly, But a journalist of my democratic tendencies cannot let such an opportunity as this slip. The bubble of official infallibility must be pricked. This superstition must be destroyed, like any other.

Dr Stockmann. I am whole-heartedly with you in that, Mr. Hovstad; if it is a superstition, away with it!

Hovstad. I should be very reluctant to bring the Mayor into it, because he is your brother. But I am sure you will agree with me that truth should be the first consideration.

Dr Stockmann. That goes without saying. [With sudden emphasis.] Yes, but — but —

Hovstad. You must not misjudge me. I am neither more self-interested nor more ambitious than most men.

Dr Stockmann. My dear fellow — who suggests anything of the kind?

Hovstad. I am of humble origin, as you know; and that has given me opportunities of knowing what is the most crying need in the humbler ranks of life. It is that they should be allowed some part in the direction of public affairs, Doctor. That is what will develop their faculties and intelligence and self respect —

Dr Stockmann. I quite appreciate that.

Hovstad. Yes — and in my opinion a journalist incurs a heavy responsibility if he neglects a favourable opportunity of emancipating the masses — the humble and oppressed. I know well enough that in exalted circles I shall be called an agitator, and all that sort of thing; but they may call what they like. If only my conscience doesn't reproach me, then —

Dr Stockmann. Quite right! Quite right, Mr. Hovstad. But all the same — devil take it! [A knock is heard at the door.] Come in!

[ASLAKSEN appears at the door. He is poorly but decently dressed, in black, with a slightly crumpled white neckcloth; he wears gloves and has a felt hat in his hand.]

Aslaksen [bowing]. Excuse my taking the liberty, Doctor —

Dr Stockmann [getting up]. Ah, it is you, Aslaksen!

Aslaksen. Yes, Doctor.

Hovstad [standing up]. Is it me you want, Aslaksen?

Aslaksen. No; I didn't know I should find you here. No, it was the Doctor I—

Dr Stockmann. I am quite at your service. What is it?

Aslaksen. Is what I heard from Mr. Billing true, sir — that you mean to improve our water supply?

Dr Stockmann. Yes, for the Baths.

Aslaksen. Quite so, I understand. Well, I have come to say that I will back that up by every means in my power.

Hovstad [to the DOCTOR]. You see!

Dr Stockmann. I shall be very grateful to you, but —

Aslaksen. Because it may be no bad thing to have us small tradesmen at your back. We form, as it were, a compact majority in the town — if we choose. And it is always a good thing to have the majority with you, Doctor.

Dr Stockmann. That is undeniably true; but I confess I don't see why such unusual precautions should be necessary in this case. It seems to me that such a plain, straightforward thing.

Aslaksen. Oh, it may be very desirable, all the same. I know our local authorities so well; officials are not generally very ready to act on proposals that come from other people. That is why I think it would not be at all amiss if we made a little demonstration.

Hovstad. That's right.

Dr Stockmann. Demonstration, did you say? What on earth are you going to make a demonstration about?

Aslaksen. We shall proceed with the greatest moderation, Doctor. Moderation is always my aim; it is the greatest virtue in a citizen — at least, I think so.

Dr Stockmann. It is well known to be a characteristic of yours, Mr. Aslaksen.

Aslaksen. Yes, I think I may pride myself on that. And this matter of the water supply is of the greatest importance to us small tradesmen. The Baths promise to be a regular gold-mine for the town. We shall all make our living out of them, especially those of us who are householders. That is why we will back up the project as strongly as possible. And as I am at present Chairman of the Householders' Association.

Dr Stockmann. Yes —?

Aslaksen. And, what is more, local secretary of the Temperance Society — you know, sir, I suppose, that I am a worker in the temperance cause?

Dr Stockmann. Of course, of course.

Aslaksen. Well, you can understand that I come into contact with a great many people. And as I have the reputation of a temperate and law-abiding citizen — like yourself, Doctor — I have a certain influence in the town, a little bit of power, if I may be allowed to say so.

Dr Stockmann. I know that quite well, Mr. Aslaksen.

Aslaksen. So you see it would be an easy matter for me to set on foot some testimonial, if necessary.

Dr Stockmann. A testimonial?

Aslaksen. Yes, some kind of an address of thanks from the townsmen for your share in a matter of such importance to the community. I need scarcely say that it would have to be drawn up with the greatest regard to moderation, so as not to offend the authorities — who, after all, have the reins in their hands. If we pay strict attention to that, no one can take it amiss, I should think!

Hovstad. Well, and even supposing they didn't like it —

Aslaksen. No, no, no; there must be no discourtesy to the authorities, Mr. Hovstad. It is no use falling foul of those upon whom our welfare so closely depends. I have done that in my time, and no good ever comes of it. But no one can take exception to a reasonable and frank expression of a citizen's views.

Dr Stockmann [shaking him by the hand]. I can't tell you, dear Mr. Aslaksen, how extremely pleased I am to find such hearty support among my fellow-citizens. I am delighted — delighted! Now, you will take a small glass of sherry, eh?

Aslaksen. No, thank you; I never drink alcohol of that kind.

Dr Stockmann. Well, what do you say to a glass of beer, then?

Aslaksen. Nor that either, thank you, Doctor. I never drink anything as early as this. I am going into town now to talk this over with one or two householders, and prepare the ground.

Dr Stockmann. It is tremendously kind of you, Mr. Aslaksen; but I really cannot understand the necessity for all these precautions. It seems to me that the thing should go of itself.

Aslaksen. The authorities are somewhat slow to move, Doctor. Far be it from me to seem to blame them —

Hovstad. We are going to stir them up in the paper tomorrow, Aslaksen.

Aslaksen. But not violently, I trust, Mr. Hovstad. Proceed with moderation, or you will do nothing with them. You may take my advice; I have gathered my experience in the school of life. Well, I must say goodbye, Doctor. You know now that we small tradesmen are at your back at all events, like a solid wall. You have the compact majority on your side Doctor.

Dr Stockmann. I am very much obliged, dear Mr. Aslaksen, [Shakes hands with him.] Goodbye, goodbye.

Aslaksen. Are you going my way, towards the printing-office. Mr. Hovstad?

Hovstad. I will come later; I have something to settle up first.

Aslaksen. Very well. [Bows and goes out; STOCKMANN follows him into the hall.]

Hovstad [as STOCKMANN comes in again]. Well, what do you think of that, Doctor? Don't you think it is high time we stirred a little life into all this slackness and vacillation and cowardice?

Dr Stockmann. Are you referring to Aslaksen?

Hovstad. Yes, I am. He is one of those who are floundering in a bog — decent enough fellow though he may be, otherwise. And most of the people here are in just the same case — see-sawing and edging first to one side and then to the other, so overcome with caution and scruple that they never dare to take any decided step.

Dr Stockmann. Yes, but Aslaksen seemed to me so thoroughly well-intentioned.

Hovstad. There is one thing I esteem higher than that; and that is for a man to be self-reliant and sure of himself.

Dr Stockmann. I think you are perfectly right there.

Hovstad. That is why I want to seize this opportunity, and try if I cannot manage to put a little virility into these well-intentioned people for once. The idol of Authority must be shattered in this town. This gross and inexcusable blunder about the water supply must be brought home to the mind of every municipal voter.

Dr Stockmann. Very well; if you are of opinion that it is for the good of the community, so be it. But not until I have had a talk with my brother.

Hovstad. Anyway, I will get a leading article ready; and if the Mayor refuses to take the matter up —

Dr Stockmann. How can you suppose such a thing possible!

Hovstad. It is conceivable. And in that case —

Dr Stockmann. In that case I promise you —. Look here, in that case you may print my report — every word of it.

Hovstad. May I? Have I your word for it?

Dr Stockmann [giving him the MS.]. Here it is; take it with you. It can do no harm for you to read it through, and you can give it me back later on.

Hovstad. Good, good! That is what I will do. And now goodbye, Doctor.

Dr Stockmann. Goodbye, goodbye. You will see everything will run quite smoothly, Mr. Hovstad — quite smoothly.

Hovstad. Hm! — we shall see. [Bows and goes out.]

Dr Stockmann [opens the dining-room door and looks in]. Katherine! Oh, you are back, Petra?

Petra [coming in]. Yes, I have just come from the school.

Mrs Stockmann [coming in]. Has he not been here yet?

Dr Stockmann. Peter? No, but I have had a long talk with Hovstad. He is quite excited about my discovery, I find it has a much wider bearing than I at first imagined. And he has put his paper at my disposal if necessity should arise.

Mrs Stockmann. Do you think it will?

Dr Stockmann. Not for a moment. But at all events it makes me feel proud to know that I have the liberal-minded independent press on my side. Yes, and just imagine — I have had a visit from the Chairman of the Householders' Association!

Mrs Stockmann. Oh! What did he want?

Dr Stockmann. To offer me his support too. They will support me in a body if it should be necessary. Katherine — do you know what I have got behind me?

Mrs Stockmann. Behind you? No, what have you got behind you?

Dr Stockmann. The compact majority.

Mrs Stockmann. Really? Is that a good thing for you Thomas?

Dr Stockmann. I should think it was a good thing. [Walks up and down rubbing his hands.] By Jove, it's a fine thing to feel this bond of brotherhood between oneself and one's fellow citizens!

Petra. And to be able to do so much that is good and useful, father!

Dr Stockmann. And for one's own native town into the bargain, my child!

Mrs Stockmann. That was a ring at the bell.

Dr Stockmann. It must be he, then. [A knock is heard at the door.] Come in!

Peter Stockmann [comes in from the hall]. Good morning.

Dr Stockmann. Glad to see you, Peter!

Mrs Stockmann. Good morning, Peter, How are you?

Peter Stockmann. So so, thank you. [To DR. STOCKMANN.] I received from you yesterday, after office hours, a report dealing with the condition of the water at the Baths.

Dr Stockmann. Yes. Have you read it?

Peter Stockmann. Yes, I have,

Dr Stockmann. And what have you to say to it?

Peter Stockmann [with a sidelong glance]. Hm! —

Mrs Stockmann. Come along, Petra. [She and PETRA go into the room on the left.]

Peter Stockmann [after a pause]. Was it necessary to make all these investigations behind my back?

Dr Stockmann. Yes, because until I was absolutely certain about it —

Peter Stockmann. Then you mean that you are absolutely certain now?

Dr Stockmann. Surely you are convinced of that.

Peter Stockmann. Is it your intention to bring this document before the Baths Committee as a sort of official communication?

Dr Stockmann. Certainly. Something must be done in the matter — and that quickly.

Peter Stockmann. As usual, you employ violent expressions in your report. You say, amongst other things, that what we offer visitors in our Baths is a permanent supply of poison.

Dr Stockmann. Well, can you describe it any other way, Peter? Just think — water that is poisonous, whether you drink it or bathe in it! And this we offer to the poor sick folk who come to us trustfully and pay us at an exorbitant rate to be made well again!

Peter Stockmann. And your reasoning leads you to this conclusion, that we must build a sewer to draw off the alleged impurities from Molledal and must relay the water conduits.

Dr Stockmann. Yes. Do you see any other way out of it? I don't.

Peter Stockmann. I made a pretext this morning to go and see the town engineer, and, as if only half seriously, broached the subject of these proposals as a thing we might perhaps have to take under consideration some time later on.

Dr Stockmann. Some time later on!

Peter Stockmann. He smiled at what he considered to be my extravagance, naturally. Have you taken the trouble to consider what your proposed alterations would cost? According to the information I obtained, the expenses would probably mount up to fifteen or twenty thousand pounds.

Dr Stockmann. Would it cost so much?

Peter Stockmann. Yes; and the worst part of it would be that the work would take at least two years.

Dr Stockmann. Two years? Two whole years?

Peter Stockmann. At least. And what are we to do with the Baths in the meantime? Close them? Indeed we should be obliged to. And do you suppose anyone would come near the place after it had got out that the water was dangerous?

Dr Stockmann. Yes but, Peter, that is what it is.

Peter Stockmann. And all this at this juncture — just as the Baths are beginning to be known. There are other towns in the neighbourhood with qualifications to attract visitors for bathing purposes. Don't you suppose they would immediately strain every nerve to divert the entire stream of strangers to themselves? Unquestionably they would; and then where should we be? We should probably have to abandon the whole thing, which has cost us so much money-and then you would have ruined your native town.

Dr Stockmann. I— should have ruined —!

Peter Stockmann. It is simply and solely through the Baths that the town has before it any future worth mentioning. You know that just as well as I.

Dr Stockmann. But what do you think ought to be done, then?

Peter Stockmann. Your report has not convinced me that the condition of the water at the Baths is as bad as you represent it to be.

Dr Stockmann. I tell you it is even worse! — or at all events it will be in summer, when the warm weather comes.

Peter Stockmann. As I said, I believe you exaggerate the matter considerably. A capable physician ought to know what measures to take — he ought to be capable of preventing injurious influences or of remedying them if they become obviously persistent.

Dr Stockmann. Well? What more?

Peter Stockmann. The water supply for the Baths is now an established fact, and in consequence must be treated as such. But probably the Committee, at its discretion, will not be disinclined to consider the question of how far it might be possible to introduce certain improvements consistently with a reasonable expenditure.

Dr Stockmann. And do you suppose that I will have anything to do with such a piece of trickery as that?

Peter Stockmann. Trickery!!

Dr Stockmann. Yes, it would be a trick — a fraud, a lie, a downright crime towards the public, towards the whole community!

Peter Stockmann. I have not, as I remarked before, been able to convince myself that there is actually any imminent danger.

Dr Stockmann. You have! It is impossible that you should not be convinced. I know I have represented the facts absolutely truthfully and fairly. And you know it very well, Peter, only you won't acknowledge it. It was owing to your action that both the Baths and the water conduits were built where they are; and that is what you won't acknowledge — that damnable blunder of yours. Pooh! — do you suppose I don't see through you?

Peter Stockmann. And even if that were true? If I perhaps guard my reputation somewhat anxiously, it is in the interests of the town. Without moral authority I am powerless to direct public affairs as seems, to my judgment, to be best for the common good. And on that account — and for various other reasons too — it appears to me to be a matter of importance that your report should not be delivered to the Committee. In the interests of the public, you must withhold it. Then, later on, I will raise the question and we will do our best, privately; but, nothing of this unfortunate affair not a single word of it — must come to the ears of the public.

Dr Stockmann. I am afraid you will not be able to prevent that now, my dear Peter.

Peter Stockmann. It must and shall be prevented.

Dr Stockmann. It is no use, I tell you. There are too many people that know about it.

Peter Stockmann. That know about it? Who? Surely you don't mean those fellows on the "People's Messenger"?

Dr Stockmann. Yes, they know. The liberal-minded independent press is going to see that you do your duty.

Peter Stockmann [after a short pause]. You are an extraordinarily independent man, Thomas. Have you given no thought to the consequences this may have for yourself?

Dr Stockmann. Consequences? — for me?

Peter Stockmann. For you and yours, yes.

Dr Stockmann. What the deuce do you mean?

Peter Stockmann. I believe I have always behaved in a brotherly way to you — haven't I always been ready to oblige or to help you?

Dr Stockmann. Yes, you have, and I am grateful to you for it.

Peter Stockmann. There is no need. Indeed, to some extent I was forced to do so — for my own sake. I always hoped that, if I helped to improve your financial position, I should be able to keep some check on you,

Dr Stockmann. What! Then it was only for your own sake —!

Peter Stockmann. Up to a certain point, yes. It is painful for a man in an official position to have his nearest relative compromising himself time after time.

Dr Stockmann. And do you consider that I do that?

Peter Stockmann. Yes, unfortunately, you do, without even being aware of it. You have a restless, pugnacious, rebellious disposition. And then there is that disastrous propensity of yours to want

305

to write about every sort of possible and impossible thing. The moment an idea comes into your head, you must needs go and write a newspaper article or a whole pamphlet about it.

Dr Stockmann. Well, but is it not the duty of a citizen to let the public share in any new ideas he may have?

Peter Stockmann. Oh, the public doesn't require any new ideas. The public is best served by the good, old established ideas it already has.

Dr Stockmann. And that is your honest opinion?

Peter Stockmann. Yes, and for once I must talk frankly to you. Hitherto I have tried to avoid doing so, because I know how irritable you are; but now I must tell you the truth, Thomas. You have no conception what an amount of harm you do yourself by your impetuosity. You complain of the authorities, you even complain of the government — you are always pulling them to pieces; you insist that you have been neglected and persecuted. But what else can such a cantankerous man as you expect?

Dr Stockmann. What next! Cantankerous, am I?

Peter Stockmann. Yes, Thomas, you are an extremely cantankerous man to work with — I know that to my cost. You disregard everything that you ought to have consideration for. You seem completely to forget that it is me you have to thank for your appointment here as medical officer to the Baths.

Dr Stockmann. I was entitled to it as a matter of course! — I and nobody else! I was the first person to see that the town could be made into a flourishing watering-place, and I was the only one who saw it at that time. I had to fight single-handed in support of the idea for many years; and I wrote and wrote —

Peter Stockmann. Undoubtedly. But things were not ripe for the scheme then — though, of course, you could not judge of that in your out-of-the-way corner up north. But as soon as the opportune moment came I— and the others — took the matter into our hands

Dr Stockmann. Yes, and made this mess of all my beautiful plan. It is pretty obvious now what clever fellows you were!

Peter Stockmann. To my mind the whole thing only seems to mean that you are seeking another outlet for your combativeness. You want to pick a quarrel with your superiors — an old habit of yours. You cannot put up with any authority over you. You look askance at anyone who occupies a superior official position; you regard him as a personal enemy, and then any stick is good enough to beat him with. But now I have called your attention to the fact that the town's interests are at stake — and, incidentally, my own too. And therefore, I must tell you, Thomas, that you will find me inexorable with regard to what I am about to require you to do.

Dr Stockmann. And what is that?

Peter Stockmann. As you have been so indiscreet as to speak of this delicate matter to outsiders, despite the fact that you ought to have treated it as entirely official and confidential, it is obviously impossible to hush it up now. All sorts of rumours will get about directly, and everybody who has a grudge against us will take care to embellish these rumours. So it will be necessary for you to refute them publicly.

Dr Stockmann. I! How? I don't understand.

Peter Stockmann. What we shall expect is that, after making further investigations, you will come to the conclusion that the matter is not by any means as dangerous or as critical as you imagined in the first instance.

Dr Stockmann. Oho! — so that is what you expect!

Peter Stockmann. And, what is more, we shall expect you to make public profession of your confidence in the Committee and in their readiness to consider fully and conscientiously what steps may be necessary to remedy any possible defects.

Dr Stockmann. But you will never be able to do that by patching and tinkering at it — never! Take my word for it, Peter; I mean what I say, as deliberately and emphatically as possible.

Peter Stockmann. As an officer under the Committee, you have no right to any individual opinion.

Dr Stockmann [amazed]. No right?

Peter Stockmann. In your official capacity, no. As a private person, it is quite another matter. But as a subordinate member of the staff of the Baths, you have no right to express any opinion which runs contrary to that of your superiors.

Dr Stockmann. This is too much! I, a doctor, a man of science, have no right to —!

Peter Stockmann. The matter in hand is not simply a scientific one. It is a complicated matter, and has its economic as well as its technical side.

Dr Stockmann. I don't care what it is! I intend to be free to express my opinion on any subject under the sun.

Peter Stockmann. As you please — but not on any subject concerning the Baths. That we forbid.

Dr Stockmann [shouting]. You forbid —! You! A pack of —

Peter Stockmann. I forbid it — I, your chief; and if I forbid it, you have to obey.

Dr Stockmann [controlling himself]. Peter — if you were not my brother —

Petra [throwing open the door]. Father, you shan't stand this!

Mrs Stockmann [coming in after her]. Petra, Petra!

Peter Stockmann. Oh, so you have been eavesdropping.

Mrs Stockmann. You were talking so loud, we couldn't help it!

Petra. Yes, I was listening.

Peter Stockmann. Well, after all, I am very glad —

Dr Stockmann [going up to him]. You were saying something about forbidding and obeying?

Peter Stockmann. You obliged me to take that tone with you.

Dr Stockmann. And so I am to give myself the lie, publicly?

Peter Stockmann. We consider it absolutely necessary that you should make some such public statement as I have asked for.

Dr Stockmann. And if I do not — obey?

Peter Stockmann. Then we shall publish a statement ourselves to reassure the public.

Dr Stockmann. Very well; but in that case I shall use my pen against you. I stick to what I have said; I will show that I am right and that you are wrong. And what will you do then?

Peter Stockmann. Then I shall not be able to prevent your being dismissed.

Dr Stockmann. What —?

Petra. Father — dismissed!

Mrs Stockmann. Dismissed!

Peter Stockmann. Dismissed from the staff of the Baths. I shall be obliged to propose that you shall immediately be given notice, and shall not be allowed any further participation in the Baths' affairs.

Dr Stockmann. You would dare to do that!

Peter Stockmann. It is you that are playing the daring game.

Petra. Uncle, that is a shameful way to treat a man like father!

Mrs Stockmann. Do hold your tongue, Petra!

Peter Stockmann [looking at PETRA]. Oh, so we volunteer our opinions already, do we? Of course. [To MRS. STOCKMANN.] Katherine, I imagine you are the most sensible person in this house. Use any influence you may have over your husband, and make him see what this will entail for his family as well as —

Dr Stockmann. My family is my own concern and nobody else's!

Peter Stockmann. — for his own family, as I was saying, as well as for the town he lives in.

Dr Stockmann. It is I who have the real good of the town at heart! I want to lay bare the defects that sooner or later must come to the light of day. I will show whether I love my native town.

Peter Stockmann. You, who in your blind obstinacy want to cut off the most important source of the town's welfare?

Dr Stockmann. The source is poisoned, man! Are you mad? We are making our living by retailing filth and corruption! The whole of our flourishing municipal life derives its sustenance from a lie!

Peter Stockmann. All imagination — or something even worse. The man who can throw out such offensive insinuations about his native town must be an enemy to our community.

Dr Stockmann [going up to him]. Do you dare to —!

Mrs Stockmann [throwing herself between them]. Thomas!

Petra [catching her father by the arm]. Don't lose your temper, father!

Peter Stockmann. I will not expose myself to violence. Now you have had a warning; so reflect on what you owe to yourself and your family. Goodbye. [Goes out.]

Dr Stockmann [walking up and down]. Am I to put up with such treatment as this? In my own house, Katherine! What do you think of that!

Mrs Stockmann. Indeed it is both shameful and absurd, Thomas —

Petra. If only I could give uncle a piece of my mind —

Dr Stockmann. It is my own fault. I ought to have flown out at him long ago! — shown my teeth! — bitten! To hear him call me an enemy to our community! Me! I shall not take that lying down, upon my soul!

Mrs Stockmann. But, dear Thomas, your brother has power on his side.

Dr Stockmann. Yes, but I have right on mine, I tell you.

Mrs Stockmann. Oh yes, right — right. What is the use of having right on your side if you have not got might?

Petra. Oh, mother! — how can you say such a thing!

Dr Stockmann. Do you imagine that in a free country it is no use having right on your side? You are absurd, Katherine. Besides, haven't I got the liberal-minded, independent press to lead the way, and the compact majority behind me? That is might enough, I should think!

Mrs Stockmann. But, good heavens, Thomas, you don't mean to?

Dr Stockmann. Don't mean to what?

Mrs Stockmann. To set yourself up in opposition to your brother.

Dr Stockmann. In God's name, what else do you suppose I should do but take my stand on right and truth?

Petra. Yes, I was just going to say that.

Mrs Stockmann. But it won't do you any earthly good. If they won't do it, they won't.

Dr Stockmann. Oho, Katherine! Just give me time, and you will see how I will carry the war into their camp.

Mrs Stockmann. Yes, you carry the war into their camp, and you get your dismissal — that is what you will do.

Dr Stockmann. In any case I shall have done my duty towards the public — towards the community, I, who am called its enemy!

Mrs Stockmann. But towards your family, Thomas? Towards your own home! Do you think that is doing your duty towards those you have to provide for?

Petra. Ah, don't think always first of us, mother.

Mrs Stockmann. Oh, it is easy for you to talk; you are able to shift for yourself, if need be. But remember the boys, Thomas; and think a little of yourself too, and of me —

Dr Stockmann. I think you are out of your senses, Katherine! If I were to be such a miserable coward as to go on my knees to Peter and his damned crew, do you suppose I should ever know an hour's peace of mind all my life afterwards?

Mrs Stockmann. I don't know anything about that; but God preserve us from the peace of mind we shall have, all the same, if you go on defying him! You will find yourself again without the means of subsistence, with no income to count upon. I should think we had had enough of that in the old days. Remember that, Thomas; think what that means.

Dr Stockmann [collecting himself with a struggle and clenching his fists]. And this is what this slavery can bring upon a free, honourable man! Isn't it horrible, Katherine?

Mrs Stockmann. Yes, it is sinful to treat you so, it is perfectly true. But, good heavens, one has to put up with so much injustice in this world. There are the boys, Thomas! Look at them! What is to become of them? Oh, no, no, you can never have the heart —. [EJLIF and MORTEN have come in, while she was speaking, with their school books in their hands.]

Dr Stockmann. The boys — I [Recovers himself suddenly.] No, even if the whole world goes to pieces, I will never bow my neck to this yokel [Goes towards his room.]

Mrs Stockmann [following him]. Thomas — what are you going to do!

Dr Stockmann [at his door]. I mean to have the right to look my sons in the face when they are grown men. [Goes into his room.]

Mrs Stockmann [bursting into tears]. God help us all!

Petra. Father is splendid! He will not give in.

[The boys look on in amazement; PETRA signs to them not to speak.]

ACT III

[SCENE. — The editorial office of the "People's Messenger." The entrance door is on the left-hand side of the back wall; on the right-hand side is another door with glass panels through which the printing room can be seen. Another door in the right-hand wall. In the middle of the room is a large table covered with papers, newspapers and books. In the foreground on the left a window, before which stands a desk and a high stool. There are a couple of easy chairs by the table, and other chairs standing along the wall. The room is dingy and uncomfortable; the furniture is old, the chairs stained and torn. In the printing room the compositors are seen at work, and a printer is working a handpress. HOVSTAD is sitting at the desk, writing. BILLING comes in from the right with DR. STOCKMANN'S manuscript in his hand.]

Billing. Well, I must say!

Hovstad [still writing]. Have you read it through?

Billing [laying the MS. on the desk]. Yes, indeed I have.

Hovstad. Don't you think the Doctor hits them pretty hard?

Billing. Hard? Bless my soul, he's crushing! Every word falls like — how shall I put it? — like the blow of a sledgehammer.

Hovstad. Yes, but they are not the people to throw up the sponge at the first blow.

Billing. That is true; and for that reason we must strike blow upon blow until the whole of this aristocracy tumbles to pieces. As I sat in there reading this, I almost seemed to see a revolution in being.

Hovstad [turning round]. Hush! — Speak so that Aslaksen cannot hear you.

Billing [lowering his voice]. Aslaksen is a chicken-hearted chap, a coward; there is nothing of the man in him. But this time you will insist on your own way, won't you? You will put the Doctor's article in?

Hovstad. Yes, and if the Mayor doesn't like it —

Billing. That will be the devil of a nuisance.

Hovstad. Well, fortunately we can turn the situation to good account, whatever happens. If the Mayor will not fall in with the Doctor's project, he will have all the small tradesmen down on him — the whole of the Householders' Association and the rest of them. And if he does fall in with it, he will fall out with the whole crowd of large shareholders in the Baths, who up to now have been his most valuable supporters —

Billing. Yes, because they will certainly have to fork out a pretty penny —

Hovstad. Yes, you may be sure they will. And in this way the ring will be broken up, you see, and then in every issue of the paper we will enlighten the public on the Mayor's incapability on one point and another, and make it clear that all the positions of trust in the town, the whole control of municipal affairs, ought to be put in the hands of the Liberals.

Billing. That is perfectly true! I see it coming — I see it coming; we are on the threshold of a revolution!

[A knock is heard at the door.]

Hovstad. Hush! [Calls out.] Come in! [DR. STOCKMANN comes in by the street door. HOVSTAD goes to meet him.] Ah, it is you, Doctor! Well?

Dr Stockmann. You may set to work and print it, Mr. Hovstad!

Hovstad. Has it come to that, then?

Billing. Hurrah!

Dr Stockmann. Yes, print away. Undoubtedly it has come to that. Now they must take what they get. There is going to be a fight in the town, Mr. Billing!

Billing. War to the knife, I hope! We will get our knives to their throats, Doctor!

Dr Stockmann. This article is only a beginning. I have already got four or five more sketched out in my head. Where is Aslaksen?

Billing [calls into the printing-room]. Aslaksen, just come here for a minute!

Hovstad. Four or five more articles, did you say? On the same subject?

Dr Stockmann. No — far from it, my dear fellow. No, they are about quite another matter. But they all spring from the question of the water supply and the drainage. One thing leads to another, you know. It is like beginning to pull down an old house, exactly.

Billing. Upon my soul, it's true; you find you are not done till you have pulled all the old rubbish down.

Aslaksen [coming in]. Pulled down? You are not thinking of pulling down the Baths surely, Doctor?

Hovstad. Far from it, don't be afraid.

Dr Stockmann. No, we meant something quite different. Well, what do you think of my article, Mr. Hovstad?

Hovstad. I think it is simply a masterpiece.

Dr Stockmann. Do you really think so? Well, I am very pleased, very pleased.

Hovstad. It is so clear and intelligible. One need have no special knowledge to understand the bearing of it. You will have every enlightened man on your side.

Aslaksen. And every prudent man too, I hope?

Billing. The prudent and the imprudent — almost the whole town.

Aslaksen. In that case we may venture to print it.

Dr Stockmann. I should think so!

Hovstad. We will put it in tomorrow morning.

Dr Stockmann. Of course — you must not lose a single day. What I wanted to ask you, Mr. Aslaksen, was if you would supervise the printing of it yourself.

Aslaksen. With pleasure.

Dr Stockmann. Take care of it as if it were a treasure! No misprints — every word is important. I will look in again a little later; perhaps you will be able to let me see a proof. I can't tell you how eager I am to see it in print, and see it burst upon the public —

Billing. Burst upon them — yes, like a flash of lightning!

Dr Stockmann. — and to have it submitted to the judgment of my intelligent fellow townsmen. You cannot imagine what I have gone through today. I have been threatened first with one thing and then with another; they have tried to rob me of my most elementary rights as a man —

Billing. What! Your rights as a man!

Dr Stockmann. — they have tried to degrade me, to make a coward of me, to force me to put personal interests before my most sacred convictions.

Billing. That is too much — I'm damned if it isn't.

Hovstad. Oh, you mustn't be surprised at anything from that quarter.

Dr Stockmann. Well, they will get the worst of it with me; they may assure themselves of that. I shall consider the "People's Messenger" my sheet-anchor now, and every single day I will bombard them with one article after another, like bombshells —

Aslaksen. Yes, but

Billing. Hurrah! — it is war, it is war!

Dr Stockmann. I shall smite them to the ground — I shall crush them — I shall break down all their defenses, before the eyes of the honest public! That is what I shall do!

Aslaksen. Yes, but in moderation, Doctor — proceed with moderation.

Billing. Not a bit of it, not a bit of it! Don't spare the dynamite!

Dr Stockmann. Because it is not merely a question of water-supply and drains now, you know. No — it is the whole of our social life that we have got to purify and disinfect —

Billing. Spoken like a deliverer!

Dr Stockmann. All the incapables must be turned out, you understand — and that in every walk of life! Endless vistas have opened themselves to my mind's eye today. I cannot see it all quite clearly yet, but I shall in time. Young and vigorous standard-bearers — those are what we need and must seek, my friends; we must have new men in command at all our outposts.

Billing. Hear hear!

Dr Stockmann. We only need to stand by one another, and it will all be perfectly easy. The revolution will be launched like a ship that runs smoothly off the stocks. Don't you think so?

Hovstad. For my part I think we have now a prospect of getting the municipal authority into the hands where it should lie.

Aslaksen. And if only we proceed with moderation, I cannot imagine that there will be any risk.

Dr Stockmann. Who the devil cares whether there is any risk or not! What I am doing, I am doing in the name of truth and for the sake of my conscience.

Hovstad. You are a man who deserves to be supported, Doctor.

Aslaksen. Yes, there is no denying that the Doctor is a true friend to the town — a real friend to the community, that he is.

Billing. Take my word for it, Aslaksen, Dr. Stockmann is a friend of the people.

Aslaksen. I fancy the Householders' Association will make use of that expression before long.

Dr Stockmann [affected, grasps their hands]. Thank you, thank you, my dear staunch friends. It is very refreshing to me to hear you say that; my brother called me something quite different. By Jove, he shall have it back, with interest! But now I must be off to see a poor devil — I will come back, as I said. Keep a very careful eye on the manuscript, Aslaksen, and don't for worlds leave out any of my notes of exclamation! Rather put one or two more in! Capital, capital! Well, good-bye for the present — goodbye, goodbye! [They show him to the door, and bow him out.]

Hovstad. He may prove an invaluably useful man to us.

Aslaksen. Yes, so long as he confines himself to this matter of the Baths. But if he goes farther afield, I don't think it would be advisable to follow him.

Hovstad. Hm! — that all depends-Billing. You are so infernally timid, Aslaksen!

Aslaksen. Timid? Yes, when it is a question of the local authorities, I am timid, Mr. Billing; it is a lesson I have learned in the school of experience, let me tell you. But try me in higher politics, in matters that concern the government itself, and then see if I am timid.

Billing. No, you aren't, I admit. But this is simply contradicting yourself.

Aslaksen. I am a man with a conscience, and that is the whole matter. If you attack the government, you don't do the community any harm, anyway; those fellows pay no attention to attacks, you see — they go on just as they are, in spite of them. But local authorities are different; they can be turned out, and then perhaps you may get an ignorant lot into office who may do irreparable harm to the householders and everybody else.

Hovstad. But what of the education of citizens by self government — don't you attach any importance to that?

Aslaksen. When a man has interests of his own to protect, he cannot think of everything, Mr. Hovstad.

Hovstad. Then I hope I shall never have interests of my own to protect!

Billing. Hear, hear!

Aslaksen [with a smile]. Hm! [Points to the desk.] Mr. Sheriff Stensgaard was your predecessor at that editorial desk.

Billing [spitting]. Bah! That turncoat.

Hovstad. I am not a weathercock — and never will be.

Aslaksen. A politician should never be too certain of anything, Mr. Hovstad. And as for you, Mr. Billing, I should think it is time for you to be taking in a reef or two in your sails, seeing that you are applying for the post of secretary to the Bench.

Billing. I—!

Hovstad. Are you, Billing?

Billing. Well, yes — but you must clearly understand I am only doing it to annoy the bigwigs.

Aslaksen. Anyhow, it is no business of mine. But if I am to be accused of timidity and of inconsistency in my principles, this is what I want to point out: my political past is an open book. I have never changed, except perhaps to become a little more moderate, you see. My heart is still with the people; but I don't deny that my reason has a certain bias towards the authorities — the local ones, I mean. [Goes into the printing room.]

Billing. Oughtn't we to try and get rid of him, Hovstad?

Hovstad. Do you know anyone else who will advance the money for our paper and printing bill?

Billing. It is an infernal nuisance that we don't possess some capital to trade on.

Hovstad [sitting down at his desk]. Yes, if we only had that, then —

Billing. Suppose you were to apply to Dr. Stockmann?

Hovstad [turning over some papers]. What is the use? He has got nothing.

Billing. No, but he has got a warm man in the background, old Morten Kiil —"the Badger," as they call him.

Hovstad [writing]. Are you so sure he has got anything?

Billing. Good Lord, of course he has! And some of it must come to the Stockmanns. Most probably he will do something for the children, at all events.

Hovstad [turning half round]. Are you counting on that?

Billing. Counting on it? Of course I am not counting on anything.

Hovstad. That is right. And I should not count on the secretaryship to the Bench either, if I were you; for I can assure you — you won't get it.

Billing. Do you think I am not quite aware of that? My object is precisely not to get it. A slight of that kind stimulates a man's fighting power — it is like getting a supply of fresh bile — and I am sure one needs that badly enough in a hole-and-corner place like this, where it is so seldom anything happens to stir one up.

Hovstad [writing]. Quite so, quite so.

Billing. Ah, I shall be heard of yet! — Now I shall go and write the appeal to the Householders' Association. [Goes into the room on the right.]

Hovstad [sitting at his desk, biting his penholder, says slowly]. Hm! — that's it, is it. [A knock is heard.] Come in! [PETRA comes in by the outer door. HOVSTAD gets up.] What, you! — here?

Petra. Yes, you must forgive me —

Hovstad [pulling a chair forward]. Won't you sit down?

Petra. No, thank you; I must go again in a moment.

Hovstad. Have you come with a message from your father, by any chance?

Petra. No, I have come on my own account. [Takes a book out of her coat pocket.] Here is the English story.

Hovstad. Why have you brought it back?

Petra. Because I am not going to translate it.

Hovstad. But you promised me faithfully.

Petra. Yes, but then I had not read it, I don't suppose you have read it either?

Hovstad. No, you know quite well I don't understand English; but —

Petra. Quite so. That is why I wanted to tell you that you must find something else. [Lays the book on the table.] You can't use this for the "People's Messenger."

Hovstad. Why not?

Petra. Because it conflicts with all your opinions.

Hovstad. Oh, for that matter —

Petra. You don't understand me. The burden of this story is that there is a supernatural power that looks after the so-called good people in this world and makes everything happen for the best in their case — while all the so-called bad people are punished.

Hovstad. Well, but that is all right. That is just what our readers want.

Petra. And are you going to be the one to give it to them? For myself, I do not believe a word of it. You know quite well that things do not happen so in reality.

Hovstad. You are perfectly right; but an editor cannot always act as he would prefer. He is often obliged to bow to the wishes of the public in unimportant matters. Politics are the most important thing in life — for a newspaper, anyway; and if I want to carry my public with me on the path that leads to liberty and progress, I must not frighten them away. If they find a moral tale of this sort in the serial at the bottom of the page, they will be all the more ready to read what is printed above it; they feel more secure, as it were.

Petra. For shame! You would never go and set a snare like that for your readers; you are not a spider!

Hovstad [smiling]. Thank you for having such a good opinion of me. No; as a matter of fact that is Billing's idea and not mine.

Petra. Billing's!

Hovstad. Yes; anyway, he propounded that theory here one day. And it is Billing who is so anxious to have that story in the paper; I don't know anything about the book.

Petra. But how can Billing, with his emancipated views —

Hovstad. Oh, Billing is a many-sided man. He is applying for the post of secretary to the Bench, too, I hear.

Petra. I don't believe it, Mr. Hovstad. How could he possibly bring himself to do such a thing?

Hovstad. Ah, you must ask him that.

Petra. I should never have thought it of him.

Hovstad [looking more closely at her]. No? Does it really surprise you so much?

Petra. Yes. Or perhaps not altogether. Really, I don't quite know

Hovstad. We journalists are not much worth, Miss Stockmann.

Petra. Do you really mean that?

Hovstad. I think so sometimes.

Petra. Yes, in the ordinary affairs of everyday life, perhaps; I can understand that. But now, when you have taken a weighty matter in hand —

Hovstad. This matter of your father's, you mean?

Petra. Exactly. It seems to me that now you must feel you are a man worth more than most.

Hovstad. Yes, today I do feel something of that sort.

Petra. Of course you do, don't you? It is a splendid vocation you have chosen — to smooth the way for the march of unappreciated truths, and new and courageous lines of thought. If it were nothing more than because you stand fearlessly in the open and take up the cause of an injured man —

Hovstad. Especially when that injured man is — ahem! — I don't rightly know how to —

Petra. When that man is so upright and so honest, you mean?

Hovstad [more gently]. Especially when he is your father I meant.

Petra [suddenly checked]. That?

Hovstad. Yes, Petra — Miss Petra.

Petra. Is it that, that is first and foremost with you? Not the matter itself? Not the truth? — not my father's big generous heart?

Hovstad. Certainly — of course — that too.

Petra. No, thank you; you have betrayed yourself, Mr. Hovstad, and now I shall never trust you again in anything.

Hovstad. Can you really take it so amiss in me that it is mostly for your sake —?

Petra. What I am angry with you for, is for not having been honest with my father. You talked to him as if the truth and the good of the community were what lay nearest to your heart. You have made fools of both my father and me. You are not the man you made yourself out to be. And that I shall never forgive you-never!

Hovstad. You ought not to speak so bitterly, Miss Petra — least of all now.

Petra. Why not now, especially?

Hovstad. Because your father cannot do without my help.

Petra [looking him up and down]. Are you that sort of man too? For shame!

Hovstad. No, no, I am not. This came upon me so unexpectedly — you must believe that.

Petra. I know what to believe. Goodbye.

Aslaksen [coming from the printing room, hurriedly and with an air of mystery]. Damnation, Hovstad! —[Sees PETRA.] Oh, this is awkward —

Petra. There is the book; you must give it to some one else. [Goes towards the door.]

Hovstad [following her]. But, Miss Stockmann —

Petra. Goodbye. [Goes out.]

Aslaksen. I say — Mr, Hovstad —

Hovstad. Well well! — what is it?

Aslaksen. The Mayor is outside in the printing room.

Hovstad. The Mayor, did you say?

Aslaksen. Yes he wants to speak to you. He came in by the back door — didn't want to be seen, you understand.

Hovstad. What can he want? Wait a bit — I will go myself. [Goes to the door of the printing room, opens it, bows and invites PETER STOCKMANN in.] Just see, Aslaksen, that no one —

Aslaksen. Quite so. [Goes into the printing-room.]

Peter Stockmann. You did not expect to see me here, Mr. Hovstad?

Hovstad. No, I confess I did not.

Peter Stockmann [looking round]. You are very snug in here — very nice indeed.

Hovstad. Oh —

Peter Stockmann. And here I come, without any notice, to take up your time!

Hovstad. By all means, Mr. Mayor. I am at your service. But let me relieve you of your —[takes STOCKMANN's hat and stick and puts them on a chair]. Won't you sit down?

Peter Stockmann [sitting down by the table]. Thank you. [HOVSTAD sits down.] I have had an extremely annoying experience today, Mr. Hovstad.

Hovstad. Really? Ah well, I expect with all the various business you have to attend to —

Peter Stockmann. The Medical Officer of the Baths is responsible for what happened today.

Hovstad. Indeed? The Doctor?

Peter Stockmann. He has addressed a kind of report to the Baths Committee on the subject of certain supposed defects in the Baths.

Hovstad. Has he indeed?

Peter Stockmann. Yes — has he not told you? I thought he said —

Hovstad. Ah, yes — it is true he did mention something about —

Aslaksen [coming from the printing-room]. I ought to have that copy.

Hovstad [angrily]. Ahem! — there it is on the desk.

Aslaksen [taking it]. Right.

Peter Stockmann. But look there — that is the thing I was speaking of!

Aslaksen. Yes, that is the Doctor's article, Mr. Mayor.

Hovstad. Oh, is THAT what you were speaking about?

Peter Stockmann. Yes, that is it. What do you think of it?

Hovstad. Oh, I am only a layman — and I have only taken a very cursory glance at it.

Peter Stockmann. But you are going to print it?

Hovstad. I cannot very well refuse a distinguished man.

Aslaksen. I have nothing to do with editing the paper, Mr. Mayor —

Peter Stockmann. I understand.

Aslaksen. I merely print what is put into my hands.

Peter Stockmann. Quite so.

Aslaksen. And so I must — [moves off towards the printing-room].

Peter Stockmann. No, but wait a moment, Mr. Aslaksen. You will allow me, Mr. Hovstad?

Hovstad. If you please, Mr. Mayor.

Peter Stockmann. You are a discreet and thoughtful man, Mr. Aslaksen.

Aslaksen. I am delighted to hear you think so, sir.

Peter Stockmann. And a man of very considerable influence.

Aslaksen. Chiefly among the small tradesmen, sir.

Peter Stockmann. The small tax-payers are the majority — here as everywhere else.

Aslaksen. That is true.

Peter Stockmann. And I have no doubt you know the general trend of opinion among them, don't you?

Aslaksen. Yes I think I may say I do, Mr. Mayor.

Peter Stockmann. Yes. Well, since there is such a praiseworthy spirit of self-sacrifice among the less wealthy citizens of our town —

Aslaksen. What?

Hovstad. Self-sacrifice?

Peter Stockmann. It is pleasing evidence of a public-spirited feeling, extremely pleasing evidence. I might almost say I hardly expected it. But you have a closer knowledge of public opinion than I.

Aslaksen. But, Mr. Mayor–Peter Stockmann. And indeed it is no small sacrifice that the town is going to make.

Hovstad. The town?

Aslaksen. But I don't understand. Is it the Baths —?

Peter Stockmann. At a provisional estimate, the alterations that the Medical Officer asserts to be desirable will cost somewhere about twenty thousand pounds.

Aslaksen. That is a lot of money, but —

Peter Stockmann. Of course it will be necessary to raise a municipal loan.

Hovstad [getting up]. Surely you never mean that the town must pay —?

Aslaksen. Do you mean that it must come out of the municipal funds? — out of the ill-filled pockets of the small tradesmen?

Peter Stockmann. Well, my dear Mr. Aslaksen, where else is the money to come from?

Aslaksen. The gentlemen who own the Baths ought to provide that.

Peter Stockmann. The proprietors of the Baths are not in a position to incur any further expense.

Aslaksen. Is that absolutely certain, Mr. Mayor?

Peter Stockmann. I have satisfied myself that it is so. If the town wants these very extensive alterations, it will have to pay for them.

Aslaksen. But, damn it all — I beg your pardon — this is quite another matter, Mr, Hovstad!

Hovstad. It is, indeed.

Peter Stockmann. The most fatal part of it is that we shall be obliged to shut the Baths for a couple of years.

Hovstad. Shut them? Shut them altogether?

Aslaksen. For two years?

Peter Stockmann. Yes, the work will take as long as that — at least.

Aslaksen. I'm damned if we will stand that, Mr. Mayor! What are we householders to live upon in the meantime?

Peter Stockmann. Unfortunately, that is an extremely difficult question to answer, Mr. Aslaksen. But what would you have us do? Do you suppose we shall have a single visitor in the town, if we go about proclaiming that our water is polluted, that we are living over a plague spot, that the entire town —

Aslaksen. And the whole thing is merely imagination?

Peter Stockmann. With the best will in the world, I have not been able to come to any other conclusion.

Aslaksen. Well then I must say it is absolutely unjustifiable of Dr. Stockmann — I beg your pardon, Mr. Mayor.

Peter Stockmann. What you say is lamentably true, Mr. Aslaksen. My brother has unfortunately always been a headstrong man.

Aslaksen. After this, do you mean to give him your support, Mr. Hovstad?

Hovstad. Can you suppose for a moment that I—?

Peter Stockmann. I have drawn up a short resume of the situation as it appears from a reasonable man's point of view. In it I have indicated how certain possible defects might suitably be remedied without outrunning the resources of the Baths Committee.

Hovstad. Have you got it with you, Mr. Mayor?

Peter Stockmann [fumbling in his pocket]. Yes, I brought it with me in case you should —

Aslaksen. Good Lord, there he is!

Peter Stockmann. Who? My brother?

Hovstad. Where? Where?

Aslaksen. He has just gone through the printing room.

Peter Stockmann. How unlucky! I don't want to meet him here, and I had still several things to speak to you about.

Hovstad [pointing to the door on the right]. Go in there for the present.

Peter Stockmann. But —?

Hovstad. You will only find Billing in there.

Aslaksen. Quick, quick, Mr. Mayor — he is just coming.

Peter Stockmann. Yes, very well; but see that you get rid of him quickly. [Goes out through the door on the right, which ASLAKSEN opens for him and shuts after him.]

Hovstad. Pretend to be doing something, Aslaksen. [Sits down and writes. ASLAKSEN begins foraging among a heap of newspapers that are lying on a chair.]

Dr Stockmann [coming in from the printing room]. Here I am again. [Puts down his hat and stick.]

Hovstad [writing]. Already, Doctor? Hurry up with what we were speaking about, Aslaksen. We are very pressed for time today.

Dr Stockmann [to ASLAKSEN]. No proof for me to see yet, I hear.

Aslaksen [without turning round]. You couldn't expect it yet, Doctor.

Dr Stockmann. No, no; but I am impatient, as you can understand. I shall not know a moment's peace of mind until I see it in print.

Hovstad. Hm! — It will take a good while yet, won't it, Aslaksen?

Aslaksen. Yes, I am almost afraid it will.

Dr Stockmann. All right, my dear friends; I will come back. I do not mind coming back twice if necessary. A matter of such great importance — the welfare of the town at stake — it is no time to shirk trouble, [is just going, but stops and comes back.] Look here — there is one thing more I want to speak to you about.

Hovstad. Excuse me, but could it not wait till some other time?

Dr Stockmann. I can tell you in half a dozen words. It is only this. When my article is read tomorrow and it is realised that I have been quietly working the whole winter for the welfare of the town —

Hovstad. Yes but, Doctor —

Dr Stockmann. I know what you are going to say. You don't see how on earth it was any more than my duty — my obvious duty as a citizen. Of course it wasn't; I know that as well as you. But my fellow citizens, you know —! Good Lord, think of all the good souls who think so highly of me —!

Aslaksen. Yes, our townsfolk have had a very high opinion of you so far, Doctor.

Dr Stockmann. Yes, and that is just why I am afraid they —. Well, this is the point; when this reaches them, especially the poorer classes, and sounds in their ears like a summons to take the town's affairs into their own hands for the future . . .

Hovstad [getting up]. Ahem I Doctor, I won't conceal from you the fact —

Dr Stockmann. Ah I— I knew there was something in the wind! But I won't hear a word of it. If anything of that sort is being set on foot —

Hovstad. Of what sort?

Dr Stockmann. Well, whatever it is — whether it is a demonstration in my honour, or a banquet, or a subscription list for some presentation to me — whatever it is, you most promise me solemnly and faithfully to put a stop to it. You too, Mr. Aslaksen; do you understand?

Hovstad. You must forgive me, Doctor, but sooner or later we must tell you the plain truth —

[He is interrupted by the entrance Of MRS. STOCKMANN, who comes in from the street door.]

Mrs Stockmann [seeing her husband]. Just as I thought!

Hovstad [going towards her]. You too, Mrs. Stockmann?

Dr Stockmann. What on earth do you want here, Katherine?

Mrs Stockmann. I should think you know very well what I want.

Hovstad. Won't you sit down? Or perhaps —

Mrs Stockmann. No, thank you; don't trouble. And you must not be offended at my coming to fetch my husband; I am the mother of three children, you know.

Dr Stockmann. Nonsense! — we know all about that.

Mrs Stockmann. Well, one would not give you credit for much thought for your wife and children today; if you had had that, you would not have gone and dragged us all into misfortune.

Dr Stockmann. Are you out of your senses, Katherine! Because a man has a wife and children, is he not to be allowed to proclaim the truth-is he not to be allowed to be an actively useful citizen — is he not to be allowed to do a service to his native town!

Mrs Stockmann. Yes, Thomas — in reason.

Aslaksen. Just what I say. Moderation in everything.

Mrs Stockmann. And that is why you wrong us, Mr. Hovstad, in enticing my husband away from his home and making a dupe of him in all this.

Hovstad. I certainly am making a dupe of no one —

Dr Stockmann. Making a dupe of me! Do you suppose I should allow myself to be duped!

Mrs Stockmann. It is just what you do. I know quite well you have more brains than anyone in the town, but you are extremely easily duped, Thomas. [To Hovstad.] Please do realise that he loses his post at the Baths if you print what he has written.

Aslaksen. What!

Hovstad. Look here, Doctor!

Dr Stockmann [laughing]. Ha-ha! — just let them try! No, no — they will take good care not to. I have got the compact majority behind me, let me tell you!

Mrs Stockmann. Yes, that is just the worst of it — your having any such horrid thing behind you.

Dr Stockmann. Rubbish, Katherine! — Go home and look after your house and leave me to look after the community. How can you be so afraid, when I am so confident and happy? [Walks up and down, rubbing his hands.] Truth and the People will win the fight, you may be certain! I see the whole of the broad-minded middle class marching like a victorious army —! [Stops beside a chair.] What the deuce is that lying there?

Aslaksen. Good Lord!

Hovstad. Ahem!

Dr Stockmann. Here we have the topmost pinnacle of authority! [Takes the Mayor's official hat carefully between his finger-tips and holds it up in the air.]

Mrs Stockmann. The Mayor's hat!

Dr Stockmann. And here is the staff of office too. How in the name of all that's wonderful —?

Hovstad. Well, you see —

Dr Stockmann. Oh, I understand. He has been here trying to talk you over. Ha-ha! — he made rather a mistake there! And as soon as he caught sight of me in the printing room. [Bursts out laughing.] Did he run away, Mr. Aslaksen?

Aslaksen [hurriedly]. Yes, he ran away, Doctor.

Dr Stockmann. Ran away without his stick or his —. Fiddlesticks! Peter doesn't run away and leave his belongings behind him. But what the deuce have you done with him? Ah! — in there, of course. Now you shall see, Katherine!

Mrs Stockmann. Thomas — please don't —!

Aslaksen. Don't be rash, Doctor.

[DR. STOCKMANN has put on the Mayor's hat and taken his stick in his hand. He goes up to the door, opens it, and stands with his hand to his hat at the salute. PETER STOCKMANN comes in, red with anger. BILLING follows him.]

Peter Stockmann. What does this tomfoolery mean?

Dr Stockmann. Be respectful, my good Peter. I am the chief authority in the town now. [Walks up and down.]

Mrs Stockmann [almost in tears]. Really, Thomas!

Peter Stockmann [following him about]. Give me my hat and stick.

Dr Stockmann [in the same tone as before]. If you are chief constable, let me tell you that I am the Mayor — I am the master of the whole town, please understand!

Peter Stockmann. Take off my hat, I tell you. Remember it is part of an official uniform.

Dr Stockmann. Pooh! Do you think the newly awakened lionhearted people are going to be frightened by an official hat? There is going to be a revolution in the town tomorrow, let me tell you. You thought you could turn me out; but now I shall turn you out — turn you out of all your various offices. Do you think I cannot? Listen to me. I have triumphant social forces behind me. Hovstad and Billing will thunder in the "People's Messenger," and Aslaksen will take the field at the head of the whole Householders' Association —

Aslaksen. That I won't, Doctor.

Dr Stockmann. Of course you will —

Peter Stockmann. Ah! — may I ask then if Mr. Hovstad intends to join this agitation?

Hovstad. No, Mr. Mayor.

Aslaksen. No, Mr. Hovstad is not such a fool as to go and ruin his paper and himself for the sake of an imaginary grievance.

Dr Stockmann [looking round him]. What does this mean?

Hovstad. You have represented your case in a false light, Doctor, and therefore I am unable to give you my support.

Billing. And after what the Mayor was so kind as to tell me just now, I—

Dr Stockmann. A false light! Leave that part of it to me. Only print my article; I am quite capable of defending it.

Hovstad. I am not going to print it. I cannot and will not and dare not print it.

Dr Stockmann. You dare not? What nonsense! — you are the editor; and an editor controls his paper, I suppose!

Aslaksen. No, it is the subscribers, Doctor.

Peter Stockmann. Fortunately, yes.

Aslaksen. It is public opinion — the enlightened public — householders and people of that kind; they control the newspapers.

Dr Stockmann [composedly]. And I have all these influences against me?

Aslaksen. Yes, you have. It would mean the absolute ruin of the community if your article were to appear.

Dr Stockmann. Indeed.

Peter Stockmann. My hat and stick, if you please. [DR. STOCKMANN takes off the hat and lays it on the table with the stick. PETER STOCKMANN takes them up.] Your authority as mayor has come to an untimely end.

Dr Stockmann. We have not got to the end yet. [To HOVSTAD.] Then it is quite impossible for you to print my article in the "People's Messenger"?

Hovstad. Quite impossible — out of regard for your family as well.

Mrs Stockmann. You need not concern yourself about his family, thank you, Mr. Hovstad.

Peter Stockmann [taking a paper from his pocket]. It will be sufficient, for the guidance of the public, if this appears. It is an official statement. May I trouble you?

Hovstad [taking the paper]. Certainly; I will see that it is printed.

Dr Stockmann. But not mine. Do you imagine that you can silence me and stifle the truth! You will not find it so easy as you suppose. Mr. Aslaksen, kindly take my manuscript at once and print it as a pamphlet — at my expense. I will have four hundred copies — no, five or six hundred.

Aslaksen. If you offered me its weight in gold, I could not lend my press for any such purpose, Doctor. It would be flying in the face of public opinion. You will not get it printed anywhere in the town.

Dr Stockmann. Then give it me back.

Hovstad [giving him the MS.]. Here it is.

Dr Stockmann [taking his hat and stick]. It shall be made public all the same. I will read it out at a mass meeting of the townspeople. All my fellow-citizens shall hear the voice of truth!

Peter Stockmann. You will not find any public body in the town that will give you the use of their hall for such a purpose.

Aslaksen. Not a single one, I am certain.

Billing. No, I'm damned if you will find one.

Mrs Stockmann. But this is too shameful! Why should every one turn against you like that?

Dr Stockmann [angrily]. I will tell you why. It is because all the men in this town are old women — like you; they all think of nothing but their families, and never of the community.

Mrs Stockmann [putting her arm into his]. Then I will show them that an old woman can be a man for once. I am going to stand by you, Thomas!

Dr Stockmann. Bravely said, Katherine! It shall be made public — as I am a living soul! If I can't hire a hall, I shall hire a drum, and parade the town with it and read it at every street-corner.

Peter Stockmann. You are surely not such an errant fool as that!

Dr Stockmann. Yes, I am.

Aslaksen. You won't find a single man in the whole town to go with you.

Billing. No, I'm damned if you will.

Mrs Stockmann. Don't give in, Thomas. I will tell the boys to go with you.

Dr Stockmann. That is a splendid idea!

Mrs Stockmann. Morten will be delighted; and Ejlif will do whatever he does.

Dr Stockmann. Yes, and Petra! — and you too, Katherine!

Mrs Stockmann. No, I won't do that; but I will stand at the window and watch you, that's what I will do.

Dr Stockmann [puts his arms round her and kisses her]. Thank you, my dear! Now you and I are going to try a fall, my fine gentlemen! I am going to see whether a pack of cowards can succeed in gagging a patriot who wants to purify society! [He and his wife go out by the street door.]

Peter Stockmann [shaking his head seriously]. Now he has sent her out of her senses, too.

ACT IV

[SCENE. — A big old-fashioned room in CAPTAIN HORSTER'S house. At the back folding-doors, which are standing open, lead to an ante-room. Three windows in the left-hand wall. In the middle of the opposite wall a platform has been erected. On this is a small table with two candles, a water-bottle and glass, and a bell. The room is lit by lamps placed between the windows. In the foreground on the left there is a table with candles and a chair. To the right is a door and some chairs standing near it. The room is nearly filled with a crowd of townspeople of all sorts, a few women and schoolboys being amongst them. People are still streaming in from the back, and the room is soon filled.]

1st Citizen [meeting another]. Hullo, Lamstad! You here too?

2nd Citizen. I go to every public meeting, I do.

3rd Citizen. Brought your whistle too, I expect!

2nd Citizen. I should think so. Haven't you?

3rd Citizen. Rather! And old Evensen said he was going to bring a cow-horn, he did.

2nd Citizen. Good old Evensen! [Laughter among the crowd.]

4th Citizen [coming up to them]. I say, tell me what is going on here tonight?

2nd Citizen. Dr. Stockmann is going to deliver an address attacking the Mayor.

4th Citizen. But the Mayor is his brother.

1st Citizen. That doesn't matter; Dr. Stockmann's not the chap to be afraid.

Peter Stockmann. For various reasons, which you will easily understand, I must beg to be excused. But fortunately we have amongst us a man who I think will be acceptable to you all. I refer to the President of the Householders' Association, Mr. Aslaksen.

Several voices. Yes — Aslaksen! Bravo Aslaksen!

[DR. STOCKMANN takes up his MS. and walks up and down the platform.]

Aslaksen. Since my fellow-citizens choose to entrust me with this duty, I cannot refuse.

[Loud applause. ASLAKSEN mounts the platform.]

Billing [writing], "Mr. Aslaksen was elected with enthusiasm."

Aslaksen. And now, as I am in this position, I should like to say a few brief words. I am a quiet and peaceable man, who believes in discreet moderation, and — and — in moderate discretion. All my friends can bear witness to that.

Several Voices. That's right! That's right, Aslaksen!

Aslaksen. I have learned in the school of life and experience that moderation is the most valuable virtue a citizen can possess —

Peter Stockmann. Hear, hear!

Aslaksen. — And moreover, that discretion and moderation are what enable a man to be of most service to the community. I would therefore suggest to our esteemed fellow-citizen, who has called this meeting, that he should strive to keep strictly within the bounds of moderation.

A Man by the door. Three cheers for the Moderation Society!

A Voice. Shame!

Several Voices. Sh!-Sh!

Aslaksen. No interruptions, gentlemen, please! Does anyone wish to make any remarks?

Peter Stockmann. Mr. Chairman.

Aslaksen. The Mayor will address the meeting.

Peter Stockmann. In consideration of the close relationship in which, as you all know, I stand to the present Medical Officer of the Baths, I should have preferred not to speak this evening. But my official position with regard to the Baths and my solicitude for the vital interests of the town compel me to bring forward a motion. I venture to presume that there is not a single one of our citizens present who considers it desirable that unreliable and exaggerated accounts of the sanitary condition of the Baths and the town should be spread abroad.

Several Voices. No, no! Certainly not! We protest against it!

Peter Stockmann. Therefore, I should like to propose that the meeting should not permit the Medical Officer either to read or to comment on his proposed lecture.

Dr Stockmann [impatiently]. Not permit —! What the devil —!

Mrs Stockmann [coughing]. Ahem!-ahem!

Dr Stockmann [collecting himself]. Very well, Go ahead!

Peter Stockmann. In my communication to the "People's Messenger," I have put the essential facts before the public in such a way that every fair-minded citizen can easily form his own opinion. From it you will see that the main result of the Medical Officer's proposals — apart from their constituting a vote of censure on the leading men of the town — would be to saddle the ratepayers with an unnecessary expenditure of at least some thousands of pounds.

[Sounds of disapproval among the audience, and some cat-calls.]

Aslaksen [ringing his bell]. Silence, please, gentlemen! I beg to support the Mayor's motion. I quite agree with him that there is something behind this agitation started by the Doctor. He talks about the Baths; but it is a revolution he is aiming at — he wants to get the administration of the town put into new hands. No one doubts the honesty of the Doctor's intentions — no one will suggest that there can be any two opinions as to that, I myself am a believer in self-government for the people, provided it does not fall too heavily on the ratepayers. But that would be the case here; and that is why I will see Dr. Stockmann damned — I beg your pardon — before I go with him in the matter. You can pay too dearly for a thing sometimes; that is my opinion.

[Loud applause on all sides.]

Hovstad. I, too, feel called upon to explain my position. Dr. Stockmann's agitation appeared to be gaining a certain amount of sympathy at first, so I supported it as impartially as I could. But presently we had reason to suspect that we had allowed ourselves to be misled by misrepresentation of the state of affairs —

Dr Stockmann. Misrepresentation —!

Hovstad. Well, let us say a not entirely trustworthy representation. The Mayor's statement has proved that. I hope no one here has any doubt as to my liberal principles; the attitude of the "People's Messenger" towards important political questions is well known to everyone. But the advice of experienced and thoughtful men has convinced me that in purely local matters a newspaper ought to proceed with a certain caution.

Aslaksen. I entirely agree with the speaker.

Hovstad. And, in the matter before us, it is now an undoubted fact that Dr. Stockmann has public opinion against him. Now, what is an editor's first and most obvious duty, gentlemen? Is it not to work in harmony with his readers? Has he not received a sort of tacit mandate to work persistently and assiduously for the welfare of those whose opinions he represents? Or is it possible I am mistaken in that?

Voices from the crowd. No, no! You are quite right!

Hovstad. It has cost me a severe struggle to break with a man in whose house I have been lately a frequent guest — a man who till today has been able to pride himself on the undivided goodwill of his fellow-citizens — a man whose only, or at all events whose essential, failing is that he is swayed by his heart rather than his head.

A few scattered voices. That is true! Bravo, Stockmann!

Hovstad. But my duty to the community obliged me to break with him. And there is another consideration that impels me to oppose him, and, as far as possible, to arrest him on the perilous course he has adopted; that is, consideration for his family —

Dr Stockmann. Please stick to the water-supply and drainage!

Hovstad. — consideration, I repeat, for his wife and his children for whom he has made no provision.

Morten. Is that us, mother?

Mrs Stockmann. Hush!

Aslaksen. I will now put the Mayor's proposition to the vote.

Dr Stockmann. There is no necessity! Tonight I have no intention of dealing with all that filth down at the Baths. No; I have something quite different to say to you.

Peter Stockmann [aside]. What is coming now?

A Drunken Man [by the entrance door]. I am a ratepayer! And therefore, I have a right to speak too! And my entire — firm — inconceivable opinion is —

A number of voices. Be quiet, at the back there!

Others. He is drunk! Turn him out! [They turn him out.]

Dr Stockmann. Am I allowed to speak?

Aslaksen [ringing his bell]. Dr. Stockmann will address the meeting.

Dr Stockmann. I should like to have seen anyone, a few days ago, dare to attempt to silence me as has been done tonight! I would have defended my sacred rights as a man, like a lion! But now it is all one to me; I have something of even weightier importance to say to you. [The crowd presses nearer to him, MORTEN Kiil conspicuous among them.]

Dr Stockmann [continuing]. I have thought and pondered a great deal, these last few days — pondered over such a variety of things that in the end my head seemed too full to hold them —

Peter Stockmann [with a cough]. Ahem!

Dr Stockmann. — but I got them clear in my mind at last, and then I saw the whole situation lucidly. And that is why I am standing here to-night. I have a great revelation to make to you, my fellow-citizens! I will impart to you a discovery of a far wider scope than the trifling matter that our water supply is poisoned and our medicinal Baths are standing on pestiferous soil.

A number of voices [shouting]. Don't talk about the Baths! We won't hear you! None of that!

Dr Stockmann. I have already told you that what I want to speak about is the great discovery I have made lately — the discovery that all the sources of our moral life are poisoned and that the whole fabric of our civic community is founded on the pestiferous soil of falsehood.

Voices of disconcerted Citizens. What is that he says?

Peter Stockmann. Such an insinuation —!

Aslaksen [with his hand on his bell]. I call upon the speaker to moderate his language.

Dr Stockmann. I have always loved my native town as a man only can love the home of his youthful days. I was not old when I went away from here; and exile, longing and memories cast as it were an additional halo over both the town and its inhabitants. [Some clapping and applause.] And there I stayed, for many years, in a horrible hole far away up north. When I came into contact with some of the people that lived scattered about among the rocks, I often thought it would of been more service to the poor half-starved creatures if a veterinary doctor had been sent up there, instead of a man like me. [Murmurs among the crowd.]

Billing [laying down his pen]. I'm damned if I have ever heard —!

Hovstad. It is an insult to a respectable population!

Dr Stockmann. Wait a bit! I do not think anyone will charge me with having forgotten my native town up there. I was like one of the cider-ducks brooding on its nest, and what I hatched was the plans for these Baths. [Applause and protests.] And then when fate at last decreed for me the great happiness of coming home again — I assure you, gentlemen, I thought I had nothing more in the world to wish for. Or rather, there was one thing I wished for — eagerly, untiringly, ardently — and that was to be able to be of service to my native town and the good of the community.

Peter Stockmann [looking at the ceiling]. You chose a strange way of doing it — ahem!

Dr Stockmann. And so, with my eyes blinded to the real facts, I revelled in happiness. But yesterday morning — no, to be precise, it was yesterday afternoon — the eyes of my mind were opened wide, and the first thing I realised was the colossal stupidity of the authorities —. [Uproar, shouts and laughter, MRS. STOCKMANN coughs persistently.]

Peter Stockmann. Mr. Chairman!

Aslaksen [ringing his bell]. By virtue of my authority —!

Dr Stockmann. It is a petty thing to catch me up on a word, Mr. Aslaksen. What I mean is only that I got scent of the unbelievable piggishness our leading men had been responsible for down at the Baths. I can't stand leading men at any price! — I have had enough of such people in my time. They are like billy-goats on a young plantation; they do mischief everywhere. They stand in a free man's way, whichever way he turns, and what I should like best would be to see them exterminated like any other vermin —. [Uproar.]

Peter Stockmann. Mr. Chairman, can we allow such expressions to pass?

Aslaksen [with his hand on his bell]. Doctor —!

Dr Stockmann. I cannot understand how it is that I have only now acquired a clear conception of what these gentry are, when I had almost daily before my eyes in this town such an excellent specimen of them — my brother Peter — slow-witted and hide-bound in prejudice —. [Laughter, uproar and hisses. MRS. STOCKMANN Sits coughing assiduously. ASLAKSEN rings his bell violently.]

The Drunken Man [who has got in again]. Is it me he is talking about? My name's Petersen, all right — but devil take me if I—

Angry Voices. Turn out that drunken man! Turn him out. [He is turned out again.]

Peter Stockmann. Who was that person?

1st Citizen. I don't know who he is, Mr. Mayor.

2nd Citizen. He doesn't belong here.

3rd Citizen. I expect he is a navvy from over at —[the rest is inaudible].

Aslaksen. He had obviously had too much beer. Proceed, Doctor; but please strive to be moderate in your language.

Dr Stockmann. Very well, gentlemen, I will say no more about our leading men. And if anyone imagines, from what I have just said, that my object is to attack these people this evening, he is wrong — absolutely wide of the mark. For I cherish the comforting conviction that these parasites — all these venerable relics of a dying school of thought — are most admirably paving the way for their own extinction; they need no doctor's help to hasten their end. Nor is it folk of that kind who constitute the most pressing danger to the community. It is not they who are most instrumental in poisoning the sources of our moral life and infecting the ground on which we stand. It is not they who are the most dangerous enemies of truth and freedom amongst us.

Shouts from all sides. Who then? Who is it? Name! Name!

Dr Stockmann. You may depend upon it — I shall name them! That is precisely the great discovery I made yesterday. [Raises his voice.] The most dangerous enemy of truth and freedom amongst us is the compact majority — yes, the damned compact Liberal majority — that is it! Now you know!

[Tremendous uproar. Most of the crowd are shouting, stamping and hissing. Some of the older men among them exchange stolen glances and seem to be enjoying themselves. MRS. STOCKMANN gets up, looking anxious. EJLIF and MORTEN advance threateningly upon some schoolboys who are playing pranks. ASLAKSEN rings his bell and begs for silence. HOVSTAD and BILLING both talk at once, but are inaudible. At last quiet is restored.]

Aslaksen. As Chairman, I call upon the speaker to withdraw the ill-considered expressions he has just used.

Dr Stockmann. Never, Mr. Aslaksen! It is the majority in our community that denies me my freedom and seeks to prevent my speaking the truth.

Hovstad. The majority always has right on its side.

Billing. And truth too, by God!

Dr Stockmann. The majority never has right on its side. Never, I say! That is one of these social lies against which an independent, intelligent man must wage war. Who is it that constitute the majority of the population in a country? Is it the clever folk, or the stupid? I don't imagine you will dispute the fact that at present the stupid people are in an absolutely overwhelming majority all the world over. But, good Lord! — you can never pretend that it is right that the stupid folk should govern the clever ones I [Uproar and cries.] Oh, yes — you can shout me down, I know! But you cannot answer me. The majority has might on its side — unfortunately; but right it has not. I am in the right — I and a few other scattered individuals. The minority is always in the right. [Renewed uproar.]

Hovstad. Aha! — so Dr. Stockmann has become an aristocrat since the day before yesterday!

Dr Stockmann. I have already said that I don't intend to waste a word on the puny, narrow-chested, short-winded crew whom we are leaving astern. Pulsating life no longer concerns itself with them. I am thinking of the few, the scattered few amongst us, who have absorbed new and vigorous truths. Such men stand, as it were, at the outposts, so far ahead that the compact majority has not yet been able to come up with them; and there they are fighting for truths that are too newly-born into the world of consciousness to have any considerable number of people on their side as yet.

Hovstad. So the Doctor is a revolutionary now!

Dr Stockmann. Good heavens — of course I am, Mr. Hovstad! I propose to raise a revolution against the lie that the majority has the monopoly of the truth. What sort of truths are they that the majority usually supports? They are truths that are of such advanced age that they are beginning to break up. And if a truth is as old as that, it is also in a fair way to become a lie, gentlemen. [Laughter and mocking cries.] Yes, believe me or not, as you like; but truths are by no means as long-lived at Methuselah — as some folk imagine. A normally constituted truth lives, let us say, as a rule seventeen or eighteen, or at most twenty years — seldom longer. But truths as aged as that are always worn frightfully thin, and nevertheless it is only then that the majority recognises them and recommends them to the community as wholesome moral nourishment. There is no great nutritive value in that sort of fare, I can assure you; and, as a doctor, I ought to know. These "majority truths" are like last year's cured meat — like rancid, tainted ham; and they are the origin of the moral scurvy that is rampant in our communities.

Aslaksen. It appears to me that the speaker is wandering a long way from his subject.

Peter Stockmann. I quite agree with the Chairman.

Dr Stockmann. Have you gone clean out of your senses, Peter? I am sticking as closely to my subject as I can; for my subject is precisely this, that it is the masses, the majority — this infernal compact majority — that poisons the sources of our moral life and infects the ground we stand on.

Hovstad. And all this because the great, broadminded majority of the people is prudent enough to show deference only to well-ascertained and well-approved truths?

Dr Stockmann. Ah, my good Mr. Hovstad, don't talk nonsense about well-ascertained truths! The truths of which the masses now approve are the very truths that the fighters at the outposts held to in the days of our grandfathers. We fighters at the outposts nowadays no longer approve of them; and I do not believe there is any other well-ascertained truth except this, that no community can live a healthy life if it is nourished only on such old marrowless truths.

Hovstad. But, instead of standing there using vague generalities, it would be interesting if you would tell us what these old marrowless truths are, that we are nourished on.

[Applause from many quarters.]

Dr Stockmann. Oh, I could give you a whole string of such abominations; but to begin with I will confine myself to one well-approved truth, which at bottom is a foul lie, but upon which nevertheless Mr. Hovstad and the "People's Messenger" and all the "Messenger's" supporters are nourished.

Hovstad. And that is —?

Dr Stockmann. That is, the doctrine you have inherited from your forefathers and proclaim thoughtlessly far and wide — the doctrine that the public, the crowd, the masses, are the essential part of the population — that they constitute the People — that the common folk, the ignorant and incomplete element in the community, have the same right to pronounce judgment and to, approve, to direct and to govern, as the isolated, intellectually superior personalities in it.

Billing. Well, damn me if ever I—

Hovstad [at the same time, shouting out]. Fellow-citizens, take good note of that!

A number of voices [angrily]. Oho! — we are not the People! Only the superior folk are to govern, are they!

A Workman. Turn the fellow out for talking such rubbish!

Another. Out with him!

Another [calling out]. Blow your horn, Evensen!

[A horn is blown loudly, amidst hisses and an angry uproar.]

Dr Stockmann [when the noise has somewhat abated]. Be reasonable! Can't you stand hearing the voice of truth for once? I don't in the least expect you to agree with me all at once; but I must say I did expect Mr. Hovstad to admit I was right, when he had recovered his composure a little. He claims to be a freethinker —

Voices [in murmurs of astonishment]. Freethinker, did he say? Is Hovstad a freethinker?

Hovstad [shouting]. Prove it, Dr. Stockmann! When have I said so in print?

Dr Stockmann [reflecting]. No, confound it, you are right! — you have never had the courage to. Well, I won't put you in a hole, Mr. Hovstad. Let us say it is I that am the freethinker, then. I am going to prove to you, scientifically, that the "People's Messenger" leads you by the nose in a shameful manner when it tells you that you — that the common people, the crowd, the masses, are the real essence of the People. That is only a newspaper lie, I tell you! The common people are nothing more than the raw material of which a People is made. [Groans, laughter and uproar.] Well, isn't that the case? Isn't there an enormous difference between a well-bred and an ill-bred strain of animals? Take, for instance, a common barn-door hen. What sort of eating do you get from a shrivelled up old scrag of a fowl like that? Not much, do you! And what sort of eggs does it lay? A fairly good crow or a raven can lay pretty nearly as good an egg. But take a well-bred Spanish or Japanese hen, or a good pheasant or a turkey — then you will see the difference. Or take the case of dogs, with whom we humans are on such intimate terms. Think first of an ordinary common cur — I mean one of the horrible, coarse-haired, low-bred curs that do nothing but run about the streets and befoul the walls of the houses. Compare one of these curs with a poodle whose sires for many generations have been bred in a gentleman's house, where they have had the best of food and had the opportunity of hearing soft voices and music. Do you not think that the poodle's brain is developed to quite a different degree from that of the cur? Of course it is. It is puppies of well-bred poodles like that, that showmen train to do incredibly clever tricks — things that a common cur could never learn to do even if it stood on its head. [Uproar and mocking cries.]

A Citizen [calls out]. Are you going to make out we are dogs, now?

Another Citizen. We are not animals, Doctor!

Dr Stockmann. Yes but, bless my soul, we are, my friend! It is true we are the finest animals anyone could wish for; but, even among us, exceptionally fine animals are rare. There is a tremendous difference between poodle-men and cur-men. And the amusing part of it is, that Mr. Hovstad quite agrees with me as long as it is a question of four-footed animals —

Hovstad. Yes, it is true enough as far as they are concerned.

Dr Stockmann. Very well. But as soon as I extend the principle and apply it to two-legged animals, Mr. Hovstad stops short. He no longer dares to think independently, or to pursue his ideas to their logical conclusion; so, he turns the whole theory upside down and proclaims in the "People's Messenger" that it is the barn-door hens and street curs that are the finest specimens in the menagerie. But that is always the way, as long as a man retains the traces of common origin and has not worked his way up to intellectual distinction.

Hovstad. I lay no claim to any sort of distinction, I am the son of humble country-folk, and I am proud that the stock I come from is rooted deep among the common people he insults.

Voices. Bravo, Hovstad! Bravo! Bravo!

Dr Stockmann. The kind of common people I mean are not only to be found low down in the social scale; they crawl and swarm all around us — even in the highest social positions. You have only to look at your own fine, distinguished Mayor! My brother Peter is every bit as plebeian as anyone that walks in two shoes — [laughter and hisses]

Peter Stockmann. I protest against personal allusions of this kind.

Dr Stockmann [imperturbably]. — and that, not because he is like myself, descended from some old rascal of a pirate from Pomerania or thereabouts — because that is who we are descended from —

Peter Stockmann. An absurd legend. I deny it!

Dr Stockmann. — but because he thinks what his superiors think, and holds the same opinions as they, People who do that are, intellectually speaking, common people; and, that is why my magnificent brother Peter is in reality so very far from any distinction — and consequently also so far from being liberal-minded.

Peter Stockmann. Mr. Chairman —!

Hovstad. So it is only the distinguished men that are liberal-minded in this country? We are learning something quite new! [Laughter.]

Dr Stockmann. Yes, that is part of my new discovery too. And another part of it is that broad-mindedness is almost precisely the same thing as morality. That is why I maintain that it is absolutely inexcusable in the "People's Messenger" to proclaim, day in and day out, the false doctrine that it is the masses, the crowd, the compact majority, that have the monopoly of broad-mindedness and morality — and that vice and corruption and every kind of intellectual depravity are the result of culture, just as all the filth that is draining into our Baths is the result of the tanneries up at Molledal! [Uproar and interruptions. DR. STOCKMANN is undisturbed, and goes on, carried away by his ardour, with a smile.] And yet this same "People's Messenger" can go on preaching that the masses ought to be elevated to higher conditions of life! But, bless my soul, if the "Messenger's" teaching is to be depended upon, this very raising up the masses would mean nothing more or less than setting them straightway upon the paths of depravity! Happily the theory that culture demoralises is only an old falsehood that our forefathers believed in and we have inherited. No, it is ignorance, poverty, ugly conditions of life, that do the devil's work! In a house which does not get aired and swept every day — my wife Katherine maintains that the floor ought to be scrubbed as well, but that is a debatable question — in such a house, let me tell you, people will lose within two or three years the power of thinking or acting in a moral manner. Lack of oxygen weakens the conscience. And there must be a plentiful lack of oxygen in very many houses in this town, I should think, judging from the fact that the whole compact majority

339

can be unconscientious enough to wish to build the town's prosperity on a quagmire of falsehood and deceit.

Aslaksen. We cannot allow such a grave accusation to be flung at a citizen community.

A Citizen. I move that the Chairman direct the speaker to sit down.

Voices [angrily]. Hear, hear! Quite right! Make him sit down!

Dr Stockmann [losing his self-control]. Then I will go and shout the truth at every street corner! I will write it in other towns' newspapers! The whole country shall know what is going on here!

Hovstad. It almost seems as if Dr. Stockmann's intention were to ruin the town.

Dr Stockmann. Yes, my native town is so dear to me that I would rather ruin it than see it flourishing upon a lie.

Aslaksen. This is really serious. [Uproar and cat-calls MRS. STOCKMANN coughs, but to no purpose; her husband does not listen to her any longer.]

Hovstad [shouting above the din]. A man must be a public enemy to wish to ruin a whole community!

Dr Stockmann [with growing fervor]. What does the destruction of a community matter, if it lives on lies? It ought to be razed to the ground. I tell you — All who live by lies ought to be exterminated like vermin! You will end by infecting the whole country; you will bring about such a state of things that the whole country will deserve to be ruined. And if things come to that pass, I shall say from the bottom of my heart: Let the whole country perish, let all these people be exterminated!

Voices from the crowd. That is talking like an out-and-out enemy of the people!

Billing. There sounded the voice of the people, by all that's holy!

The whole crowd. [shouting]. Yes, yes! He is an enemy of the people! He hates his country! He hates his own people!

Aslaksen. Both as a citizen and as an individual, I am profoundly disturbed by what we have had to listen to. Dr. Stockmann has shown himself in a light I should never have dreamed of. I am unhappily obliged to subscribe to the opinion which I have just heard my estimable fellow-citizens utter; and I propose that we should give expression to that opinion in a resolution. I propose a resolution as follows: "This meeting declares that it considers Dr. Thomas Stockmann, Medical Officer of the Baths, to be an enemy of the people." [A storm of cheers and applause. A number of men surround the DOCTOR and hiss him. MRS. STOCKMANN and PETRA have got up from their seats. MORTEN and EJLIF are fighting the other schoolboys for hissing; some of their elders separate them.]

Dr Stockmann [to the men who are hissing him]. Oh, you fools! I tell you that —

Aslaksen [ringing his bell]. We cannot hear you now, Doctor. A formal vote is about to be taken; but, out of regard for personal feelings, it shall be by ballot and not verbal. Have you any clean paper, Mr. Billing?

Billing. I have both blue and white here.

Aslaksen [going to him]. That will do nicely; we shall get on more quickly that way. Cut it up into small strips — yes, that's it. [To the meeting.] Blue means no; white means yes. I will come round myself and collect votes. [PETER STOCKMANN leaves the hall. ASLAKSEN and one or two others go round the room with the slips of paper in their hats.]

1st Citizen [to HOVSTAD]. I say, what has come to the Doctor? What are we to think of it?

Hovstad. Oh, you know how headstrong he is.

2nd Citizen [to BILLING]. Billing, you go to their house — have you ever noticed if the fellow drinks?

Billing. Well I'm hanged if I know what to say. There are always spirits on the table when you go.

3rd Citizen. I rather think he goes quite off his head sometimes.

1st Citizen. I wonder if there is any madness in his family?

Billing. I shouldn't wonder if there were.

4th Citizen. No, it is nothing more than sheer malice; he wants to get even with somebody for something or other.

Billing. Well certainly he suggested a rise in his salary on one occasion lately, and did not get it.

The Citizens [together]. Ah! — then it is easy to understand how it is!

The Drunken Man [who has got among the audience again]. I want a blue one, I do! And I want a white one too!

Voices. It's that drunken chap again! Turn him out!

Morten Kiil. [going up to DR. STOCKMANN]. Well, Stockmann, do you see what these monkey tricks of yours lead to?

Dr Stockmann. I have done my duty.

Morten Kiil. What was that you said about the tanneries at Molledal?

Dr Stockmann. You heard well enough. I said they were the source of all the filth.

Morten Kiil. My tannery too?

Dr Stockmann. Unfortunately your tannery is by far the worst.

Morten Kiil. Are you going to put that in the papers?

Dr Stockmann. I shall conceal nothing.

Morten Kiil. That may cost you dearly, Stockmann. [Goes out.]

A Stout Man [going UP to CAPTAIN HORSTER, Without taking any notice of the ladies]. Well, Captain, so you lend your house to enemies of the people?

Horster. I imagine I can do what I like with my own possessions, Mr. Vik.

The Stout Man. Then you can have no objection to my doing the same with mine.

Horster. What do you mean, sir?

The Stout Man. You shall hear from me in the morning. [Turns his back on him and moves off.]

Petra. Was that not your owner, Captain Horster?

Horster. Yes, that was Mr. Vik the shipowner.

Aslaksen [with the voting-papers in his hands, gets up on to the platform and rings his bell]. Gentlemen, allow me to announce the result. By the votes of every one here except one person —

A Young Man. That is the drunk chap!

Aslaksen. By the votes of everyone here except a tipsy man, this meeting of citizens declares Dr. Thomas Stockmann to be an enemy of the people. [Shouts and applause.] Three cheers for our ancient and honourable citizen community! [Renewed applause.] Three cheers for our able and energetic Mayor, who has so loyally suppressed the promptings of family feeling! [Cheers.] The meeting is dissolved. [Gets down.]

Billing. Three cheers for the Chairman!

The whole crowd. Three cheers for Aslaksen! Hurrah!

Dr Stockmann. My hat and coat, Petra! Captain, have you room on your ship for passengers to the New World?

Horster. For you and yours we will make room, Doctor.

Dr Stockmann [as PETRA helps him into his coat], Good. Come, Katherine! Come, boys!

Mrs Stockmann [in an undertone]. Thomas, dear, let us go out by the back way.

Dr Stockmann. No back ways for me, Katherine, [Raising his voice.] You will hear more of this enemy of the people, before he shakes the dust off his shoes upon you! I am not so forgiving as a certain Person; I do not say: "I forgive you, for ye know not what ye do."

Aslaksen [shouting]. That is a blasphemous comparison, Dr. Stockmann!

Billing. It is, by God! It's dreadful for an earnest man to listen to.

A Coarse Voice. Threatens us now, does he!

Other Voices [excitedly]. Let's go and break his windows! Duck him in the fjord!

Another Voice. Blow your horn, Evensen! Pip, pip!

[Horn-blowing, hisses, and wild cries. DR. STOCKMANN goes out through the hall with his family, HORSTER elbowing a way for them.]

The Whole Crowd [howling after them as they go]. Enemy of the People! Enemy of the People!

Billing [as he puts his papers together]. Well, I'm damned if I go and drink toddy with the Stockmanns tonight!

[The crowd press towards the exit. The uproar continues outside; shouts of "Enemy of the People!" are heard from without.]

ACT V

[SCENE. — DR. STOCKMANN'S study. Bookcases and cabinets containing specimens, line the walls. At the back is a door leading to the hall; in the foreground on the left, a door leading to the sitting-room. In the righthand wall are two windows, of which all the panes are broken. The DOCTOR'S desk, littered with books and papers, stands in the middle of the room, which is in disorder. It is morning. DR. STOCKMANN in dressing-gown, slippers and a smoking-cap, is bending down and raking with an umbrella under one of the cabinets. After a little while he rakes out a stone.]

Dr Stockmann [calling through the open sitting-room door]. Katherine, I have found another one.

Mrs Stockmann [from the sitting-room]. Oh, you will find a lot more yet, I expect.

Dr Stockmann [adding the stone to a heap of others on the table]. I shall treasure these stones as relics. Ejlif and Morten shall look at them everyday, and when they are grown up they shall inherit them as heirlooms. [Rakes about under a bookcase.] Hasn't — what the deuce is her name? — the girl, you know — hasn't she been to fetch the glazier yet?

Mrs Stockmann [coming in]. Yes, but he said he didn't know if he would be able to come today.

Dr Stockmann. You will see he won't dare to come.

Mrs Stockmann. Well, that is just what Randine thought — that he didn't dare to, on account of the neighbours. [Calls into the sitting-room.] What is it you want, Randine? Give it to me. [Goes in, and comes out again directly.] Here is a letter for you, Thomas.

Dr Stockmann. Let me see it. [Opens and reads it.] Ah! — of course.

Mrs Stockmann. Who is it from?

Dr Stockmann. From the landlord. Notice to quit.

Mrs Stockmann. Is it possible? Such a nice man

Dr Stockmann [looking at the letter]. Does not dare do otherwise, he says. Doesn't like doing it, but dare not do otherwise — on account of his fellow-citizens — out of regard for public opinion. Is in a dependent position — dares not offend certain influential men.

Mrs Stockmann. There, you see, Thomas!

Dr Stockmann. Yes, yes, I see well enough; the whole lot of them in the town are cowards; not a man among them dares do anything for fear of the others. [Throws the letter on to the table.] But it doesn't matter to us, Katherine. We are going to sail away to the New World, and —

Mrs Stockmann. But, Thomas, are you sure we are well advised to take this step?

Dr Stockmann. Are you suggesting that I should stay here, where they have pilloried me as an enemy of the people — branded me — broken my windows! And just look here, Katherine — they have torn a great rent in my black trousers too!

Mrs Stockmann. Oh, dear! — and they are the best pair you have got!

Dr Stockmann. You should never wear your best trousers when you go out to fight for freedom and truth. It is not that I care so much about the trousers, you know; you can always sew them up again for me. But that the common herd should dare to make this attack on me, as if they were my equals — that is what I cannot, for the life of me, swallow!

Mrs Stockmann. There is no doubt they have behaved very ill toward you, Thomas; but is that sufficient reason for our leaving our native country for good and all?

Dr Stockmann. If we went to another town, do you suppose we should not find the common people just as insolent as they are here? Depend upon it, there is not much to choose between them. Oh, well, let the curs snap — that is not the worst part of it. The worst is that, from one end of this country to the other, every man is the slave of his Party. Although, as far as that goes, I daresay it is not much better in the free West either; the compact majority, and liberal public opinion, and all that infernal old bag of tricks are probably rampant there too. But there things are done on a larger scale, you see. They may kill you, but they won't put you to death by slow torture. They don't squeeze a free man's soul in a vice, as they do here. And, if need be, one can live in solitude. [Walks up and down.] If only I knew where there was a virgin forest or a small South Sea island for sale, cheap —

Mrs Stockmann. But think of the boys, Thomas!

Dr Stockmann [standing still]. What a strange woman you are, Katherine! Would you prefer to have the boys grow up in a society like this? You saw for yourself last night that half the population are out of their minds; and if the other half have not lost their senses, it is because they are mere brutes, with no sense to lose.

Mrs Stockmann. But, Thomas dear, the imprudent things you said had something to do with it, you know.

Dr Stockmann. Well, isn't what I said perfectly true? Don't they turn every idea topsy-turvy? Don't they make a regular hotchpotch of right and wrong? Don't they say that the things I know are true, are lies? The craziest part of it all is the fact of these "liberals," men of full age, going about in crowds imagining that they are the broad-minded party! Did you ever hear anything like it, Katherine!

Mrs Stockmann. Yes, yes, it's mad enough of them, certainly; but —[PETRA comes in from the silting-room]. Back from school already?

Petra. Yes. I have been given notice of dismissal.

Mrs Stockmann. Dismissal?

Dr Stockmann. You too?

Petra. Mrs. Busk gave me my notice; so I thought it was best to go at once.

Dr Stockmann. You were perfectly right, too!

Mrs Stockmann. Who would have thought Mrs. Busk was a woman like that!

Petra. Mrs. Busk isn't a bit like that, mother; I saw quite plainly how it hurt her to do it. But she didn't dare do otherwise, she said; and so I got my notice.

Dr Stockmann [laughing and rubbing his hands]. She didn't dare do otherwise, either! It's delicious!

Mrs Stockmann. Well, after the dreadful scenes last night —

Petra. It was not only that. Just listen to this, father!

Dr Stockmann. Well?

Petra. Mrs. Busk showed me no less than three letters she received this morning —

Dr Stockmann. Anonymous, I suppose?

Petra. Yes.

Dr Stockmann. Yes, because they didn't dare to risk signing their names, Katherine!

Petra. And two of them were to the effect that a man, who has been our guest here, was declaring last night at the Club that my views on various subjects are extremely emancipated —

Dr Stockmann. You did not deny that, I hope?

Petra. No, you know I wouldn't. Mrs. Busk's own views are tolerably emancipated, when we are alone together; but now that this report about me is being spread, she dare not keep me on any longer.

Mrs Stockmann. And someone who had been a guest of ours! That shows you the return you get for your hospitality, Thomas!

Dr Stockmann. We won't live in such a disgusting hole any longer. Pack up as quickly as you can, Katherine; the sooner we can get away, the better.

Mrs Stockmann. Be quiet — I think I hear someone in the hall. See who it is, Petra.

Petra [opening the door]. Oh, it's you, Captain Horster! Do come in.

Horster [coming in]. Good morning. I thought I would just come in and see how you were.

Dr Stockmann [shaking his hand]. Thanks — that is really kind of you.

Mrs Stockmann. And thank you, too, for helping us through the crowd, Captain Horster.

Petra. How did you manage to get home again?

Horster. Oh, somehow or other. I am fairly strong, and there is more sound than fury about these folk.

Dr Stockmann. Yes, isn't their swinish cowardice astonishing? Look here, I will show you something! There are all the stones they have thrown through my windows. Just look at them! I'm hanged if there are more than two decently large bits of hard stone in the whole heap; the rest are nothing but gravel — wretched little things. And yet they stood out there bawling and swearing that they would do me some violence; but as for doing anything — you don't see much of that in this town.

Horster. Just as well for you this time, doctor!

Dr Stockmann. True enough. But it makes one angry all the same; because if some day it should be a question of a national fight in real earnest, you will see that public opinion will be in favour of taking to one's heels, and the compact majority will turn tail like a flock of sheep, Captain Horster. That is what is so mournful to think of; it gives me so much concern, that —. No, devil take it, it is ridiculous to care about it! They have called me an enemy of the people, so an enemy of the people let me be!

Mrs Stockmann. You will never be that, Thomas.

Dr Stockmann. Don't swear to that, Katherine. To be called an ugly name may have the same effect as a pin-scratch in the lung. And that hateful name — I can't get quit of it. It is sticking here in the pit of my stomach, eating into me like a corrosive acid. And no magnesia will remove it.

Petra. Bah! — you should only laugh at them, father,

Horster. They will change their minds some day, Doctor.

Mrs Stockmann. Yes, Thomas, as sure as you are standing here.

Dr Stockmann. Perhaps, when it is too late. Much good may it do them! They may wallow in their filth then and rue the day when they drove a patriot into exile. When do you sail, Captain Horster?

Horster. Hm! — that was just what I had come to speak about —

Dr Stockmann. Why, has anything gone wrong with the ship?

Horster. No; but what has happened is that I am not to sail in it.

Petra. Do you mean that you have been dismissed from your command?

Horster [smiling]. Yes, that's just it.

Petra. You too.

Mrs Stockmann. There, you see, Thomas!

Dr Stockmann. And that for the truth's sake! Oh, if I had thought such a thing possible —

Horster. You mustn't take it to heart; I shall be sure to find a job with some ship-owner or other, elsewhere.

Dr Stockmann. And that is this man Vik — a wealthy man, independent of everyone and everything —! Shame on him!

Horster. He is quite an excellent fellow otherwise; he told me himself he would willingly have kept me on, if only he had dared —

Dr Stockmann. But he didn't dare? No, of course not.

Horster. It is not such an easy matter, he said, for a party man —

Dr Stockmann. The worthy man spoke the truth. A party is like a sausage machine; it mashes up all sorts of heads together into the same mincemeat — fatheads and blockheads, all in one mash!

Mrs Stockmann. Come, come, Thomas dear!

Petra [to HORSTER]. If only you had not come home with us, things might not have come to this pass.

Horster. I do not regret it.

Petra [holding out her hand to him]. Thank you for that!

Horster [to DR. STOCKMANN]. And so what I came to say was that if you are determined to go away, I have thought of another plan —

Dr Stockmann. That's splendid! — if only we can get away at once.

Mrs Stockmann. Hush! — wasn't that some one knocking?

Petra. That is uncle, surely.

Dr Stockmann. Aha! [Calls out.] Come in!

Mrs Stockmann. Dear Thomas, promise me definitely —. [PETER STOCKMANN comes in from the hall.]

Peter Stockmann. Oh, you are engaged. In that case, I will —

Dr Stockmann. No, no, come in.

Peter Stockmann. But I wanted to speak to you alone.

Mrs Stockmann. We will go into the sitting-room in the meanwhile.

Horster. And I will look in again later.

Dr Stockmann. No, go in there with them, Captain Horster; I want to hear more about —.

Horster. Very well, I will wait, then. [He follows MRS. STOCKMANN and PETRA into the sitting-room.]

Dr Stockmann. I daresay you find it rather draughty here today. Put your hat on.

Peter Stockmann. Thank you, if I may. [Does so.] I think I caught cold last night; I stood and shivered —

Dr Stockmann. Really? I found it warm enough.

Peter Stockmann. I regret that it was not in my power to prevent those excesses last night.

Dr Stockmann. Have you anything in particular to say to me besides that?

Peter Stockmann [taking a big letter from his pocket]. I have this document for you, from the Baths Committee.

Dr Stockmann. My dismissal?

Peter Stockmann. Yes, dating from today. [Lays the letter on the table.] It gives us pain to do it; but, to speak frankly, we dared not do otherwise on account of public opinion.

Dr Stockmann [smiling]. Dared not? I seem to have heard that word before, today.

Peter Stockmann. I must beg you to understand your position clearly. For the future you must not count on any practice whatever in the town.

Dr Stockmann. Devil take the practice! But why are you so sure of that?

Peter Stockmann. The Householders' Association is circulating a list from house to house. All right-minded citizens are being called upon to give up employing you; and I can assure you that not a single head of a family will risk refusing his signature. They simply dare not.

Dr Stockmann. No, no; I don't doubt it. But what then?

Peter Stockmann. If I might advise you, it would be best to leave the place for a little while —

Dr Stockmann. Yes, the propriety of leaving the place has occurred to me.

Peter Stockmann. Good. And then, when you have had six months to think things over, if, after mature consideration, you can persuade yourself to write a few words of regret, acknowledging your error —

Dr Stockmann. I might have my appointment restored to me, do you mean?

Peter Stockmann. Perhaps. It is not at all impossible.

Dr Stockmann. But what about public opinion, then? Surely you would not dare to do it on account of public feeling . . .

Peter Stockmann. Public opinion is an extremely mutable thing. And, to be quite candid with you, it is a matter of great importance to us to have some admission of that sort from you in writing.

Dr Stockmann. Oh, that's what you are after, is it! I will just trouble you to remember what I said to you lately about foxy tricks of that sort!

Peter Stockmann. Your position was quite different then. At that time you had reason to suppose you had the whole town at your back —

Dr Stockmann. Yes, and now I feel I have the whole town ON my back —[flaring up]. I would not do it if I had the devil and his dam on my back —! Never — never, I tell you!

Peter Stockmann. A man with a family has no right to behave as you do. You have no right to do it, Thomas.

Dr Stockmann. I have no right! There is only one single thing in the world a free man has no right to do. Do you know what that is?

Peter Stockmann. No.

Dr Stockmann. Of course you don't, but I will tell you. A free man has no right to soil himself with filth; he has no right to behave in a way that would justify his spitting in his own face.

Peter Stockmann. This sort of thing sounds extremely plausible, of course; and if there were no other explanation for your obstinacy —. But as it happens that there is.

Dr Stockmann. What do you mean?

Peter Stockmann. You understand, very well what I mean. But, as your brother and as a man of discretion, I advise you not to build too much upon expectations and prospects that may so very easily fail you.

Dr Stockmann. What in the world is all this about?

Peter Stockmann. Do you really ask me to believe that you are ignorant of the terms of Mr. Kiil's will?

Dr Stockmann. I know that the small amount he possesses is to go to an institution for indigent old workpeople. How does that concern me?

Peter Stockmann. In the first place, it is by no means a small amount that is in question. Mr. Kiil is a fairly wealthy man.

Dr Stockmann. I had no notion of that!

Peter Stockmann. Hm! — hadn't you really? Then I suppose you had no notion, either, that a considerable portion of his wealth will come to your children, you and your wife having a life-rent of the capital. Has he never told you so?

Dr Stockmann. Never, on my honour! Quite the reverse; he has consistently done nothing but fume at being so unconscionably heavily taxed. But are you perfectly certain of this, Peter?

Peter Stockmann. I have it from an absolutely reliable source.

Dr Stockmann. Then, thank God, Katherine is provided for — and the children too! I must tell her this at once —[calls out] Katherine, Katherine!

Peter Stockmann [restraining him]. Hush, don't say a word yet!

351

Mrs Stockmann [opening the door]. What is the matter?

Dr Stockmann. Oh, nothing, nothing; you can go back. [She shuts the door. DR. STOCKMANN walks up and down in his excitement.] Provided for! — Just think of it, we are all provided for! And for life! What a blessed feeling it is to know one is provided for!

Peter Stockmann. Yes, but that is just exactly what you are not. Mr. Kiil can alter his will any day he likes.

Dr Stockmann. But he won't do that, my dear Peter. The "Badger" is much too delighted at my attack on you and your wise friends.

Peter Stockmann [starts and looks intently at him]. Ali, that throws a light on various things.

Dr Stockmann. What things?

Peter Stockmann. I see that the whole thing was a combined manoeuvre on your part and his. These violent, reckless attacks that you have made against the leading men of the town, under the pretence that it was in the name of truth —

Dr Stockmann. What about them?

Peter Stockmann. I see that they were nothing else than the stipulated price for that vindictive old man's will.

Dr Stockmann [almost speechless]. Peter — you are the most disgusting plebeian I have ever met in all my life.

Peter Stockmann. All is over between us. Your dismissal is irrevocable — we have a weapon against you now. [Goes out.]

Dr Stockmann. For shame! For shame! [Calls out.] Katherine, you must have the floor scrubbed after him! Let — what's her name — devil take it, the girl who has always got soot on her nose —

Mrs Stockmann. [in the sitting-room]. Hush, Thomas, be quiet!

Petra [coming to the door]. Father, grandfather is here, asking if he may speak to you alone.

Dr Stockmann. Certainly he may. [Going to the door.] Come in, Mr. Kiil. [MORTEN KIIL comes in. DR. STOCKMANN shuts the door after him.] What can I do for you? Won't you sit down?

Morten Kiil. I won't sit. [Looks around.] You look very comfortable here today, Thomas.

Dr Stockmann. Yes, don't we!

Morten Kiil. Very comfortable — plenty of fresh air. I should think you have got enough today of that oxygen you were talking about yesterday. Your conscience must be in splendid order today, I should think.

Dr Stockmann. It is.

Morten Kiil. So I should think. [Taps his chest.] Do you know what I have got here?

Dr Stockmann. A good conscience, too, I hope.

Morten Kiil. Bah! — No, it is something better than that. [He takes a thick pocket-book from his breast-pocket, opens it, and displays a packet of papers.]

Dr Stockmann [looking at him in astonishment]. Shares in the Baths?

Morten Kiil. They were not difficult to get today.

Dr Stockmann. And you have been buying —?

Morten Kiil. As many as I could pay for.

Dr Stockmann. But, my dear Mr. Kiil — consider the state of the Baths' affairs!

Morten Kiil. If you behave like a reasonable man, you can soon set the Baths on their feet again.

Dr Stockmann. Well, you can see for yourself that I have done all I can, but —. They are all mad in this town!

Morten Kiil. You said yesterday that the worst of this pollution came from my tannery. If that is true, then my grandfather and my father before me, and I myself, for many years past, have been poisoning the town like three destroying angels. Do you think I am going to sit quiet under that reproach?

Dr Stockmann. Unfortunately I am afraid you will have to.

Morten Kiil. No, thank you. I am jealous of my name and reputation. They call me "the Badger," I am told. A badger is a kind of pig, I believe; but I am not going to give them the right to call me that. I mean to live and die a clean man.

Dr Stockmann. And how are you going to set about it?

Morten Kiil. You shall cleanse me, Thomas.

Dr Stockmann. I!

Morten Kiil. Do you know what money I have bought these shares with? No, of course you can't know — but I will tell you. It is the money that Katherine and Petra and the boys will have when I am gone. Because I have been able to save a little bit after all, you know.

Dr Stockmann [flaring up]. And you have gone and taken Katherine's money for this!

Morten Kiil. Yes, the whole of the money is invested in the Baths now. And now I just want to see whether you are quite stark, staring mad, Thomas! If you still make out that these animals and other nasty things of that sort come from my tannery, it will be exactly as if you were to flay broad strips of skin from Katherine's body, and Petra's, and the boys'; and no decent man would do that — unless he were mad.

Dr Stockmann [walking up and down]. Yes, but I am mad; I am mad!

353

Morten Kiil. You cannot be so absurdly mad as all that, when it is a question of your wife and children.

Dr Stockmann [standing still in front of him]. Why couldn't you consult me about it, before you went and bought all that trash?

Morten Kiil. What is done cannot be undone.

Dr Stockmann [walks about uneasily]. If only I were not so certain about it —! But I am absolutely convinced that I am right.

Morten Kiil [weighing the pocket-book in his hand]. If you stick to your mad idea, this won't be worth much, you know. [Puts the pocket-book in his pocket.]

Dr Stockmann. But, hang it all! It might be possible for science to discover some prophylactic, I should think — or some antidote of some kind —

Morten Kiil. To kill these animals, do you mean?

Dr Stockmann. Yes, or to make them innocuous.

Morten Kiil. Couldn't you try some rat's-bane?

Dr Stockmann. Don't talk nonsense! They all say it is only imagination, you know. Well, let it go at that! Let them have their own way about it! Haven't the ignorant, narrow-minded curs reviled me as an enemy of the people? — and haven't they been ready to tear the clothes off my back too?

Morten Kiil. And broken all your windows to pieces!

Dr Stockmann. And then there is my duty to my family. I must talk it over with Katherine; she is great on those things,

Morten Kiil. That is right; be guided by a reasonable woman's advice.

Dr Stockmann [advancing towards him]. To think you could do such a preposterous thing! Risking Katherine's money in this way, and putting me in such a horribly painful dilemma! When I look at you, I think I see the devil himself —.

Morten Kiil. Then I had better go. But I must have an answer from you before two o'clock — yes or no. If it is no, the shares go to a charity, and that this very day.

Dr Stockmann. And what does Katherine get?

Morten Kiil. Not a halfpenny. [The door leading to the hall opens, and HOVSTAD and ASLAKSEN make their appearance.] Look at those two!

Dr Stockmann [staring at them]. What the devil! — have YOU actually the face to come into my house?

Hovstad. Certainly.

Aslaksen. We have something to say to you, you see.

Morten Kiil [in a whisper]. Yes or no — before two o'clock.

Aslaksen [glancing at HOVSTAD]. Aha! [MORTEN KIIL goes out.]

Dr Stockmann. Well, what do you want with me? Be brief.

Hovstad. I can quite understand that you are annoyed with us for our attitude at the meeting yesterday.

Dr Stockmann. Attitude, do you call it? Yes, it was a charming attitude! I call it weak, womanish — damnably shameful!

Hovstad. Call it what you like, we could not do otherwise.

Dr Stockmann. You DARED not do otherwise — isn't that it?

Hovstad. Well, if you like to put it that way.

Aslaksen. But why did you not let us have word of it beforehand? — just a hint to Mr. Hovstad or to me?

Dr Stockmann. A hint? Of what?

Aslaksen. Of what was behind it all.

Dr Stockmann. I don't understand you in the least —

Aslaksen [with a confidential nod]. Oh yes, you do, Dr. Stockmann.

Hovstad. It is no good making a mystery of it any longer.

Dr Stockmann [looking first at one of them and then at the other]. What the devil do you both mean?

Aslaksen. May I ask if your father-inlaw is not going round the town buying up all the shares in the Baths?

Dr Stockmann. Yes, he has been buying Baths shares today; but —

Aslaksen. It would have been more prudent to get someone else to do it — someone less nearly related to you.

Hovstad. And you should not have let your name appear in the affair. There was no need for anyone to know that the attack on the Baths came from you. You ought to have consulted me, Dr. Stockmann.

Dr Stockmann [looks in front of him; then a light seems to dawn on him and he says in amazement.] Are such things conceivable? Are such things possible?

Aslaksen [with a smile]. Evidently they are. But it is better to use a little finesse, you know.

Hovstad. And it is much better to have several persons in a thing of that sort; because the responsibility of each individual is lessened, when there are others with him.

Dr Stockmann [composedly]. Come to the point, gentlemen. What do you want?

Aslaksen. Perhaps Mr. Hovstad had better —

Hovstad. No, you tell him, Aslaksen.

Aslaksen. Well, the fact is that, now we know the bearings of the whole affair, we think we might venture to put the "People's Messenger" at your disposal.

Dr Stockmann. Do you dare do that now? What about public opinion? Are you not afraid of a storm breaking upon our heads?

Hovstad. We will try to weather it.

Aslaksen. And you must be ready to go off quickly on a new tack, Doctor. As soon as your invective has done its work —

Dr Stockmann. Do you mean, as soon as my father-inlaw and I have got hold of the shares at a low figure?

Hovstad. Your reasons for wishing to get the control of the Baths are mainly scientific, I take it.

Dr Stockmann. Of course; it was for scientific reasons that I persuaded the old "Badger" to stand in with me in the matter. So we will tinker at the conduit-pipes a little, and dig up a little bit of the shore, and it shan't cost the town a sixpence. That will be all right — eh?

Hovstad. I think so — if you have the "People's Messenger" behind you.

Aslaksen. The Press is a power in a free community. Doctor.

Dr Stockmann. Quite so. And so is public opinion. And you, Mr. Aslaksen — I suppose you will be answerable for the Householders' Association?

Aslaksen. Yes, and for the Temperance Society. You may rely on that.

Dr Stockmann. But, gentlemen — I really am ashamed to ask the question — but, what return do you —?

Hovstad. We should prefer to help you without any return whatever, believe me. But the "People's Messenger" is in rather a shaky condition; it doesn't go really well; and I should be very unwilling to suspend the paper now, when there is so much work to do here in the political way.

Dr Stockmann. Quite so; that would be a great trial to such a friend of the people as you are. [Flares up.] But I am an enemy of the people, remember! [Walks about the room.] Where have I put my stick? Where the devil is my stick?

Hovstad. What's that?

Aslaksen. Surely you never mean —

Dr Stockmann [standing still.] And suppose I don't give you a single penny of all I get out of it? Money is not very easy to get out of us rich folk, please to remember!

Hovstad. And you please to remember that this affair of the shares can be represented in two ways!

Dr Stockmann. Yes, and you are just the man to do it. If I don't come to the rescue of the "People's Messenger," you will certainly take an evil view of the affair; you will hunt me down, I can well imagine — pursue me — try to throttle me as a dog does a hare.

Hovstad. It is a natural law; every animal must fight for its own livelihood.

Aslaksen. And get its food where it can, you know.

Dr Stockmann [walking about the room]. Then you go and look for yours in the gutter; because I am going to show you which is the strongest animal of us three! [Finds an umbrella and brandishes it above his head.] Ah, now —!

Hovstad. You are surely not going to use violence!

Aslaksen. Take care what you are doing with that umbrella.

Dr Stockmann. Out of the window with you, Mr. Hovstad!

Hovstad [edging to the door]. Are you quite mad!

Dr Stockmann. Out of the window, Mr. Aslaksen! Jump, I tell you! You will have to do it, sooner or later.

Aslaksen [running round the writing-table]. Moderation, Doctor — I am a delicate man — I can stand so little —[calls out] help, help!

[MRS. STOCKMANN, PETRA and HORSTER come in from the sitting-room.]

Mrs Stockmann. Good gracious, Thomas! What is happening?

Dr Stockmann [brandishing the umbrella]. Jump out, I tell you! Out into the gutter!

Hovstad. An assault on an unoffending man! I call you to witness, Captain Horster. [Hurries out through the hall.]

Aslaksen [irresolutely]. If only I knew the way about here —. [Steals out through the sitting-room.]

Mrs Stockmann [holding her husband back]. Control yourself, Thomas!

Dr Stockmann [throwing down the umbrella]. Upon my soul, they have escaped after all.

Mrs Stockmann. What did they want you to do?

Dr Stockmann. I will tell you later on; I have something else to think about now. [Goes to the table and writes something on a calling-card.] Look there, Katherine; what is written there?

Mrs Stockmann. Three big Noes; what does that mean.

Dr Stockmann. I will tell you that too, later on. [Holds out the card to PETRA.] There, Petra; tell sooty-face to run over to the "Badger's" with that, as quick as she can. Hurry up! [PETRA takes the card and goes out to the hall.]

Dr Stockmann. Well, I think I have had a visit from every one of the devil's messengers today! But now I am going to sharpen my pen till they can feel its point; I shall dip it in venom and gall; I shall hurl my inkpot at their heads!

Mrs Stockmann. Yes, but we are going away, you know, Thomas.

[PETRA comes back.]

Dr Stockmann. Well?

Petra. She has gone with it.

Dr Stockmann. Good. — Going away, did you say? No, I'll be hanged if we are going away! We are going to stay where we are, Katherine!

Petra. Stay here?

Mrs Stockmann. Here, in the town?

Dr Stockmann. Yes, here. This is the field of battle — this is where the fight will be. This is where I shall triumph! As soon as I have had my trousers sewn up I shall go out and look for another house. We must have a roof over our heads for the winter.

Horster. That you shall have in my house.

Dr Stockmann. Can I?

Horster. Yes, quite well. I have plenty of room, and I am almost never at home.

Mrs Stockmann. How good of you, Captain Horster!

Petra. Thank you!

Dr Stockmann [grasping his hand]. Thank you, thank you! That is one trouble over! Now I can set to work in earnest at once. There is an endless amount of things to look through here, Katherine! Luckily I shall have all my time at my disposal; because I have been dismissed from the Baths, you know.

Mrs Stockmann [with a sigh]. Oh yes, I expected that.

Dr Stockmann. And they want to take my practice away from me too. Let them! I have got the poor people to fall back upon, anyway — those that don't pay anything; and, after all, they need me most, too. But, by Jove, they will have to listen to me; I shall preach to them in season and out of season, as it says somewhere.

Mrs Stockmann. But, dear Thomas, I should have thought events had showed you what use it is to preach.

Dr Stockmann. You are really ridiculous, Katherine. Do you want me to let myself be beaten off the field by public opinion and the compact majority and all that devilry? No, thank you! And what I want to do is so simple and clear and straightforward. I only want to drum into the heads of these curs the fact that the liberals are the most insidious enemies of freedom — that party programmes strangle every young and vigorous truth — that considerations of expediency turn morality and justice upside down — and that they will end by making life here unbearable. Don't you think, Captain Horster, that I ought to be able to make people understand that?

Horster. Very likely; I don't know much about such things myself.

Dr Stockmann. Well, look here — I will explain! It is the party leaders that must be exterminated. A party leader is like a wolf, you see — like a voracious wolf. He requires a certain number of smaller victims to prey upon every year, if he is to live. Just look at Hovstad and Aslaksen! How many smaller victims have they not put an end to — or at any rate maimed and mangled until they are fit for nothing except to be householders or subscribers to the "People's Messenger"! [Sits down on the edge of the table.] Come here, Katherine — look how beautifully the sun shines today! And this lovely spring air I am drinking in!

Mrs Stockmann. Yes, if only we could live on sunshine and spring air, Thomas.

Dr Stockmann. Oh, you will have to pinch and save a bit — then we shall get along. That gives me very little concern. What is much worse is, that I know of no one who is liberal-minded and high-minded enough to venture to take up my work after me.

Petra. Don't think about that, father; you have plenty of time before you. — Hello, here are the boys already!

[EJLIF and MORTEN come in from the sitting-room.]

Mrs Stockmann. Have you got a holiday?

Morten. No; but we were fighting with the other boys between lessons —

Ejlif. That isn't true; it was the other boys were fighting with us.

Morten. Well, and then Mr. Rorlund said we had better stay at home for a day or two.

Dr Stockmann [snapping his fingers and getting up from the table]. I have it! I have it, by Jove! You shall never set foot in the school again!

The Boys. No more school!

Mrs Stockmann. But, Thomas —

Dr Stockmann. Never, I say. I will educate you myself; that is to say, you shan't learn a blessed thing —

Morten. Hooray!

Dr Stockmann. — but I will make liberal-minded and high-minded men of you. You must help me with that, Petra.

Petra. Yes, father, you may be sure I will.

Dr Stockmann. And my school shall be in the room where they insulted me and called me an enemy of the people. But we are too few as we are; I must have at least twelve boys to begin with.

Mrs Stockmann. You will certainly never get them in this town.

Dr Stockmann. We shall. [To the boys.] Don't you know any street urchins — regular ragamuffins —?

Morten. Yes, father, I know lots!

Dr Stockmann. That's capital! Bring me some specimens of them. I am going to experiment with curs, just for once; there may be some exceptional heads among them.

Morten. And what are we going to do, when you have made liberal-minded and high-minded men of us?

Dr Stockmann. Then you shall drive all the wolves out of the country, my boys!

[EJLIF looks rather doubtful about it; MORTEN jumps about crying "Hurrah!"]

Mrs Stockmann. Let us hope it won't be the wolves that will drive you out of the country, Thomas.

Dr Stockmann. Are you out of your mind, Katherine? Drive me out! Now — when I am the strongest man in the town!

Mrs Stockmann. The strongest — now?

Dr Stockmann. Yes, and I will go so far as to say that now I am the strongest man in the whole world.

Morten. I say!

Dr Stockmann [lowering his voice]. Hush! You mustn't say anything about it yet; but I have made a great discovery.

Mrs Stockmann. Another one?

Dr Stockmann. Yes. [Gathers them round him, and says confidentially:] It is this, let me tell you — that the strongest man in the world is he who stands most alone.

Mrs Stockmann [smiling and shaking her head]. Oh, Thomas, Thomas!

Petra [encouragingly, as she grasps her father's hands]. Father!